The Second British Empire

CRITICAL ISSUES IN WORLD AND INTERNATIONAL HISTORY
Series Editor: Morris Rossabi

The Second British Empire

In the Crucible of the Twentieth Century

Timothy H. Parsons

ROWMAN & LITTLEFIELD
Lanham • Boulder • New York • London

Published by Rowman & Littlefield
A wholly owned subsidary of The Rowman & Littlefield Publishing Company, Inc.
4501 Forbes Boulevard, Suite 200, Lanham, Maryland 20706
www.rowman.com

16 Carlisle Street, London W1D 3BT, United Kingdom

British Library Cataloguing in Publication Information Available

Library of Congress Cataloging-in-Publication Data
Parsons, Timothy, 1962–
The second British Empire : in the crucible of the twentieth century / Timothy H. Parsons.
pages cm. — (Critical issues in world and international history)
Includes bibliographical references and index.
ISBN 978-0-7425-2050-9 (cloth : alk. paper) — ISBN 978-1-4422-3529-8 (electronic)
1. Great Britain—Colonies—History. 2. Commonwealth countries—History. 3. Imperialism—History. I. Title.
DA16.P3178 2014
909.09'71241082—dc23
2014007971

♾ ™ The paper used in this publication meets the minimum requirements of American
National Standard for Information Sciences Permanence of Paper for Printed Library
Materials, ANSI/NISO Z39.48-1992.

Printed in the United States of America

For Annie, as always,
and for Richard Davis, mentor, colleague, and dear friend

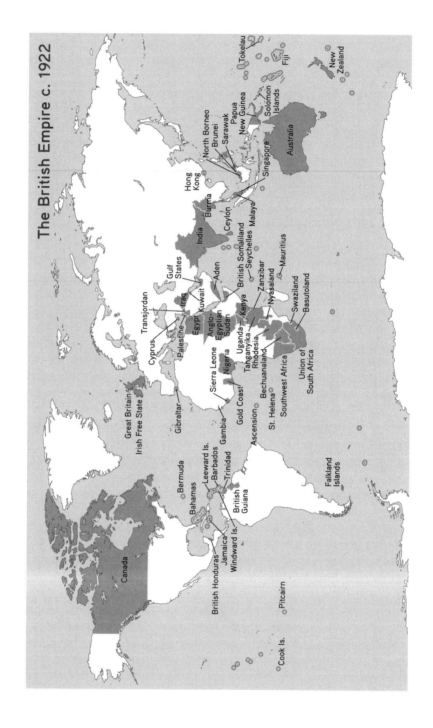

The British Empire c. 1922

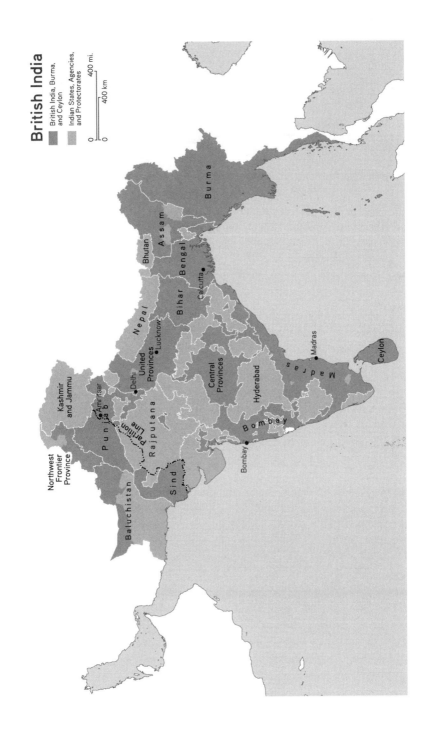

British India

- British India, Burma, and Ceylon
- Indian States, Agencies, and Protectorates

0   400 mi.
0   400 km

Burma

Assam

Bhutan

Bengal

Bihar

Calcutta

Nepal

Lucknow

United Provinces

Delhi

Central Provinces

Madras

Madras

Ceylon

Hyderabad

Kashmir and Jammu

Amritsar

Punjab

Partition Line

Rajputana

Bombay

Bombay

Northwest Frontier Province

Baluchistan

Sind

Contents

Acknowledgments

It is no easy task to write about empire on a global scale, and several colleagues and scholars merit special mention for their kind assistance in helping me puzzle out the complexities of British imperial rule in the twentieth century. Peter Crooks introduced me to Ireland and, most important, reminded me how central Irish history is to the larger history of empire. I am also indebted to Mike Rowe for patiently explaining how and why cricket generates so much passion in Britain and the Commonwealth. Philip Murphy has my very grateful thanks for generously helping me work through the enormously complex history of the Central African Federation.

In St. Louis, Richard Davis made this book possible by convincing me that the British Empire is a suitable topic for an Africanist historian. Jean Allman also had a significant influence on the scope and arguments of the book by inspiring me to consider less conventional interpretations of decolonization and national independence. Gabriella Alvarez, Lauren Henley, Rosa Johnson, and the rest of the staff of the African and African American Studies Program office merit special thanks for their invaluable assistance, as does Karl Topp of the Olin Library Interlibrary Loan Office. My friends and colleagues in the International and Area Studies Program were also wonderfully supportive and encouraging as I struggled to find time to finish this manuscript. And a note of special thanks to Celina della Croce for making it possible for me to take so many research trips abroad.

I am also grateful to the Rowman & Littlefield external reviewer for drawing my attention to the inevitable glitches that creep into all manuscripts and for pushing me to be clearer and more precise in my arguments. And finally, many, many thanks to my editor, Susan McEachern. This book is very much a testament to her enthusiasm, wisdom, and considerable patience. But as always, I am solely responsible for any errors of fact or interpretation that may persist after all this generous help and support.

Chapter One

Introduction

EMPIRE AT MIDNIGHT AND MIDDAY

If Hong Kong was Britain's last significant imperial possession, then the British Empire ended in the driving rain. Acquired from China at gunpoint in the 1842 Treaty of Nanking, the colony became one of the empire's most important economic and military outposts in the Far East. Through an 1898 treaty that legitimized the seizure of sovereign Chinese territory, Britain acquired a ninety-nine-year lease on the Kowloon Peninsula (or New Territories) that vastly expanded its original holding on Hong Kong Island. This lease remained in force over the course of the next century as one British imperial territory after another became independent nation-states. Although the Chinese authorities never surrendered their claim to the colony, the wars and civil upheaval that beset China during the twentieth century meant that the communist regime did not try to break the lease by military force. But the People's Republic of China also had no intention of renewing it when it expired, and so under the terms of a 1984 accord, Hong Kong formally became a self-governing territory under Chinese sovereignty at the stroke of midnight on July 30, 1997.

Although the wider British Empire was largely gone at this point, the surrender of Hong Kong was an emotional transition for many Britons. First, it appeared to mark the demise of an institution that could theoretically be dated to the assertion of English power over its Celtic neighbors in the British Isles some eight centuries earlier. Additionally, Hong Kong's prosperity and democratic institutions in 1997, particularly in contrast to mainland China under communist rule, seemed to affirm romantic conceptions of the British Empire as progressively benevolent. In his final speech to the Hong Kong legislature, the last British governor, Christopher Patton, labeled the colony an "astonishing Chinese success story," but he went on to assert that it was "a success story with British characteristics. . . . What Britain has helped provide . . . is a framework within which . . . ordinary Chinese men and women have been able to do extraordinary things."[1]

The transfer-of-power ceremony itself followed a ceremonial template that successive British governments had perfected in Africa, Asia, the Middle East, and the West Indies over the previous three decades. Lasting only fifteen minutes and conducted in English and Mandarin (most of the colony's population spoke Cantonese), it entailed the lowering and rising of national flags, the replacement of British imperial insignia and icons, and the inevitable speeches by key dignitaries and concluded with a massive fireworks display. As *Times of London* correspondent Simon Jenkins saw it,

> The weather was awful but the ceremonial superb. The Pacific Empire went out on the completion of a property contract, in a swirl of pipes and a rattle of drums. The massed bands defied the thunderstorms sweeping down from The Peak, and played "The Day Thou Gavest Lord Has Ended." The flag dipped and a lone piper played the lament. The audience sang Auld Lang Syne, the tears mingling with the rain. The Governor [Christopher Patton] admitted he had long run out of handkerchiefs. [The British prime minister] Tony Blair looked bemused, the Prince of Wales [as the representative of his mother, Queen Elizabeth II] merely wet.[2]

In Jenkins's opinion, "The Prince of Wales made a dull speech, standing in what appeared to be a waterfall," but the *Times* correspondent cheered Patton's declaration that "Hong Kong people are now to run Hong Kong. . . . That is the promise and that is the unshakeable destiny." The subtext to this assessment was that the transfer of power to communist China safeguarded the liberal political institutions that Britain had bestowed upon the colony. But an elderly man named Mr. Lam, who had likely spent most of his life as a British subject, complicated this comforting image when he told an American journalist, "It's a good thing we can finally get rid of the imperialists. We're all Chinese. I feel great. This land belongs to China."[3] Most of Britain's former subjects would have probably voiced similar sentiments at their independence ceremonies, which helps to explain why the twentieth-century British Empire was much more ephemeral and inherently unpopular than its mourners in Hong Kong imagined.

Although this reality may have appeared obvious to most of the rain-soaked crowd who watched the Union Jack come down at midnight on July 30, 1997, the members of the audience gathered in the blazing bright sun of noontime Delhi to witness the imperial majesty and grandeur of King George V's Coronation Durbar on December 12, 1911, would have never imagined that the British Empire would prove so short-lived and fragile. Originally "durbar" was the term for the Mughal court, but the British government of

India, popularly known as the Raj, reimagined it in the late nineteenth century as a spectacular pageant that affirmed Britain's will and determination to rule India. Faced with growing Indian opposition to foreign rule, particularly over a highly unpopular decision to divide Bengal into two provinces, Herbert Asquith's Liberal government used the ascent of George V to the throne as an excuse to stage the largest and most grandiose durbar to date.

Although he had already been crowned at Westminster in June 1911, King George then traveled to India six months later to receive the direct homage of his subjects as the king-emperor of the Raj. This made him the first reigning British monarch to visit India. Planned in extensive and full-scale detail at Windsor Castle for months in advance, the durbar was a prodigious imperial undertaking. The king's party, which sailed on a thirteen-thousand-ton luxury steamer escorted by four Royal Navy cruisers, made a powerful political statement as it visited Britain's main Mediterranean naval bases before passing through the Suez Canal on the way to Aden and then Bombay. The tented Durbar Camp in Delhi was an impressively massive complex covering twenty-five square miles that had its own hospital, stables, dairy, and market. A waterworks consisting of 101 miles of pipes supplied 5 million gallons of filtered water per day, and the camp's power station, which daily required three thousand tons of coal, generated twenty-four hundred kilowatts of electricity to light its streets.

The durbar itself began at 11 a.m. on the hot, sunny morning of December 12 on a twenty-foot-high platform in the center of two amphitheaters. The smaller was for twelve thousand official guests consisting of senior imperial officials, high-ranking military officers, and Indian princes, and the other accommodated fifty thousand members of the general public. Some twenty thousand British and Indian troops looked on as well. The event opened with a flourish of trumpets and drum rolls, and the king and his consort, Queen Mary, arrived wearing heavily embroidered satin and velvet robes (which must have been extremely hot under the Delhi sun). George wore an Imperial Crown of India, worth some £60,000, made especially for the occasion. They took their seats on crimson and gold thrones under a golden dome supported by four marble pillars and shaded by a canopy of crimson velvet.

Following the carefully choreographed plan, the king and queen first received "homage" from the official guests in the inner amphitheater. The most important of these were the rulers of the Indian princely states, who, according to the official durbar historian, were "resplendent in gorgeous robes, hung with priceless jewels, and employing every variety of salutation."[4] The British monarchs then moved to a pavilion in the center of the larger arena to address the general public. A chief herald read out a proclamation by the king-emperor that was entirely consistent with Governor Patton's last address to the Hong Kong legislature. In it he assured his Indian subjects of "the deep affection with which We regard Our Indian Empire, the

welfare and prosperity of which are, and ever will be, Our constant concern."
The viceroy of India then read out a lengthy list of "boons" that the king had
awarded his loyal subjects. These included medals and titles for the princes,
more education funding for the general public, extra pay for soldiers and civil
servants, and pardons for minor criminals. George V himself then surprised
the crowd by personally reading a pronouncement declaring the reunification
of Bengal and the relocation of the imperial capital of India from Calcutta to
Delhi. The durbar concluded with the British national anthem, "God Save the
King," three cheers for the king-emperor and his queen, and a 101-gun salute.

At first glance, the Delhi Coronation Durbar seemed to capture the power
and resilience of the British Empire. As was the case in Hong Kong eighty-
six years later, a correspondent from the *Times* was on hand to chronicle the
proceedings, but he was in a much better mood than the sodden Simon
Jenkins: "The ceremony . . . exactly typified the Oriental conception of the
ultimate repositories of imperial power. The Monarchs sat alone, remote but
beneficent, raised far above the multitude, but visible to all, clad in rich
vestments, flanked by radiant emblems of authority, guarded by a glittering
array of troops, the cynosure of the proudest Princes of India. . . . Not a soul
who witnessed it, not even the poorest coolie who stood fascinated and awed
upon the outskirts of the throng, can have been unresponsive to its profound
significance."[5] Costing the British and Indian governments more than
£750,000, the durbar created the appearance of durability, confidence, and
dominance. The cheering crowds and dutiful Indian princes suggested that
the empire commanded the loyalty of its subjects.

Yet King George's greatest boon, the construction of a new imperial
capital on the plains of Delhi, could not conceal the reality that the Raj had
retreated from the plan to dilute Indian political opposition by partitioning
Bengal. In this sense, the durbar was an admission of weakness cloaked in a
massively opulent display of imperial pomp. Moreover, even in 1911 plenty
of attendees shared the sentiments of Hong Kong's Mr. Lam. One of these
was Maharaja Sayajirao III of Baroda, who as the third most senior Indian
prince and a grand knight commander of the Order of the Star of India, might
have been expected to be an enthusiastic participant in the ceremony. Yet,
according to an English observer, the maharaja refused to pay proper homage
to the king; instead, he bowed improperly and then turned his back on the
monarch as he strode away, twirling a walking stick nonchalantly.[6] In hindsight, the durbar did not have much of a lasting impact on Indian politics or
aspirations, and within two decades Indian antipathy to foreign rule was so
great that the Raj canceled durbars for George's sons Edward VIII and
George VI.

THE SECOND BRITISH EMPIRE

These two seemingly disparate ceremonies, held more than eight decades apart, reveal fundamental realities about the nature of the later British Empire. Great Britain itself was a relatively small nation with a population of only 41.5 million at the turn of the twentieth century, but it claimed to rule over 12 million square miles (roughly one-quarter of the habitable world) and boasted over 400 million people.[7] In 1911, this empire was a seemingly deep-rooted great military and economic superpower. By 1997, it was essentially gone. This is in contrast to the empires of the ancient, medieval, and early-modern eras, which spanned much greater swaths of time.

Yet it is not productive to search for a cause of Britain's imperial "decline." Tempting as it may be to compare ancient Rome with the twentieth-century British Empire, the common usage of the English word "empire," which comes from the Latin *imperare* (to command), for large political units ruling diverse groups of people creates a false sense of continuity and implies that all imperial entities followed similar trajectories of rise and fall. The term "imperialism" has much more recent origins. The British press coined the term in the 1840s to attack Napoleon III's declaration of a second French empire. It acquired mixed meanings in the twentieth century, but after World War II, it largely became a synonym for exploitation and authoritarian rule.[8] Although empires, by definition, entailed the formal, direct, and authoritarian rule by one group of people over another, the scope and method of this rule changed considerably over time. By the twentieth century, it had become much harder to maintain control over restive and unwilling subject populations. In the cases of Hong Kong and the Raj, the Chinese and the Indians rejected foreign imperial rule, and it did not matter how benevolent or well-meaning the foreigners claimed to be. Thus, the transfer of Britain's last significant imperial possession to Chinese sovereignty did not so much signify the fall of the British Empire as it demonstrated that formal empire itself was no longer a viable institution in the contemporary world.

Moreover, the British Empire that wound down on that rainy night in Hong Kong was not the same "empire" that began in the twelfth century with the English conquest of Ireland. In fact, there were several British empires that ended at different times and for different reasons. Some historians date the end of the "first" British Empire to the loss of the thirteen North American colonies. The transition of the remaining settlement colonies, in what would become Canada, Australia, New Zealand, and the South African Cape Colony, to local self-government over the course of the nineteenth century further suggested that the era of formal empire was over. Additionally, Ireland and India, which were Britain's most important remaining imperial possessions, followed their own separate and unique paths to independence. The "second" British Empire was born of the "new imperialism" of the late nineteenth century when Britain took part in the European conquest of Africa, consolidated its hold on Malaya, and claimed new territories in the South Pacific. This was the empire celebrated by the Raj at the 1911 Coronation Durbar and packed up in Hong Kong in 1997.

Imperial partisans were sure that their revived and expanded empire made them a great power, but ironically Great Britain was much more secure in its wealth and global influence in the mid-nineteenth century when it had far fewer colonies and protectorates. During this era of "informal empire," Britain emerged from the turmoil of the Napoleonic Wars as the world's foremost manufacturing and trading nation. Much of its wealth came from foreign investment, overseas insurance, and global shipping, which historians refer to as "invisible trade." Confident in the supremacy of the Royal Navy and of laissez-faire capitalism and lacking significant economic or political competitors, British free traders, Christian evangelicals, and budget-conscious politicians and military strategists viewed most of the overseas remnants of the first British Empire as an unnecessary expense. They noted that by mid-century military outlays accounted for more than 70 percent of national spending and that overseas bases consumed more than one-third of the army's budget. Why spend the resources and manpower to conquer and govern exotic non-Western societies when British merchants, backed by Royal Navy gunboats, easily found new opportunities for lucrative trade and investment in Latin America, Africa, the Middle East, and Asia on their own? In the 1860s, Sir Charles Adderley and the supporters of free trade in the British parliament even demanded that Britain relinquish its few official West African possessions because they were an unacceptable drain on the Treasury and drew the nation into unnecessary wars in defense of special interests. In answering the missionaries who lobbied against the recommendation, Adderley's ally Lord Stanley declared, "If we talk of civilising the Africans I am afraid we had better first look at home. We have not to go five miles from the place in which we are sitting [in London] to find plenty of persons who stand as much in need of civilising and who have as little done for them as the negro."[9]

The formal rule of non-Western and overseas populations was both expensive and unnecessary when Britain was the nineteenth century's premier commercial power and its trade and investments flowed freely. This is why Britain joined the wider scramble for new imperial territory reluctantly. The primary concern of British statesmen, strategists, and financiers was to protect their global interests from economic and military challenges posed by the emerging industrialized powers of continental Europe, the United States, and eventually Japan. Faced with a punishing depression in the 1870s sparked primarily by industrial overproduction and haunted by fears that rival empires might close off access to important markets and raw materials, successive British governments claimed vast stretches of territory in Africa and Asia in the 1880s. In some instances, as in Egypt and the Suez Canal, they intervened in localized conflicts to defend specific strategic or economic interests, then found that the new era of international competition made it extremely difficult to withdraw.

For the most part, however, the government in London committed surprisingly few resources to the new imperial scramble, and irregular "native militias" raised by chartered companies or Indian army units played the most active role in seizing new territories. Put another way, metropolitan Britain acquired over 4.7 million square miles of territory and some 90 million new subjects on the cheap by contracting out much of the new imperial scramble to private commercial concerns and the Indian subempire. Conducted beyond the boundaries of metropolitan oversight, the "small wars" that expanded the formal British Empire were often bloody and brutal. On the whole, the shift from the secure informal empire of the mid-nineteenth century to this "modern" or second British Empire of the twentieth century was born of anxiety and weakness. Indeed, very few of the new acquisitions had immediate economic worth. The British government allowed its representatives to claim them for the Crown to protect existing commercial interests and on the possibility that the new territories might one day prove economically or strategically valuable.

These realities were extremely difficult to recognize in metropolitan Britain at the turn of the twentieth century. Although they disagreed sharply on specific policy issues, the rival Conservative (Tory) and Liberal parties saw the revived formal empire as a measure of British greatness and a force for good in the world. They also hoped to bind the increasingly wayward self-governing settlement colonies born of the first British Empire more closely to the metropole in a vibrant network of open commerce and shared defense. British rule over territories acquired during the late nineteenth century would provide more land for settlement and additional markets for British goods while putting a final end to slave trading and exercising benevolent trusteeship over the backward races of Africa and Asia. Imperial enthusiasts excused the bloodshed resulting from this enterprise by depicting the non-Westerners who refused to recognize the benefits of British rule as barbaric savages.

This mutually beneficial concept of empire, which featured prominently in King George V's 1911 Coronation Durbar, was an absolutely essential legitimizing ideology for British imperial rule. Earlier generations of empire builders rarely felt the need to justify their demands for tribute and submission. Late-nineteenth-century Britain, however, was a liberal democracy that imagined itself as a force for good in contrast to the oriental despotism of the Russian, Ottoman, and Chinese empires. Yet African and Asian states and communities defended their political and economic autonomy tenaciously. No one voluntarily joined the British Empire. As one veteran of the West

African "bush wars" admitted in 1903, "It is a fact incontrovertible that our expansion of Empire has been very largely brought about by the subjugation of the savage and lawless races who were the original inhabitants of the soil."[10] Most people became imperial subjects when British forces conquered them. There is also no disguising the brutality of these small but vicious wars, particularly when they involved seizing land for European settlement. Writing of Ndebele resistors in what would become Southern Rhodesia (modern Zimbabwe), a British deputy commissioner confessed, "It would offer me sincere and lasting satisfaction if I could see the Matabele Matjaha cut down by our own rifles and machine guns like a cornfield by a reaping machine and I would not spare a single one if I could have my way."[11] The records of this period are sketchy, but in the highlands of central Kenya, the famine and disease that accompanied the Imperial British East Africa Company's wars of conquest most likely killed off 10 to 30 percent of the population.

The journalists, missionaries, and military officers who witnessed these messy realities of empire building reassured the metropolitan public that their enemies in these "pacification campaigns" were, at worst, pirates, slave raiders, cannibals, and other sorts of dangerous barbarians and, at best, tradition-bound tribesmen who did not understand that British rule brought "modernity." Depicting Britain's non-Western subjects as "lesser races" or "savage natives" made it possible for a liberal democratic nation to have an authoritarian empire. In this sense, British imperial rule was an early form of "development" that provided both moral and material uplift. The second British Empire became a project that evangelicals and humanitarians could support because it brought prosperity and Western Christian civilization to heathen peoples. Although they acknowledged the cultural achievements of earlier Chinese, South Asian, and Near Eastern empires, the empire lobby argued that the descendants of these great civilizations had become so degenerate and corrupt that they too needed the guiding hand of British rule. This was particularly true in the case of African and Asian women, who had to be "saved" from child marriage and prostitution, polygamy, female infanticide, and genital mutilation. Conveniently missing from this narrative was the West's own history of slave trading, religious hatred and warfare, exploitation of poorly paid industrial workers living in barbaric conditions, and treatment of women as marginal and second-class.

Moreover, the darkest side of the new imperialism's legitimizing imperial rhetoric was that it treated non-Westerners as culturally, if not racially, inferior. Writing to a friend in 1900, Viceroy of India Lord Curzon showed how these assumptions could justify authoritarianism: "We cannot take the natives [i.e., Indians] up into the administration. They are crooked-minded and corrupt. We have got therefore to go on ruling them and we can only do it with success by being both kindly and virtuous. I dare say I am talking rather like a schoolmaster; but after all the millions I have to manage are less than school children."[12] Twenty years later, pioneer soldier and administrator Frederick Lugard was only slightly more diplomatic when he asserted that Britain followed a "dual mandate" that opened Africa for economic development by the "white races" while simultaneously and without any conflict of interest "devoting our energies to raising the ignorant millions to a higher plane by a system of education suited to their needs." Even as late as 1951, Margery Perham, a highly respected Oxford professor and expert on African history, could still characterize preconquest Africans as so "uncivilised and tribal" that they were trapped in a "state of mind which militates against reason and moderation."[13] At the turn of the twentieth century, many, if not most, educated Westerners accepted the social Darwinist premise that humanity was made up of more and less advanced "races," and there was little stigma attached to sweeping generalizations about the strengths and weaknesses of one "race" or another. Nevertheless, it was only a short jump from the paternalistically authoritarian racial and cultural distinctions of Lugard and Perham to the more pernicious, often vicious, racism that opened the way for blatant forms of political discrimination and economic exploitation. Thus, the notorious Kenyan settler Ewart Grogan justified land seizures and forced labor on the grounds that it was "patent to all who have observed the African native, that he is fundamentally inferior in mental development and ethical possibilities (call it a soul if you will) to the white man."[14] In this sense, the empire's non-Western subjects were an exploitable resource that had little more standing than draft animals.

Although it is easy to dismiss Grogan's blatant racism as simply self-serving, the larger reality was that reconciling authoritarian rule in the empire with liberal democracy at home meant it was essential to depict subject peoples as inherently unable to master the complexities of the modern world. This is why the westernized and often highly educated African elites who ran the small British West African coastal territories that Sir Charles Adderley found so unnecessarily expensive had to go. In the Gold Coast colonial administration in the 1880s, the lieutenant governor, seven district commissioners, the acting secretary for native affairs, and a government surveyor were all Africans. Africans also held commissions in the local militia and were some of the most prominent doctors, lawyers, and journalists in the colony. By the turn of the twentieth century, they had all disappeared from government service. Under the inherent racism that underpinned the new imperialism, they were "trousered natives" who aped the trappings of Western culture without ever really understanding it. It had to be this way because the second British Empire would not have been tenable if imperial partisans acknowledged their subjects as civilized equals. Doing so would have meant that there was no moral or legitimate reason to deny them full equality with metropolitan Britons or not to grant them the dignity of ruling themselves.

Imperial partisans therefore claimed that it would take generations, if not centuries, to advance non-Western subjects to the stage where they could govern themselves and assume responsibility for their own economic development. Just as it took ancient Rome four centuries to civilize their barbaric Celtic ancestors, in time the second British Empire would transform simple tribes into great nations. However, this could only happen if conquered populations were sufficiently patient and trusting. But unlike the ancient Romans, or their French contemporaries for that matter, British imperialists had no intention of assimilating Africans or Asians. As Evelyn Baring, the British consul general and de facto ruler of Egypt, explained to the Classical Association in 1910, while Rome practiced an "easy-going polytheism" that could accommodate a wide variety of beliefs, "[as Christians] our habits are insular, and our social customs render us . . . unduly exclusive."[15] As there was no room for outsiders and racially distinct populations in the modern British nation-state, British imperial rule would produce culturally distinct "modern" Africans and Asians rather than expanding the definition of what it meant to be British beyond racial conceptions of nationalism. Thus, at least in theory, Britain's barbaric subjects could be kept at arm's length, but as chapter 6 will show, the empire would change the meaning of what it means to be British. Nevertheless, the men who ran the second British Empire reassured themselves that the point at which they would have to surrender power to civilized tribal peoples or reformed Asians was comfortably in the future. A plaque on the secretariat buildings in the Raj's new capital of New Delhi made this clear: "Liberty does not descend to a people. A people must raise themselves to liberty. It is a blessing that must be earned before it can be enjoyed."

In contrast, the new imperialists accepted that Britain's "white" settler colonies were entitled to at least some measure of self-government. Unlike an empire, which entailed the direct and unequal rule of one people over another, a colony (from the Latin *colonia*) was the permanent settlement of the lands of a defeated people by their conquerors. In this sense, "colonialism" differed from "imperialism." In the North American and Australian settlement colonies, colonialism entailed the near extermination, by both accident and design, of the original Amerindian and Aboriginal populations. By the social Darwinist reasoning of the new imperialism, these groups simply suffered the inevitable fate of "inferior races." The Maori of New Zealand and Bantu-speaking southern Africans, who were conquered in the nineteenth century, were better able to survive foreign rule and an influx of European colonists. Nevertheless, the most oppressive and virulently racist imperial societies in British Africa emerged in the temperate regions of Africa where new groups of Westerners sought to build settler colonies on this earlier model. Thankfully it was no longer possible or defensible to kill off entire populations, but the new imperialism consigned Africans and their

Maori counterparts in New Zealand to second-class status in Western polities that considered themselves cultural extensions of Britain itself.

The American Revolution demonstrated that these overseas settlements of "kith and kin" could not be classified as subordinate subjects of the imperial metropole. British colonists would not tolerate being treated like less civilized Indians, much less like native tribesmen. During the heyday of informal empire in the mid-nineteenth century, economy-minded metropolitan politicians were content to allow the colonies a greater measure of self-government so long as they also shouldered more of the costs of their administration and defense. Grouping individual colonies into larger and more economical federations, which became a central feature of British imperial policy, generated even greater efficiency and savings. Thus, the British North America Act created a united Canada in 1867, and similar federation-building exercises produced Australia in 1901 and the Union of South Africa in 1910.

Theoretically, "Crown colonies" enjoyed some measure of self-government through locally elected legislative councils. This was even true for the non-European populations in the Caribbean and West African coastal enclaves, like Freetown in Sierra Leone, that were holdovers from the first British Empire. By contrast, most of the territories Britain acquired during the new imperial era had the legal status of "protectorates," which meant that imperial officials exercised authority through cooperative local rulers who accepted the protection of the British Crown. Although there was little practical difference between colonies and protectorates in terms of day-to-day administration (Kenya was actually both), as "British-protected persons" Africans and Asians lacked the rights of British settlers, who enjoyed considerably more status and privileges as subjects of the Crown.

In time, the British came to call Canada, Australia, New Zealand, and the Union of South Africa "dominions," which by strict definition meant territories or realms under the sovereignty of the Crown. The ideal was that Britain and her imperial possessions, both old and new, constituted a larger commonwealth bound together, regardless of their inherent differences, by a mutual allegiance and loyalty to the royal family. By this reasoning, the Commonwealth was, in the words of a metropolitan parliamentarian, "a great, loyal confederation of people, enjoying in each individual part self-government and liberty unexampled in the history of the Empires of the world."[16] Imperial enthusiasts proudly pointed to the Commonwealth and the dominions as evidence that it was possible for overseas populations (albeit populations of European descent) to fulfill their nationalist ambitions within the British Empire.

Yet, at the turn of the twentieth century, this was still not true in practice, and there was considerable friction over what self-government actually meant. The dominions had their own elected legislatures, but under the terms of the 1865 Colonial Laws Validity Act, any legislation that conflicted with

British statute law was automatically "null and avoid." Similarly, dominion leaders disliked having to acknowledge the authority of imperial governors who still exercised considerable influence as the representatives of the Crown. They balked at subordinating their economies to the needs of Britain and rejected metropolitan proposals to place their armed forces under a unified imperial command. Giving voice to this increased dominion assertiveness, Canadian prime minister W. L. Mackenzie King famously and unabashedly declared, "My first duty is to Canada."

These tensions became more pronounced in 1910 when Asquith's government tried to reconcile with the defeated Afrikaners after the bloody South African War by creating the Union of South Africa. Allowing Afrikaners to play the leading role in this federation of the Cape Colony and Natal with the Afrikaner republics of the Transvaal and the Orange Free State meant abandoning Britain's long-standing paternal commitment to safeguarding native rights, but the hope was that uniting the two white races in a self-governing dominion would provide a cost-effective means of solidifying British control of the strategically important region. Afrikaner nationalists, however, remained embittered by their defeat and sought continually to slip the bonds of imperial control.

Ireland was an even greater obstacle to the ideal of imperial unity and Commonwealth loyalty. Technically one of the four nonsovereign nations that comprised the United Kingdom, along with England, Wales, and Scotland, Ireland first came under English rule in the twelfth century. But unlike the Welsh and Scots, who eventually came to terms with their inclusion in Great Britain after suffering military reverses, the Irish remained much more distinct and separate. This was due in part to the incomplete attempt at colonization by English and Scottish settlers in the early seventeenth century, which left behind a powerful class of Anglo-Irish landlords who treated the larger population as an exploitable resource. Seeking to better integrate Ireland into the United Kingdom and resolve the simmering Irish discontent that led to a serious rebellion in 1798 and Irish support for France during the Napoleonic Wars, British prime minister William Pitt pushed through the 1801 Act of Union that abolished the Irish parliament and granted Ireland one hundred seats in the House of Commons at Westminster. Theoretically, the resulting United Kingdom of Great Britain and Ireland constituted a single economic unit and encouraged the assimilation of Irish Catholics by diluting their distinctiveness through incorporation into the larger British population.

The Act of Union's promised equality never materialized. The British and Irish public finances and national debt remained separate, and a viceroy (the lord lieutenant) and an imperial-style chief secretary remained in residence at the seat of government in Dublin Castle. More significantly, strong anti-Catholicism in Britain and the determination by Protestant elites to retain power in Ireland meant that a great many Irishmen remained unassimilated and intensely dissatisfied with British rule. Dissolution of the Act of Union and "home rule," which essentially amounted to dominion status, became increasingly popular demands over the course of the nineteenth century. Ironically, sharp divisions in the House of Commons meant that Irish members of Parliament (MPs) often held the balance of power between the rival Conservative and Liberal parties. As the century drew to a close, this political leverage gave the Irish Parliamentary Party the means to force their Liberal allies to introduce a pair of home rule bills. These floundered in the House of Lords, and most Irishmen remained as restive as the empire's Indian and Afrikaner subjects.

IMPERIAL IDEALS AND IMPERIAL REALITIES

In 1911, a group of private investors bankrolled by wealthy Conservative politician the Earl of Plymouth staged a Festival of Empire that mirrored the Delhi Durbar in celebrating the coronation of George V. The earl, who was a direct descendant of Robert Clive, the clerk turned general who conquered Bengal for the British East India Company in the eighteenth century, staged the festival at the famous Crystal Palace exhibition hall in Sydenham. A replacement for the original Crystal Palace in Hyde Park, it was the world's largest building at the time. Inside, the festival celebrated Britain's commercial supremacy with an "All British Imperial Exhibition of Arts and Industry and Applied Chemistry." But the "All Red Route," an electric railway named for red Royal Mail steamships, best represented British conceptions of their empire. Running some 1.5 miles, it took passengers on an imperial tour of painted murals, three hundred specially constructed buildings, and live displays of the empire's exotic animals and tribal subjects. During the twenty-minute tour, passengers saw Canadian mountains, a Jamaican sugar plantation, an Irish cottage, a Delhi temple, Malayan huts, Sydney Harbor, and a Maori village. There were even three-quarter-sized scale models of the dominion parliament buildings. The festival drew only two hundred thousand visitors and left the Earl of Plymouth with a £250,000 loss, but those who took the twenty minutes to ride the All Red Route could quite logically have concluded proudly that they were the subjects of an ancient, wealthy, and vital empire. In the following decades, British politicians, diplomats, and imperial partisans would echo the same theme, and play upon this general ignorance, in insisting the British Empire was a stable and unified international entity.

This was an understandable conclusion, but the empire's apparent coherence was illusory. Although the second British Empire included territories that Britain had held for centuries, its organization and systems of rule were the products of the late-nineteenth-century new imperialism. Even more important, it was, like the other European empires born of the same era, an outmoded anachronism built in large part by old-fashioned chartered companies and "native levies" despite its claims to modernity. The American Revolution, the progress of Western settlement colonies toward self-government, Napoleon's resounding fall at the hands of the Sixth and Seventh coalitions, and the vitality of the British "empire of influence" at mid-century were all indications that formal empires were no longer viable. But Westerners took their success in claiming large sections of the globe in the late nineteenth century as evidence of their cultural, if not moral, superiority. Placing themselves at the apex of a pseudoevolutionary racial pyramid on the basis of military victories and rapid industrialization, they promised the new empires would modernize the world's backward races. They failed to realize that the new imperialism was the result of short-term global economic and technological imbalances. In 1911, the passengers on the All Red Route and the dignitaries at the Delhi Coronation Durbar may have been certain that their empire would last for centuries, but the wet and gloomy transfer of power in Hong Kong at the close of the century shows that it took only decades for these global disparities to even out.

This, however, is only clear in hindsight. At its noontime, the empire's promoters imagined it as a coherent global community of diverse peoples bound together by shared allegiance to the British Crown and the just political and social institutions it represented. In fact, the empire was not a coherent administrative or economic unit. Instead of a single imperial system, there were multiple and overlapping subempires that employed vastly different political and social policies and followed substantially different trajectories. The Act of Union aimed to integrate Ireland more tightly into the United Kingdom, but its failure meant that Britain's oldest and most unique imperial possession was already slipping away at the turn of the twentieth century. The Indian Raj was an imperial power in its own right that, with its own army and navy, exercised substantial influence over East Africa, the Persian Gulf, Arabia, Burma, Ceylon, and Malaya. Covering 1.8 million miles, it was larger than the Roman Empire and boasted a population of 300 million people. The self-governing "white" dominions were well on their way to nationhood and similarly followed their own expansionist policies. The West Indian sugar colonies were vestiges of the first British Empire, whereas private chartered companies administered many of the territories in Africa and the Pacific. From its stronghold in Hong Kong, Britain exerted informal influence over China, and Argentina, Brazil, and Chile, which were never British possessions, were still more important trading partners and recipients of British investment than most of the new imperial acquisitions.

In terms of administration, the Colonial Office in London, which answered to the British parliament, was only responsible for a portion of the empire. Organized into geographical and functional departments, its primary role was to oversee the colonial civil service. It had no jurisdiction over the Indian Civil Service (which was under the separate India Office), the Sudan Political Service, or, after 1926, the self-governing dominions. The Indian Civil Service did not even directly administer all of India. One-third of the South Asian subcontinent consisted of princely states, which were governed by Indian rulers under the careful supervision of a British resident. British Malaya was a similarly confusing hodgepodge of nine protected Malay sultanates, four federated Malay states, three "straits settlements," and the great port city of Singapore. The Treasury and board of trade exercised considerable influence over the sovereign states in the empire's informal commercial orbit through their management of trade and investment policy. Moreover, although the Colonial Office appointed, trained, and assigned members of the colonial service, the individual territories paid their salaries and pensions. This meant that the colonial secretary and his staff had little direct authority over colonial governors and legislatures. Instead the authorities in London usually relied on persuasion to implement colonial policy, and colonial governors and settlers were often able to undermine or even thwart directives from London that they did not agree with. At times, candid metropolitan politicians acknowledged these irrational administrative realities. Speaking in a debate on the 1948 British Nationality Bill, Lord Alrincham, who had served as governor of Kenya as Edward Grigg, declared, "The Empire has always been an untidy Empire, and I think that is the chief reason why it still exists. Let us not rely too much on logic, for I verily believe that that would spell the decadence and demise of our greatest asset."[17]

At the imperial center, metropolitan Britons knew very little about what actually went on in the untidy empire. This may seem odd given that imperial governance generated an enormous body of statistics, commission reports, and other forms of official knowledge that appeared to provide a full and detailed representation of how it functioned. However, a great many of these reports and findings actually reflected official discord among the various imperial experts and did not provide a realistic picture of life in the wider empire. More often than not, the role of official reports and fact-finding commissions was to manufacture as much as to uncover truth. These realities allowed various groups to make wide-ranging and often contradictory claims about the empire that were difficult to sort out in the metropole. Social imperialists, for example, promised that the new imperial territories would replace markets lost to rival industrial powers and dampen the appeal of socialism by raising living standards for the British working classes. Yet relatively few ordinary Britons paid much attention to this pro-empire propaganda. The Earl of Plymouth lost a substantial investment because his Festival of Empire was so poorly attended, and there is little evidence that imperial promises had much of an impact on British elections. In 1951, the Government Social Survey Unit poll found that 59 percent of the electorate could not name a single British colony and that 80 percent did not know the difference between a dominion and colony.[18]

Still, some segments of metropolitan society did care deeply about the empire. For most politicians empire building was a bipartisan project. Although MPs often asked hard questions about imperial policies to embarrass rivals or pursue various causes, most generally agreed that, as an institution, the empire was a matter of national interest and therefore above party politics. Most significantly, manufacturers, who were struggling to keep pace with European and American rivals by the beginning of the twentieth century, embraced the idea of imperial protectionism and sought to use their political influence to block Indian entrepreneurs from setting up competing businesses in the Raj or British East Africa. The general public, however, was largely unconcerned with the specific details of imperial rule and investment, and most people accepted the vague notion, driven home by imperial partisans in the press, popular literature, music halls, and eventually movies and radio broadcasts, that there was no inherent conflict between liberal democracy and empire.

Not all Britons accepted this premise, and there was always a vocal minority in Britain that opposed every aspect of empire building. Many of the proponents of informal empire in the mid-nineteenth century distrusted the new imperialism, and they worried that Prime Minister Benjamin Disraeli's decision to crown Victoria empress of India would lead to Roman or Napoleonic despotism at home. Similarly, these critics noted that the metropolitan parliament had no direct control of the vast Indian army. Others objected to the fortunes speculators made in the empire by using privileged connections to secure guaranteed loans, grants, and subsidies. Charging that these concessions came at the expense of the metropolitan taxpayer, they portrayed the second British Empire as a covert mechanism for enriching segments of the upper classes at the expense of the rest of British society. In this vein journalist J. A. Hobson claimed that a cabal of capitalists had instigated the South African War to protect their investments. Additionally, secular philanthropic organizations like the Aborigines Rights Protection Society and Protestant evangelical groups, which often worked closely with left-wing politicians, championed the cause of subject peoples and criticized specific exploitive imperial policies vehemently. Even so, few of these metropolitan critics would have favored dismantling the empire. Rather, this "humanitarian lobby" wanted it to live up to its high ideals.

These conflicting perspectives were even sharper in the wider empire, where a diverse range of Britons played significantly different roles in the imperial enterprise. Critics of the new imperialism often portrayed it as a scramble for riches, but in reality the second British Empire was remarkably unprofitable for all but a select few. Recognizing the expensive and risky speculative nature of empire building, most industrialists and private investors preferred to put their capital in the United States, Latin America, and the dominions. Of the £1.2 billion that Britons invested in the empire between 1865 and 1914, less than 10 percent went to the non-self-governing "dependent territories."[19] This is why the metropolitan government relied so heavily on private chartered companies to claim territory. Speculators willing to undertake the risk of financing private armies and colonial bureaucracies stood to become extremely rich if their companies acquired the rights to administer regions with easily exploitable resources like precious metals or marketable agricultural commodities, but the windfall profits of Cecil Rhodes's British South Africa Company and George Goldie's Royal Niger Company were exceptional. The bankruptcy suffered by William MacKinnon's Imperial British East Africa Company, which floundered trying to run the Uganda and East Africa (Kenya) protectorates, was much more typical. Still, there was money to be made in imperial enterprises like Malayan tin and rubber, Fijian and Jamaican sugar, and Northern Rhodesian copper if investors could reduce their labor expenses sufficiently to compensate for high shipping costs, insufficient infrastructure, and undercapitalization.

In the public sphere, the colonial service provided rewarding careers for the graduates of top British universities who were ready to embrace the ideology of the new imperialism. For most of the twentieth century, Sir Ralph Furse and a pair of assistants in the Colonial Office sought gifted athletes from good families to serve as field administrators in remote corners of the empire. The empire's critics, in turn, charged that the men who actually joined the colonial service were primarily mediocre students from established landed families. The Colonial Office recruiters preferred graduates with degrees in classics and modern history but would settle for men with training in literature or geography. They were not impressed with credentials in the sciences and avoided the unmanly spectacled chap entirely. Those who made the cut faced an arduous and lonely job serving as often the sole voice of imperial authority in rural Africa or Asia. As compensation, a district officer was, in the words of an unofficial historian of the colonial service, "king of all he surveys." Few would have disputed a former Kenyan district officer's claim that he and his fellow field administrators were the "elite corps of an elite system, created for the benevolent exercise of paternal power."[20]

The empire also offered military officers opportunities for glory and career advancement. In the decades before World War I, a time when Britain was largely at peace with the rest of Europe, imperial wars of conquest were often the only way for military officers to distinguish themselves. This often meant "secondment" from the regular British army to colonial militias and the irregular native forces of the private chartered companies. Ambitious men like Frederick Lugard, William Robertson, and Robert Baden Powell earned rapid promotion by fighting Afrikaners, Africans, and Asians. Robertson, who began his military career as a private and retired a field marshal, won his commission in the Indian army and his fame in the South African War. Lugard was also an Indian army officer, but his career path took him into the service of African private chartered company armies and then the colonial service. After serving as governor of Nigeria, he retired as Baron Lugard of Abinger. Robert Baden Powell also made his reputation during Britain's African wars, but it was his role in founding the Boy Scout movement that earned him the title First Baron Baden Powell of Gilwell. Given these examples, it is hardly surprising that the rush for glory and decorations became a problem. Civil officials in British East Africa grumbled that each new officer should be awarded two medals upon arriving in the colony with the threat that he would lose one for each minor war (punitive expedition) he started.

In the eastern, central, and southern African highlands, relatively temperate regions attracted migrants who believed it was still possible to establish old-fashioned settlement colonies at the expense of the indigenous population. Their leaders tended to come from elite backgrounds, and many of these restless nobles aspired to create a version of the aristocratic social order of privilege and deference of an imaginary English countryside. Although the settlers liked to portray themselves as rugged frontiersmen, they acquired their land at the expense of local people and relied heavily on their forced labor to remain solvent. Similarly, most Western corporations, which focused primarily on mining and plantation agriculture, also needed cheap labor to compensate for underinvestment and minimal infrastructure. These economic limitations, coupled with institutionalized racial segregation in the settler colonies, known as the "colour bar," made a nonsense of the paternalistic promises of the new imperialism.

These realities were obvious to those who looked closely at daily life in the imperial periphery, and one of the untidy aspects of the new British Empire was that the various imperial interest groups had substantially contradictory agendas. The Protestant mission societies and leftist secular reformers in the humanitarian lobby often pressed the Colonial Office and the metropolitan parliament to rein in settler racism and inhuman labor policies. W. McGregor Ross, an ex-administrator turned imperial critic, was brutally honest in his description of the origins of the Kenya colony: "We got the country not by conquest nor cession. We went there under the terms of treaties, and as protectors of the natives. We have stolen immense quantities of land, and indulged in unblushing exploitation of many native tribes."[21]

The reformers' attacks on specific abusive policies did not mean that they disagreed with the underlying assumptions of the new imperialism. Although many administrative officers considered missionaries intrusive meddlers, the missions received significant government funding to run most of the empire's schools and hospitals. This quasi-official role enhanced their status and proved immensely useful as they sought converts among subject populations. With no significant economic stake in the new territories, the reformers had little to lose in pushing to make imperial rule more humane and less lucrative. Moreover, like the colonial military and administrative services, the missions provided good careers for university graduates. This held true for women as well as men. At a time when middle-class notions of domesticity confined women to the home in metropolitan Britain, the empire offered them a measure of independence as missionaries, teachers, social welfare experts, and farmers. The colour bar in colonial societies also meant that Western women had de facto authority over African and Asian men by virtue of their race. These non-Western males became permanent "boys" who were too immature and undisciplined to assume adult responsibilities.

Most of the Britons who governed, fought, invested, traded, preached, taught, or settled in the empire understood very little of the people among whom they lived and worked. Nevertheless, administrators, missionaries, and all sorts of professional and amateur ethnographers were quite certain that they did. Under the rhetoric of the new imperialism, they spent an enormous amount of time and effort classifying conquered populations as natives, tribesmen, clansmen, Asiatics, "Mohammedans" (Muslims), and members of Hindu castes. The population of Lord Alrincham's untidy empire was incredibly diverse, but for British imperialists there were common denominators. Unlike the "modern" individuals in the settlement colonies or dominions, non-Westerners were members of rigidly organic corporate groups whose lives were governed by unchanging tradition. This fiction helped justify imperial authoritarianism by suggesting that the empire's subjects did not understand or expect individual rights and liberties. It also had practical administrative and security applications. Although the 1907 Hague Convention banned collective punishment in Western nations, many British territories had ordinances empowering the authorities to demand communal labor or punish groups suspected of harboring law breakers.

Although no state has the power to impose identity on unwilling populations, the empire's exotic collective identities were largely products of the imperial imagination. The English word "tribe" is from the Latin *tribus*, which described the three original communities of ancient Rome. Similarly, "caste" was a Spanish and Portuguese derivative of the Latin *castus*, which meant pure and unpolluted. Westerners turned these terms into defining categories of subjecthood to make sense of confusing and seemingly chaotic Amerindian, Asian, and African identities during the first and second imperial eras. By this reasoning, "tribe" became a lower order of political or social organization that might one day, perhaps under the guiding hand of British rule, evolve into a nation. Under the Raj, "caste" became a fundamental social ideology that determined an individual's status, worldview, and inher-

ent behavioral characteristics. Government surveys and censuses spelled out
the size and nature of each group in precise detail. After World War I, British
administrators similarly adapted Ottoman religious categories to organize
and classify the population of the Palestine Mandate. Throughout the empire,
civil officials and military officers developed a set of ethnographic stereotypes that labeled specific communities as simple peasants, "warrior races,"
"criminal tribes," pastoral traditionalists, religious fanatics, or untrustworthy
political subversives.

This is not to say that the imperialists fabricated tribal and caste identities.
British rule made tribe, caste, and religion the language of politics, economic
enterprise, and social legitimacy. Administrators, missionaries, and ethnographers framed the high political culture and dominant economic order of the
empire, but their subjects determined what these concepts actually meant in
daily practice. This meant that British officials, who often fancied themselves
experts on native culture, could be manipulated by ethnic impostors, religious authorities, or self-styled traditional elders.

Tight economies of the new imperialism produced financial and manpower shortages that forced administrators to seek allies among subject populations. Having built the second British Empire largely on speculation and
outsourcing to private chartered companies, the metropolitan government ran
most of the new territories on a shoestring. In 1926, the European administration of Nigeria, a colony of 20 million people, consisted of less than twenty-
two hundred district officers, policemen, soldiers, teachers, and technical
experts, and during the same decade there were only about 156,000 Britons
in all of India. [22] Rather than exporting metropolitan models of direct administration to the wider empire, district officers governed by co-opting and
adapting African and Asian cultures. In recruiting native policemen, soldiers,
translators, and clerks, they had to share power in order to exercise power.
The most important of these proxies were subordinate bureaucrats that British officials termed chiefs or headmen to maintain the illusion that their
administrative systems were in harmony with native cultures. However, most
of these "native authorities" were imperial appointees, and they faced the
difficult prospect of maintaining enough respect among the general population to govern while collecting taxes and enforcing unpopular imperial policies.

Imperial experts like Frederick Lugard put a positive spin on this system
of "indirect rule" by claiming that the aim was to help the empire's subjects
follow their own culturally distinct path to modernity. As governor of Uganda, Philip Mitchell asserted that indirect rule was intended "to train and
develop the African inhabitants of the country, so that their ancient tribal
organisations may be modernised and adapted by them in such a manner as
to serve the present, and the future, as they have served the past." [23] Remi-
niscing nostalgically several decades after Kenyan independence, former ad-

ministrator Terence Gavaghan insisted that "development was the pre-occupation, the pride and the pleasure of almost every administrative officer."[24] In reality, indirect rule was an unspoken admission by British officials that they lacked the resources and popular support to make good on the developmentalist promises of the new imperialism. By appointing themselves guardians of primitive cultures and allying with conservative native authorities, they created weak and anachronistic state systems that could not provide the basic social services that were the norm in most nations by the mid-twentieth century.

These tensions show that the central tenets of the second British Empire were contradictory and often irrational. In theory, the empire was compatible with Britain's liberal ideals because it civilized and modernized less fortunate people. Yet, although district officers recruited laborers for Western investors and settlers, their reliance on native authorities to govern meant that they distrusted private enterprise and laissez-faire capitalism on the grounds that it weakened the communal bonds of customary society by promoting dangerous individualism. In fact, many African colonial governments even allowed slavery to continue for several decades because they worried abolition would cause undue economic and social disruption. This pragmatism put them at odds with the missionaries and secular humanitarians who provided the moral legitimacy for the imperial enterprise. The missions and their allies also criticized exploitive labor practices and settler racism, but most still believed that Africans and Asians could not speak for themselves. In this they shared the colonial service's faith that, on the whole, imperial rule was moral and benevolent. More often than not, however, the empire's political, economic, and moral representatives worked at cross-purposes.

THE UNSEEN EMPIRE

To the twentieth-century contemporary observer, the second British Empire was a strong and unified engine of political, economic, and social change, but its inherent untidiness obscured its actual consequences. Over the last century, anticolonial nationalists, imperial apologists, and historians of all stripes have debated whether a stereotypically monolithic British Empire was a "good" or "bad" institution. But the empire was never actually so coherent, and so it is much more productive to ask who benefited from British rule and who did not. Empire building was a form of historical change, and any such large-scale change invariably profited some people while harming others. The character and impact of imperial rule therefore depended largely on a person's perspective, geographic location, and social status.

The diversity of these subject experiences defies generalization or easy categorization. In India, the British members of the Indian Civil Service saw themselves as the platonic guardians of simple South Asian peasants and craftsmen. But the political activism of highly educated members of the Indian National Congress (INC) and the emerging class of prosperous industrialists, like the Tata family, punctured these romantic stereotypes. Maharaja Sayajirao's defiant behavior at the Delhi Coronation Durbar also showed that the Indian princes were not always the loyal allies that the British imagined them to be. Moreover, South Asians experienced imperial rule in markedly different and often conflicting ways. This is why the growing Indian working classes were just as likely to strike against Indian employers as against foreign capitalists, and when INC politicians gained a measure of self-rule in the 1930s, they enacted legislation that restricted unionization and gave rural landlords greater authority over their tenants. Most fundamentally, while South Asians from all walks of life became increasingly certain that they wanted an end to the Raj, they struggled to agree on what should replace it.

Similar tensions and contradictions were in play throughout the empire. Educated Asians, Africans, and West Indians followed the Indian National Congress's example in claiming the leadership of anti-imperial nationalist movements. Like the Indian princes, the Malayan sultans, Bugandan *kabakas*, Hausa emirs, and other assorted "traditional authorities" used their importance under indirect rule to defend their aristocratic privilege against challenges from this emerging national elite. Trinidadian oil field workers, Guyanese sugar plantation laborers, Sierra Leonian longshoremen, South African gold miners, Kenyan bus drivers, and countless other groups who survived by selling their labor took collective action to demand better wages and working conditions. And in virtually every corner of the empire, peasant farmers demonstrated that they were not as conservative or backward as British authorities imagined by increasing yields and producing for the market when given sufficient access to land, credit, and transportation. Rural women rejected Western conceptions of domestic femininity and defied the patriarchal authority of the imperial regime's "traditional" allies by taking control of cash crop production or setting up informal and often illegal urban businesses. Similarly, young men from pastoral communities, which imperial ethnographers assumed were the most tradition-bound peoples in the entire empire, willingly entered the cash economy on their own terms as soldiers, policemen, and livestock rustlers. In all of these cases, British rule resulted in a series of unexpected and unintended consequences that brought both hardship and opportunity.

When confronted with these developments, the imperial authorities were often more reactive than proactive. Although the empire appeared powerful and coherent in London, most territorial governments lacked the resources and manpower to direct the course of modernization. Their monopoly on lethal force meant that they had the police and soldiers to deal violently with mass unrest or overt challenges to imperial authority, but most of the time, particularly before World War II, it was relatively easy for ordinary people to avoid, circumvent, or even ignore imperial authority. This ironically meant that the second British Empire was most tolerable and stable when it was weak, and it was no accident that the era of more intrusive development imperialism in the late 1940s and 1950s coincided with the increased popularity of anti-imperial nationalism.

This is not to say that the empire was not a powerful instrument of change, just that it was not the instrument of change that British imperialists intended it to be. The consequences of the new imperialism were often unexpected, difficult to recognize, and driven by local forces. As the Delhi Coronation Durbar demonstrated, subject peoples who made a grand show of adopting British institutions and professing their loyalty to the empire sometimes used such displays as vehicles for protest and criticism because they had no other recognized means of political expression under its system of authoritarian paternalism. In creating their own churches, schools, sports teams, and social organizations, imperial subjects claimed the symbols of legitimacy and respectability without necessarily trying to become Western. The imperial authorities reassured themselves that these institutions were childish imitations, but in reality independent Ugandan Protestant churches, Trinidadian cricket teams, youth movements like the Indian Girl Messenger Service, curry, ska music, and other variations on British imperial norms were dynamic innovations resulting from cross-cultural borrowing. They demonstrated that the imperial regime's equation of modernization with westernization was ethnocentric and simplistic.

The twentieth-century British Empire was not as British as it appeared in the Festival of Empire. As core possessions that bridged the first and second British empires, Ireland and India were the model for British imperial policy and assumptions. After London, Dublin was the "second city of the empire," and Irish administrative and policing methods were a central point of reference for centuries. Irishmen also traveled throughout the empire as migrants, soldiers, merchants, and missionaries. The same was true for Indians. Poorly paid Indian soldiers made the new imperial conquests of the late nineteenth century affordable, and indirect rule, as an institution, had its origins in the Indian princely states before British administrators exported it to Africa, the Pacific, and the rest of Asia. Recruits from northern India formed the backbone of many imperial police forces, which meant, as Thomas Metcalf has observed, "for Africans and Asians, the turbaned Sikh, as much as the Englishman with his sun helmet, made visible their colonial subjugation."[25]

Even more important, Indian migrants and indentured laborers followed imperial commercial and transportation networks to settle in Burma, Malaya, Fiji, East Africa, Trinidad, and even Canada. By 1914, there were more than 1.3 million Indians living permanently in the wider empire. Although British officials, merchants, and settlers often denigrated, belittled, and persecuted these South Asian diasporic communities, they relied heavily on their entrepreneurial capital, commercial acumen, artisanal skills, clerical assistance, and coercive muscle. This meant that Indian values and norms had a direct and profound impact on British imperial culture. Although the Kenyan settlers liked to claim that Nairobi was a "white man's city," Indians played the key role in funding it, building it, and keeping it running.

Although imperial chauvinists would never admit it, the cultural reach of Indians and other non-Western subject populations extended to metropolitan Britain. Indirect rule and Christian evangelism required British administrators and missionaries to become intimately familiar with new values, languages, traditions, commodities, and ways of life. These expatriates brought many of these novel ideas and products back to Britain, where the imperial pageants and displays helped create a popular appetite for romanticized and exoticized manifestations of non-Western cultures. The West Indians, Africans, and Asians who traveled to Britain as diplomats, politicians, students, soldiers, sailors, religious pilgrims, and tourists further drove this imperial cross-pollination. At first these groups found the imperial metropole a generally welcoming place because British liberal values ensured that they enjoyed the same political rights and civil liberties as ordinary British citizens, but as they came by the tens of thousands as guest workers and then semipermanent settlers in the 1950s and 1960s, many Britons began to worry that they themselves were being colonized. In this sense the second British Empire was part of an evolving hybrid global culture that sprang from the intimate cross-cultural interaction between Britons and their non-Western subjects. The new imperial partisans promised to modernize the backward regions of the world, but they did not recognize that the forces they unleashed would also globalize their own culture and society.

NEW QUESTIONS

During the heyday of the new imperialism in the decades leading up to World War I, few people in Britain realized that the processes of empire building cut in so many unexpected ways. From the perspective of the metropolitan taxpayer, the empire paid relatively few tangible dividends. The self-governing dominions refused to play a subordinate economic role, and by the end of World War II, India had become one of Britain's primary creditors. Moreover, with the exception of a few successful export-producing colonies like Malaya, Uganda, and the Gold Coast, most of the new imperial territories were not economically viable and often had to draw on support from the metropolitan Treasury to remain solvent. And although the Indian army made Britain a great power, expensive counterinsurgency operations in Malaya, Kenya, and Cyprus in the 1950s were a heavy drain on limited metro-politan military and economic resources.

Similarly, the empire had very little to offer its subjects. In return for the ephemeral promise that British tutelage would lead to political maturity and economic development at some point in the vaguely defined future, the ma-jority of ordinary people had to endure authoritarian rule, put up with exploi-tive labor and land policies that benefited foreign commercial interests and alien settlers, and accept the humiliation of being labeled savage natives and tribal primitives. Even the educated elites and traditional authorities who benefited personally from their roles in the empire grew impatient with its inherent racism, condescension, and double standards.

In time, more and more people throughout the British Empire came to question its legitimacy. The largely unseen horizontal networks of communi-cation and commerce that bound the empire together also allowed imperial subjects to share ideas, and in the early decades of the twentieth century, Irish, Afrikaner, and Indian nationalists studied each other's tactics closely. This cooperative anti-imperialism was never a direct threat to the empire, but it marked the beginning of a growing unwillingness of the larger subject population to be ruled by foreigners. A bloody anti-imperial war gave Ireland dominion status and de facto independence in 1922, and the Raj came to an end twenty-five years later in 1947. The British Empire never fell in the stereotypical Roman sense. Instead, in the decade and a half following World War II, the expense of imperial rule, coupled with the rising expense of counterinsurgency operations and the diplomatic costs of trying to maintain an empire when anti-imperial nationalism was becoming the global norm, led Britain to grant its remaining West Indian, Asian, and African territories independence in fairly rapid succession.

The "white" dominions never formally severed their ties with the British metropole, but their assertiveness forced imperial partisans to seize upon the Commonwealth as the logical end point of empire. In defining this Common-wealth as a "free association" of independent nations bound together by common ties to the Crown, they hoped to preserve as much of the economic, strategic, and diplomatic benefits of the second British Empire as possible. Central to this project was a revisionist narrative that asserted "nation build-ing" had always been the ultimate goal of British imperial rule. In the 1920s, Lugard would have agreed with this statement in principle, but in the years after World War II, his successors advanced his timetable considerably. De-nying that they had given in to outside pressure in dismantling the empire, imperial partisans held up the self-governing nations in the Commonwealth as evidence that they had successfully executed a planned transfer of power. Unspoken in this argument was the presumption that the African, Asian, and West Indian nationalists were to blame for any political instability, economic underdevelopment, or social turmoil in the former British possessions.

This debate obscures the fundamental reality that all of the empires born of the late nineteenth century were inherently unstable. The Delhi Coronation Durbar's projection of imperial vitality and stability was illusionary. The global political and military imbalance that gave Britain and other industrial powers the means to claim new territories in Africa and Asia at minimal cost was temporary. History shows that these sorts of global fluctuations in knowledge and technology even out fairly quickly, and so it is unproductive to argue about how and why the British Empire "fell." It is much more rewarding to explore its legacy. In most territories anti-imperial nationalists were united in wanting British rule to end, but they rarely could agree on what should replace it. Turning a colony born of foreign conquest into a nation-state was no easy matter, and the empire's political heirs had to confront thorny questions of whether to keep imperial boundaries, how to determine who was a citizen, and whether they should retain British institutions or seek to recover the pre-imperial past. Equally interesting and complex is the question of how becoming a twentieth-century imperial power changed Britain itself. The rainy ceremony in Hong Kong may have marked the surrender of Britain's last significant imperial possession, but the legacy of the empire lives on in Britain's twenty-first-century diverse multicultural society. This new Britain, which would most likely have horrified many of the architects of the new imperialism, shows that the empires of the last century were short-lived engines of globalization that left behind new and vital networks of migration, commerce, and cultural exchange.

Chapter Two

The Empire at High Tide

HAM MUKASA MEETS THE KING

On August 8, 1902, Ham Mukasa found himself at Windsor Castle awaiting an audience with King Edward VII. Mukasa, a nobleman from the Kingdom of Buganda, was at the palace in his capacity as the personal secretary of the Bugandan *katikiro* (prime minister) Apolo Kagwa. The Gandans were part of a larger delegation of African and Asian aristocrats who were to witness Edward's official coronation in a few days' time. In this sense, Mukasa's visit to see the king was a more intimate version of his son George V's massive durbar a decade later. As was the case with the elaborate rituals in Delhi in 1911, the imperial authorities aimed to demonstrate the power and majesty of the empire by inviting their most aristocratic subjects to witness the pageantry of the coronation and the technical and cultural supremacy of Britain itself.

At first glance, Mukasa's personal diary appeared to show that the Gandans were indeed overawed by what they saw in the imperial metropole. They arrived at Windsor Castle in a "very fine carriage" and walked through "many passages and rooms, each with its own doorkeeper," until they came to "a very large door, which was covered with gold." Conducted through this grand portal by Lord Lansdowne, the secretary of state for foreign affairs, they met "the Father of the Nation," King Edward, "sitting upon his throne, dressed in a magnificent kingly raiment." During the polite conversation that followed, the king asked Apolo Kagwa, "Do you like this country very much?" And the Gandan *katikiro* replied, "It is a very fine country and the work which is done in this country of yours is most wonderful. I am amazed at the houses and streets, and the people like locusts in numbers, and the railway trains go marvelously fast." Mukasa recorded that the king gravely responded, "Yes, that is true, these things are wonderful."[1] Kagwa and his secretary also had prime seats at Edward's coronation at Westminster Abbey. Here again, British readers of Mukasa's diary would have been well satisfied that their African visitors were suitably impressed. Writing of the pageantry, he gushed, "He who had one eye would have liked two, and he who had two would have liked four, that he might see better than he could with two. . . . [The ceremony] was a marvelous thing, and one's hair stood on end on account of the exceeding glory!"[2]

The British government's grand treatment of them indicated that the Gandan aristocrats were distinguished visitors from a strategically important East African state. Located on the shores of Lake Victoria/Nyanza, which is the source of the Nile River, the Kingdom of Buganda was a significant prize. Beginning in the 1860s, rival factions of Gandan nobles became enmeshed in a competition for power that led them to forge alliances with Muslim Swahili traders, "explorers" like Henry Morton Stanley, and rival French and British empire builders. In the 1880s, a Gandan prince named Mwanga became *kabaka* (king) with the aid of Frederick Lugard, who was then an employee of the Imperial British East Africa Company, and Lugard's maxim gun. But Mwanga eventually revolted against his sponsors when he found that the alliance meant that the Westerners claimed the right to control land in the kingdom. After a series of violent skirmishes, the British replaced him with his infant son Daudi Chwa under the regency of three cooperative Protestant Gandan noblemen, one of whom was Apolo Kagwa. Under the terms of a 1900 treaty signed by these regents, the Kingdom of Buganda became a province of the larger Uganda Protectorate, which profited Apolo Kagwa and the rest of the elites in the pro-British faction substantially. In addition to allowances for Gandan royal family members and gun licenses for all the significant nobles, Kagwa and the aristocratic members of the Gandan *lukiko* (parliament) received 50 percent of the land in the kingdom to share out among themselves. This was in contrast to the preconquest arrangement where Gandan clans had title to the land.

Kagwa was one of Britain's most important African allies, and his visit to London was intended both to reward and to intimidate his ruling Anglican faction. Writing in the introduction to the English-language translation of Mukasa's diary, Sir Harry Johnston, the first "special commissioner" of Uganda, frankly acknowledged, "It is our business as an Imperial race to show all those people who are British subjects or British-protected persons, and who dwell outside the limits of the white man's lands, that it is to their interest and advantage to remain of their own free will a part of that British Empire which should develop as time goes on into a vast league of peace and good will, unhampered commerce, tolerant beliefs, and unbounded knowledge."[3] The Gandan nobles were thus part of a steady stream of elite African and Asian visitors who traveled to Britain at government expense at the turn of the twentieth century, and Mukasa and Kagwa even bumped into Ras Makonnen, the prime minister of Ethiopia, during their tour of Windsor Castle. In fact, they were not even the first Gandans to have an audience with a reigning British monarch, for Anglican missionaries had already brought two earlier Gandan delegations to meet Queen Victoria. Direct access to the royal family and the centers of power in London often paid handsome dividends to cooperative African leaders. Khama III solidified his status as *kgosi* (king) of the Bamangwato (in present-day Botswana) and fended off incursions by the Germans, Afrikaners, and Cecil Rhodes by personally convincing Victoria to establish a British protectorate over what became known as Bechuanaland.

The standard template for these visits showed off Britain's technological and cultural superiority through tours of factories, printing works, subways, museums, and churches. In addition to having an audience with the sovereign, the delegations usually also visited the homes of the missionaries and administrators who had served in their country. Lest the visitors miss the subtle nuances of this imperial propaganda, the British authorities were also ready to deliver a more explicit message. After dutifully listing the various wonders that had "astonished" them in Britain, Kagwa and Mukasa received the following advice from Sir Clement Hill of the Foreign Office: "Work hard at cultivation and at learning everything that brings money to your country. . . . We were like you are once, or even worse off, and you too if you work hard will be like we are now."[4]

Yet Mukasa's English-language account of these proceedings did not convey the subtle nuances of his impressions of Britain. The book's editor and translator, Ernest Millar, was an Anglican missionary who admitted to cutting out observations "that might have caused pain to some, or that were of a too personal nature."[5] And Sir Harry Johnston, who wrote its introduction, took offense at a passage that Millar left in where Mukasa characterized English dancing as immoral. "When they dance they jump up and down and twist round, men and women holding on to each other in pairs; for my own part I preferred the music to the dancing, which I thought was a shameful thing, for men and women to dance thus together."[6] Although the Gandan delegation was unquestionably impressed by Britain's wealth and technological achievements, they were not as overawed as their hosts intended. This was evident in another of Mukasa's carefully worded critiques that survived Millar's editorial purge. Cagily alerting his readers that he was aware of the propagandistic overtones of their endless itinerary of factory visits, middle-class tea parties, and royal audiences, Mukasa observed, "If you agreed to everything the English beg you to do, you would get ill and die a sudden death, because they are so kind they want you to see everything, and to talk to you all day long; and so their kindness tires you before you know it, and you are like a reed which is burning at both ends and so gets burned up quickly."[7]

At first glance, Ham Mukasa and Apolo Kagwa seemed just the sort of elite allies that made British rule possible and cost-effective in the remote corners of the empire. They were highly educated, enthusiastic Anglicans who, upon their return to East Africa, built Western-style houses, purchased automobiles, and sent their children to elite mission schools. But the British readers who took satisfaction in Mukasa's numerous expressions of wonderment and empire loyalty missed the reality that the Gandan noblemen did not believe that his people needed foreign help to become "modern."

Mukasa clearly took offense at British insinuations that his country was backward and primitive. In the 1930s, he was particularly provoked by an article in the *Uganda Journal* by Sir John Gray, a colonial jurist and amateur historian, that described Kabaka Mutesa, the last independent Gandan sovereign, as "an absolute ruler of a sycophant race, a man of regal bearing but a superlative egoist, always capricious and at times revoltingly cruel."[8] In an era when it was unwise and potentially dangerous to openly challenge British rule, Mukasa chose to respond to Gray's insult in kind. Offering his own alternative history of Buganda in a pair of articles in the same journal, he credited Mutesa with showing the celebrated explorer John Hanning Speke that Lake Victoria/Nyanza was the source of the Nile. In an inversion of his seeming wonderment in his own published account of Edwardian Britain, he drew on Gandan oral history to quote Speke as marveling at "the greatness of the cultivation of the Baganda" and declaring, "The masses of people I have seen in Buganda resemble the crowds to be seen on our roads in Europe." More significantly, Mukasa included a clear critique of the British conquest and subjugation of his country by having visiting Muslim merchants caution Mutesa on the consequences of allowing Westerners to gain a toehold in his kingdom. Warning that soldiers and administrators would follow on the heels of seemingly humble missionaries, they foretold that the empire builders would "eat up" his country. Although Mukasa embraced Western material culture in his own personal life, his Muslim proxies depicted Christianity and industrial technology as dangerous lures that would lead to imperial subjugation: "When a fish has swallowed the hook, baited with a piece of meat, there is nothing left to do except to pull it in; its strength is finished."[9]

It is quite likely that Mukasa's account of this prescient warning was apocryphal and that no such conversation between Mutesa and some Muslim advisors took place. But the story itself was not unusual in imperial Africa. Indeed, a great many African communities credited their own prophets and religious figures with similarly foretelling the European conquest of Africa. Jomo Kenyatta included a satirical parable of the British conquest and colonization of Kenya in *Facing Mount Kenya: The Tribal Life of the Gikuyu* that remarkably paralleled the style and content of the warnings issued by the

Muslim traders in Mukasa's story.[10] These similarities were not accidental. As was the case with Maharaja Sayajirao at the Delhi Coronation Durbar, Mukasa's alternative and subtly subversive history of Buganda and the widespread popularity of prophetic predictions of the new imperial conquests revealed a fundamental dissatisfaction with foreign rule among Britain's imperial subjects. Although it would take decades for these rumblings to turn into overt anti-imperial nationalism, Ham Mukasa's quiet defiance showed that Britain's hold over its new imperial territories was never as strong as its spectacles and pageants suggested.

A TOUR OF THE BRITISH EMPIRE IN THE TIME OF HAM MUKASA, CA. 1900 TO 1914

Some Britons actually sensed this reality at the turn of the twentieth century. Indeed, the grand pageantry of the Delhi Coronation Durbar, the Festival of Empire, and the coronation ceremonies masked a deep insecurity that Britain might suffer the fate of the later Roman Empire. Politicians, strategists, merchants, bankers, and imperial enthusiasts all worried that an aging industrial base, competition from continental and American rivals, and waning national morality and vigor made Britain an empire in decline. The second British Empire was feasible in the 1880s because the cost of conquering new territories was surprisingly low, but when Ham Mukasa arrived in London roughly two decades later, the price of formal empire was considerably higher.

Challenged by continental European powers, the United States, Japan, and increasing unrest in India, Britain now had to devote considerably more effort to policing and defending its sprawling transcontinental empire. This was at a time when its status as a global economic power was substantially diminished. In 1870, British industry produced one-third of the world's manufacturing output, but by 1914 this had fallen to just one-seventh. The nation's status as the first industrial power gave it a head start over its competitors in the early nineteenth century, but this early lead also meant that British manufacturers were less ready to exploit the new opportunities in steel, chemicals, and electrical goods that represented a second Industrial Revolution. Moreover, protected imperial markets gradually weakened Britain's industrial base by sparing industrialists the pain of modernizing their factories and competing in the global marketplace.

Distracted by grand propagandistic displays like coronation celebrations and the Festival of Empire, most metropolitan taxpayers did not realize how little the empire contributed to the Treasury. In the decade and a half before the outbreak of World War I, Britain's primary trading partners were in Europe and North America, not in the empire. Since Britain imported 50 percent more goods than it exported in 1900, it took foreign investments and "invisible" export earnings from shipping, banking, insurance, engineering, and consulting to make up the imbalance. The British pound sterling remained the favored currency of investors and traders around the world because it was based on gold but, unlike gold, could earn interest. London was the world's banking center because investors knew that the British government backed the sterling deposits in its banks. Although imperial enthusiasts took comfort in the vast stretches of territory marked out in British red on maps in their studies and parlors, London's preeminence as a center of global finance and banking was as important a source of British power and influence as colonies and armies. As trade declined, the value of the nation's overseas holdings rose from £700 million to £2 billion during the last three decades of the nineteenth century. These investments were worth nearly £4 billion by 1913 and produced £200 million per year in earnings, which constituted 10 percent of Britain's total national income. [11] Only a small fraction of this considerable wealth came from formal imperial territories. Nevertheless, manufacturers and protectionist politicians like the Liberal colonial secretary Joseph Chamberlain still believed that turning the empire into a closed mercantilistic trading system was the best way to preserve Britain's global economic influence.

In terms of imperial security, British strategists were most concerned about Germany's aspirations to become a sea power. They were not particularly alarmed in the 1880s when Chancellor Otto von Bismarck claimed African colonies during the new imperial scramble, but after the turn of the twentieth century, the increasingly powerful German navy threatened imperial shipping and communication links and exposed the vulnerability of Britain's lightly defended overseas possessions. The result was an expensive arms race in which Britain and Germany competed to build ever-more powerful battleships. To make matters worse, the growing Russian military presence in Central Asia led British commanders in India to ask for £2 million to expand and modernize the Indian army. Faced with the need to reduce defense costs and concentrate the Royal Navy in European waters, the Foreign Office tried to protect British interests in Asia by forging a formal alliance with the expanding Japanese Empire.

In Africa, the South African War of 1899 to 1902, which brought the entire southern tip of the continent under British rule, constituted an even more serious drain on British resources. The three-year conflict with a far weaker opponent tied down 750,000 imperial soldiers who were needed elsewhere and produced twenty-two thousand casualties. Moreover, the £270 million it took to defeat the Afrikaners, who were descended primarily from Dutch settlers, represented 14 percent of the national income of 1902. [12] Equally troubling was the extremely high rate of medical rejection by the armed services of members of the British working classes for a range of relatively simple health problems associated with poverty. This included the three thousand urban recruits whose teeth were so bad that they were unfit to serve. Sensational newspaper reports of these mass disqualifications, which suggested national weakness, led anxious Britons to worry that they might suffer the fate of a declining ancient Rome.

Unrest among substantial populations in Ireland and India, two of Britain's oldest and most important imperial possessions, gave substance to these fears. This was particularly true in Ireland, where the 1801 Act of Union failed to win popular acceptance of British rule. Even though there were 750,000 Irishmen living in Britain and Irishmen constituted almost one-third of the rank-and-file soldiers in the British army at the midpoint of the nineteenth century, the fundamental inequities of Ireland's imperial relationship with Britain remained. The Irish Parliamentary Party had the capacity to shift the balance of power between the Liberal and Conservative parties in the House of Commons, but Conservatives still blocked the Liberals' relatively halfhearted efforts to pass a home rule bill. Moreover, Irish political influence in London did not improve standards of living in Ireland. On the eve of World War I, Dublin remained one of the most impoverished cities in western Europe. Although imperial partisans bragged that it was the second city of the empire, some twenty-one thousand of its families lived in one-room tenements that lacked running water and basic sanitation.[13]

Consequently, increasing numbers of Irish Catholics and even a significant number of Protestants were more determined than ever to seek a solution to Ireland's problems by asserting some form of autonomy. Frustrated by the Irish Parliamentary Party's inability to win home rule, the separatists first sought to reassert an Irish national identity. The Gaelic Athletic Association promoted "ancient" Irish sports in place of humiliating foreign (i.e., British) games, and the Gaelic League worked to replace English with the Irish language in government, schools, and even the post office. In time, these cultural movements gradually merged with more militant groups, like the Irish Republican Brotherhood, to explicitly call for severing all ties with Britain by creating a democratic Irish republic. This was still a much too radical step for most Irishmen at this point. Arthur Griffith's Sinn Féin party, which called for separate national status for Ireland under the British Crown, seemed a more feasible option.

Attitudes began to shift after Herbert Asquith's Liberal government finally passed an Irish home rule bill in 1912 that would have reestablished a separate Irish parliament. Alarmed by the prospect of being governed by a republican-minded Catholic majority, Irish Protestants and committed unionists threatened to contest the law through violent extralegal means. In 1913, fifty-eight British army officers at the Curragh camp in County Kildare (just over one hundred kilometers from Dublin) threatened to resign their commissions if the British government ordered them to move against the unionist militia. To make matters worse, the Ulster Unionist Council laid the groundwork for the secession of six of the nine counties in the northern province of Ulster by creating the paramilitary Ulster Volunteer Force (UVF), which was armed with twenty-five thousand smuggled rifles. The home rule opponents had the unspoken support of many die-hard imperialists in the Conservative Party who feared that making political concessions in Ireland would set a precedent for India and the rest of the overseas empire. Faced with the prospect of armed resistance in the north, the Irish republicans formed the Irish Volunteer Movement to counter the UVF. Only the outbreak of World War I, which delayed full implementation of home rule, saved Ireland from a civil war that could have destabilized the entire empire.

This certainly would have been the case in India, where almost three centuries of British rule had produced a small but influential class of West-ern-educated Indians who watched the events in Ireland closely. Many held degrees from British universities and were accomplished doctors, lawyers, and educators. Only a few of these professionals and intellectuals thought of India as a potentially independent nation-state at this point, but as a group they were certain that they were entitled to an equal voice in administration and business. Ironically, it was easier for Indians to participate in the politics of the empire in Britain than it was in India. By the time Ham Mukasa arrived in London, a few expatriates, like mathematics professor Dadabhai Naoroji, actually held seats representing English constituencies in Parlia-ment.

In India, conversely, these educated elites were largely disenfranchised. They could do little to challenge unpopular imperial policies, like the Raj's practice of favoring British manufacturers, traders, and investors over local Indian interests. In 1913, Britons had Indian holdings totaling roughly £380 million, almost 20 percent of total British investment in the overseas empire. Most of this money went into the Indian railway system, which had about thirty-four thousand miles of track in 1913. The Raj financed this impressive construction program by guaranteeing foreign investors at least a 4.5 percent profit and had to borrow at extremely high rates of interest to make good on this promise in years when the railways were not sufficiently profitable. British India also spent roughly £53 million per year in 1913 (65 percent of its overall budget) on civil administration and the Indian army.[14] These funds either went directly to the Treasury in London or to the salaries and pensions of civil servants, thus providing a comfortable income for educated upper-middle-class Britons. In effect, India's primary contribution to the empire was to buy British goods, pay interest on British loans, provide opportunities for British investment, and cover the costs of the Indian army, which num-bered some 150,000 men in the pre–World War I era. Indians paid for these imperial subsidies through taxes on land, salt, and other commodities and through customs and excise duties. The leaders of the Indian National Con-gress (INC) complained bitterly that these "home charges" and discriminatory fiscal policies "drained" India of the wealth and resources needed for economic development. They also blamed mounting peasant unrest on unreasonably high taxes.

The INC's vocal opposition to the home charges and other imperial expenditures obscured the fact that metropolitan industrialists were actually losing their share of the Indian market to foreign and local Indian competition. The Manchester textile mills, which were heavily reliant on India in the nineteenth century, saw their share of the Indian market begin to shrink markedly at a time when Indian-owned industry was becoming a significant national and global force. British manufacturers tried to choke off this competition by using their political connections to prevent the Raj from emulating the "white" self-governing dominions by increasing import duties to protect developing domestic industries. Nevertheless, entrepreneurs like J. N. Tata, the founder of the Tata Iron and Steel Company, managed to survive and prosper without government assistance. Raising operating capital from some eight thousand Indian investors, Tata exploited the Raj's decision to end restrictions on local iron production in response to increased imports from Germany and Belgium. In 1907, he established a state-of-the-art steel plant at Jamshedpur in Bihar Province with £1.6 million provided by family members, princes, and Indian businessmen after London investors shunned the project. The plant had an annual output of 155,000 tons of pig iron and 78,000 tons of steel just seven years after it opened. Tata won a standing order from the Raj for steel rails and soon branched out into other industries, like textile production. By the outbreak of World War I, Tata and his colleagues had made India the world's fourth-largest cotton manufacturer. [15]

Yet the architects of this economic boom lacked a political voice. Falling back on racist caricatures of educated Indians, the imperial authorities claimed that they were insufficiently Western for full citizenship but too Western to represent the average uneducated Indian. At best, the men who ran the Raj allowed Indians to elect a few representatives to local legislative bodies. Keeping with the overall philosophy of British rule, they dismissed the Indian graduates of their own universities and considered "traditional" Indian princes, aristocrats, and large landowners natural allies. Although the Indian Civil Service (ICS) was technically open to Indians, it only held its annual competitive entrance exam in London. Few Indian candidates had the resources to make such an expensive journey, which meant that 95 percent of the ICS cadets recruited between 1904 and 1913 were British. [16]

Faced with this entrenched and systematic discrimination, INC leaders became considerably more aggressive in demanding equal rights for all Indians. Some, like the radical journalist Bal Gangadhar Tilak, even followed the Irish example by calling for swaraj, or self-rule. Viceroy Lord Curzon, a self-described benevolent tyrant, would have none of this. Firmly rejecting the INC's demands for more democracy, in 1905 he attempted to fragment the Indian political elite by splitting Bengal, which was a center of anti-imperial agitation, into two separate provinces with borders based on religious and ethnic divisions.

Curzon's strategy backfired. It alienated moderates who were still willing to pursue self-rule within the limited political framework of the Raj and prompted a younger generation to turn to violence. Inspired by Japan's victory in the 1905 Russo-Japanese War, sensational acts of violence by Russian anarchists, and Irish republicanism, a small group of middle-class Bengalis attempted to spark a mass anti-British uprising in South Asia. Their secret societies derailed trains and made contacts with sympathetic would-be revolutionaries in Indian communities abroad who were largely beyond the Raj's reach. The radicals' most successful act of violence actually took place in London in 1909 when an Indian student named Madan Lal Dhingra assassinated Sir William Curzon Wyllie, the political aide-de-camp to the secretary of state for India.

Although the imperial authorities would have never acknowledged it, they were unable to smother what amounted to the most serious challenge to British rule in South Asia since the 1857 Indian Mutiny because their empire was, in effect, also an Indian empire. Over the course of the nineteenth century, Indians had traveled Britain's global networks as diplomats, soldiers, settlers, merchants, indentured workers, wives, and students. Indeed, the second British Empire would not have been possible without Indian investment, military manpower, clerical assistance, and labor. Borrowed Indian army battalions made it possible for private chartered company armies to conquer East and Central Africa, and Punjabi Sikh and Muslim police constables enforced imperial law and order from Nairobi to Hong Kong. South Asian unskilled laborers and craftsmen built the Mombasa-to-Buganda railway, tended Fijian and Mauritian sugar plantations, and provided much of the workforce in the British West Indies. Big investors, small-scale entrepreneurs, and simple shopkeepers helped keep precarious economies afloat from the Caribbean to Malaya and from the Union of South Africa to Ham Mukasa's Uganda Protectorate. In addition to pursuing higher education in metropolitan Britain, Indians also established a presence at universities in the United States and Canada as both students and academics. These broad population shifts included both men and women, which meant that small but vibrant South Asian communities sprang up in virtually every corner of the empire in the decades before World War I. Alarmed by the unexpected influx of Punjabis in British Columbia, the Canadian government tried to gain better control of imperial communication and travel networks in 1910 by passing legislation that allowed immigration officers to bar entry to "Asiatics" lacking proper documentation and sufficient financial resources.

These measures did not prevent the Indian revolutionaries from exploiting the empire's horizontal ties because the authorities lacked the knowledge, resources, and manpower to fully police the imperial networks. In 1904, the Raj established a Department of Criminal Intelligence (DCI) to collect reports on subversive activity from local governments, monitor Indian newspapers both at home and abroad, and recruit a small group of Indian agents to spy on the revolutionaries and nationalists. However, the DCI only had a staff of twenty-six men and a tiny budget. The Special Branch of the Metropolitan Police at Scotland Yard provided some assistance in monitoring the revolutionary activities of South Asian students in London, but Lord Morley, the secretary of state for India, refused to expand the surveillance operations on the grounds that the activists were degenerates who spent more time pursuing English women than plotting revolution.

Consequently, the overseas Indian opponents of the empire operated relatively freely in the decade before World War I. This was particularly true in foreign nations where the DCI's small handful of agents risked provoking an anti-British backlash if they were too open in pursuing the revolutionaries. In Japan, Indian students created an international incident in 1907 by convincing leading political figures like Count Okuma to attend a nationalist festival celebrating the Maratha hero Shivaji Bhonsle. British diplomatic pressure convinced the Japanese government to be more circumspect in its support for the radicals, but the United States provided an even more hospitable base of operations. Qualifying as British subjects under an 1818 Anglo-American treaty, Indian students and other migrants were legally entitled to enter the country. The Vedenta Society's India House in New York City was a meeting place for Indian and Irish nationalists, but the most politically active Indian communities were in the Pacific Northwest. The DCI reported that Indian students studying science and technology at Western universities were learning to build bombs and that scholars like Lala Har Dayal, who taught South Asian philosophy and Sanskrit at Stanford University, were organizing subversive plots. There was some truth to this. Har Dayal and several like-minded intellectuals founded the Ghadr (mutiny) movement in San Francisco, which openly plotted to overthrow the Raj by touching off a revolution in India in the years before World War I. In Vancouver, like-minded Sikhs challenged restrictive Canadian immigration policies by secretly chartering a Japanese freighter to bring several hundred would-be settlers into the port. The result was a violent "affray" that injured twenty-two Canadian policemen, and when the British authorities forcibly repatriated the passengers to India, another major riot ensued.

The Indian government tamped down these challenges with a flurry of aggressive legislation that gave the police the authority to censor seditious newspapers, spy on nationalists, and detain suspected revolutionaries. Turning to Ireland for inspiration, the police created new armed paramilitary units based on the Royal Irish Constabulary. Extensive censorship laws empowering officials to ban books and punish newsmen who published "subversive

articles" helped limit the revolutionary contagion. Overseas, nationalist attacks against suspected DCI informers and the outbreak of World War I
compelled the American government to finally take action against the Ghadr
leaders, leading several of them to flee to Latin America, Europe, and Japan.

Although these reactionary measures suppressed the immediate nationalist threat, the British authorities recognized that they lacked the resources and
manpower to hold India by force. In 1909, Lord Minto, Curzon's replacement as viceroy, tried to win back the moderates through the Morley-Minto
reforms, which added Indians to the Viceroy's Legislative Council and gave
Indian representatives on provincial legislatures greater power to propose
resolutions and question the budget. Three years later, Lord Hardinge used
the pageantry of George V's Coronation Durbar in Delhi as cover to rescind
Curzon's partition of Bengal. Not surprisingly, these reforms did not satisfy
the hard-core nationalists; nor did they placate the Indian National Congress
leadership, which continued to call for a truly equal voice in governing the
Raj. Britain's hold on India on the eve of World War I was therefore intact
but precarious.

There were also assertions of local autonomy, if not outright nationalism,
in the settlement colonies, but these caused considerably less consternation in
metropolitan Britain. Having granted Australia, Canada, and New Zealand
self-government with their own elected parliaments and prime ministers, the
authorities in London were willing to recognize them as embryonic nations
so long as they retained some form of tie to Britain. South Africa, however,
was another matter. Although Britain went to enormous expense to win the
South African War, mounting tensions in Europe meant that it could not
afford to rule the Afrikaners by force. In 1907, the Liberal government in
London therefore reached an accord with its former enemies whereby the
Transvaal and the Orange Free State joined Britain's Cape and Natal colonies
in the Union of South Africa. Formed in 1910, the new federation became the
empire's fourth dominion. The constitution also included a provision for the
union to absorb what became known as the High Commission Territories.
These included the Swaziland and Basutoland protectorates and Khama's
kingdom in Bechuanaland.

In return for accepting imperial control over their diplomatic relations and
economic policy, the Afrikaners won the right to local self-government. By
allying with working-class English speakers and reaching an accord with the
foreign investors who controlled the mining industry, Afrikaner nationalists
took control of the union and excluded the African majority from the political process, thereby laying the foundations of apartheid. Previously, the Cape
Colony government had made property rather than race the criteria for voting
rights under British rule, but under the terms of the union agreement, Britain
sacrificed its supposed duty to its African subjects to placate its former
Afrikaner adversaries. The British architects of the union hoped that these

concessions would convince the two "white races" (English and Afrikaans speakers) of South Africa to settle for dominion status within the empire, but like the Irish, the Afrikaners chaffed under British authority, and most still aspired to turn the union into an independent sovereign republic.

Dismissing this defiant nationalism, imperial enthusiasts instead spoke optimistically of linking the overseas settlements into a global federation with a unified economy, a single army and navy, and an imperial council or parliament. None of the dominions, however, were willing to surrender their growing political and economic autonomy to an institution that surely would have been dominated by Britain. Indeed, Australia and New Zealand had already become de facto imperial powers when they acquired administrative authority over Britain's scattered territories in the South Pacific, including the Gilbert, Ellice, Cook, and Solomon Islands. The union government similarly looked to assert its influence over the British settlement colonies in southern Africa. Although they contributed funds to the Royal Navy and provided troops for imperial conflicts, the dominion prime ministers only agreed to take part in nonbinding consultations with the metropolitan government. Known first as colonial and then as imperial conferences, the London summits laid the groundwork for what would become the British Commonwealth of Nations.

Although these conferences created an impression of imperial unity, stability, and security, there were disruptive currents of dissent for those who took the time to look for them. This was certainly the case in the West Indies, where Britain's sugar-producing colonies had fallen on hard times due to competition from other territories in the Caribbean and subsidies to European sugar beet growers. Although most people in these colonies were descended from African slaves and, to a lesser extent, South Asian migrant laborers, political power lay in the hands of a small class of European planters, businessmen, and administrators. In the nineteenth century, these territories appeared to be following the larger settler federations on the path to representative local self-government. The abolition of slavery, however, created a free non-European majority that would have dominated any democratic government by their weight of numbers.

The elite planters in most West Indian territories therefore took the extraordinary step of giving up their right to representative self-government to become more conventional Crown colonies. This meant that a governor chosen by the Colonial Office and an assembly comprised primarily of appointed civil servants had the power to legislate. With the exception of Barbados, Bermuda, and the Bahamas, elected local members were gone from West Indian legislative councils by 1900. Colonial officials claimed that these changes protected less educated "blacks" from abuse by the privileged "white" minority, but this was largely an excuse to remove the non-European majority from the political arena. Barbados was the only territory not to shift to Crown colony status, but it kept government in the hands of the planters through strict voting requirements based on wealth, occupation, and education that excluded most of the island's majority. But these discriminatory measures did not do much to bolster the waning influence and status of the West Indian planter aristocracy. Although their political power was still secure, they needed protective tariffs and preferences to compete with more efficient foreign sugar producers and direct grants from the metropolitan Treasury to cover the costs of day-to-day administration. Moreover, there were few viable employment opportunities for West Indian workers, and many left to work as migrants in Central America and the United States.

In the Middle East, where Britain's interests were more strategic than economic, imperial planners worried most about protecting the routes to India. For most of the nineteenth century, they did this by defending the Ottoman Empire to block the Russians and French from acquiring too much influence in the Mediterranean. During the era of informal empire, it was cheaper and more effective to let their Ottoman allies bear the cost of protecting British interests in the region. In 1878, however, the Conservative prime minister Benjamin Disraeli brokered a treaty with the Ottomans that gave Britain direct administrative control over the strategically important island of Cyprus to ensure that the Royal Navy could close the Dardanelles to the Russians in the event of war. Disraeli's successor and Liberal rival, William Gladstone, went a step further in 1882 by invading Egypt to protect the Suez Canal and other British investments from a popular revolt by Egyptian nationalists who blamed the Turkish-speaking ruler Muhammad Tawfiq Pasha for leaving the country open to economic and political exploitation by Westerners. Although Gladstone intended this to be a temporary operation to restore Tawfiq's cooperative regime to power, the occupation stretched into decades as Egypt became a British protectorate and a de facto part of the empire.

Britain's consul general was theoretically only an advisor to the Egyptian cabinet, but he and a raft of British administrators on loan to key government ministries essentially ran Egypt's financial, diplomatic, and military affairs. This also allowed Britain to claim the Sudan, which was technically an Egyptian possession, and transfer the costs of its administration to the Egyptian government. The British civil service, which numbered only about a thousand men, tried to build popular support among the Egyptian peasantry for this awkward arrangement through a program of good government that included lowering taxes, abolishing flogging and forced labor, and expanding the irrigation system. Consul General Evelyn Baring (Earl of Cromer) tried to win over Egyptian nationalists, who vehemently opposed the British occupation, by adopting measures similar to the Indian Morley-Minto reforms, increasing Egyptian participation on provincial counsels and in the general assembly.

These concessions, however, did little to appease the Egyptians, and imperial strategists continued to fret about the security of the Suez Canal. The Royal Navy's shift from coal to oil in 1911 compounded these worries and gave them an even stronger reason to seek some form of control over the petroleum-producing regions of the Middle East. Many of the sheikdoms in the Persian Gulf became formal British protectorates, largely in response to the Raj's concerns about the security of its main east-west transportation and communication arteries, in the early decades of the twentieth century, but Russian interests in Central Asia prevented Britain from adding Persia to the empire. Instead the two imperial powers divided the country into dual spheres of influence. British strategists were never comfortable with this arrangement, and they were ever mindful of the Russian threat to their strategic oil reserves and India's vulnerable northwest frontier.

On the whole, Britain's new African colonies appeared to be the most secure and stable imperial territories in the decades before World War I. Despite Sir Clement Hill's promise that British rule would bring modernity to the Kingdom of Buganda, it was rather ironic that old-fashioned chartered companies, which were products of the early-modern era, undertook the initial conquest, administration, and economic development of British Africa. This meant that private speculators gambled that running colonies under the legitimacy of a royal charter would bring a sufficient return on what was often a substantial but risky investment. As quasi-governmental institutions, chartered companies allowed Britain to claim African territory at no cost to the metropolitan taxpayer. Their backers and investors, however, were usually disappointed, and only Cecil Rhodes's British South Africa Company managed to produce significant profits. As a result, many companies went bankrupt, and the metropolitan government eventually assumed control of all the African colonies.

At first, most territories (as was the case with Uganda) were protectorates run by the Foreign Office, but the Colonial Office eventually took them over as Crown colonies. Many of the first generation of African colonial officials began their careers under the Raj, and they pragmatically introduced to British Africa the inexpensive South Asian model of governing through local rulers, like the Gandan *kabaka*. In communities lacking powerful princes or sultans, the imperial authorities appointed cooperative African allies as chiefs or headmen. In eastern and southern African territories with favorable climates, the authorities encouraged European settlement to defray the cost of colonial administration and economic development. In Kenya, Nyasaland (Malawi), and the Rhodesias (Zimbabwe and Zambia), these settlers used metropolitan political connections to seize African land, and they guarded their privileges jealously by making race the basis for access to politics and civil society. So, despite the promises that British rule would bring modernity, the settlement colonies treated Africans as primitive tribesmen who were supposedly incapable of participating in a representative Western government.

The conquerors of British Africa liked to portray themselves as hardy, independent pioneers, but the men who sought their fortunes in the new territories needed cheap labor to develop the colonies' agricultural and mineral resources. Faced with high production costs and an inability to attract sufficient foreign investment, they demanded government help in getting people to work for the lowest possible wages. Africans had little incentive to work for European employers, however, because their largely sufficient agrarian and pastoral economies meant that money was only good for buying imported luxuries. Settler farmers, plantation owners, and mining interests therefore tried to free up labor for colonial enterprises by wiping away local systems of production.

British administrators supported these private efforts because the Treasury insisted that the new colonies had to be self-supporting. This was one of the reasons why the governments of Nigeria, the Gambia, and Kenya (known as the East Africa Protectorate until 1920) took so long to free slaves in their colonies. Ultimately, they needed to keep Africans working. These pragmatic policies drew harsh criticism from the missionaries and metropolitan humanitarian lobby, which pushed administrators to look for a civilized way of compelling Africans to work. Some colonial governments initially experimented with requiring work on municipal projects or private European estates as a form of taxation, but this veered uncomfortably close to slavery. By World War I, most realized that requiring people to pay their taxes in cash was the most efficient and defensible way to drag Africans into the colonial economy, as tax resistance was a crime in every modern nation-state. The British authorities used armed force to seize the crops of communities that would or could not pay their taxes in cash, thereby forcing them to work or starve.

The South African, Southern Rhodesian, and Kenyan governments, which faced additional pressure to supply cheap "native labor" to mines and settler farms, took the extra step of confiscating enormous swaths of fertile land. They organized the remaining territory into "native reserves" that theoretically protected unsophisticated communities from Western speculators by barring individuals from selling "tribal" land. These rural ghettos conveniently generated cheap African labor by limiting the number of families that could survive through farming or pastoralism. The reserves in South Africa constituted just 13 percent of the dominion's arable land, while Africans made up 70 percent of the union's population. In Kenya, Africans were over 80 percent of the population, but their reserves included just 20 percent of the usable land in the colony. [17]

The situation was slightly better in West Africa, where African entrepreneurs and commodity producers provided one of the few bright spots in Britain's new African empire. Cocoa farmers and palm oil planters in these territories were already integrated into the world economy before the European conquest of the continent. Nigeria and the Gold Coast (Ghana) were therefore largely self-supporting colonies because African growers had already pioneered the mass production and export of cash crops in the preconquest era. The two territories accounted for almost one-quarter of global cocoa production by 1915. These local producers were so efficient that the colonial authorities turned away Sir William Lever when he asked for permission to set up a palm oil plantation in Nigeria in 1907. Tariffs on the export of African-produced cash crops generated so much revenue that the Gold Coast and Nigeria did not need to tax the African population directly until the 1930s.

DAILY LIFE THROUGHOUT THE EMPIRE

Imperial partisans celebrated the diversity of the second British Empire and used it to justify governing their imperial subjects differently. [18] In their view, it was inappropriate and unwise to treat primitive Gandan tribesmen like the civilized populations of the dominions and settlement colonies, and Sir Clement Hill had promised Mukasa and his colleagues that British rule would help them achieve an indigenous Gandan version of modernity. Ham Mukasa clearly doubted the sincerity and intent of these assertions, and critics of the empire, both at home and in the colonies, pointed out that the imperial authorities self-servingly assumed that this process of "native uplift" would take centuries. Inevitably, these differing perspectives turned into debates over whether the British Empire was a "good" or "bad" institution.

It was not possible to make such broad characterizations, for the diverse populations of the empire experienced it in markedly different ways. Fundamentally, imperial rule was a form of political, economic, and social change that brought both predictable outcomes and unintended consequences. The British Empire, both by design and by accident, transformed local communities as it integrated them into wider global networks of commerce, investment, and culture. Imperial rule inevitably modified established patterns of political power and social authority, thereby allowing some people to profit from these changes while others suffered from them considerably. The individuals and groups who benefited most from British rule were those who became local allies and intermediaries, acquired some form of Western education, or tapped into the empire's broader markets and economic networks. Mukasa's pro-British faction came to power in Buganda by allying with the Imperial British East Africa Company. Conversely, people who were unwilling or unable to adapt to the sweeping changes suffered political disenfranchisement, economic exploitation, and loss of social status.

In South Asia, Indian agricultural entrepreneurs and industrial magnates like the Tatas prospered under the Raj. New railways give them access to world markets, and by 1900 India sent significant quantities of raw cotton, jute, tea, wheat, and hides overseas. India replaced China as the world's leading tea exporter, and the province of Assam alone devoted almost six hundred thousand acres to tea production in 1915. Britons owned most of the tea estates, but Indian agriculturalists who secured loans to expand production also prospered. To the west, Punjabi farmers in particular exploited new agrarian technologies and improved irrigation to expand their production of wheat, cotton, and sugar cane for export. Between 1891 and 1921, the per capita production of crops in the Punjab increased by 45 percent. Indian landlords and small-scale investors, or moneylenders, also profited by extending land and credit to these prosperous farmers. On the negative side, changing fashions, cheap imported textiles from Britain and Japan, and competition from new Indian-owned textile mills drove most hand-loom weavers out of business by the turn of the twentieth century.[19]

Although these sorts of conventional political and economic shifts were relatively obvious, the British Empire also brought subtler, more unexpected changes that were much harder to recognize. Few contemporary observers noticed the extent to which the globalizing processes of imperial rule altered the physical environment. In South Asia, the Indian railway system accelerated deforestation as it consumed large amounts of wood for construction and fuel. In the Punjab, the extensive irrigation system diverted water from rivers, waterlogged low-lying regions, increased the salinity of the land, and created breeding grounds for malaria-bearing mosquitoes. The situation was much the same in British Africa, where imperial rule made it difficult for local communities to control the tsetse fly, the primary vector for trypanosomiasis (sleeping sickness). Wars of conquest, pacification campaigns, and even game parks prevented people from clearing brush to destroy the fly's habitat and hunting the wild animals that carried the disease. In the Uganda Protectorate, sleeping sickness killed about 250,000 people at the turn of the century.

British administrators and doctors did not understand their role in this tragedy, which allowed imperial partisans like Sir Clement Hill to point proudly to Western medicine as one of Britain's gifts to its subjects. A great many well-meaning Britons would have been surprised and dismayed at these unforeseen consequences of imperial rule. For the most part, the metropolitan public viewed imperial wars and paternalistic authoritarianism as necessary evils that brought civilization, modernization, reform, moral uplift, and Christianity to backward peoples.

Christian missions, which operated freely throughout the British Empire, played a central role in reinforcing these perceptions. The Catholic Church was extremely active in the imperial field, but Protestants in Britain and the

United States sponsored the empire's most influential missions. In 1899, these Protestant churches were spending roughly £2 million per year to support the activities of some fifty thousand missionaries operating around the world. This enormous sum equaled British government spending on metropolitan civil service salaries.[20] In addition to preaching, the missions drew potential converts by offering health care and a Western education. In East Africa, missionaries used medicine to demonstrate the power of their religious message and kept Muslim patients hospitalized longer to provide greater opportunities for evangelism. Religious educators also used Western schooling, which opened the door to more lucrative white-collar jobs, to attract converts. The quality of these institutions varied considerably, and many evangelically focused organizations, like Kenya's African Inland Mission, provided only enough instruction to ensure converts could read the Bible. In most cases, their ultimate goal was to establish self-financing "native churches" that would continue the expensive task of mass evangelization on their own.

Although the missions played a key role in exposing imperial scandals and challenging governmental and commercial mistreatment of subject peoples as part of the humanitarian lobby, they also maintained a close working relationship with the colonial state to gain privileged access to non-Christians. In doing so they reduced administrative costs in the colonies and provided imperial partisans with proof that the empire was fulfilling its obligation to civilize its backward subjects. Moreover, mission schools also played an important economic and administrative role. The limited economic returns of imperial rule forced entrepreneurs and administrators to rely on educated native clerks and tradesmen. Most colonial governments therefore subsidized the missions' educational and medical projects with direct grants.

Yet this church-state alliance also complicated the overall imperial enterprise. In theory, if non-Europeans became westernized Christians, they could demand political and social equality with metropolitan Britons. Ham Mukasa and Apolo Kagwa became deeply pious Anglicans (which explains Mukasa's disapproval of Western dancing), but they were not the sort of obedient converts that the missions expected. Similarly, in the Gold Coast converts rejected the authority of "pagan" chiefs who were key imperial allies, and in Nyasaland a Baptist pastor named John Chilembwe founded his own Providence Industrial Mission to challenge the Western monopoly on Christianity. Alarmed by this pervasive disobedience, administrators, missionaries, and teachers throughout the empire took the experience of education and evangelism in India as a cautionary tale. Believing that attempts to westernize Indians in the nineteenth century had produced the class of politically frustrated elites who led the Indian National Congress, they developed an education system based on the African American industrial curriculum of the segregated American South that used "tribal tradition" to train students in skills tailored to rural life. Not surprisingly, most people rejected this "adapted" schooling as inferior. The Gandan nobles used their considerable resources to provide for the Western education of their children by founding King's School at Budo, which they modeled on an elite English public school. In central Kenya, the first generation of upwardly mobile Kikuyu converts, who often came from marginalized segments of society, similarly insisted on a conventional Western literary education.

Troubled by this resistance, many missionaries questioned whether it was worthwhile to be so closely tied to the colonial state. They were also deeply frustrated by their inability to make significant progress among the empire's Hindu and Muslim communities. By 1911, they had only about 3.8 million Indian converts, who came almost entirely from the lower classes, to show for over a century of evangelism. This amounted to a little more than 1 percent of the Indian population. Britain had roughly 94 million Muslim subjects at the turn of the century, and the missions were deeply critical of the pragmatism of indirect rule that turned Muslim sultans and emirs and other "pagan" rulers into imperial allies. Much to the Christian missions' frustration, Islam spread easily throughout the empire as Muslim clerics and traders took advantage of its new and safer trade and communication links and Muslim noncommissioned officers in imperial armies converted new recruits.

Some missionaries were also deeply embarrassed by the inherent economic exploitation of imperial rule and the open racism of settler societies. Many were passionate defenders of the rights of subject communities. A few, like Joseph Booth, an American Baptist missionary in Nyasaland who was John Chilembwe's patron, stepped over the line in challenging British imperial authority by preaching a message of "Africa for the Africans" and were deported. Most, however, shared the paternalistic views of Archdeacon W. E. Owen, whose defense of "native interests" so incensed the Kenyan settlers that they referred to him as "Archdemon Owen." Owen criticized colonial policy in Kenya but was not ready to call for full African political rights. He worried that the missions were teaching their students and converts a dangerous and immoral form of individualism and materialism that promoted social disintegration by undermining the best elements of communal tribal life.

The archdeacon's attempt to create an explicitly Christian form of tribal culture reflected a larger imperial social agenda. Assuming that the empire would be stronger if Africans and Asians became Christians, the missions worked with their secular allies in the imperial administration to spread British middle-class notions of morality. Ideally, these Edwardian gender norms turned men into proper husbands and protected women by consigning them to the domestic sphere.

This promise of moral uplift sounded grand in London, but it ran aground on the gendered economic realities of imperial rule. The need for tax revenues and low-cost labor meant that, as was the case in early industrial Britain, imperial administrators and investors viewed most subject women as potential workers. In southern and eastern Africa, the pressure of taxation drove men to leave their wives at home while they traveled great distances to look for paid employment. Mine and plantation owners kept their salaries low on the grounds that these African workers did not need a living wage because their wives were at home working the land. Contrary to the promise of imperial development, rural African women essentially subsidized Western employers and investors. These coercive labor policies propped up failing imperial business ventures and helped keep the undercapitalized African colonies afloat, but they were entirely incompatible with the idealized Western gender norms that legitimized the second British Empire.

Moreover, British imperial rule had a number of other unexpected gender consequences that further complicated the imperial social agenda. Taxation and the native reserve system in settler colonies made it difficult for young African males to become the kind of men who could provide for a family and household. In precolonial times, they would have qualified for adult status by acquiring enough land and bridewealth cattle to marry and establish a family, but the slow transformation of rural economies through settler land seizures and the pressures of migrant labor made this difficult. The result was a generational crisis among communities like South Africa's Zulu people, whose young men had previously accepted the authority of their elders in return for assistance in acquiring land and cattle. By 1900, Zulus had little reason to defer to the old men who had failed to prevent the British conquest. Instead, the most successful migrants could buy cattle and marry with the money they earned in the South African mines.

There were also new opportunities for African women under British rule if, like the female cocoa growers in West Africa, they could acquire enough access to land, labor, and markets to shift from food to cash crop production. This relatively small group of wealthy female entrepreneurs hardly fit the mission ideal of a dutiful, homebound wife. More often than not, however, women became a means for chiefs and elders to reassert control over junior men. By raising bridewealth prices and using official connections to marry multiple young wives, they monopolized access to fertile women. British district officers supported the elders' opportunistic reinterpretation of tribal law to reinforce the authority of their chiefly partners. Put another way, colonial governments used young women to reward key rural allies. African women thus became an important cornerstone of indirect rule, and fleeing to the nontribal towns and cities was usually their best hope of escape.

These complications exposed a fundamental gender contradiction in the empire's legitimizing ideology. Imperial partisans justified their conquests in part by promising to protect Asian and African women from degrading and inhumane local social customs. Yet these same women often suffered sexual exploitation under British rule. In India, government officials accepted these realities and defended the racially stratified social order by creating a state-regulated two-tiered system of brothels to ensure that perceptibly "white" women would only have commercial sex with European men. The authorities justified this blatant disregard for Christian morality by arguing that intimate contacts with Westerners would undermine the perceptions of racial superiority that made British rule in India possible.[21]

This implausible racist reasoning did not prevent British men from using the privileges of empire to gratify themselves. Indulging in informal extra-marital contacts that would have been socially unacceptable at home, administrators, soldiers, traders, and settlers sought sexual release with local people of both genders. Some of the more notorious incidents included a provincial governor in Malaya molesting girls in a local orphanage and a pair of district officers in Southern Rhodesia acquiring multiple African "wives" by threatening their families with arrest.[22] In another highly publicized case, General Sir Hector MacDonald, a much-decorated hero of the imperial wars in Africa, committed suicide when faced with dismissal and possible prosecution for having sex with Ceylonese boys. By 1909, these incidents were so embarrassing that the Colonial Office issued a blanket declaration ordering its employees not to have sexual contact with non-Westerners on the grounds that it diminished European prestige and status. This ban often meant little in practice. District officers used the need to learn local languages as an excuse to take native mistresses, and in a memoir published later in life, a former Kenyan official credited one such woman with teaching him exotic "intricacies of sex."[23]

Although British administrators risked official sanction when they violated the Colonial Office directive openly, subject men who dared to have intimate contact with European women faced prosecution and execution for "rape." It did not matter if the female in question was a consenting partner. In Kenya, a white woman convicted of voluntarily engaging in an "unlawful carnal connection with a native" could be imprisoned for five years, and the police actively investigated women whose conjugal contacts with non-Western men made them a "menace to the white community."[24] These draconian and invasive laws, which embodied pernicious stereotypes about the dangerous, unquenchable sexuality of non-European men, underpinned the racial privileges of settler societies. The virtue of European women reinforced sharp racial and social boundaries that were central to the colour bar and imperial order.

Although official rhetoric described the imperial project as a partnership between the British and their subjects, these attitudes reflected the fact that few Britons believed Arabs, Asians, Africans, and West Indians could ever become equal members of the empire. At best, some missionaries and liberals assumed that non-Westerners might become fully civilized after a lengthy period of British rule. Robert Baden Powell, hero of the South African War and founder of the Boy Scouts, considered that young Africans could grow up to be "white men with black skins" with the proper education and exposure to Scouting. Other imperial ideologues, however, believed that Africans were biologically inferior to the "white races." In Kenya, the eugenicist Dr. H. L. Gordon weighed the brains of corpses to "prove" that Africans lacked the mental capacity to master European culture and education. To be sure, this pseudoscientific racism was not unique to the British Empire, and many segregationists in the United States held similar views of African Americans. The mining magnate Cecil Rhodes famously declared that he favored equal rights for all civilized men in southern Africa, but in practice institutionalized racism allowed the imperial governments to treat non-Westerners as "protected persons" incapable of exercising full political rights. This even applied to Ham Mukasa and his colleagues, despite their elite status, for many Edwardian Britons saw them as little more than black tribesmen in Western dress.

This dehumanizing racism and lack of political representation made British imperial rule, no matter how well intentioned, much harder to tolerate. Lacking the capacity to resist through conventional military methods, Africans, Asians, and West Indians asserted their rights and autonomy through legal and extralegal means. As would be expected, educated and upper-class people usually worked through politics and the courts. Pressure from the Indian National Congress was a key factor in convincing the Raj to grant Indians greater political representation under the Morley-Minto reforms. In the Gold Coast, the Aborigines Rights Protection Society (ARPS) blocked the government's attempt to classify all unused land in the colony as Crown land by taking its grievances to London. Even Kenya's Maasai people, who stood out in the imperial imagination (and contemporary Western advertising) as the most tribal and simplistic community in British Africa, hired British lawyers to contest settler land seizures and defend rights that Britain had guaranteed them by treaty. Unfortunately, the settlers' political influence in London trumped the Maasai's strong legal case, and the South African Native National Congress was similarly unsuccessful in using political and legal means to oppose the union's creation of native reserves. Nevertheless, the ARPS's small victory demonstrated that it was possible to challenge abusive imperial policies if they came to the attention of the metropolitan government and British public.

Lawsuits and petitions were really only viable tactics for educated and wealthy elites. Most territories tried to limit the ability of their subjects to acquire firearms, but for ordinary people evasion and occasional violence remained options for opposing imperial misrule. Young Hindu men assassinated administrators in Bengal who enforced unpopular health regulations that clashed with local conceptions of morality. In 1906, excessive taxation in South Africa escalated into a full-scale revolt among the Zulu that led to the deaths of twenty-five European soldiers and over three thousand rebels. In Somalia, Muhammad Abdulla, whom the British disparagingly called the "Mad Mullah," fought the colonial authorities to a standstill. Using the vast Somali deserts as cover, he waged a long-running guerrilla war for two decades before British air and land forces finally ran him to ground. The Somali case demonstrates that often it was simply easier to evade imperial authority instead of confronting it directly. Given the futility and risk of armed resistance, it usually made more sense to retreat to the countryside or even neighboring colonies when expecting a visit from a tax collector or labor recruiter.

Indeed, the capacity of imperial officials to impose their will on subject populations at the turn of the century was actually quite limited. With the metropolitan British army concentrated in Europe to face a growing German threat, they had limited military resources at their disposal. The dominions raised their own all-European infantry battalions, but most of the new protectorates and colonies had to rely on the poorly trained militias inherited from bankrupt chartered companies. And most of these formations consisted of soldiers recruited from subject non-Western populations. The colonial police forces were equally dependent on local people to fill out their ranks and were concentrated primarily in urban areas. Even the Indian police, whose Department of Criminal Intelligence and sophisticated provincial criminal intelligence departments dealt with terrorism and political subversion, had a limited rural presence.

British administrators were therefore highly dependent on local allies to deal with anti-imperial resistance. The authority of an isolated district officer usually depended mostly on imperial grandeur or, as one former official put it, "blanco [a detergent cake used to clean military equipment], brass bands, and bullshit."[25] Educated Africans learned about kindly "Kingi Georgi" in schools, while ordinary people throughout the empire encountered him on their stamps and money. In effect, imperial officials liked to think that the monarch was the omnipresent and thus omnipotent symbol of the British authority that stood behind the lone district office.

However, frequent transfers meant that these field officers often did not have as much knowledge or power as they assumed. This was particularly the case in India, where the Raj relied on some twenty thousand lower-level Indian civil servants to actually govern, which meant that imperial authority in rural India was never particularly strong. Lacking direct supervision, Indian policemen in the countryside relied so heavily on brutality to maintain law and order that it became a scandal in metropolitan Britain. Parliamentary investigators, who uncovered hundreds of cases of police abuse and torture of suspects and witnesses between 1906 and 1911, concluded that the Indian police were "a terror to the people."[26]

THE EMPIRE IN THE GREAT WAR

The British Empire's relatively tenuous bonds held well enough in peacetime, but World War I stretched them to the limit. Although the conflict took place primarily in Europe, imperial subjects played a vital role in the British war effort. The wider empire provided the financing, raw materials, and manpower that helped Britain sustain four brutal years of total war. Moreover, British efforts to protect the far-reaching imperial networks of trade and communication made the Great War of 1914 to 1918 a truly world war. From a global perspective, there was a stark contrast between the tragic stalemate in western Europe and the successes British forces achieved overseas. Working with their French allies, British imperial formations easily overran Germany's colonies in West and Southwest Africa. German East Africa held out until the end of the war, but the German territories in the Pacific put up minimal resistance. It took considerably more effort and bloodshed to subdue the Germans' Ottoman ally, particularly in Iraq, Arabia, Syria, and Turkey itself. But the Allied victory led directly to the dismemberment of the Ottoman Empire.

The concessions and pragmatic decisions that it took to win the war changed the British Empire considerably. On August 4, 1914, King George V declared war on behalf of all his subjects, but the dominions exacted a high price in return for turning their ships over to the Royal Navy and raising expeditionary forces for imperial service. Canadian prime minister Sir Robert Borden spoke for his counterparts in Australia, New Zealand, and South Africa when he protested the imperial government's failure to consult the self-governing territories in taking the empire to war. Noting Canada's substantial imperial contributions, he stated, "It can hardly be expected that we shall put 400,000 or 500,000 men in the field and willingly accept the position of having no more voice and receiving no more consideration than if we were toy automata."[27] It was impossible to argue with this logic, and the dominions' contributions to the Allied victory set them on the path to full autonomy and eventual nationhood.

Although the imperial authorities were relatively comfortable in relying on the dominions for military support, they were far less willing to mobilize their non-European subjects. Fearing that imperial military service would allow Asians, Africans, and West Indians to demand greater political and economic rights, British strategists at first hoped to limit their participation in the war. They had no choice, however, but to lean more heavily on the wider empire as the fighting in northwestern France intensified. In 1914, the British army had only six regular divisions, while the Germans and the French had ninety-eight and seventy-two divisions, respectively. This is how Indian forces came to fight on the battlefields of France. They served in western Europe until 1915, when mounting losses due to cold and disease forced their redeployment to warmer climates. During the remainder of the war, Indian army units played a central role in campaigns in Gallipoli, Mesopotamia (Iraq), Palestine, East and West Africa, northern China, and the Persian Gulf. The Royal West Indies Regiment served in France and Egypt, while East Africa's King's African Rifles and the Royal West African Frontier Force fought only in Africa. Combat operations in these African theaters, where there were few railways and serviceable roads, required several hundred thousand conscripted African men and women to carry supplies and ammunition. Tens of thousands of them died of disease and neglect during the course of the fighting.[28]

The imperial authorities accepted these noncombatant losses as militarily necessary, but the colonial governments were extremely reluctant to allow their soldiers to fight in Europe on the grounds that they would lose respect for white authority if they learned to kill Germans and Austrians or became too familiar with Western women. The Union of South Africa grudgingly allowed several thousand of its subjects to serve in unarmed labor units in western France on the condition that British generals promised to keep them strictly segregated from French civilians and other Allied soldiers. In setting this condition the South African authorities sought to ensure that African servicemen did not acquire the military training or notions of equality that would threaten the racially segregated social order they were laboring to build in the union.

This was not an entirely unreasonable fear, for the war strained the empire's precarious bonds so severely that revolts broke out in territories that had chaffed most under British rule in peacetime. In South Africa itself, where die-hard Afrikaner nationalists were still bitter over their defeat in the South African War, Prime Minister Louis Botha's decision to stand by their former enemy touched off a civil war. Careful to keep British troops out of the conflict, Botha used the new Union Defence Force to crush the rebellion during the fall of 1914. One year later, the African missionary John Chilembwe led an armed uprising in southern Nyasaland to protest the abuse of African laborers on settler farms and the mass conscription of military laborers.

The war similarly inflamed the ongoing and deep-seated debate over Ireland's status within the British Empire. At first, the hostilities temporarily defused the controversy over whether the Third Irish Home Rule Bill would apply to Northern Ireland, and John Redmond's Irish Parliamentary Party, which had fought hard for Irish self-rule in peacetime, even offered to have the Irish Volunteer Movement (IVM) guard Ireland to demonstrate that home rule was compatible with loyalty to the larger empire. In making the offer Redmond gambled that wartime service would unite all Irishmen, but radical members of the Irish Republican Brotherhood (IRB) and the IVM refused to support what they regarded as British imperial aggression. In 1916, the IRB's military council calculated that it would be possible to wrench Ireland out of the empire if it backed its declaration of a republic up with a credible display of military force. But their seizure of the General Post Office and other strong points throughout Dublin on the Monday following Easter failed to produce a popular uprising. After a week of bloody fighting with the British army that led to roughly 450 deaths and thousands of injuries, the imperial authorities stifled the republican movement with martial law and mass detentions of suspected nationalists. In this sense the leaders of the rising succeeded in building popular support for independence by provoking the imperial authorities into using indefensibly violent tactics.

Not surprisingly, many Indians paid close attention to the events in Ireland. With the Raj playing a central role in the imperial war effort, tensions rose as the wartime economy subjected civilians to higher taxes, shortages of key commodities, and rising prices. A small number of Indian companies, like the Tata Iron and Steel Company, won lucrative government contracts, but huge price increases and the failure of the monsoon rains led to grain riots by the end of the war. Indian Muslims were particularly unwilling to oppose the Ottoman Empire because they considered the Turkish sultan to be the spiritual head of the global Islamic community. With roughly 1.5 million Indians serving in the imperial forces and the Raj's entire financial wartime contributions totaling almost £500 million, the Indian National Congress and other relatively moderate political leaders, like Muhammad Ali Jinnah, called for India to achieve self-governing dominion status on par with Canada, South Africa, Australia, and New Zealand.[29] A small but militant faction of nationalists, however, would only settle for a complete break with the empire. As a pamphlet by the Indian National Party, which was essentially part of the Ghadr movement, declared, "The Indian people have never been reconciled to the British rule. . . . The Indian has come to see that independence is the panacea for all his evils. He will therefore even swim in a sea of blood to reach his goal."[30] True to their word, the revolutionaries plotted to attack key imperial installations and inspire a mass uprising through spectacular acts of violence. In 1915, some four thousand Ghadr members living abroad snuck back into India to join the revolt. The revolutionaries convinced a few Indian army units in Singapore to mutiny, but the Indian police broke up their main plot relatively easily.

The Raj took this subversion seriously, and as in Ireland, it instituted draconian steps to maintain security. The 1915 Defence of India Act empowered the authorities to detain suspects without trial for the duration of the war, but this increased security came at a high political price. The extralegal measures alienated the moderate politicians, who had been more inclined to accept British promises that the empire could accommodate their aspirations for self-determination. One year later, the leaders of the Indian National Congress and the Muslim League issued a joint declaration, known as the

Lucknow Pact, that stopped just short of calling for full home rule on the Irish model. But Secretary of State for India Edwin Montagu's 1917 declaration that the British government "had in view the gradual development of free institutions in India with a view to self-government" was not the promise of full dominion status, which carried the implicit authority to leave the empire, that the moderates expected.

In the Middle East, the war was equally disruptive. The Ottoman entry into the conflict ended conclusively Britain's nineteenth-century strategy of propping up the Ottoman Empire to protect the routes to India. Instead, imperial strategists used the war to expand British influence in the region, often at cross-purposes. Foreign Office officials drew up a secret accord with the French, known as the Sykes-Picot Agreement, dividing the region into French and British spheres. Unaware of these negotiations, the British high commissioner in Egypt promised the Hashemite dynasty that governed the Arabian holy cities of Mecca and Medina under the Ottomans that Britain would sponsor an independent Arab state if they revolted. To complicate matters further, Foreign Secretary Arthur Balfour courted worldwide Jewish support by promising Lord Rothschild, leader of the British Jewish community, that Britain would support Zionist plans to create a "national home for the Jewish people" in Palestine. These conflicting agreements were more the result of poorly coordinated imperialism and diplomacy rather than intentional British perfidy. They added considerable territory to the postwar British Empire, but the unsustainable and contradictory wartime promises led to intractable Jewish and Arab unrest in interwar Palestine.

In 1918, the British Empire emerged from World War I as a global superpower, but its apparent strength was illusory. The war set the dominions on the path to eventual nationhood, and although they continued to support Britain politically and militarily, they became much more assertive in looking out for their own economic interests in the postwar era. Much more seriously, the war weakened the empire's hold on Ireland and India. This was fairly obvious in Ireland, where republicanism was widely popular by 1918, but it was also true in India, even though the imperial authorities appeared to have beaten back the revolutionary challenge successfully. The Raj's increasing authoritarianism actually made large numbers of Indians much more willing to follow Mohandas Gandhi's call to peaceably but forcefully reject the legitimacy of foreign imperial rule. British Africa and the West Indies appeared far more stable, but the anti-imperial agitation in India and Ireland would ripple across the empire's weblike networks of commerce, communication, and travel in the interwar decades.

Chapter Three

The Empire between the Wars, 1918 to 1939

TWO PERSPECTIVES ON EMPIRE

World War I dealt a devastating blow to the metropolitan British economy and nearly destroyed an entire generation of young Britons, but the British Empire grew as a result of the conflict. Hypocritically casting the Germans as unsuitable colonial rulers, the Allied powers turned Germany's African and Pacific colonies over to the British, French, and Japanese as League of Nations mandates. Similarly, the league dismembered the Ottoman Empire and transferred its Arab provinces to Britain and France as mandates. Britain's share of this windfall in Africa included Tanganyika (Tanzania) and parts of Cameroon and Togo. Southwest Africa (Namibia) went to Britain as well, but in practice it came under South African control. In the Middle East, Mesopotamia (Iraq), Transjordan (Jordan), and Palestine (Israel) became British mandates. These acquisitions, coupled with informal dominance over nominally independent Arabia and Persia, made the Indian Ocean a de facto British lake. With the influence of Soviet Russia temporarily on the wane in the Caucasus and Central Asia, India was secure. All told, in early 1919 the British Empire had roughly 450 million subjects and ruled territories covering 13 million square miles on six continents.[1] With isolationism taking hold in the United States, western Europe laid waste by war, and the tsarist Russian and Ottoman empires consigned to history, Britain appeared to be the sole global superpower.

From this perspective, the architects of British Africa had good reason to feel confident in the decade that followed. This was particularly true for Frederick Lugard, the former Indian army officer of relatively humble middle-class origins whose military and administrative exploits in Africa earned him a peerage as Baron Lugard of Abinger. Having helped to transform the semiprivate armies of British chartered companies in Central, East, and West Africa into conventional military units and then serving as the governor of Hong Kong, he famously oversaw the amalgamation of northern and southern Nigeria into a single colony during World War I. Upon his return to Britain, he served as the British representative on the League of Nations' Permanent Mandates Commission.

In 1922, Lugard published the seminal manifesto (and apologia) for British rule in Africa as *The Dual Mandate in British Tropical Africa*. Responding to a wave of popular anti-imperial sentiment that grew out of revulsion for empires and militarism in the immediate postwar years, the book offered an idealized view of the British imperial project. To rebut American, Soviet, and British socialist charges that British rule was exploitive, Lugard claimed that it was possible to develop African resources for the greater good of Britain and the global economy while simultaneously acting as the "trustee for the welfare of the [native] masses."[2] By this view the imperial enterprise could be both profitable and humanitarian because working for Europeans was inherently civilizing: "The primitive savage in contact with civilization learns the discipline of work, and the result of cooperation. He learns on a plantation new methods of cultivation which he can apply to his own fields."[3]

Lugard's doctrine of the dual mandate thus rested on the implicit assumption that the majority of Africans were inherently incapable of managing their own government or economic development. Trusteeship assumed that it would take centuries of British tutelage for the native races to reach the stage where they could look after their own affairs. With independence "not yet visible on the horizon of time," it was the job of the British district officer to "clothe his principles in the garb of evolution, not revolution."[4] Ironically, but predictably, there was no room for Western-educated Africans in this system of indirect rule, for westernization alienated them from their fellow tribesmen. Lugard was much more comfortable with "primitive pagans" and Muslim potentates than with educated Christians, and he was particularly contemptuous of the highly educated elites who ran Britain's small West African possessions in the era of informal empire. Dismissing their political aspirations as counter to the "natural tendencies of tribal evolution," he confidently declared that "native lawyers" were "not representative of the masses, and know less about them, their language and their needs than the District Officer."[5]

This division of subject populations into "masses and classes" typified British imperial thinking during the interwar years. The vast majority of Africans and Asians were simple but good-hearted primitives who would develop their own unique and organic forms of modernity and civilization after centuries of British rule. In the meantime they needed protection from the small but disruptive, individualistic political, clerical, and mercantile classes that would surely exploit them. Native lawyers, journalists, and businessmen appeared civilized, but they were only capable of aping Western norms. Although the African version of indirect rule appeared to run counter to the ultimate goal of the British imperial mission in that it discriminated against Western-educated Africans, Lugard and his disciples pointed to the postwar turmoil in the rest of the empire to make their case. "Prosperity, combined with a wrong system of education and widespread illiteracy, has indeed, like in Ireland, in Egypt, and in India, invariably given rise to unrest and sedition."[6] Lugard, like many administrators who began their careers under the Raj, believed that applying lessons learned in India to the new African colonies would ensure that the British Empire would last for centuries.

But in the immediate aftermath of World War I, stability was a matter of perspective. Lugard's confident assessment of Britain's imperial prospects stood in stark contrast to the increasing panic that gripped the men who struggled to govern India in the postwar era. Whereas British Africa appeared solid and durable, the Raj faced growing opposition from all quarters as anger over imperial demands for Indian soldiers, taxes, and raw materials during the war led to peacetime inflation, food shortages, higher taxes, and frustrated expectations for greater political participation. A great many Indians found the 1919 Government of India Act, which grew out of Secretary of State for India Edwin Montagu's 1917 promise to set India on the path to self-government within the empire, entirely unsatisfying. It enfranchised less than 4 percent of the population and only gave elected Indian politicians control over minor government ministries and noncontroversial provincial legislation. These Montagu-Chelmsford reforms (named for Montagu and wartime viceroy of India Lord Chelmsford) kept the Raj's key political, military, and economic institutions in British hands.

Ghadr revolutionaries like Taraknath Das considered the newly expanded legislative assembly "little more . . . than a debating society." Declaring that the nationalist revolution that began with the 1905 uprising in Bengal had now "passed the Boston Tea Party stage," Das asserted that the radicals were following the example of the early Roman Christians by creating a "state within the state."[7] This was largely wishful thinking as most Indians preferred to challenge the Raj through more conventional constitutional means, which made Mohandas Gandhi's call to achieve swaraj, or self-rule, through nonviolent mass resistance more appealing. A former London-trained barrister, who became a leading force in the Indian National Congress (INC) upon his return from overseas in 1915, Gandhi argued that it was possible to make India ungovernable by organizing Indians to withdraw their tacit cooperation with the empire and its institutions. Calling his philosophy of nonviolent opposition to injustice satyagraha, or truth force, Gandhi sought to create a mass movement. His goal was not simply to remake India into a Western-style nation-state. Rather, he believed that Indians could only free themselves fully from foreign domination by addressing the divisive moral and social failings that made British rule possible in the first place. Rejecting social and material status, Gandhi argued that wealth entailed a form of trusteeship and should be used to benefit all of society. He considered sectarianism particularly dangerous and strove to include Muslims in his movement. Although the INC leadership was predominately Hindu, in 1919 Gandhi forged a working alliance with the Khilafat movement, which organized Indian Muslims to defend the dignity of Islam and to oppose Allied plans to depose the Ottoman sultan and partition his empire. Although they did not share his views on class, most Indian moderates were more comfortable with Gandhi's call for mass noncooperation because they worried revolutionary violence might threaten their interests by inspiring peasants and workers to challenge the established social order.

The British authorities considered the swaraj movement seditious and treasonous. They worried that wartime demands on the Indian army had left the Raj vulnerable by reducing the ratio of British to Indian troops in India from one in two to one in sixteen. The Hindu-Muslim cooperation at the core of the INC Khilafat alliance was unsettling, and Gandhi's increasing influence over Indians from all walks of life raised the alarming prospect that the "masses and classes" might actually heed to his call to unite. Although Gandhi intended this campaign to be resolutely nonviolent, widespread but uncoordinated acts of local violence opposing Britain's wartime policies gave the Raj the opening it needed to extend World War I–era security measures into 1919. This was done over the vehement and universal objections of Indian legislators. In March 1919, the Anarchical and Revolutionary Crimes Act (also known as the Rowlatt Act) suspended conventional rules of evidence and arrest and empowered the security forces to detain suspects for one year without trial. The law also allowed judges to deny Indians charged with political crimes jury trials and the right of appeal.

The backlash against this extremely foolish piece of legislation was immediate and resounding. The Muslim leader Muhammad Ali Jinnah resigned his seat on the Imperial Legislative Council in a scathing letter to the viceroy: "By passing this Bill, Your Excellency's Government have . . . ruthlessly trampled upon the principles for which Great Britain avowedly fought [World War I]. . . . A Government that passes or sanctions such a law in times of peace forfeits its claim to be called a civilised Government."[8] Widespread rumors that the Rowlatt Act empowered the Raj to arrest groups of more than three people, tax marriages and burials, and seize land and crops without compensation generated popular support for the noncooperation movement and, despite Gandhi's call for peaceful mass strikes, touched off antigovernment riots from Delhi to the Afghan frontier in late March and early April of 1919. The unrest, which included the murder of local officials, arson attacks on government buildings, and the sabotage of railway and telegraph lines, was so widespread, particularly in the Punjab, that it took the army to restore order.

Nowhere was the situation more serious than in Amritsar, where the civil authorities lost control of the city for two days. Angered by the government's decision to detain and deport a pair of influential local INC leaders, Indians gathered on the morning of April 10 to lodge a formal protest with the city's deputy commissioner. Accounts vary as to whether they intended to resort to violence, but when the group reached the bridges leading to the European section of the city, a small detachment of outnumbered policemen and soldiers turned them back with rifle fire. The crowd then grew into an enraged mob that killed five Europeans while looting and burning the city's main banks, post offices, government offices, and Christian churches. Most ominously from the British perspective, the victims included a European missionary named Marcella Sherwood, whom a group of men beat and left for dead. This attack, which violated the fundamental principle of imperial rule that held all European women sacred and inviolate, led the panicked authorities to believe that they were facing the most serious outbreak of anti-British violence since the 1857 Indian Mutiny. [9]

Concluding that they had to act quickly to prevent the unrest from spreading to the countryside, the civil authorities in Amritsar turned over control to the military. Indian army detachments restored control by April 12, and Brigadier General Reginald Dyer arrived to take command of the city and oversee the arrest of the rioters. One of his first acts was to issue a proclamation that banned public meetings and warned that "unlawful assemblies" would be "dispersed by force of arms if necessary." When Dyer learned that a crowd of several thousand people was gathering at a public square known as the Jallianwala Bagh on April 13 in defiance of this order, he acted quickly. Leading a force of approximately one hundred Indian and Gurkha soldiers and two armored cars equipped with machine guns, the general reached the assembly in the late afternoon. As the three gates that led into the two-hundred-square-yard meeting ground were too narrow for vehicles, he left the armored cars behind and marched his detachment into the square, where he encountered between five and twenty thousand adult men. Some were there to listen to speakers criticize the government crackdown, whereas others had apparently come into the city to visit a cattle market and observe a religious festival. With no warning or command to disperse, Dyer ordered his men to take positions and open fire. Over the next ten minutes, he carefully directed the troops to shoot at the largest concentrations of people. The distance was about 100 to 150 yards. Dyer's troops expended 1,650 rounds of 303 Mark VI ammunition and executed, by official tally, 379 of King George V's Indian subjects. The general then marched the detachment out of the square without making any arrangements for the approximately twelve hundred wounded to receive medical treatment. Upon making a full report of the events at the Jallianwala Bagh to his military superiors, he received a telegram stating, "Your action correct and Lieutenant-Governor [of the Punjab Sir Michael O'Dwyer] approves."[10]

The widespread application of martial law throughout northeastern India smothered the unrest by the end of April 1919. Although investigators never found any conclusive evidence that organized conspirators like Russian Bolsheviks and Egyptian pan-Islamicists were responsible for the violence, Dyer claimed that his decisive action had saved the Raj. In a detailed report to his division commander written several months later, he baldly stated,

> There was no reason to further parley with the mob, evidently they were there to defy the arm of the law. . . . My duty and my military instincts told me fire. My conscience was also clear on that point. . . . I fired and continued to fire until the crowd dispersed and I consider this is the least amount of firing which would produce the necessary moral, and widespread effect it was my duty to produce, if I was to justify my action. If more troops had been at hand the casualties would have been greater in proportion. It was no longer a question of merely dispersing the crowd; but one of producing a sufficient moral effect.[11]

Dyer further admitted that he had decided to give the order to shoot when he first heard of the public meeting. Testifying before the Hunter Committee, which the Raj convened to investigate the mass unrest of spring 1919, Dyer declared that his actions were "the only means of saving life" and that "any reasonable man with justice in his mind would realize that I had done the right thing." In admitting that he would have used the machine guns on the armored cars to kill even more people if he could have, he remarkably called his order to fire a "merciful act" and asserted that he should be thanked for undertaking such a "horrible duty."[12]

Although Dyer may appear deranged by today's standards, there was a sad imperial logic to his statements. Much as Frederick Lugard thought that British district commissioners understood tribal culture better than educated Africans, Dyer believed that he had a special understanding of "the Indian mind." He confidentially told the Hunter Committee, "I was born in India and have served in Punjab Regiments all my service, I know the language very well and I consider I am an authority on what was going on in and around Amritsar."[13] This expertise told him that the entire population of the Punjab would rise in revolt if he did not quickly and conclusively demonstrate the folly of challenging the Raj. As in 1857, tens, if not hundreds, of thousands of people would die in the crackdown that would be necessary to restore imperial control. Thus, it was merciful and necessary to sacrifice a few hundred suspected subversives and uninvolved bystanders to save many

more innocent lives. Implicit in this chilling logic was the assumption that
British rule in India would be over the minute the majority of Indians concluded that they could defy imperial authority successfully. When the Indian
members of the Hunter Committee asked Dyer if it was his intention "to
strike terror" into the general population, he responded, "Call it what you
like. I was going to punish them. My idea from the military point of view was
to make a wide impression . . . throughout the Punjab."[14] Having taken it
upon himself to shoulder the burden of such a "horrible duty," Dyer was
absolutely confident that he had saved the Raj and, by extension, the British
Empire.

In addressing the recriminations that followed the Amritsar massacre, the
governments of India and Britain insisted categorically that Dyer's actions
did not reflect official imperial policy. But a great many Britons in northwestern India shared Dyer's panic that a mass revolt was in the offing.
Consequently, the Hunter Committee's investigation found that the general
was not the only official to overstep his authority and the limits of metropolitan British morality in enforcing martial law in the Punjab. Royal Air Force
(RAF) officers admitted to machine-gunning crowds that gathered outside
the city of Gujranwala also to achieve a "moral effect," and armored trains
similarly discouraged railway sabotage by firing indiscriminately into suspect villages. In Lahore, the army's Order No. 1 warned that imperial troops
would destroy all property surrounding sites where bombs or rifle fire
wounded a British soldier. Army officers coerced fugitives into surrendering
by turning their families into the street, while in the countryside mobile
columns seized hostages and flogged suspects to dissuade villagers from
harboring railway saboteurs.[15]

In reviewing the events of March and April, the Hunter Committee found
that the military authorities had treated the entire population as if it were at
war with the British Empire. Many officers seemed more concerned with
humiliating and intimidating educated Indians than with restoring law and
order. Students were a favored target. Enraged by their "truculence" and
insubordination, British officials strove to restore the prestige of the Raj by
flogging them, marching them for miles in the hot sun, revoking their schol-
arships, and even expelling them from school altogether. In some districts the
emergency regulations required all Indians to salute any passing civil or
military officer by placing their heads on the ground. The authors of these
unorthodox orders later justified them as necessary to teach the general population "respect." As the senior commander in Amritsar, Dyer added to the
notoriety he earned at the Jallianwala Bagh by issuing the infamous "crawl-
ing order" that required any Indian passing on the street where Marcella
Sherwood was attacked do so on hands and knees. He later justified this
humiliating pronouncement to the Hunter Committee by claiming that it
impacted relatively few people, and since the missionary teacher's blood had

made the street "holy ground," it was necessary for passersby "to go on all fours in an attitude well understood by natives of India in relation to holy places."[16]

Although most British residents of India found Dyer's tactics just and necessary, the general almost single-handedly derailed the Raj's efforts to win over Indian moderates through the Government of India Act. Gandhi, who broke off negotiations with the government, declaring that he could not cooperate with a "satanic regime," used the massacre to justify the INC's call to boycott the reformed legislative councils. This pressure was a key factor in Montagu's decision to convene the Hunter Committee to investigate the causes and resolution of the unrest. The committee, which had both British and Indian members, disagreed over whether there was an actual conspiracy behind the violence and whether wartime excesses by Sir Michael O'Dwyer's administration in the Punjab had provoked it, but they were unanimous in their condemnation of Dyer's actions. Moreover, the Indian minority report explicitly compared the Amritsar executions to the war crimes, or "frightfulness," that the Germans had inflicted on Belgium during World War I: "The plea of military necessity is the plea that has always been advanced in justification of the Prussian atrocities."[17]

Dyer's graphic and unapologetic testimony that he explicitly intended to kill as many people at the Jallianwala Bagh as possible made him a political liability. Although Montagu's legal advisors found that there was sufficient evidence to charge Dyer with culpable homicide, they advised against prosecution on the grounds that no British jury would convict him. Instead, the secretary of state for India directed the Indian army to order the general to resign his commission and issued a formal statement disavowing his conduct: "His Majesty's Government repudiate emphatically the doctrine of 'frightfulness' upon which Brigadier-General Dyer based his action."[18]

These developments shocked Dyer, particularly as he had been promoted twice since giving the order to open fire in Amritsar, and he fought to clear his name and resume his military career upon returning to Britain in July 1920. In both public statements to the metropolitan press and in an appeal to the Army Council, Dyer backed away from his testimony before the Hunter Committee that the crowd at the Jallianwala Bagh was not aggressive and now claimed that it had been threatening and armed with iron-tipped heavy wooden sticks. Although British fact-finding commissions were not judicial bodies, he also protested that he had been denied the rights of due process by the Indian committee members, who unexpectedly cross-examined him without legal counsel present. In addition to ignoring the reality that the military authorities did not need an excuse to retire him forcibly (this was the fate of thousands of wartime officers as the British army shrank to peacetime levels), Dyer's attempt to portray himself as the victim of shifty Indian lawyers also conveniently overlooked the fact that he himself was an expert in military law.[19]

Nonetheless, a large section of the British public, which did not learn of the events at Amritsar for eight months, rallied to the general's defense when his account reached the metropolitan press. This gave imperial partisans in Parliament an excuse to attack Montagu's reformist policies in India. In their eyes, the rebellion in the Punjab was part of a global anti-British conspiracy, and they hailed Dyer as the savior of the Raj. More significantly, the debate over whether the government had unfairly scapegoated a heroic soldier turned on a sharp disagreement over the true nature of the British Empire. In the House of Lords, Lord Harris rejected Montagu's claim that Britain did not rule India by force: "Every country in the Empire is held by the sword. I happen very much to prefer the expression 'the iron hand in the velvet glove,' but . . . we have eventually to come back to force to secure obedience to the law." Brigadier General Herbert Surtees, Harris's Conservative colleague in the Commons, declared that this force actually held the empire together: "There are vast areas in Africa and the Pacific, where the sole British representative is . . . one white man. . . . Once you destroy [his] prestige, then the Empire will collapse like a house of cards, and with it all that trade which feeds, clothes, and gives employment to our people."[20] This argument struck a chord with the public and the British expatriate community in India, and Dyer went grudgingly into retirement with donations totaling more than £26,000 to fund his continued efforts to clear his name.

Like Dyer, Baron Lugard was also a product of the Raj, and so he most likely would have agreed with these assertions that the British Empire was held together by force. There was no other way that his district commissioners, who liked to imagine themselves as philosopher kings and platonic guardians, could have ruled the subject millions of British Africa without the underlying threat that organized resistance would be met with ruthless state violence. But in the interwar era, it was still possible to burnish the empire's humanitarian veneer in Africa because the poorly funded and understaffed colonial administrations made relatively few demands on ordinary people. In contrast, the unrest in northwestern India that forced Dyer to expose the inherent violence behind imperial rule stemmed from Indian anger over the weight of the empire's heavy wartime demands and a growing impatience with the pace of political change after several centuries of British rule. Clearly, at this pivotal point in the history of the British Empire, the question of whether an imperial enthusiast was confident or anxious about the long viability of the empire depended on where she or he stood.

THE EMPIRE IN CRISIS, 1918 TO 1922

In the short term, there was little question that victory in the Great War had strained the empire enormously regardless of its superpower status. In addition to the economic consequences of the massive war effort, the global conflagration produced new imperial problems and complicated long-standing ones. The dominions expected considerably more autonomy in return for their substantial financial and military contributions to imperial defense. As the regular British army shrank from a wartime high of 3.5 million to 370,000 men by 1921, Britain's military challenges in India, the Middle East, Central Asia, and Europe grew and intertwined. Strategic tensions in Asia mounted as the need to forge closer ties to the United States led the British government not to renew its alliance with Japan. At home, Special Branch reports that radical groups of World War I veterans who remained angry about insufficient demobilization benefits and widespread unemployment were contemplating revolt raised fears that Britain might experience its own Bolshevik revolution. To further complicate matters, the shrinking metropolitan budget and intense public opposition to restoring conscription made it impossible to expand the British army to deal with the domestic and global threats.

The dominions could have helped alleviate the crisis, but the trauma of World War I left them wary of being drawn into yet another war in the service of the empire. In 1917, Prime Minister David Lloyd George acknowledged these sentiments by giving the dominion leaders a more direct role in wartime planning and diplomacy by creating an Imperial War Cabinet in London that met several times between 1917 and 1921. Moreover, Canada, South Africa, Australia, New Zealand, and even the Raj were signatories at the postwar peace conferences with the status of near sovereign nations. Wartime service and sacrifice strengthened national sentiments among dominion voters, and although they remained loyal to the idea of the empire, they soundly rejected metropolitan proposals to create a more integrated postwar imperial federation. As chapter 6 will discuss, the 1922 Empire Settlement Act, which aimed to change these views and strengthen imperial bonds by sponsoring the emigration of 450,000 war veterans and their families, was an overly optimistic failure. That same year, the Canadian prime minister W. L. Mackenzie King made it clear that there would be no dominion troops for postwar imperial projects by refusing to support Lloyd George's attempt to intimidate the Turkish government into accepting the onerous terms of the Treaty of Sevres by threatening war.

Consequently, imperial strategists became increasingly concerned as even the more stable corners of the empire seemed precarious in the immediate aftermath of the war. Apart from the Somaliland Protectorate, where a defiant shaykh named Muhammad Abdille Hassan resumed his long-standing insurgent war against British rule in 1920, the African colonies were relatively tranquil. Even so, administrators and missionaries worried that African military participation in the war had encouraged the spread of bolshevism and Pan-Africanist "Ethiopianism" in the urban areas and, in the words of Lugard, dangerously "lowered [European] racial prestige by appealing to the coloured races to kill white men." Trouble also appeared to be brewing in the British Caribbean colonies. In December 1918, rank-and-file members of the Royal West Indies Regiment went on strike at their base in Taranto, Italy, to protest demeaning duty cleaning latrines and bed linens. Encouraged by a nationally minded officer from the European planter class named A. A. Cipriani, they challenged segregated hospitals and social facilities by defying a South African camp commander who openly called them "n--gers." The group resolved to seek greater rights and self-government when its members returned home after the war.[21]

These expectations were understandable given that the Allied powers' claim to be fighting for freedom and democracy complicated the inherent authoritarianism of imperial rule in peacetime. Although he was referring primarily to the territories of the defunct Russian, Austro-Hungarian, and Ottoman empires, Woodrow Wilson's insistence on respecting the national wishes of subject peoples in his famed Fourteen Points caught the attention of educated people in the British Empire. Most were not ready to call for full independence on the Wilsonian model, but they expected Britain to adhere to the spirit of this declaration by creating greater opportunities for political participation. When the victors convened the Paris Peace Conference in 1919 to determine the fate of the Central powers and their empires, Africans, West Indians, and African Americans convened a Pan-Africanist Congress under the leadership of the noted African American activist W. E. B. DuBois to lobby the conferees to extend Wilson's program to Africa. Instead, the great powers divided among themselves the remnants of the German and Ottoman empires in Africa, the Middle East, and the South Pacific as League of Nations mandates, but, as in India, the political aspirations of their educated subjects became harder to ignore.

These global challenges to the empire were the larger context for the panic in the Punjab and Dyer's decision to fire on unarmed Indian civilians. In the two years following World War I, the widespread unrest in northwestern India coincided with mounting violence and opposition to imperial authority in Egypt, Somalia, India, Iraq, Palestine, Persia, Afghanistan, Burma, and, most important, Ireland. In Egypt, nationalist unrest during the war forced British officials to declare martial law and replace Khedive Abbas Hilmi with a succession of more cooperative relatives. This overly ambitious attempt to impose a protectorate on the former Ottoman viceroyalty by arresting and deporting leading Egyptian nationalists and politicians provoked a mass uprising. As in the Punjab, the authorities had to resort to martial law, military action, and indiscriminate collective punishment to regain control over the countryside. Across the border in Palestine, the Arab and Jewish confrontation over the character of the new mandate required British intervention to maintain civil order. To the east, Arab and Iranian resistance rendered unworkable plans to control strategically important oil fields by claiming a League of Nations mandate over Iraq and adding Persia and Arabia to Britain's informal sphere of imperial influence.

This was particularly true in Iraq, where the nationalists refused to acknowledge the legitimacy of the new mandate, and British administrators overestimated the ability of cooperative shaykhs to control the general population. In July 1920, a successful jailbreak by an anti-British shaykh touched off a full-scale revolt that cut off the imperial garrison in central Iraq. Unable to keep the railway and telegraph lines open, the mandate government had to call in a full Indian army division as reinforcements at a time when the Raj could barely spare military resources already stretched thin in northern India. Internal divisions among the nationalists, coupled with heavy RAF bombing, brought an end to the Iraqi insurrection by November at the staggering cost of £40 million. More ominously, Montagu declared that the Raj could spare no further troops or money for Iraq and warned that there would be "grave political consequences" if Indian Muslims perceived that Britain was trying to carve up the Ottoman Empire using "Indian mercenaries." Faced with these seemingly connected events, nervous imperial officials concluded there were sinister forces behind such widespread challenges. In a secret report to the British cabinet, a special intelligence officer in the India Office warned that "Turkish nationalists and Arab extremists" were plotting with the German Foreign Office and the Soviet Union to send trained revolutionaries to instigate anti-British revolts throughout central and southern Asia. [22]

Such a fanciful alliance of Britain's various imperial enemies made no ideological sense, but it never occurred to the British strategists that imperial rule was simply unacceptable to their would-be subjects. Lacking the resources to tamp down this opposition through military means, they instead fell back on the hope that they could detach the elite Arab "classes" from "Nationalist-Bolshevist" control by demonstrating their "honesty of purpose." This was the same thinking behind the Montagu-Chelmsford reforms that led to the 1919 Government of India Act. In Egypt, the Colonial Secretary Viscount Milner believed that Britain could protect its interests by winning over "the better elements of [Egyptian] nationalism" through a treaty that would give them limited sovereignty in return for allowing the empire to retain control of their defense and foreign relations. [23] This was how the Commonwealth was supposed to work, but in Asia the ideal that subject populations would accept any form of foreign rule was another exercise in wishful thinking.

Much closer to home, a great many Irishmen had also lost faith in Britain's honesty of purpose. Although the 1916 Easter Rising failed to produce a popular revolution, the crackdown that followed won a substantial portion of the population over to militant republicanism. Under the leadership of Éamon de Valera, Sinn Féin absorbed what remained of the Irish Republican Brotherhood and abandoned Arthur Griffith's relatively moderate call for separate national status for Ireland under the British Crown. Instead, having reorganized and adopted a more radical agenda in 1917, Sinn Féin won a huge victory in the December 1918 general election by calling for an independent Irish nation-state, and rather than taking their seats in the British parliament, its elected representatives convened a separate Irish parliament (Dáil Éireann) in Dublin to draft a new constitution. David Lloyd George's coalition government, which was dominated by Conservative Party unionists, took this as a declaration of war and responded in force by outlawing Sinn Féin as a terrorist organization.

The result was a short but vicious anti-imperial war that was far more serious than the uprisings in Iraq, Egypt, or India. Lasting from 1919 to 1921, it consisted primarily of republican guerrilla raids on government installations in Ireland and targeted assassinations of Irish unionists and British political and military leaders that the Royal Irish Constabulary (RIC) and the British army garrison, which numbered roughly 110,000 men, could not contain. As in India and the Punjab, the civil government declared martial law, but when conventional counterinsurgency tactics failed, senior British generals contemplated creating free-fire zones and sending RAF bombers against nationalist strongholds. They also raised a special police auxiliary division consisting primarily of recently discharged war veterans to reinforce the overstretched RIC. Known as "the Black and Tans" for its members' military-style khaki uniforms, the new unit's poorly trained and undersupervised paramilitary companies damaged the unionist cause substantially by engaging in tit-for-tat terrorism with the equally violent Irish Republican Army (IRA). In November 1920, their attack on a Dublin Gaelic football crowd in retaliation for the IRA's execution of eleven British officers created uncomfortable parallels with General Dyer's actions in Amritsar one year earlier.

The viciousness of the fight eventually exhausted both sides. Although the IRA received substantial financial and military aid from its supporters in the United States, the security forces were able to round up more than three-quarters of its seventy-five hundred active members. On the government side, the war cost the British Treasury roughly £20 million per year, and military strategists warned that they did not have the manpower resources to continue the war in Ireland and properly garrison the wider empire during the global crisis.[24] Unionist diehards still believed that they could defeat the insurgents and win the Irish population back through the offer of self-government within the empire, but pragmatists realized that it was time to negotiate with the republicans. The 1920 Government of Ireland Act, which created separate parliaments for the six northern provinces with significant Protestant populations and the twenty-six remaining, largely Catholic southern provinces, made this much easier.

During the fall of 1921, the two sides testily hammered out an agreement that turned southern Ireland into a de facto dominion as the Irish Free State (Saorstát Éireann). King George V remained the head of state, but English landowners had to give up their large estates with very little compensation. More significantly, the British military garrison withdrew, and the Free State acquired fiscal autonomy and unqualified home rule. But the agreement split the Sinn Féin leadership because it left Northern Ireland in the United Kingdom, and continued membership in the Commonwealth required Irish leaders to pledge their loyalty to the Crown. The IRA commander Michael Collins grudgingly accepted the arrangement on the grounds that it brought the "freedom to achieve freedom" at some point in the not too distant future. De Valera, however, rejected it, and the treaty only passed the Dáil Éireann with a slim margin of seven votes. Unable to resolve these deep and acrimonious divisions, the republicans fought a de facto civil war between 1922 and 1923 that cost roughly £17 million and killed four to five thousand people.[25] Michael Collins died in the fighting, but the new Free State army, which was essentially the core of the old IRA, prevailed over the more militant faction through martial law and draconian security measures that rivaled British imperial methods in severity and brutality. At the same time, the unionists solidified their hold on the six northern counties through a violent crackdown on the IRA and discriminatory legislation against Catholics.

Quite understandably, the Anglo-Irish Treaty had repercussions throughout the empire. Although the Irish Free State was born of a tragic civil war, it demonstrated that it was possible for subject peoples to win a measure of independence. Lloyd George's negotiators recognized this and tried to avoid setting a precedent by insisting that Ireland remain a member of the Commonwealth. Nevertheless, the Afrikaners paid close attention to events in Ireland, and Jawaharlal Nehru, who would become independent India's first prime minister, praised the Irish nationalists' determination to fight rather than "begging for favors" through negotiation.

The events in Ireland profoundly influenced how imperial partisans viewed the crises in the Middle East and Asia. The unionist leader Sir Edward Carson was one of General Dyer's strongest defenders in the Commons, and he emphatically declared that he was proud that Lieutenant Governor of the Punjab Michael O'Dwyer was an Irishman. Indeed, although Conservatives in Parliament were genuinely outraged by Dyer's forced retirement, much of the debate over his fate was really about Ireland. Dyer's unionist supporters wanted to ensure that a censure of the general and his tactics did not tie their hands in Ireland, particularly in the north. Conversely, in condemning the Amritsar shootings, the Liberal leader J. C. Wedgwood charged that metropolitan support for Dyer was making the Indian populace "anti-English and Sinn Féin," and he warned that if Dyer's actions succeeded in subverting the reforms of the 1919 Government of India Act, "you may carry on for a few years, but in the end you will find yourselves where the Irish Government is to-day—and without an Ulster!"[26]

THE RETURN TO STABILITY, 1922 TO 1929

In time, Wedgwood's warning would prove prescient, but the men who ruled the empire brought it safely through the postwar crisis years by finding the right mix of concession and repression. They gave up the unrealistic attempt to extend Britain's informal sphere of influence in the peripheral regions of the Middle East and Asia, and they made the strategic manpower shortage disappear by deciding arbitrarily that the empire would not face a significant military challenge from a foreign power for at least a decade. The Royal Navy seemed more than sufficient to safeguard British interests around the world. In 1924, the massive battle cruiser HMS *Hood* led a Special Service Squadron on a global cruise to remind both friends and enemies that British naval supremacy remained intact. Most important, postwar constitutional reforms and power-sharing arrangements offered the hope that a reasonably attractive alternative to the Irish brand of radical nationalism might mean that Dyer's "frightfulness" was not needed to hold together the interwar empire.

This was even true in the Raj, where Indian moderates were sufficiently alarmed by the violence of 1919 to give the Montagu-Chelmsford reforms a chance to succeed. The Government of India Act introduced into the provinces the concept of dyarchy, or dual rule, whereby Indian ministers and legislators, 70 percent of whom were elected, assumed responsibility for agriculture, education, and sanitation, while Britons retained control over finances and the police. Soldiers and the small group of civilians who met a fairly high property requirement also gained the right to vote, enfranchising about 10 percent of adult men and 1 percent of adult women. A Chamber of Princes became a conservative counterweight to this new legislative class. Radicals like Taraknath Das may have dismissed the provincial councils as mere debating societies, but the restructured assemblies could influence government policy through their power to tax. Diverting resources to the provinces created opportunities for patronage and drained revenue from the central government. This in turn made it harder to fund the Indian army and its operations abroad, and it checked the expansion of the police and internal security forces. Moreover, the Raj's need to raise customs duties on imports to make up for budget shortfalls hurt metropolitan British manufacturers by making their goods more expensive. These tariffs also offered a substantial measure of protection for a growing domestic industrial sector.

Gandhi and his allies were not satisfied with these constitutional concessions and were still determined to win full self-rule. Their aspiration for an independent Indian nation-state conflicted directly with the ideal of the liberal empire embodied in the Montagu-Chelmsford reforms. In 1920, they convinced the INC leadership to boycott the first elections under the Government of India Act and launched an ambitious noncooperation campaign that called on all Indians to withdraw from government schools, courts, and local administration, to boycott British goods, and to refuse to pay their taxes. Gandhi himself publicly defied the salt tax, which provided 4 percent of the Raj's revenue, by marching to the sea to illegally evaporate seawater to make salt. In willingly accepting punishment for his symbolic "crime," he sought to show that it was possible to render imperial rule impotent and illegitimate through collective action.

Initially, the noncooperation movement succeeded in reducing cloth imports, cutting school attendance, and convincing some Indian judges and legislators to resign their posts. Gandhi's problem, however, was that his call to reject the Raj's authority opened the way for impatient radical nationalists and militant labor leaders to take matters into their own hands. As at Amritsar, strikes and protests that were supposed to be peaceable often turned violent once civil order broke down. This growing unrest exposed the fallacy of Dyer's claims that his exercise in terrorism had demonstrated the futility of violent resistance to British rule. In early 1922, Gandhi suspended the noncooperation campaign after a mob in a small town in the northern United Provinces burned twenty-two policemen to death by setting fire to their police station. Considering the violence immoral despite reports that the police had fired first, he worried that the riot would give the Raj a seemingly legitimate reason to crack down more violently on the nationalist movement.

This created an opportunity to split Gandhi's coalition. Although his passive resistance campaign held the promise of success, the government finally realized that it could undercut his efforts by showing more restraint. Overruling the objections of the Indian army high command, whose continuing calls for expanding martial law showed that they still favored Dyer's tactics, Viceroy Lord Chelmsford recognized that using force against Gandhi's followers would weaken the moderates willing to give the new constitutional reforms a chance. This softer approach worked because there were limits to the Indian populace's willingness to withdraw from imperial society. Students went back to school because education was the key to social mobility, and many politicians took part in regional elections because the Government of India Act created real opportunities for them to exercise power at the local level. Nor was Gandhi able to convince the radicals to renounce violence. The Ghadr movement revived in 1922, and other nationalist groups robbed banks to raise funds, bombed the legislative assembly in Delhi, assassinated police-men and civil officials, and plotted to destroy the viceroy's train.

By the mid-1920s, the Raj's new policy of restraint bore fruit as educated and elite Indians came to disagree over whether it was best to test the prom-ise of the Montagu-Chelmsford reforms or to undermine them in hopes of achieving self-rule. Maharaja Sayajirao III, who had famously turned his back on King George V at the Delhi Coronation Durbar, made his peace with British rule and became a knight grand commander of the Order of the Indian Army. Even Lala Har Dayal, one of the founders of the Ghadr movement, had a change of heart. In a 1919 journal article he deemed the British Empire "reformable" and called for it to evolve into a "British-Oriental-African Commonwealth of the future."[27] The Khilafat movement's audacious but unrealistic attempt to radicalize Muslims in the Indian army gave the author-ities an excuse to arrest its more militant leaders, which helped bring an end to the interfaith alliance at the core of Gandhi's noncooperation campaign. The democratic concessions in the Government of India Act were also a factor in the Hindu-Muslim split, for they raised the possibility that larger groups might monopolize the spoils of elected government if they voted as a block. Muslims, who were a numerical minority, worried that they might eventually find themselves living in a Hindu-dominated state, particularly because the Muslim League was not as well organized or popular as the largely Hindu Indian National Congress.

The Government of India Act was thus a short-term success because it drew the Indian National Congress into politics by inspiring it to reorganize itself as a popular political party to compete in the new elections. After some initial elite male opposition in Bengal, the constitutional reforms even al-lowed propertied and educated women to vote in the elections for the provin-cial legislative assemblies. The postwar era also opened new opportunities for Indians in government service. Recognizing that career restrictions in the Indian Civil Service (ICS) angered educated Indians, the Raj pledged that the imperial bureaucracy would be half Indian by 1939. The authorities framed this concession as a reform, but in reality the ICS faced enormous difficulties in the interwar years recruiting British university graduates, who correctly perceived that foreign rule in India could not last much longer. Although substantial improvements in the ICS's terms of service raised the annual recruitment intake from three to thirty-seven new cadets between 1924 and 1927, there was no getting around the reality that Britain would need even more senior Indian bureaucrats to actually rule India. The Raj faced similar problems recruiting for the army and police, and the military authorities reported over ninety separate attempts to "subvert" the Indian soldiery in the early 1920s. Granting soldiers and their families better pay and extra privi-leges helped defuse this threat, and the army commissioned its first regular Indian officers in 1918.

Although imperial partisans tried to limit the scope of these reforms to India, the Raj's concessions of the 1920s inspired other Asians to demand similar privileges. This was particularly true in Burma, where Indian radicals seeking refuge from the government's postwar crackdown brought news of the changes next door. Under the leadership of the General Council of Buddhist Associations, nationalists successfully pushed British officials to extend the dyarchy reforms to Burma. The Ceylonese government also enacted constitutional changes increasing local participation on its legislative council, but it used the London County Council system rather than the Government of India Act as its model.

It was more difficult to grant an equal measure of self-rule to Malaya because Chinese merchants and artisans outnumbered Malays and Indians in the urban areas. The prosperous and well-organized Chinese community would most likely have controlled elected local councils, thereby provoking the Malays, who considered them aliens. British officials in Malaya also preferred to believe that the Malayan Chinese were temporary immigrants. But most Chinese were in Malaya to stay. Moreover, many Chinese merchants and bankers embraced their status as imperial subjects to better exploit the empire's economic potential. They played a leading role in developing the Malayan tin mines and building Singapore into a global financial center and a major imperial naval base.

As with the friction between Hindus and Muslims in India, the constitutional reforms of the 1920s tended to exacerbate ethnic and communal tensions throughout Asia. The Malayan sultans, who were central to British rule, refused to consider any political role for Chinese or Indians. In Burma and Ceylon, friction between expatriate Indian merchants and landowners and host communities complicated the reform process. This was also the case in Fiji, which also had a large Indian diasporic population. Most had arrived in the colony as sugar plantation workers, but in the post–World War I era, their support for Gandhi's self-rule movement in India and demands for land and equal Fijian citizenship alarmed and alienated both the imperial authorities and the indigenous population.

Winning moderate support for imperial rule through limited and localized constitutional concessions proved equally difficult and complicated in the Middle East. Once the Egyptian and Iraqi revolts had demonstrated that it was not possible to stifle nationalist ambitions through military force, imperial strategists instead hoped to install friendly dependent governments in the Palestine, Transjordan, and Iraq mandates and an independent Egyptian constitutional monarchy. Their primary goal was to find a low-cost way to protect the routes to India through the Suez Canal and control the Middle Eastern oil reserves. In essence, they hoped to recreate Britain's informal empire in the region by forming good relationships with cooperative monarchs and shaykhs, but this plan was entirely out of step with the aspirations of most people in the region.

When the Western powers drew the borders of the modern Middle East at the 1920 San Remo conference, they gave birth to artificial states that held little favor with the Arab populace. Many intellectuals hoped the Allies would allow them to establish a unified Arab state or even recreate the early caliphate as a reward for their revolt against the Ottomans during the Great War. Writing in the 1940s, the passionate Arabist historian George Antonius captured the hope and optimism of the immediate postwar era: "For the first time in its history the Arab national movement stood abreast of its destiny. . . . All the Arabic-speaking provinces of the Ottoman Empire . . . were at last rid of the alien yoke that lain upon them for four stifling centuries."[28] When the Allies instead favored their own interests by creating the mandates, many disillusioned nationalists came to view Britain's Arab political partners as illegitimate puppets.

The imperial authorities therefore looked for ways to win popular support and rebut charges that they had cynically exploited Arab nationalist sentiments during the war. Faced with the conflict between Britain's agreement with the French to partition the region and its promise to support Husayn, the head of the Hashemite dynasty and nominal leader of the Arab revolt, in his efforts to create a pan-Arab state, they opportunistically chose to cooperate with the French. To soften the blow, Britain's Arab experts installed Husayn's son Faysal as king of Iraq after the French drove him out of their Syrian mandate. Faysal's older brother Abdullah became ruler of the Transjordan when he opportunistically arrived in Aman, the only significant urban center in a land that was mostly desert, and forced the British to carve a kingdom for him out of territory that was technically part of the Palestine Mandate. Britain could thus claim to have fulfilled its obligations to Husayn and his family and therefore did not intervene when the Saudis overthrew the Hashemites in Arabia. Concerned primarily with protecting the Suez Canal and gaining access to Arabian oil reserves, Britain self-servingly recognized Ibn Saud as the king of Arabia in 1927. The British government further negotiated loose protectorates with the small Arab shaykhdoms on the Persian Gulf, and oil-rich Kuwait became a separate British protectorate.

Oil was also the primary reason for Britain's interest in Iraq. Realizing they could not rule the mandate directly after the 1920 revolt, the imperial authorities created the modern nation of Iraq by combining the Ottoman provinces of Mosul, Baghdad, and Basra and setting up Faysal as its constitutional monarch. Although the British depicted themselves as liberators, Iraqi opposition to foreign rule required a significant imperial military presence to keep Faysal in power. The 1929 treaty that formally terminated the mandate did little to build popular support for the Hashemite regime because it gave Britain continued access to Iraq's military bases and oil reserves.

The mandate in Palestine proved an even more complex problem. British strategists coveted the region, which had been cobbled together by the San Remo conferees out of three separate Ottoman districts, as an alternative to their increasingly precarious military bases in Egypt. Yet conflicting wartime promises about the future of the Middle East came back to haunt British governments throughout the interwar era. The Balfour Declaration committed Britain to opening Palestine to Jewish settlement, and the British authorities allowed roughly eighteen thousand Jewish immigrants into the mandate between 1919 and 1921. Taking little comfort in Foreign Secretary Arthur Balfour's assurances that "nothing shall be done which may prejudice the civil and religious rights of existing non-Jewish communities in Palestine," local Arabs feared they might become a minority in a Zionist state. Their violent opposition forced the British government to issue a formal statement in 1922 promising to limit further immigration to match the economic capacity of the mandate. British officials also promised that only part of Palestine would become the Jewish national home. Their attempt at compromise offended both Arabs and Jews, and British authorities in Palestine strained to keep the peace between the two irreconcilable nationalist factions.

Egypt was not a mandate, but here too anti-imperialism complicated Britain's attempt to exert influence by treaties with cooperative local rulers. In 1922, the British government tried to follow through on Milner's accommodationist strategy of demonstrating its good intentions to the nationalists by granting Egypt a limited form of independence, but it required the Egyptians to endure continued British responsibility for Egyptian defense, protection of minority populations, administration of the Sudan (a shared Anglo-Egyptian co-dominion), and control of the Suez. The Egyptian nationalist leader Said Zaghul and his allies accepted this watered-down sovereignty to end the widely detested wartime protectorate. In 1922, Egypt became formally independent, with King Faud as its constitutional monarch. But two years later British High Commissioner Field Marshall Lord Allenby used conflict over the control of the Sudan and the assassination of the British head of the Egyptian army as an excuse to reduce substantially the Egyptian role in their shared colonial possession. Far from being an entirely sovereign nation, Egypt had a great deal in common with the Indian princely states. The Egyptian nationalists found this relationship intolerable, and Britain's influence in the country depended largely on its ability to keep King Faud in power.

In the Western Hemisphere, constitutional reform and limited political concessions proved an equally imperfect means of bringing long-term security to British imperial interests in the postwar West Indies. As expected, the Great War had a significant impact on the British Empire in the Caribbean. The veterans of the Royal West Indies Regiment, particularly the participants in the December 1918 strike in Italy, returned to local economies suffering from a 145 percent increase in basic food prices due to wartime inflation.

Making good on their Italian resolutions, they played a central role in the mass protests and strikes for higher wages that spread throughout the West Indies in the immediate postwar years. Overtaxed colonial governments throughout the region struggled to contain this mass unrest. On Trinidad, planters and businessmen formed vigilante groups, and the situation grew so tense that the government had to call in British troops to restore order and back up the local police.

This West Indian unrest was driven primarily by economic rather than political grievances. The strikers and rioters did not have a strong connection to the middle classes, which shared their dissatisfaction with British rule but were not as interested in changing the social and economic order. Whereas the unskilled laborers and veterans sought higher wages, these teachers, journalists, lawyers, and small business owners wanted a greater political voice, if not true autonomy on the Irish model. Some envisioned a federation of territories with self-governing dominion status. In 1921, a senior Colonial Office official visited the West Indies to investigate whether this would be possible but concluded that participatory democracy would not work in the racially divided societies of the Caribbean. Arguing poverty and underdevelopment would produce an oligarchy rather than a truly representative government, he insisted that the backward peoples of the islands depended on the British Crown as their trustee. Left unsaid was the reality that Britain felt the need to retain direct control over its West Indian territories to protect British investments and prevent local commercial interests from forming ties with American competitors.

As in India, the colonial governments recognized the need to win over the moderate middle classes, and they adopted a policy of gradually introducing elected members to local executive and legislative councils. But they granted these concessions with numerous caveats. British officials retained full control of the territorial governments by ensuring that appointed civil servants outnumbered the new elected "unofficial" representatives. Stiff property requirements for voting also meant that less than 10 percent of the population had the franchise on most islands. The Colonial Office further promised to gradually increase local representation until West Indians eventually had self-governing institutions elected on the basis of universal suffrage. As in British Africa, however, the timeline for these reforms remained undefined and far off.

Unlike in British Africa, the imperial authorities in the Caribbean did not share Lugard's confidence and comfort because they worried that radical nationalists, socialists, or even Soviet-directed Bolsheviks might take control of the growing labor movement. On Trinidad, they were fortunate that A. A. Cipriani, a member of a prominent planter family, emerged as the president of the Trinidad Workingmen's Association. Cipriani was the officer in the Royal West Indies Regiment during the war who won over his men by serving as their spokesman during the Taranto strike. Capitalizing on the respect he earned among urban workers for standing up to the racist military authorities, he captured the legislative council seat for the Port of Spain in the 1925 election.

Cipriani's agenda typified the position of many liberals in the interwar empire. He sided with poor West Indians against exploitive employers, but he believed in the imperial system and was not willing to address the underlying economic and political factors that led to these abuses. His only real accomplishment on the legislative council was to win slightly better pay and a shorter workday for Trinidadian laborers. Moreover, Cipriani's unwillingness to push for more radical measures angered West Indian intellectuals, and he had only limited success in steering the Trinidad Workingmen's Association away from a more radical agenda.

Gradualism and reform were not much of a substitute for a living wage, and the West Indian governments had to fall back on more draconian security measures to deal with overt anti-imperialism and labor unrest. Police officers monitored the Barbados Workingmen's Association's meetings for signs of communism, and Trinidad's Sedition Ordinance of 1920 empowered the governor to ban books and close newspapers that spread "subversion." As in the Raj, the colonial authorities went to great lengths to keep news of the Russian Bolshevik revolution out of the West Indies and confiscated books and magazines that were freely available in metropolitan Britain. These were stopgap measures at best, and the security of British rule in the Caribbean depended ultimately on the extent to which the constitutional reforms gave middle- and working-class people a reason to work within the imperial system.

By comparison, British Africa did seem truly stable and secure in the 1920s. Having been imperial subjects for only three to four decades, most Africans were still adjusting to the realities of British rule. Imperial experts therefore assumed they had ample time to develop a rational system of rule for Africa. Whereas most colonies ran on shoestring budgets before the war, Lugard and his disciples set out to develop standardized economic and administrative policies that could be applied to all the African territories. Cognizant of growing anti-imperial nationalism in India and, to a lesser extent, the West Indies, they hoped to learn from their mistakes in the remnants of the first British Empire.

Yet Lugard's ideal of ruling through local native authorities on the Indian model never worked as well as he suggested in *The Dual Mandate in British Tropical Africa* because most Africans lived in stateless societies that had diffuse and often overlapping centers of power. These sophisticated but unfamiliar institutions limited the formation of centralized states in the preconquest era, and the British complicated efforts to introduce indirect rule to Africa. As the pioneer South African administrator Theophilus Shepstone learned in nineteenth-century Natal, Lugard found that he had to appoint cooperative local allies as chiefs for stateless communities. Theoretically, these men were native rulers, but they held power only as long as they could execute imperial policy. More often than not, colonial administrators had to invent symbols of authority for them in the form of medals, staffs of office, and special chiefly clothing.

Nor did indirect rule make for a coherent administrative system. A convenient fig leaf, it legitimized the pragmatic steps that British officials had to take in running the African colonies with limited economic and political means. By making native tradition the basis of chiefly authority, Lugard and his fellow bureaucrats ensured that the African "tribe" as we know it today was largely a product of the twentieth-century colonial imagination. Under imperial rule a tribe was a lower order of political and social organization that was less than a nation, and as such it became the central administrative unit of British Africa. Assuming that every tribe conveniently had its own unchanging traditions, British district officers set out to make native custom the basis of local administration. No society, however, has a single set of unchanging norms and values, and each new generation reinvents its traditions to reflect changing patterns of wealth and power. In British Africa, this meant privileging one form of authority over another, which empowered the African allies who became successful tribal chiefs in ways that experts like Lugard never imagined.

Never completely aware of the full implications of these realities, colonial administrators strove to ensure that the globalizing forces of capitalism and Western culture did not damage native custom. This meant learning from the Raj's mistakes to avoid creating a class of African Gandhis. As a British expert on native education put it, "In India there has grown an educated class of varying caste which can find no place in an oriental social scheme. . . . In part of West Africa the agitator and resister have already made their appearance."[29] To ensure education did not produce any more of these unwanted political consequences, ethnographers worked in cooperation with mission educators sponsored by the American philanthropic Phelps-Stokes Fund, which claimed expertise in African American rural education, to design a new adapted curriculum that theoretically harmonized a Western curriculum with native law and custom. The goal of adapted education was to create "a better native," which the authorities defined as a dutiful Christian graduate with useful economic skills who would not challenge British rule and would accept his or her place in tribal village society. There was a strong element of unapologetic racism and chauvinism in the new curriculum. Speaking at a Tanganyikan education conference in the mid-1920s, a colonial official candidly asked, "Does anyone who sees the Europeanised African believe him to be genuine? Too often he seems only a caricature of a European and an insult to his own race."[30]

More significantly, Lugard's concept of indirect rule and its commitment to evolutionary uplift, which sounded so grand in the pages of *The Dual Mandate*, was entirely at odds with the promised economic modernization and humanitarian liberalism that made the new imperialism seem legitimate in metropolitan Britain. Christian conversion and turning African tribesmen into wage laborers was inherently and radically transformative and disruptive, and there was little that the imperial experts could do to actually manage the pace or trajectory of social change in the African colonies. Overextended British administrators had to govern as African rulers and needed African help to run the colonial state and economy. In 1925, just two hundred district officers were responsible for uplifting 20 million Nigerians, which worked out to one expatriate official per hundred thousand people. The reach of these solitary Britons was quite limited regardless of how much imperial force stood behind them, and they tended to act like school headmasters who left day-to-day matters of discipline to the senior student prefects or, in the imperial case, African chiefs and clerks. Regardless of the pronouncements of General Dyer's defenders in Parliament, the colonial chief usually had the most influence in his fiefdom, not the British district officer, and as such was generally responsible for collecting taxes, upholding law and order, recruiting laborers, and maintaining roads. These local allies, who often also served as interpreters for their imperial patrons, had considerable authority. In eastern Nigeria, African clerks and messengers ran the native courts and had the power to issue summonses and arrest warrants, while in Kenya a court translator terrorized a community in the western Gusii highlands through his ability to manipulate a succession of essentially oblivious district commissioners.

In a few places, powerful centralized rulers, who were relatively rare in preconquest Africa, became colonial allies. This was the case for Kabaka Mutesa's heirs in the Kingdom of Buganda, as well as for the royal families of the southern High Commission Territories (Swaziland, Bechuanaland, and Basutoland). In West Africa, the imperial authorities allowed the Asantehene, who once ruled the powerful Asante confederacy, to return from exile to the Gold Coast once he demonstrated that he was willing to follow orders. As in India, the British preferred to work through these kinds of nobles and aristocrats on the grounds that they were more conservative and less likely to ally with popular nationalists. They would have liked to ignore the educated elites because westernized Africans were living proof that the stereotype of African backwardness was a lie. Yet these African doctors, lawyers, journalists, and prosperous cash crop farmers could not be ignored, and the colonial authorities allowed them to elect representatives to the legislative assemblies in Nigeria, the Gold Coast, and Sierra Leone in the 1920s.

Having deemed these westernized elites unacceptable partners, the imperial authorities tried to create chiefs by lumping together culturally similar stateless societies. Even Lugard acknowledged this when he recommended grouping "small tribes, or sections of a tribe" together "so as to form a single administrative unit" whose chiefs could constitute a "native authority."[31] In East Africa, Sir Donald Cameron, who served under Lugard in Nigeria, put this policy into practice in Tanganyika by joining stateless societies together under a single paramount chiefdom, thereby ignoring the reality that many communities preferred to remain stateless. Cameron claimed that this exercise in ethnic engineering fulfilled the obligations of Britain's League of Nations mandate in Tanganyika, which required Britain to prepare subject peoples for eventual nationhood. The colonial governments also created native councils to provide chiefs and other African dignitaries with rudimentary training in local administration. These appointed bodies theoretically could make regulations and collect taxes for use in local development. In Kenya, however, district officers, who were the presidents of the councils, blocked councilors from spending money on Western-style schools on the grounds that roads and other infrastructure improvements were greater priorities.

The settler communities in eastern, central, and southern Africa presented the most significant complication for the doctrine of indirect rule. They were able to flout the humanitarian justifications for British rule in Africa because they had considerable sway in both local governments and metropolitan Britain. Many of the most influential Kenyan settlers, like Hugh Cholmondeley, Third Baron Delamere, came from the lesser British nobility. Seeking to ensure that Kenya remained an aristocratic preserve, the government deported poor and indigent Europeans to India under the Distressed British Subjects Act to maintain white prestige. The resourceful and self-sufficient emigrants that the Kenyans coveted largely preferred to go to the dominions, where prospects were much better, than to stake their futures in the economically precarious African colonies. In the postwar years, the Kenyan government therefore launched a Soldier Settlement Scheme, which opened fifty thousand acres of fertile African land to commissioned British veterans of the Great War. Over two thousand members of the Nandi community, many of whom had also fought for Britain during the war, lost their land to these former officers.

By the early 1920s, the settlers had the privilege of electing two unofficial representatives to the legislative and executive councils, which gave them a deciding voice in financial matters. They used this to create a larger imperial crisis by pushing through laws that restricted Indian immigration. Having long viewed East Africa as a de facto Indian colony, Indian nationalists seized on the issue as another example of racial discrimination in the empire. This was at the time when the Raj was desperately trying to win over moderates through the constitutional reforms in the Government of India Act. Although the metropolitan British government defused the controversy temporarily by issuing a formal statement in 1923 declaring Kenya a territory where the interests of "African natives must be paramount," the settlers continued to impose their will on the Kenyan government, even though there were less than ten thousand of them in the colony. One of their great aspirations was to join Kenya with Uganda and Tanganyika in an East African federation that might one day qualify for dominion status. African opposition and the Great Depression sank the scheme in the 1930s, but the settlers never stopped thinking of Kenya as a "white man's country."

The situation was much the same in central and southern Africa, where white settlers inherited power when the British South Africa Company, the last and most profitable of the early chartered companies, turned Northern and Southern Rhodesia over to the Crown in 1924. European settlers were 5 percent of the population in Southern Rhodesia (Zimbabwe) and 2 percent of the total population of Northern Rhodesia (Zambia). Seeking a counterweight to the Afrikaner-dominated Union of South Africa, Britain granted the Southern Rhodesians the privilege of local self-government with an elected legislature and prime minister even though they were not economically self-sufficient. Although British administrators retained responsibility for "native affairs," the Rhodesian settlers confined the Shona and Ndebele majority to native reserves and appropriated most of the colony's best land for themselves.

Colonial officials justified this privileged treatment of the settler minorities by claiming that they had a moral obligation under the second tenet of Lugard's dual mandate to develop the African colonies. They also followed Lugard's lead in suggesting that the European immigrants would teach Africans better agricultural techniques. Yet most settlers proved embarrassingly poor farmers. In Kenya, they had only 10 percent of the "white highlands" under cultivation because it was more profitable to speculate on the future value of the land than it was to actually farm it. Those who tried often went bankrupt because they had little actual agricultural experience and could not reduce their production costs enough to compete on the world market.

Settler farmers therefore needed government subsidies and low-cost African labor to survive. But Africans also recognized the potential of commercial agriculture and moved into cash crop production on their own. In central Kenya, members of Kikuyu communities with access to sufficient land and the railway or urban markets in Nairobi were far more successful than their European competitors because they had greater agricultural experience and lower labor costs. The settler farmers' only solution was to press the colonial authorities to solve their labor problems for them. In 1919, the Kenyan governor directed his district officers to encourage Africans to work for private employers and to record the names of chiefs who were not sufficiently helpful in producing the necessary laborers. The implications of this veiled threat were clear: the chiefs would face retribution if they did not force enough of their people to work. The Kenyan authorities also banned Africans from growing lucrative crops like coffee on the grounds that they did not have the expertise to prevent crop diseases from spreading to European farms. This was nonsense, particularly given that Chagga farmers in neighboring Tanganyika were extremely successful coffee growers. The government's real goal was to protect settler agriculture from more efficient African competition.

In southern Africa, the Rhodesian farmers, who needed as much government assistance as their Kenyan counterparts, had to also compete with mine owners and industrialists for African labor. The lure of reasonably good wages and the pressure of taxation convinced many young men in communities from as far away as southern Tanganyika to make the long and dangerous journey south. These migrants would have preferred to work in South Africa, where wages were relatively high, but many had to settle for jobs in the Rhodesias because they ran out of money on the way. By the end of the interwar era, the Nyasaland government estimated that 30 percent of all adult African men had left the territory in search of work. The loss of one-third of the male working population had profoundly negative consequences for rural African communities in the protectorate. Food production suffered, and families splintered when migrant husbands and fathers failed to return.

This did not mean that life was better in the Union of South Africa. Although wages in the union were higher than the rest of British Africa, the government in Pretoria introduced laws segregating the cities and reserving specific occupations for Europeans. The mining and industrial interests, which were mostly British, formed an unspoken agreement with right-wing Afrikaner nationalists whereby they accepted institutionalized racism and higher wages for skilled white workers in return for the government's assistance in producing a reliable supply of low-cost African labor. There was little that the authorities in London could do to mitigate these conditions because they had granted the South Africans self-government, but South Africa's unapologetically exploitive native policies made it politically impossible for the British government to follow through on its promise to turn the High Commission Territories over to the union. Missionaries and English-speaking South African liberals also criticized the unnecessary brutality of Pretoria's land and labor policies but viewed segregation as necessary to protect backward African communities from rapid change. Much like the liberalism of A. A. Cipriani in the West Indies, these reformers accepted the underlying social inequalities of the empire. The African National Congress and Clements Kadalie's Industrial and Commercial Union worked for equal political and economic rights for non-Europeans, but the South African authorities refused to acknowledge their authority to speak for the African majority on the grounds that they were "detribalized." Moreover, the police

and security forces used violent force to break up strikes and political protests.

THE EMPIRE AS COMMONWEALTH

These complexities and inherent weaknesses of the interwar empire were not
readily apparent in metropolitan Britain. Instead, idealists in the humanitarian lobby like J. C. Wedgwood believed it was possible to create a modern
liberal empire through the kind of gradualist constitutional reforms embodied
in the 1919 Government of India Act. In attacking Dyer's "frightfulness" at
Amritsar, he asked, "Are we to try to carry on the great position we have
today by the terrorism of subject races?" More important, he offered a vision
for the second British Empire that contrasted sharply with the pragmatism of
Dyer's Conservative defenders when he declared that he wanted to bring
subject peoples "into the British Empire on equal terms, so that Indians
should be British citizens, and have the same rights as Englishmen or Austra-
lians." To do otherwise, Wedgwood warned, meant that Britain would lose
its empire. "If you persist in treating Indians . . . as though they were an
inferior people, not equal to you and me, . . . you are ruining the British
Empire and the future cause of our country." There was even room for less
advanced or less easily assimilable people in this updated version of the
Roman Empire: "I want to see England embracing all . . . people, not only
Indians, but as they come along in the scale of civilisation, the black men of
Africa, as well as the Jews of Palestine and the Egyptians of Egypt. I want to
see them all as proud of being British citizens as the men in the Roman days
were proud of being Roman citizens."[32]

In essence, Wedgwood offered a blueprint for an empire that could accommodate the self-governing "white" dominions, the Irish Free State, the
Raj, the League of Nations mandates, the old West Indian sugar colonies, and
the new African protectorates. In this sense his vision was reconcilable with
the British hostility to formal empire that prevailed in the mid-nineteenth
century because it assumed that backward populations could advance, much
more rapidly than Lugard imagined, along the path of civilization to reach a
stage where they might join with Canada, Australia, New Zealand, and the
Union of South Africa as more equal imperial partners. Yet even this idealized version of the empire still required subject peoples to acknowledge their
less advanced state and accept continued British tutelage in the near term.
Liberal imperialists like Wedgwood believed that it was possible to overcome objections to this inferior intermediate status if they could just make
the people whom they ruled through nondemocratic authoritarian means
understand their good intentions.

This was wishful thinking in an age when the nation-state was becoming the globally recognized prerequisite for sovereignty, economic security, and human dignity. By the mid-1920s it was already readily apparent that even Britain's kith and kin in the dominions would not accept a subordinate role in the empire. Canada and South Africa blocked the Crown from conferring royal titles and honors on their citizens, and at the 1926 imperial conference the dominions refused to endorse the Treaty of Locarno, which codified the postwar European borders, because they did not want to be drawn into another continental conflict. The metropolitan government acknowledged that it had no alternative but to accept their insistence on greater independence with a declaration affirming that the dominions were "autonomous Communities within the British Empire, equal in status, in no way subordinate one to another in any aspect of their domestic or external affairs, though united by a common allegiance to the Crown, and freely associated as members of the British Commonwealth of Nations."[33] Five years later, the 1931 Statute of Westminster granted the dominions the power to change their constitutions without consulting the British parliament and affirmed that the dominions were equal self-governing institutions within the Commonwealth.

These constitutional advances went relatively smoothly in Australia, New Zealand, and Canada where economic and industrial development depended on continued investment and immigration from Britain. In the Irish Free State and the Union of South Africa, however, the promise of equal status within the Commonwealth was less believable and appealing. Neither the Irish republicans nor the Afrikaner nationalists had any desire to maintain their ties to Britain, and both intensely disliked having to swear continued loyalty to the Crown. The Free State set about severing as many economic ties with Britain as possible and embarked on an aggressive campaign to promote Irish culture by replacing English with Gaelic as the language of government and education. The Afrikaners, who never forgot that twenty thousand of their women and children had died of disease and neglect in British detention camps during the South African War, would have liked to have done the same, but they could not make as sharp a break with the empire because British investors provided much of the capital for the dominion's mines and emerging industries. Still, these economic bonds also made the British government less inclined to challenge their openly discriminatory "native policies."

From the metropolitan perspective, the British taxpayer could also legitimately question the value of the new constitutional arrangements as the nation struggled to recover from a war that had disrupted the worldwide networks of trade and investment that were the true source of Britain's global strength and influence. Prewar Russia had been a major recipient of British investment, but the Soviet Union repudiated these debts. Even worse, the necessity of selling off most of its remaining foreign investments to pay for the war reduced Britain's overall assets by roughly £1 billion. Faced with the decline of its enormously profitable "invisible" economy of banking and investment, the postwar government struggled to find ways to make its formal empire pay through more conventional means.

For many empire boosters, this meant abandoning Britain's nineteenth-century commitment to free trade and retreating behind the walls of imperial protectionism. An aging manufacturing base and emerging competition from the United States made the overseas possessions appear increasingly more important to the interwar British economy. The formal empire's share of British exports rose from 35 to 41 percent between 1913 and 1938, while imports from the empire into Britain grew from 27 to 42 percent during the same period.[34] This trade became more significant as Britain's postwar debts made it impossible for it to reconstruct its more lucrative global network of lending and investment. Beginning in 1919, David Lloyd George's coalition government began to address this problem by enacting a few limited protective tariffs that encouraged greater trade between metropolitan Britain and the empire. In the 1920s, the Conservative colonial secretary Leopold Amery dreamed of knitting the diverse imperial territories together into an integrated global economy that he compared to a reciprocating steam engine. This was not feasible given that international agreements made it difficult for the Colonial Office to order the colonies to place higher tariffs on non-British imports, and it took careful negotiation to convince the self-governing dominions to grant even limited preferences to British goods in their markets.

Lacking the legal and diplomatic means to create a closed imperial network, interwar British governments tried to overcome the growing economic nationalism in the dominions by encouraging voluntary imperial economic cooperation through a media campaign that touted the mutual economic benefits of the empire and Commonwealth. In 1924 and 1925, the British Empire Exhibition in London drew roughly 27 million people to exhibits designed to create new markets and to introduce the "races" of the empire to each other. The Empire Marketing Board continued these efforts with a £3 million budget to develop and promote imperial products. It used books, pamphlets, postcards, and posters in the London Underground to get this message across. The British Broadcasting Company also celebrated the empire through imperial-themed programs and by providing coverage of events like the empire exhibition and the monarch's greetings to colonial listeners around the globe. The emerging British movie industry played a similar role by producing films like *Gold Coast Cocoa* and *Cargo from Jamaica*.

Nevertheless, the British public was at best lukewarm to the protective preferences of the 1920s because higher tariffs on nonimperial imports drove up prices, and the government had removed most of the key protectionist measures by the end of the decade. The dominions, conversely, were concerned primarily with protecting their own developing economies, even though Britain remained the primary customer for their exports. As aspiring industrial powers, they had also no intention of fully opening their markets to more advanced metropolitan competitors. The Raj had the authority to impose preferences by decree, but nationalist opposition, particularly after the 1919 constitutional reforms, made it politically risky to do so. Rejecting the suggestion that India should favor imports from Britain and the dominions, an Indian legislative council member rightly noted, "At present I am treated as an inferior and I am not going to consider whether I will take part in any of the economic discussions when I have no right to discuss political issues and have a say of my own."[35] Budget shortfalls in the 1920s further required the Raj to increase tariffs to raise revenue regardless of Amery's plans for a closed global imperial market.

African interests were easier to ignore because Africans had fewer constitutional rights, but their captive economies were not large enough to be of significant value to the empire's postwar recovery. The newer colonies took less than 3 percent of total British exports during the interwar era, and Japanese and Indian exporters did a much better job of capturing African markets. The Colonial Development Act of 1929, which was supposed to provide £1 million per year to stimulate colonial development, did little to promote real economic growth because much of the money went to paying the colonies' debts to Britain.

Finally, imperial preferences actually undermined the metropolitan industrial base. The barriers to foreign imports made British goods less competitive by allowing manufacturers to put off the pain of modernizing aging industries. Contrary to contemporary historians who celebrate the second British Empire as a global engine of free trade, the interwar empire was actually an exercise in failed protectionism and ultimately a reflection of Britain's growing economic and industrial weakness.

CRISIS ONCE MORE: THE EMPIRE IN THE 1930S

Although the British Empire appeared outwardly strong and well organized once the turmoil of the immediate postwar years subsided, the global economic collapse of 1929 once again exposed underlying structural problems that threatened its long-term viability. Most fundamentally, the depression gravely damaged the global networks of trade and investment that underpinned the empire. Faced with alarming revenue shortfalls, individual colonial states cut back on administration, economic development, social services, internal security, and defense. These draconian steps limited severely the empire's ability to deal with the international fascist threat, the continued growth of anti-imperial nationalism in more advanced colonies, strikes by underpaid workers, and the emergence of new popular challenges to imperial rule among subject populations.

Contrary to metropolitan hopes that the empire might provide some economic relief from the depression, the economies of the dominions, colonies, protectorates, and mandates were particularly vulnerable to worldwide downturns in commerce, investment, and the bulk exports that were the main sources of revenue in most colonies. Sugar production, still the economic backbone of most West Indian territories, suffered from a drop in prices from £23 per ton in 1923 to just £5 per ton in 1934.[36] Plunging global commodity prices were also particularly damaging to African economies as falling returns from exports led to drastic wage cuts for unskilled laborers. For the Raj, the loss of revenue from trade tariffs produced severe budget problems. Throughout the empire, the resulting cuts in social services and tax increases provoked revolts and other forms of popular resistance.

These imperial economic woes also had significant consequences for metropolitan Britain. By the 1930s, one of India's main economic contributions to the empire was to pay foreign investors and balance Britain's external trade with funds generated by the export of raw materials and simple manufactures. In other words, it was still profitable to invest in India as long as the Raj could generate enough export revenue to pay its obligations. But the metropolitan taxpayer would have to assume India's £350 million in foreign debt if the Indian government went bankrupt from the depression. Britain's economic health became increasingly dependent on India's ability to make good on its financial obligations. It was therefore essential that the Raj erect significant tariffs on imports to protect developing local industries that generated revenue by producing profitable exports. This was a significant reason why the British share of India's overall imports decreased from 62 to 30 percent between 1914 and 1939.[37]

These pragmatic policies came at the expense of outmoded British manufacturers, particularly in the textile sector, who lost even more of the Indian market to American, Japanese, and domestic Indian competitors over the course of the 1930s. In contrast, Indian farmers with access to land, water, and transportation actually prospered during the economic downturn by taking advantage of the growing domestic demand for agricultural goods. In the industrial sector, the Tata Iron and Steel Company produced two-thirds of all the steel used in India by the end of the decade, and the company negotiated reciprocal agreements with its metropolitan competitors to gain access to the British market. Indian entrepreneurs further expanded into cement, paper, sugar, and textile production during this period. Some of them also started shipping companies and airlines.

Failing to recognize the full implications of these changes and the negative consequences of imperial protectionism for the British metropole, imperial partisans still hoped to turn the empire into a closed market to provide some relief from the depression. Although the dominions were also in precarious economic shape in the 1930s, the protectionists proposed to link their economies more tightly to the imperial center in a reciprocal free trade zone. This proved unworkable because the dominions would not lower their tariff walls, even to imports from the "motherland." When the dominion leaders met in Ottawa in 1932, the British national coalition government granted imperial goods free entry into the metropolitan market but received no uniform concessions from the dominions in return. Instead, it had to negotiate separate and unequal agreements with each dominion. This did little to create new markets for British exports and increased Britain's trade deficit with the empire.

Although the returns of the Ottawa Agreement were disappointing, Britain derived much greater economic benefit by convincing sovereign foreign nations dependent on the British market to tie the value of their currencies to the pound and to hold their currency reserves in metropolitan banks. The British government already required the Crown colonies to link their money to the pound and to keep enough gold and securities on deposit in Britain to cover the full value of all paper money and coins they issued. In the 1930s, Britain built this existing system into a semiformal "sterling area," which included the majority of the protectorates, colonies, and dominions (Canada and British Honduras tied their currencies to the U.S. dollar), as well as Portugal and most of the Scandinavian and Baltic countries. In 1933, Denmark alone sent 64 percent of its exports to Britain. More important than the formal empire, this sterling area helped Britain survive the Great Depression by protecting its international trade and ensuring that London remained the center of global finance for the rest of the interwar years. [38]

Refusing to play the role of dutiful subjects, dominion leaders became even more determined to assert their political and military independence as the depression deepened. The waxing political influence of right-wing Afrikaner nationalists made the South African government particularly unwilling to support imperial projects, while Ireland spent much of the 1930s locked in a trade war with metropolitan Britain. The Free State also used the abdication of King Edward VIII in favor of George VI as an opportunity to sever more of its political and diplomatic ties to the empire. The new Constitution of Ireland (1937) abolished the position of governor-general and turned Ireland into a de facto republic by making an elected president its head of state. There was little that the British government could do about this, apart from continuing to treat Ireland as a member of the Commonwealth for the purposes of citizenship and emigration. The six counties constituting Northern Ireland remained part of Great Britain with their own separate parliament and twelve representatives in the British parliament who voted on external and imperial matters.

Canada, Australia, and New Zealand still professed their loyalty to the empire, but in 1937 they joined South Africa in refusing to offer unqualified support to Britain in its confrontation with Nazi Germany because they did not want to be drawn into another European war. In India, nationalist opposition to increased military spending in the expanded legislative assemblies forced Britain to assume more of the cost of modernizing the Indian army and to promise not to deploy Indian forces overseas without consulting Indian leaders. These restrictions made it difficult to counter the growing military influence of Japan in China, where Britain still had significant economic interests, and the rest of the Far East. Lacking support from the resolutely isolationist United States, imperial strategists spent precious resources developing Singapore into a major base.

Given the continued importance of South Asia, many imperially minded British politicians, civil servants, and military officers believed that further constitutional concessions were excessive and damaging to the security and stability of the Raj. Debates over how to manage India therefore became a focal point of metropolitan British politics in the 1920s. In 1927, the Conservative government's Simon Commission concluded that power-sharing reforms had actually increased opposition to British rule by giving the nationalists access to a wider segment of Indian society. Conversely, the Labour Party held fast to Wedgwood's vision of a liberal empire and was more willing to grant Indians greater political rights within the imperial system. When the Labourites came to power in the late 1920s, the Viceroy Lord Irwin issued a declaration that India was destined for full dominion status and called a roundtable conference for Indian political leaders to discuss further reforms.

As in Ireland, the promise of greater autonomy within the Commonwealth held little appeal for committed anti-imperial nationalists. Members of the Hindustan Socialist Republic Association built secret bomb factories and sent their members abroad for military training. In 1929, a pair of prominent Punjabi radicals, Bhagat Singh and B. K. Dutt, attacked the legislative assembly in New Delhi with bombs and then passively turned over their pistols when the police moved in to arrest them. Their aim was to make the point that their actions were motived by political concerns. The attack was part of a renewed wave of spectacular anti-imperial violence that the revolutionaries hoped would trigger their long-hoped-for mass uprising. Many of these activists ended up in prison, where they adopted the Irish tactic of using hunger strikes to call attention to their cause and their demand to be treated as political prisoners rather than common criminals. Prison officials, who did not want their captives to become martyrs, did their best to keep them alive, but Jatindra Nath Das achieved national attention by successfully starving himself to death in 1929.[39] Violent challenges to imperial authority became even more widespread between 1930 and 1933 as bands of armed men (and some women) raided police stations, telegraph offices, and a European club. The radicals also assassinated the police inspector general, the inspector general of prisons, senior civil servants, and district judges, but their attempts to kill three provincial governors failed. This renewed violence took place at a time when the Indian government continued to struggle to meet its European recruiting quotas for senior positions in the civil service and police.

More troubling for the future of the empire, there was a steady erosion of moderate support for the Raj over the course of the interwar era. When the grand inauguration of New Delhi, which King George V had announced at his Coronation Durbar, finally took place in 1931, far fewer people were swayed or intimidated by its massive state buildings or propagandistic monuments celebrating the Raj's place in the empire. Relatively few Indians took part in the official ceremonies, and a heavy military and police presence, reflecting rising concerns about security, forced most of the local population to watch from a distance. Impatient with the slow pace of political change and worried that mounting political violence would spiral out of control, Gandhi embarked on a renewed noncooperation campaign that drew considerable popular support. British officials initially hoped to isolate him and the rest of the Indian National Congress leadership by forming a partnership with more pragmatic politicians willing to work with the Raj in return for a greater measure of self-rule, and the mounting violence of the early 1930s gave them a strong incentive to make further concessions to moderate Indian nationalism, regardless of Conservative opposition in Britain.

Building on the reforms of the 1920s, Lord Irwin used his roundtable conferences in London to map out India's move to full self-rule under a dominion-style government. Congress leaders boycotted the 1930 conference, which consisted of fifty delegates chosen by the viceroy and sixteen princes. Gandhi also initially refused to take part in the constitutional negotiations because he worried radical nationalists would leave the INC if he accepted anything less than full independence. His goal was to maintain unity and bridge class differences between wealthy anti-imperialists, who wanted to acquire political power without changing the existing economic and social order that was the basis of their elite status, and ordinary farmers and workers, who expected independence to bring a significant improvement in the material realities of their daily lives. As chapter 5 will show, many African nationalists would also confront this problem during the decolonization era after World War II. Additionally, Gandhi also struggled to keep his coalition from splitting along Hindu-Muslim lines. Mindful of these pressing concerns, Gandhi agreed to participate in a second London conference in return for Irwin's promise that the Raj would have an executive government that was responsible to an Indian electorate. This angered Winston Churchill, who opposed all negotiations with what he termed a "seditious Middle Temple lawyer now posing as a fakir [religious authority] of a type well known in the East."[40]

In the short term, Churchill need not have worried, for Irwin's conference quickly deadlocked. His successor as viceroy jailed Gandhi and resorted to mass arrests under a state of emergency when the noncooperation campaign resumed in January 1932. The central and ultimately intractable issues complicating the roundtable talks were the status of the princely states and political representation for Muslims and other non-Hindu minorities. In 1933, the All-India Muslim Conference called for separate electoral rolls and constitutional status for Muslims, reserved seats in all legislatures, and the creation of new Muslim-majority provinces. The Sikh and Hindu untouchable communities backed their demands. Gandhi, however, insisted on a single voting system with no special provisions for religion, caste, or ethnicity. Fearing that communal divisions would lead to violence and help the British stay in power, he attacked discrimination against lower-caste and minority groups and insisted that all Indians were equal. The Congress leadership was also opposed to preserving the political authority of the Raj's princely allies.

Gandhi's boycott of the ongoing negotiations allowed the British and their Indian partners to ignore the more militant Congress position. In 1935, they reached an accord that led to another Government of India Act, one that now granted autonomous self-government to the provinces and introduced the dyarchal system to the central administration by making most state ministries responsible to an elected legislature. New franchise rules allowed 30 million people, roughly 15 percent of the total population, to vote. British officials worried this would empower the Indian National Congress but hoped Congress leaders would become distracted with the processes of winning elections, governing the provinces, and dispensing patronage. As an additional safeguard Britain retained control of India's security forces, finances, defense, and foreign affairs, and the legislation preserved separate communal voting rolls for Muslims and other minorities. The reforms neither mentioned dominion status nor spelled out how Indians might attain it. The leaders of the Raj also hoped to use the princes to check the power of the INC, but their plans to federate the provinces with the princely states fell apart when the princes refused to give up any of their authority under the new political arrangements.

Not surprisingly, the Indian National Congress won the first elections under the Government of India Act handily in 1937. Its record of sacrifice and civil disobedience in the interwar decades had transformed it from an elite movement into a popular political party that used sophisticated electoral tactics and superior financing to defeat disorganized and underfunded opponents. Sweeping aside minor Hindu parties and the Muslim League, the Congress took total control of five of the eleven provinces and won enough legislative seats to become a significant influence in the others. Muslim leaders were alarmed by the INC's success and its use of Hindu idioms to win elections and concluded that they needed to create a unified Islamic movement and build the Muslim League, which had been a largely elite organization, into a mass party to protect their communal and political interests.

To some degree, the 1937 elections succeeded in tempering the INC's radicalism, just as the constitutional reformers had hoped. Congress was now in the difficult position of being a ruling party that opposed the very political system that brought it to power. Moreover, the INC's close ties to Indian businessmen and the necessity of courting foreign investment and trade forced Congress leaders to back away from radical populism and promises to delink the rupee from the pound and renounce India's foreign debt. Squeezed for revenue in the provinces and beholden to the influential business class, the Congress-controlled legislatures increased taxes on basic commodities and passed laws restricting strikes and unionization. The power-sharing reforms thus bought Britain some time by splitting Gandhi's anti-imperial coalition. The INC ran local affairs in India for only the next two years until it withdrew from the government in protest over Britain's arbitrary decision to take India into World War II.

Elsewhere in Asia, the political changes in India once again had widespread repercussions. The Raj was a powerful subempire in its own right, and the growing prosperity and influence of expatriate Indian moneylenders, landowners, merchants, and migrant laborers in Burma and Ceylon alarmed local nationalist leaders and ordinary workers and sparked popular unrest in both colonies. The Government of Burma Act of 1935 granted Burma self-government on the Indian model, but student nationalists led by Aung San, father of famed civil rights activist Aung San Suu Kyi, and U Nu brought down the first elected local government with their demands that Burma become a republic by severing its ties to India and, by extension, Britain. Elected leaders in Ceylon were more secure, but they too used their new authority to discourage further migration and distance themselves from India.

Although constitutional reform was a reasonably effective stopgap response to anti-imperial resistance in South Asia, British diplomats and advisors had far fewer options in dealing with Arab nationalism at a time when the Italian conquest of Ethiopia in 1935 threatened strategic interests in the Middle East. The treaties of the 1920s that granted a degree of independence to most British territories in the region meant that the empire's extensive network of military bases in Egypt, Iraq, Jordan, Palestine, and Cyprus depended largely on the cooperation and goodwill of local client rulers. Under the 1936 Anglo-Egyptian Treaty, the British military garrison withdrew to a special zone around the Suez Canal in return for a twenty-year defense pact recognizing Egypt as an independent nation. The Hashemite regime in Iraq also had to open its bases to British forces. Arab rulers understood that their nominal sovereignty depended on their willingness to accommodate Britain's strategic interests, but these compromises undermined their legitimacy in the eyes of Arab public opinion.

As with the constitutional negotiations in the Raj, the British government realized that it needed to make further concessions to Arab nationalism to bolster its Arab allies and safeguard Britain's Middle Eastern strategic interests. In 1936, this became even more difficult as the Palestine Mandate spiraled into open and bloody intercommunal violence. Angered by continuing Jewish immigration and land purchases, the Arab National Committee called a general strike to demand full representative government. When this tactic failed, armed bands, assisted by paramilitary volunteers from Syria and Iraq, attacked Jewish settlements throughout the mandate. Italian and German propaganda helped instigate the revolt by depicting Britain as an ally of global Zionism.

The government's security forces, which relied heavily on both Jewish and Arab policemen, were entirely unprepared to deal with such a massive Arab challenge to the British mandate. It took two full army divisions, plus a special police unit of British veterans of World War I, to reestablish imperial authority. Many of the new paramilitaries, who joined a police force already largely comprised of former members of the Royal Irish Constabulary, had extensive experience fighting the Irish republican forces in 1918 and 1919, and in 1938 the mandate high commissioner, Sir Harold MacMichael, admitted that they had "black and tan tendencies." This meant that they used Arab civilians as human shields and minesweepers and tortured and executed suspects.[41] The state of emergency also allowed the mandate authorities to ban the main Arab nationalist groups and dismiss key leaders, like the Mufti of Jerusalem, from local positions of authority.

These draconian tactics restored a measure of order by 1938, but the metropolitan government realized it could not afford such a massive military commitment in the Middle East as the growing power of Nazi Germany made the situation in Europe more precarious. Consequently, the mandate authorities again tried to broker a compromise by offering to divide Palestine into Arab and Jewish states. The Jewish Agency appeared receptive, but Arab leaders refused to surrender any territory. Unable to please both factions, British officials opportunistically sided with the Arabs in the hope of winning wider popular support throughout the region. Disregarding the twelve thousand Jewish militiamen who had supported the imperial security forces during the Arab Revolt, Neville Chamberlain's government issued a statement limiting further Jewish immigration to seventy-five thousand people over five years and declaring Britain's intention to surrender the mandate to an Arab regime in a decade. The Jewish community responded by stockpiling weapons, and only the outbreak of World War II saved Britain from having to deal with an armed Zionist uprising.

Although organized political anti-imperial challenges born of this complex mix of nationalism, religion, and ethnicity were limited largely to South Asia and the Middle East, the entire empire faced widespread labor unrest in the 1930s. In the Caribbean, the British government's subsidies to metropolitan sugar beet growers made the collapse of global commodity prices even worse, and plant disease and bad weather forced West Indian employers to cut wages and lay off workers. On Trinidad, endemic unemployment exacerbated poor housing and malnutrition. By 1934, conditions on the island were so bad that more than 10 percent of infants died in their first year. Dismal wages on Tobago's coconut plantations forced workers to survive on iguanas, boiled brush, and hot water tea.

Quite understandably, strikes and unrest broke out throughout the West Indies at mid-decade as desperate workers demanded jobs, lower taxes, and a living wage. Typically, the first protests began on rural plantations and spread to the docks and other urban industries, where they often turned into outright riots. Barbados, for example, experienced its first significant unrest in nearly seventy years when workers, initially angered by poor wages, went on a rampage in 1937 to protest the government's deportation of a union organizer to Trinidad. When they refused to disperse, the police broke up the mob with live ammunition and a bayonet charge that killed fourteen and injured forty-seven. Virtually every other colony in the British Caribbean experienced similar outbreaks of labor violence during this period.

These incidents took on a political dimension as middle-class elites became more interested in labor matters and labor organizations moved into politics. Noted literary figures like C. L. R. James, Albert Gomes, and Alfred Mendes used their craft to attack colonial racism and promote black pride. A. A. Cipriani and other European liberals who had worked to deflect labor activism into apolitical trade organizations lost influence when they could not convince employers and government officials to make real concessions on wages and working conditions. In 1932, Cipriani's Trinidad Workingmen's Association became the Trinidad Labour Party. Two years later Marxist-oriented activists denounced him as "Britain's best policeman in the colonies."[42] Popular anger over the empire's failure to take action against the Italian invasion of Ethiopia, which many West Indians considered their spiritual home, further radicalized the colonies. Inspired by the biblical verse "Ethiopia shall reach out its hand to God" and the coronation of Haile Selassie as the Ethiopian emperor, the Rastafarians concluded that communities of African descent in the Americas were the new Israelites, who would one day escape from bondage by returning to the African motherland.

For the most part, however, the leadership of the new, more confrontational parties came from lawyers like Norman Manley of Jamaica and Grantley Adams of Barbados, who gained fame while representing imprisoned workers. They built popular political support by focusing on labor issues. Many intellectuals, however, were still focused on winning greater local autonomy, an end to the Crown colony system, and the creation of a West Indies Federation. As in India, these issues were not necessarily as important to ordinary workers concerned with day-to-day survival. More than anything else, these people wanted old-age pensions, a shorter work-week, workers' compensation, and a sustainable minimum wage. As the hope of achieving these grew dim, many West Indians chose instead to emigrate to the United States.

Still, the mere prospect of an alliance between middle-class nationalists and radicalized workers was troubling, and the imperial authorities became even more alarmed when the militant and pervasive labor unrest of the West Indies appeared to be spreading to some of their most economically impor-tant African colonies. Between 1935 and 1940, the copper mines of Northern Rhodesia, the East African port cities of Mombasa and Dar es Salaam, and Gold Coast plantations and urban areas all experienced major strikes by African workers. There was no significant direct connection between the two corners of the empire, but West Indian merchant seamen did spread news of Caribbean events in African port cities. Many were also followers of Marcus Garvey, a Jamaican radical intellectual and founder of the Universal Negro Improvement Association, who aimed to build a united Pan-Africanist front against the empire by linking Africans with American communities of African descent.

Despite these connections, African labor unrest in the 1930s was primari-ly homegrown. The situation on the Northern Rhodesian Copperbelt became particularly tense as falling copper prices led mine owners to cut wages and tighten labor discipline to remain competitive on a global scale. Already upset by the loss of pay, African copper miners went on strike in 1935 when the Northern Rhodesian government tried to increase taxes in the mining compounds. Lacking formal unions, the protesters were led in part by mem-bers of the banned Watchtower movement, which preached that the end of the world was imminent. The Northern Rhodesia Police killed six miners in putting down the strike, but a much more serious wave of labor unrest five years later led to even more loss of life when the colonial government called in the local Northern Rhodesia Regiment to restore order.

Although the violence that beset the empire in the 1930s was mostly localized and largely unconnected, senior officials in the Colonial Office concluded that it would take significant administrative reforms to ensure the long-term viability of the British Empire. This was a marked departure from Lugard's confident pronouncements in *The Dual Mandate* a decade earlier. India was now too far down the road to self-rule, but the reformers hoped to strengthen their hold on the rest of their territories through state-directed central planning. More efficient use of resources would generate greater wealth that could be used to create better markets for British goods, improve the lives of colonial workers, and draw the politicized educated middle classes back into the imperial system.

For this to happen the empire would have to intervene more directly in the daily life of local communities. The West Indian labor riots convinced the colonial authorities that it was no longer feasible to expect individual territorial governments to be entirely self-supporting. In the late 1930s, the Colonial Secretary Malcolm MacDonald convinced the metropolitan government to invest £5 million per year for the next twenty years to promote economic development and fund social welfare in the colonies. World War II delayed the implementation of this Colonial Development and Welfare Act, and it is therefore difficult to determine whether MacDonald's initiatives would have brought about a new direction in British imperial policy. At the very least, the Colonial Office created new departments for labor, social services, education, and public relations to better coordinate the new policy initiatives. However, the imperial critic George Orwell, himself a veteran of the colonial police in Burma, dismissed the experts who staffed MacDonald's new departments as a class of "well-meaning, over-civilised men, in dark suits and black felt hats, with neatly-rolled umbrellas crooked over the left forearm," who imposed a "constipated view of life on Malaya and Nigeria, Mombasa and Mandalay."[43]

What Orwell really meant was that the Colonial Office now tried to have a greater influence on day-to-day life in the wider empire. Aiming to defuse political and economic dissent by giving subject peoples a greater stake in the economic life of the empire, MacDonald's reformers sent trade unionists to the West Indies to draw laborers away from radical politics and into organizations that would work closely with industrial advisors and local governments to improve working conditions. The Moyne Commission, which investigated the causes of the riots, tied development to political stability. It recommended diversifying the colonies' economies to make them less reliant on export plantation agriculture and devoting more resources to education and social services. Moreover, the Colonial Office finally accepted the necessity of federating the West Indian colonies to create a larger economic unit better equipped to manage and finance its development initiatives.

On the political front, MacDonald declared that the ultimate goal of British policy was to prepare the colonies for self-government. To some degree, this could be seen as the extension of the dominion model to the non-European Crown colonies, but the colonial secretary set no timetable for it. Nor did he spell out the political role of non-Europeans in the new system. Still, MacDonald's blueprint was definitely at odds with the Lugardian ideal of indirect rule. Recognizing that tribal chiefs were ill-suited to manage complex economies, the Colonial Office experts called for educational reforms to create a new generation of westernized Africans willing and able to assist in economic development. This actually meant relatively little in practice, for the members of the colonial service who actually ran British Africa largely remained committed to Lugard's tribal romanticism.

In holding fast to these prejudices, colonial administrators demonstrated both who really ran British Africa and how little they actually knew about the societies they governed. Although there were no African versions of the Tata Iron and Steel Company, African entrepreneurs were often powerful drivers of local economic development in the interwar empire. In Tanganyika, members of the Chagga community became wealthy growing coffee on the rich slopes of Mount Kilimanjaro, while cocoa and palm oil producers continued to be the backbone of the Gold Coast and Nigerian economies. Prosperous African growers throughout the continent often invested their earnings in trading and transport companies or Western education for their children. Unlike in the Indian case, however, African colonial authorities offered only lukewarm support to these entrepreneurs. European commodity brokers in West Africa blocked African growers from moving into trading by raising shipping fees and convincing metropolitan banks to deny them loans and credit. In 1925, the Chagga coffee growers formed a marketing cooperative called the Kilimanjaro Native Planters Association to bypass European and Indian middlemen, but the government forced it to become a simple agricultural cooperative when falling coffee prices during the Great Depression drove it into bankruptcy. By comparison, the Kenyan government protected European coffee planters by banning Africans from even growing the crop.

Although successful African commodity producers generated valuable export revenues for cash-strapped colonies, they competed with influential special interest groups and undermined the institutions of indirect rule. Wealthy and sophisticated African growers challenged the native custom that all land was collective tribal property rather than owned by the individuals who farmed it. In Kenya, well-paid Kamba soldiers and policemen began an agrarian and social revolution by buying plows and oxen to stake a permanent claim to communal grazing land. Commercial agriculture also created opportunities for rural women. In the Gold Coast, Asante women took up cocoa farming to acquire greater security and autonomy. Many grew wealthy enough to reject prospective husbands that their male relatives selected for them. These developments led the colonial authorities to worry that African commercial agriculture would destabilize and detribalize rural society and undercut the authority of the chiefs who used tribal custom to enforce colonial policy.

Rather than looking for ways to nurture African entrepreneurship, imperial agricultural experts warned that increased production through plowing and ranching would wear out the soil and produce an African dust bowl. Officials in Kenya, Southern Rhodesia, and South Africa were particularly worried that intensive agriculture and pastoralism would produce a political crisis by making the native reserves uninhabitable. Haunted by the environmental catastrophe that ravaged the American heartland in the 1930s, they tried to place restrictions on how Africans could use their land. Most colonial governments also tried to prevent local communities from using forest and game reserves to farm, hunt, graze livestock, or cut timber on the grounds that Africans did not understand how to protect the environment. In many cases, this environmentalism was self-serving as colonies earned considerable revenue from the sale of hunting licenses and timber concessions. Moreover, this economic opportunism masquerading as environmentalism created a public health problem.

Consequently, many Africans had ample reason to oppose British imperial policies. But in contrast to the South Asian nationalists or the West Indian unionists, in the interwar era they lacked the means and opportunity to do so in an organized and systematic fashion. In sharp contrast to the Raj, with its major constitutional reforms, colonial administrators would only deal with sanctioned tribal organizations under chiefly control. This meant anti-imperial opposition in the interwar era often targeted the chiefs and other groups of cooperative elites who helped govern British Africa. Nonelite Gandans who opposed the 1900 agreement that had essentially turned Buganda into an oligarchy formed the Bataka Association to demand a more equitable division of land and oppose other unpopular colonial policies.

Denied a formal political voice, many students and farmers resorted to less conventional means to express their opposition to authoritarian imperial policies. Formed in 1925, the London-based West African Student Union initially sought greater opportunities for educated Africans in a federated West Africa, but it became more aggressive in demanding autonomy after the 1935 Italian invasion of Ethiopia. One year later, the Gold Coast Farmers' Association used a boycott to force European exporters to pay more for their cocoa. Even art and literature could be put to political purposes. Jomo Kenyatta, the future president of independent Kenya, used scathing satire to point out the hypocrisy of the native reserve system in his short story "The Gentlemen of the Jungle." Faced with the missions' monopoly on Christianity, education, respectability, and morality, West Indians and Africans created independent churches and schools to uncouple useful elements of Western and global culture from colonialism. An elder in Western Kenya spoke for many when he declared, "We want to teach ourselves. We don't want to be taught by the Missions alone: we want our own schools."[44] Theoretically, the imperial reformers should have been cheered by these expressions of local modernity, but most governments equated independency with subversion.

This was particularly true in eastern and southern Africa, where the settler communities were deeply unnerved by any suggestion that Africans were their social equals. At first glance, these anxieties would seem unfounded given that their political preeminence remained unchallenged during the

1930s despite their poor economic record. Moreover, a series of official reports, investigations, and commissions validated and standardized the native reserve system that guaranteed their monopoly on productive land and access to cheap African labor in both Kenya and Southern Rhodesia. Nor did it particularly matter to the metropolitan authorities that the colour bar, which brought racial discrimination to virtually every aspect of colonial society, conflicted directly with the paternalistic trusteeship of Britain's oft-stated imperial mission. But most settlers still could never shake the underlying sense of insecurity, if not actual fear, that came with living as a privileged minority among a colonial majority. Writing from hindsight, the Kenyan governor Sir Edward Grigg admitted to having had an "inescapable feeling that I was administering a system so unsuited to Kenya that it must in time break down completely; and I know that the same feeling was shared by the European community."[45] The legions of poorly paid African cooks, maids, nannies, and "house boys" that made life so easy and agreeable were both a comfort and an implicit threat because they lived in close and intimate proximity to their employers, and every act of theft, housebreaking, or similar misdemeanor ratcheted up the tension. This is one of the primary reasons why the settlers often behaved so brutally in their daily interactions with people whom paternalists like Lugard cast as their wards and charges. Outlining the necessity of proper household management, the Kenyan leader Baron Cranworth demonstrated this by baldly stating that settler wives had to master the art of "managing natives" because "one could not, for instance, learn by experience in England when is the right time to have a servant beaten for rubbing silver plate on the gravel path to clean it."[46]

Although they were in fact remarkably safe during the interwar era, the rare cases of violent assaults by Africans on Europeans were absolutely terrifying as the settlers worried that any sign of weakness might inspire a native uprising. This was particularly true if the victims were "white" women. Just as the assault on Marcella Sherwood during the Amritsar rioting drove General Dyer into a rage, the settlers worried constantly that their women were vulnerable to attacks by barely civilized African men. Implicit in these overblown nightmares was the entirely irrational and fantastical assumption that natives were so sexually ravenous that they could not control themselves. But this black peril stereotype also usefully justified racial segregation. In this sense, European women were both the embodiment of settler privilege and the physical personification of Western civilization. This is why the colonial authorities generally banned them from living in African areas even if they actually had African husbands. As the Gold Coast governor explained, "I regard it as thoroughly undesirable in the interests of the colony that a European woman should be perceived to be living in a state of social degradation."[47] Ultimately, in the interwar imperial imagination racial segregation was both humane and moral.

AMRITSAR REDUX

Overall, the imperial crises and anxieties of the 1930s, much like the earlier Amritsar massacre, revealed the inherent contradictions between metropolitan idealism and the messy realities of day-to-day life in the interwar British Empire. As subject peoples became more assertive in demanding self-government, better living conditions, and basic human dignity, the imperial authorities invariably had to acknowledge that force and intimidation were inherent parts of actual imperial governance. More often than not, the "men-on-the-spot" faced the difficult task of determining when and how to use violence to sustain the empire. Imperial realists asserted unapologetically that it was essential, while liberal idealists held out hope that constitutional reforms might prove sufficiently enticing for subject populations to accept their place in an evolving commonwealth. General Dyer's unilateral decision to open fire was thus a thinly disguised attempt to resolve the debate decisively in the pragmatists' favor. Although he might not have intentionally set out to subvert the 1919 Government of India Act, he clearly rejected the accommodationist reasoning behind the Montagu-Chelmsford reforms.

This is why the secretary of state for India, Edwin Montagu, moved so swiftly and decisively to officially disavow Dyer's attempt to intimidate the Indian opponents of the Raj. During the parliamentary controversy over the government's decision to terminate the general's military career, the India secretary asked, "Are you going to keep your hold upon India by terrorism, racial humiliation and subordination, and frightfulness, or are you going to rest it upon the goodwill . . . of the people of your Indian Empire?" Even Churchill, who was no friend of Gandhi or the Indian National Congress, agreed that "frightfulness is not a remedy known to the British pharmacopoeia" and cautioned that "to shoot and to go on shooting, with all the horrors that were here involved, in order to teach somebody else a lesson, you are embarking on terrorism, to which there is no end."[48]

Dyer's parliamentary defenders declared themselves ready to accept such a risk. In crediting the general with saving the Raj, they were in effect offering a more pragmatic view of the empire. In this sense, Brigadier General Surtees's admission that "if a plebiscite were taken tomorrow as to who should govern India the result would be against us" and Lord Harris's declaration that Britain ultimately held every one of its imperial territories by the sword were frank acknowledgments that no one became or remained an imperial subject voluntarily.[49] Nor were these views limited to Conservative members of the British parliament. The commander of the Delhi Brigade told the Hunter Committee that more violence was called for against rioting crowds in the Raj's capital city: "Composed as the crowd was of the scum of Delhi city, I am of firm opinion that if they had got a bit more firing given them it would have done them a world of good . . . as force is the only thing that an Asiatic has any respect for."[50] Ironically, the Conservatives' Irish republican archnemesis, Éamon de Valera, agreed with this violent and amoral definition of empire when he told the New York Friends of Freedom for India Society, "There are a thousand native Indians to one foreigner. . . . Dyer had to shoot the people of India else the British Empire could not endure in India."[51] In the House of Commons, Churchill tried to dismiss the Amritsar shootings as "an episode . . . without precedent or parallel in the modern history of the British Empire," but a great many of the men who actually ran the empire would clearly have disagreed with him and acknowledged, perhaps grudgingly, de Valera's point.

Nonetheless, reformers like J. C. Wedgwood believed firmly in the notion that a liberal empire could evolve into an inclusive and mutually beneficial commonwealth of diverse self-governing territories. To this end, he declared himself willing to sacrifice the small European population of India. "I would rather, for the interests of our country, that English men and women had been shot down at Jallianwala by Indians than that Indians had been shot down by Englishmen. After all, lives vanish, but this country and the honour of the country remain for all time."[52] This remarkable declaration, which surely sent shockwaves through the African settler communities, was based on the assumption that most anti-imperial agitation was the work of a small group of radical conspirators or disaffected elites who did not actually represent the Asian, African, Arab, and West Indian majorities, who appreciated the impartiality and paternalistic benevolence of British rule. This "classes and masses" distinction was comforting, but it naively ignored the fundamental reasons why more and more ordinary people became increasingly dissatisfied with foreign rule during the interwar decades.

It is difficult to gauge the Amritsar massacre's impact on the long-term fate of the empire, but the personal consequences of Dyer's order to fire reverberated throughout the interwar era. When the general died relatively early in 1925, his obituary in the *Times of London* pronounced him a "breezy kind-hearted man" who "never recovered his buoyancy of mind" after the abrupt end of his military career. Sir Michael O'Dwyer, the lieutenant governor of the Punjab who explicitly endorsed Dyer's actions, made the British government distinctly uncomfortable with a successful libel suit against a moderate Indian politician for writing a book attacking Gandhi, which O'Dwyer admitted was "excellent," that also claimed O'Dwyer's Punjab administration had provoked the riots of 1919 by using "terroristic" methods to conscript Punjabi soldiers during World War I.[53] The final act in the personal histories of the men involved with the 1919 Amritsar massacre took place some twenty-one years later during World War II when an engineer named Udham Singh shot and killed O'Dwyer on the streets of London. Remarkably, Singh was at the Jallianwala Bagh when Dyer gave the order to open fire. The British press could not decide whether the killing was an act of revenge or accidental, but the presiding judge demonstrated that Amritsar remained an explosive issue when he used the wartime security laws to suppress Singh's actual final statement to the jury. [54]

Chapter Four

The 1940s

A New Kind of Empire?

CONSEQUENCES AND DISAPPOINTMENTS

On June 8, 1946, roughly ten months after the close of World War II, some 2 million Britons gathered in London to celebrate the Allied victory. This massive display of military might differed from the Peace Day commemorations that marked the formal end of World War I and the various pageants, durbars, and public coronation rituals that affirmed the power and majesty of the British Empire. The 1946 observances instead reflected the public's profound uncertainty over where Britain stood in the rapidly changing postwar world, but the ceremonies themselves were unquestionably impressive. Taking advantage of the last of the "victory holidays" that stretched over the past year, thousands of people camped overnight in St. James and Green parks to stake out prime viewing spots for what promised to be a grand spectacle. They were not disappointed. The march began as two separate parades. The first, a column consisting of representatives of all of the major Allied powers (save one) and every British and imperial military and civil arm that took part in the war effort, marched a circuitous route to the West End and back. The other was a triumphant rumbling caravan of military vehicles that circled through East London. The two came together at the center of government at Whitehall to form a nine-mile-long grand procession of men and machines that moved through Trafalgar Square past the main reviewing stand on the Mall. King George VI, who wore the uniform of an admiral of the fleet, took their salutes while the major Allied commanders sat at his feet. The Royal Air Force also conducted a flypast over the Mall. In the afternoon there were concerts, plays, and entertainments for children in the main parks, and the day concluded with dances and displays of searchlights, fireworks, and jets of colored water over the Thames. At Buckingham Palace, an enormous cheering crowd called the royal family back onto the balcony three times to prolong the celebration. [1]

As would be the case some fifty-one years later in Hong Kong, the day's ceremonies took place during a steady rain. Yet, in contrast to the air of melancholy that hung over Britain's surrender of its last significant imperial possession, most press accounts reported that the 1946 crowd cheered joyfully, spontaneously, and lustily. According to the *Times of London,* the downpour could not dampen the "unfailing good humour of the British crowd, which neither rain nor the discomfort of the journey home at midnight could quench." Among the "gay orderly crowd" were "pretty girls in funny hats," children with flags, streamers, and toy trumpets, and youths making noise with poison-gas-warning rattles. [2]

Nevertheless, it was also impossible not to acknowledge the enormous consequences of what the *Times* called "the greatest victory won by men." Wartime shortages of food and other basic necessities not only lingered but had actually grown worse since the Japanese surrender in August 1945, and on the day before the parade, Londoners faced the longest food lines to date. [3] Ominously, an ongoing controversy over the postwar government of Poland that presaged the outbreak of the Cold War led the Soviet Union to boycott the celebration. The *London Illustrated News*, which covered the various festivities extensively, also included an essay by the Irish military historian Cyril Falls titled "Aftermath of War, Victory—Consequences and Disappointments." In it, Falls surely captured the sentiments of many people in the crowd when he declared, "Recovery is hindered by physical devastation, but it is also hampered by the spirit of doubt, fear and cynicism which broods over the world." Sounding a discordant note that summarized wartime disagreements between the Allies over the legitimacy of empires, Falls further worried that the United States was not ready to help with the recovery because a "very large section of American opinion still links Britain with 'imperialism' and is determined that it shall not be buttressed by American bayonets or American dollars." [4] One of his colleagues, Arthur Bryant, went a step further in declaring that Britain, as the nation that stood longest against the Axis powers, had sacrificed its empire to save the world and Western civilization. [5]

Although the other Allied powers had their own opinions about how to share out the credit for their collective victory, Bryant correctly recognized that the strains of fighting a second global war had weakened the British Empire substantially. As in World War I, British demands for manpower, tax revenues, food, and strategic raw materials both exacerbated existing tensions in the wider empire and created new ones in formerly stable colonies. And unlike in the Great War, where most of Britain's allies were fellow imperial powers, in World War II her American and Soviet cobelligerents were openly critical of conventional empires. In the Far East, the Japanese had won allies among subject populations with their promise of a Greater East Asia Co-prosperity Sphere that would reserve "Asia for the Asians." It mattered little that the USSR's anti-imperialism was only for show, as one of Stalin's main wartime goals was to reassert Soviet control over the old tsarist empire, or that a great many disillusioned Asian nationalists found that the Japanese could be even more brutal imperial rulers than their Western opponents.

Imperially minded Britons similarly suspected the United States' motives, and many charged that its embrace of self-determination for subject peoples was a ruse to open the British colonies to American trade and investment. There was also no denying that Britain would need U.S. military and financial assistance to remain a significant imperial power. When Japan formally surrendered on September 2, 1945, it was to General Douglas MacArthur on the deck of the USS *Missouri*, the flagship of an enormous armada anchored in Tokyo Bay. British and dominion representatives were among the dignitaries who witnessed the signing ceremony, and there were two British battleships in the flotilla. Yet the presence of Lieutenant General Sir Arthur Percival, who had surrendered the great fortress at Singapore to the Japanese in 1942, was a painful reminder of one of Britain's greatest imperial setbacks. Still emaciated from his nearly three years in a Japanese prisoner-of-war camp, Percival stood alongside the equally gaunt Lieutenant General Jonathan Wainwright, who had spent even longer in Japanese captivity after the fall of the Philippines. MacArthur gave pride of place to both senior officers in the signing ceremonies in an attempt to mitigate humiliating memories of their surrender to a non-Western power. No one in attendance, though, could have failed to notice that the balance of power in Asia had shifted. The *Missouri* was one of eight American battleships on hand, and the U.S. Pacific Fleet's hundreds of warships, military transports, and supply ships that spread out across Tokyo Bay dwarfed the Royal Navy contingent.

British forces reoccupied Singapore that same afternoon of September 2, 1946, but there was no turning back the clock to the relative security of the prewar era. While the supreme commander, Lord Louis Mountbatten, confidentially asserted that his "greatest invasion force the Far East ever saw" would have recaptured Britain's lost territories without the help of the atomic bomb, the British Military Administration of Malaya was a poor substitute for the imperial regime that the Japanese overthrew in 1942. It struggled to restart rubber and tin production, alleviate widespread food shortages, tend to tens of thousands of starving former Javanese slave laborers left behind by the Japanese, and stamp out pervasive corruption among its own ranks. Initially, the military government was so underfinanced that the resurgent opium trade was its most reliable source of revenue.[6]

In India, the commander in chief of British military forces was deeply concerned about declining morale and indiscipline among the hundreds of thousands of British and imperial troops waiting impatiently in bases throughout southern Asia, where shipping problems delayed their return to civilian life. As Indian resistance to the Raj and outright demands for full independence mounted, almost every wartime military unit experienced some form of insubordination, petty crime, and general malingering. The reliability of the Indian army was also in question after thousands of Indian prisoners of war defected to the Japanese after the fall of Singapore, but the growing disaffection among the tens of thousands of African soldiers in India awaiting demobilization was a new and serious concern. An angry East African medical corpsman spoke for a great many of his comrades when he complained, "We have been told the war is finished, but that there are no ships to take us home. . . . The Europeans are selfish, most of them are demobilised."[7] Bored with sports and handicraft activities and anxious to get home, the soldiers went looking for entertainment, drink, and female companionship. Most found these diversions without incident, but the military police reported an increase in disobedience, burglary, and physical and sexual assaults on Europeans. Alarmed senior officers banned British nurses from socializing with "native" soldiers and posted armed guards and burning flares around the women's tents at night. But these incidents were by no means specific to African units. There was a much higher degree of insubordination among British troops, and military censors noted that metropolitan politicians were "targets for frequent abuse" in their letters home. British impatience with the rate of demobilization became so bad by May 1946 that an entire battalion of the elite Parachute Regiment mutinied in Malaya.[8]

Not surprisingly, the reports of unrest in the African units attracted the most concern and attention in imperial circles. Fearing that wartime military service had undermined white prestige, African governments worried that the soldiers would become subversive malcontents in civilian life because they would no longer tolerate the lack of development in their own communities. In East Africa, the authorities were particularly afraid that the ex-servicemen would not respect the racial, sexual, and social boundaries of the settler colonies. A military memorandum warned that "the relationship between African ranks and our women has certainly deteriorated during this war," while a civilian commentator was alarmed that the men who had served overseas had learned that women who "appear to be white (though we might disagree with them) can be bought for money."[9] Their overblown fears sprang primarily from the settlers' ever-present security and black peril nightmares, but they also reflected the growing recognition among civil and military officials that it would be much more difficult to manage the postwar empire.

These larger imperial insecurities lurked below the surface at the London victory celebration. At first glance, the various ceremonies included the usual confident imperial references that were an integral part of British imperial public pageantry. In reporting the presence of imperial soldiers, the *Illustrated London News* struck a typically romantic note: "The troops of the Dominions, of India and Burma, and of the Colonial Empire made up an impressive section of the great Victory Parade, their many picturesque differences of dress and equipment emphasizing the widely separated parts of the world from which they had come to march past the King in celebration of the victory to which they had contributed so gallantly."[10] The roster of forces that saluted George VI included multiple contingents from the dominions' armed forces, Indian army, Burmese army, Royal West African Frontier Force, King's African Rifles, Northern Rhodesia Regiment, Somaliland Scouts, Aden Protectorate Levies, Ceylon Light Infantry, Cyprus Regiment, Falkland Islands Defence Force, Hong Kong Pioneer Company, Malay Regiment, Fiji Infantry Regiment, Mauritius Pioneer Corps, Transjordan Frontier Force, Palestine Regiment, South African High Commission Territories Pioneer Corps, and Royal Malta Artillery. As in earlier displays of imperial pageantry, the government once again sought to impress visiting subjects with Britain's technological and cultural achievements. To this end, the Malayan Victory Contingent, which included members of both the Malay Regiment and Chinese communist guerrillas from the Malayan Peoples' Anti-Japanese Army, visited the Dagenham Ford Motor Company works, a model farm and dairy, the royal residence at Windsor Castle, Stratford-on-Avon, a match at the famed Lords Cricket Ground, and even a London dog-racing track.[11]

Overall, however, the imperial element in the 1946 parade was much more muted than in earlier national celebrations. This was due in part to concerns that the empire's subjects should not get the idea that they could expect to be rewarded for their role in saving Britain. But an equally potent reality was that the crowd was just as much concerned with recovery, prosperity, and security as with the health of an empire that most Britons had never experienced firsthand and that remained largely an abstraction.

Cyril Falls was quite right in acknowledging that empires were falling into disrepute in the new postwar era. The *New York Times*, which paid close attention to the victory celebrations, reflected these sentiments in its reporting. Observing that the "dreary weather . . . may have symbolized some dreariness in men's hearts," the American correspondent saw the beginning of the end of the formal British Empire. "The Dominions are free because they wished to be. . . . In India, over which Victoria was Empress, a British Cabinet mission is working patiently to find a formula and system for freedom. Freedom for the scattered colonies is at least envisaged as part of the future." In response, Arthur Bryant spoke for many imperial partisans when he complained in his essay on the celebrations that Britain was "giving away India, scurrying out of Egypt, jettisoning our imperial economic system to please America." Many of the Americans who were part of the crowds in London were actually much more supportive than Bryant acknowledged, and the *New York Times* openly embraced the ideals behind the Commonwealth model when it ended its reporting on an optimistic note: "As the idea of empire dies the idea of friendly association takes its place. One age passes. Another and, as we fondly hope, a better one succeeds it."[12] Such was the task facing the administrators of the British Empire. Would they be able to fashion a new, modern, and ultimately more sustainable empire out of the "consequences and disappointments" of World War II, or was the new imperial age indeed coming to a sudden end?

THE EMPIRE AT WAR

Although all of the imperial powers would have had to confront these questions sooner or later, World War II brought the inherent tensions that had bedeviled the British Empire in the interwar era to the fore. One of the most significant of these was the question of how much actual authority London had over the wider empire. In 1914, Britain's entry into the Great War meant that all its imperial territories were at war as well, but by 1939 the self-governing dominions had already made it clear that they reserved the right to decide whether to declare war for themselves, regardless of whether Britain was at war or not. The peoples of the colonies and protectorates technically still had no choice in the matter.

All of the dominions eventually made the decision to support Britain, but they did so in markedly different ways. Prime Minister R. G. Menzies interpreted Australia's diplomatic and imperial agreements with the home country to mean that if "Britain is at war, therefore Australia is at war," while his counterparts in New Zealand and Canada secured at least some form of local assent before joining the conflict. The situation was more complex in the Union of South Africa, where a significant faction of Afrikaner nationalists sympathized openly with the Nazis. Prime Minister General J. B. M. Hertzog was solidly in the antiwar camp, but the union parliament deadlocked over the question. This impasse allowed the British governor-general to block Hertzog's attempt to call new elections, thereby ensuring that the pro-British General J. C. Smuts could form a government that would bring South Africa into the war on the Allied side. The question so divided the dominion's European population that those in the South African military willing to fight for the empire took a special oath and wore a special orange tab on their uniforms indicating that they had volunteered to serve abroad. Smuts and Hertzog both opposed giving the union's non-European populations significant military training, but the South African government agreed to raise a lightly armed Native Military Corps to provide labor for its fighting formations. Service in this unit was technically voluntary, but, as in most wartime colonial units, many of its members actually had little choice but to serve.

This was also the case in India, where British viceroy Lord Linlithgow declared war and deployed the Indian army without the backing of the Indian National Congress (INC). Although this was technically legal under the 1935 Government of India Act, the viceroy's unilateral decision essentially brought the Raj's experiment with dyarchy (joint rule) to an end by provoking most Indian nationalists into withdrawing from the provincial governments. Linlithgow's attempt to win them back by offering to add Indians to his executive and war advisory councils and by making vague promises of some sort of dominion status for India after the conflict generated little popular support. The nationalists' failure to win any significant concessions for India's participation in the war stood in sharp contrast to the situation in Ireland, where the Irish government remained resolutely neutral despite Neville Chamberlain's desperate suggestion that Britain might surrender the six provinces of Northern Ireland if Éamon de Valera joined the Allies. The ability of the Irish to control their own destiny by choosing republicanism over formal dominion status was not lost on many Indians.

In practical terms, the British government did not have the luxury of respecting its subjects' nationalist sentiments. The French collapse in the spring of 1940 allowed the Nazis to overrun most of continental Europe, and in the precarious year before Hitler's ill-considered invasion of the Soviet Union, the dominions and the wider empire were Britain's only significant allies. After Chamberlain's resignation as prime minister, Winston Churchill's wartime coalition government, which consisted of hard-core imperialists and leftist critics of empire, had to sell off most of its overseas assets and devote every available resource in metropolitan Britain and the empire to the war effort.

The United States provided logistical support and military aid despite its formal neutrality, but it did not become an active ally until the Japanese attack on Pearl Harbor in December 1941. Even then the conditions the Americans attached to their aid, coupled with their insistence on including a declaration in the 1941 Atlantic Charter that "all people had a right to self-determination," led many imperial partisans to suspect that the United States was, as Arthur Bryant would later suggest in 1946, indeed scheming to break up the empire. A 1942 *Life* magazine editorial seemed to confirm these suspicions when it boldly declared, "One thing we are sure we are *not* fighting for is to hold the British Empire together. . . . If you cling to the Empire at the expense of a United Nations victory you will lose the war. Because you will lose us."[13] Much like Woodrow Wilson's anti-imperial Fourteen Points, the Atlantic Charter caught the attention of subject people throughout the

British Empire, and Churchill's attempt to "clarify" the declaration by insisting that it only applied to occupied Europe and not the colonies or India did little to dampen their postwar expectations.

The American Lend-Lease program kept Britain armed and supplied throughout the war, but British strategists assumed that they should not depend too heavily on American economic and military assistance if Churchill was to make good on his famous declaration one year later that he had not become prime minister "in order to preside over the liquidation of the British Empire." With the regular metropolitan army stretched to the limit, Britain needed colonial forces and logistical aid to defend imperial interests in the Middle East, South Asia, the Far East, and, to a lesser extent, Africa. These included the roughly forty-two thousand Irish Free State citizens who served in the British military over the course of the war, despite de Valera's unapologetic commitment to neutrality.

Japan's swift capture of Hong Kong and lightning strike into Malaya within months of its surprise attack on the United States made this assistance an absolute necessity. In a disaster that rivaled the American unpreparedness at Pearl Harbor, the Royal Navy sent two of its most powerful warships, the HMS *Repulse* and the HMS *Prince of Wales*, into the Indian Ocean unprotected by aircraft cover, where Japanese bombers quickly sank them. On land, the Japanese imperial army outflanked British troops on Malaya's Kra Isthmus to capture the great military fortress at Singapore. The designers of the city's defenses had assumed that an invader could not pass through the Kra's dense jungles, and so they failed to fortify Singapore's water supply or provide its massive fifteen-inch guns with enough shells for use against land forces. Although the Singapore garrison outnumbered the Japanese two to one, the poorly organized imperial units under General Percival surrendered on February 15, 1942. Roughly 138,000 British, Australian, and Indian troops became prisoners of war.

Britain thus had to depend heavily on Indians to defend the Raj from the Japanese forces that overran Burma and were advancing on India's eastern borders after the Singapore debacle. The Indian army grew from roughly 200,000 to over 2 million men during the war, and Indians contributed approximately £286 million worth of goods and raw materials to the Allied cause. South Asian soldiers anchored the defense of Asia and the Middle East, and nearly twenty-five thousand died in the service of the empire.

This did not mean that all Indians rallied to the empire's defense. Although indigenous Fijians fought for the empire in the Solomon Islands campaign, Fiji's Central Indian War Committee declared that they would only serve if they received the same pay and benefits as metropolitan British soldiers. In India, the steady Japanese drive through Burma in the spring of 1942 threw Bengal into a panic as merchants, clerks, laborers, and other refugees from the Indian diaspora fled west with tales of Japanese brutality against civilians. With the Raj's defenses still oriented westward toward a potential Soviet invasion through Afghanistan, wild rumors flew that the British were pulling out of India and that Japanese paratroopers and marines had landed throughout the province. In response, merchants sold off their stock at cut-rate prices, British and Indian administrators fled inland, the reserve bank of Bengal moved its gold reserves to Bombay, and keepers at the Calcutta zoo shot their most dangerous animals on the fear that they might get loose during Japanese bombing raids. [14]

British wartime demands, coupled with widespread perceptions that the Raj was about to fall, inspired the most militant faction of the Indian National Congress to launch a "Quit India" movement in August 1942 that called for immediate independence. In 1941, Mohandas Gandhi had begun another disobedience campaign to demonstrate the INC's opposition to the war and buy time for the party to develop a more unified wartime policy, but this did not appease the radical nationalists. After the fall of Singapore, INC leaders feared that internal discord over wartime policy would split the party. Consequently, Gandhi and the rest of the senior INC leaders joined the Quit India movement, which gave the British authorities little choice but to imprison them for the rest of the war. In doing so, however, they removed the restraining hand of the moderates. Freed from central control, small groups of determined activists attacked police stations, post offices, railway installations, and other symbols of imperial authority in an explosion of popular anti-imperialism that rivaled the violence of 1919. The Raj temporarily lost control over considerable stretches of territory until a military crackdown consisting of some fifty infantry battalions that were desperately needed elsewhere finally restored order in 1943. Strict censorship covered up the extent of the unrest and the reality that the army and security forces killed roughly three hundred Indian rebels.

Even more alarming, the Indian army itself became markedly less reliable as the Japanese victories mounted. Swayed by Japanese propaganda promising independence for subject Asian peoples, over thirty thousand Indians, many of whom were taken prisoner at Singapore, joined the Indian National Army (INA) to fight against the Raj. Subhas Chandra Bose, a senior INC member before the war, was its political leader. Initially a leftist, Bose would have preferred to work with the Soviets, but when they sided with Britain after the 1941 Nazi invasion of the USSR, he and a faction of like-minded Indian nationalists used Japanese support to form the Provisional Government of Free India. The Japanese accepted the aid of the INA but refused to grant this Indian government-in-exile formal recognition because an independent India conflicted with their own imperial ambitions in Asia. Nevertheless, the INA fought alongside the Japanese forces in Burma, where the nationalist leader Aung San raised a similar pro-Japanese Burma National Army. These cases of disaffection and outright defection unsettled imperial officials throughout Asia, but the radical Indian nationalists were frustrated when the bulk of the Indian army held fast and spearheaded the recapture of Burma and Malaya in 1945.

Dominion and colonial forces played an equally important role in the Middle East and Africa. In 1941, Indian units joined white South Africans and African soldiers from East, West, and Central Africa in driving the Italians out of the Horn of Africa. East Africans in the King's African Rifles also captured Madagascar from the Vichy French regime. More significantly, army divisions from South Africa, Australia, New Zealand, and India fought off Nazi attempts to seize the Suez Canal in a brutal campaign that swung back and forth through the Egyptian and Libyan deserts between 1940 and 1943. Non-European combat units did not play as much of a role in the North African campaign because imperial strategists were reluctant to use "native" soldiers against a European enemy. Instead, colonial governments from Africa, to India, to the West Indies followed the South African example by recruiting men for the auxiliary Pioneer Corps, a military labor unit that provided transport and supplies for frontline troops. Many members of these supposedly noncombat formations were killed in the fighting alongside regular imperial troops when the Germans overran the Allied lines, but the South African government insisted that fallen members of the Native Military Corps be buried in racially segregated cemeteries. As the war progressed, imperial planners became far less hesitant about using Africans in major combat roles, and in 1944 and 1945 three divisions of East and West African troops played a central role in the reconquest of Burma.

It took far more effort to get Britain's Arab subjects and nominal allies to help defend the empire. In the darkest days of the campaign, when it appeared that the Axis forces might capture Cairo and the Suez Canal, panicked imperial strategists developed a scorched-earth plan that envisioned setting fire to oil fields and refineries throughout the Middle East to prevent the Nazis from linking up with a Japanese drive on India. The nominally independent Egyptian government was obligated to stand with the Allies against the German and Italian invasion under the terms of the 1936 Anglo-Egyptian Treaty, but the Egyptian army was of little actual use because senior Egyptian military officers and cabinet officials were in active negotiations to ally with the Axis powers. Similarly, in April 1941 a group of nationalistic colonels in Iraq launched a revolt that laid siege to Baghdad. As in 1920, a rushed deployment of Indian army units put down the coup against Britain's client government and forced the Iraqis to accept imperial control. Later that year, British forces joined with the Soviets once again in occupying and partitioning Persia (Iran) to further safeguard the oil fields and open new supply routes to the Soviet Union. It did not matter that Reza Shah's government was steadfastly neutral. In Egypt, the British ambassador forced King Farouk to form a new pro-Allied Egyptian government in February 1942 by surrounding his palace with armored vehicles. This reluctance to support the British war effort did not mean that Arab leaders and populations were necessarily pro-Nazi. Most shared the Indians' sense that the war presented an opportunity to realize their nationalist ambitions, which also meant opposing Zionist efforts to build a Jewish state in Palestine.

Although it was possible for Britain's less enthusiastic subjects to avoid the dragnet for military manpower, every territory in the empire made some sort of economic contribution regardless of how the general population felt about the Allied cause. The British government used restrictive bulk-buying programs to purchase all of the crops of specific colonies at fixed prices that were substantially below world-market levels. These schemes became particularly important after the fall of Malaya and Singapore left Britain desperately short of commodities that could be sold for dollars. In 1942, the United States bought Tanganyikan sisal, a fibrous plant used to make rope, bags, and other important commodities, for three times what the British paid to Tanganyikan producers. Other territories made different sorts of important economic contributions. Middle Eastern oil was vital to the imperial war effort, and the West Indian territories loaned Britain £1.4 million and made direct contributions of £750,000 for general war purposes, £400,000 for war charities, and £425,000 for military aircraft.

Overruling domestic Indian opposition, the Raj funded the defense of India and its external interests. The British government only paid for Indian troops and wartime capital projects if they were for explicitly imperial purposes. These were largely paper payments that offered little actual compensation for India's sacrifices. The Raj covered most of its military expenses through taxation and by printing money, thereby producing an inflationary spiral as the amount of currency in circulation tripled over the course of the war. In return, the British government sent no money to India and instead simply cancelled the Raj's debts to cover the empire's share of India's expenses. Wartime financial restrictions also made it difficult for the members of the sterling area who kept their trading profits in British banks to withdraw their earnings in hard currency. This allowed Britain to delay payment on its imports, thereby freeing it of the need to balance its accounts through export earnings.

Although these unequal financial arrangements helped Britain win the war, they placed a huge burden on the subject peoples of the empire. The need for export earnings forced colonial governments to cut back on imports to ensure that their balance of trade produced a surplus that could be siphoned off for imperial purposes. In India, these cutbacks contributed to the inflationary spike that led to rationing and price controls. Farmers forced to sell their crops at artificially low levels often had to feed themselves by buying the same food back at considerably higher prices. The situation was even worse in the cities where strict rationing meant each person in Bombay had to survive on just one pound of grain per day. Food supplies became so tight by 1942 that famine broke out in Bengal when bad weather ruined harvests and the Japanese advance ended Burmese rice imports. The resulting inflation created a price famine whereby much of Bengal's rural population could no longer afford to buy increasingly scarce food. Roughly 3 million people in the province died of starvation or disease over the next three years.

The East African territories experienced similar problems when Burmese rice supplies dried up, conscription for military and civilian labor projects shrank the agricultural workforce, and the colonial government exported grain and cattle to feed the Allied forces in North Africa. Knowing full well that the 1943 shortages, which Kenyans called "the time of the rats" (*Panyu Kuu*) because they had to eat rodents to survive, were the result of imperial policy, Jomo Kenyatta blamed the colonial government for the resulting loss of life: "This famine is not sent by nature; it is the Europeans themselves who are the blight upon the land."[15] Perversely, the war actually helped the Kenyan settlers recover from the Great Depression. Facing bankruptcy a decade earlier because they could not produce crops cheaply enough to compete on the global market, the farmers now found their products in great demand. They sold to the military at inflated prices and convinced the government to supply them with forced African labor. The Colonial Office in London justified conscripting Africans for civil projects on the grounds that agriculture was an "essential undertaking" in wartime, but the Kenyan authorities opportunistically classified virtually every settler business, including coffee growing, as essential. They also forced African farmers to sell food at half the price paid to the settlers on the grounds that Africans had lower labor costs. This imbalance led many settlers to buy African corn and cattle to resell to imperial buyers at inflated prices.

These hardships and inequities invariably had political consequences. Subject peoples may not have grasped the full rationale for the war, but they understood that it made their lives more difficult. Local communities from Fiji to the West Indies struggled to cope with the absence of young men in military service and the inevitable casualties that resulted from combat and often substandard treatment in colonial units. Recognizing the need to maintain peace and stability, British administrators went to great lengths to build popular support for the war effort. In East and Central Africa, the military created a special Mobile Propaganda Unit that toured the countryside putting on pageants that balanced spectacular displays of firepower with exhibits on the military uses of local products and daily life in the army. Mobile cinema vans projected wartime propaganda films on sheets strung in rural villages, and posters showed Africans how their wartime contributions for Spitfire fighter planes and mobile food canteens helped the Allied cause. These measures had mixed results. Although people made great individual sacrifices to support the war effort, imperial propaganda also conveyed the message that the empire was vulnerable. West Indians had no love for Hitler or the Italian fascists, but Trinidadian movie crowds cheered newsreel reports of Nazi victories in Europe and North Africa on the assumption that they might lead to some form of independence.

Educated and urban people were much more aware of the scope of the war and the nature of the Axis threat. Mindful of their sacrifices for the empire, many hoped the Atlantic Charter would apply to the colonies regardless of Churchill's equivocation and British home secretary Herbert Morrison's declaration that granting "full self-government to many of the dependent territories" would be like "giving a child of ten a latch-key, a bank account, and a shot-gun."[16] Imperial propagandists tried to walk a fine line between motivating their subjects to supply more men and material without giving them a sense that these contributions helped save Britain or win the war.

Nonetheless, popular hopes for political concessions or at least some sort of tangible reward for their service remained high in most colonies after the Allied victory. The clear and obvious progress of the dominions to full autonomy, if not de facto independence, within the Commonwealth further heightened expectations. As we shall see in chapter 6, in late 1945 the trade unionists and anticolonial intellectuals from Africa, the West Indies, and the United States who gathered at the Fifth Pan-Africanist Congress in Manchester, England, followed the Indian nationalist path in finally calling for an end to imperial control. Under the leadership of men like George Padmore of Trinidad, Kwame Nkrumah of the Gold Coast, and Jomo Kenyatta of Kenya, they envisioned a socialist future by condemning the "monopoly of capital and the rule of private wealth and industry for private property alone" in the colonies. By their interpretation of the Atlantic Charter, they were entitled to "real democracy" and outright political independence.[17]

A NEW BRITAIN?

These demands clashed directly with metropolitan plans for the empire because the colonies and dependent territories seemed more important than ever to metropolitan Britain in the years following World War II. As early as 1942, the War Cabinet began to plan for postwar reconstruction by asking the economist Sir William Beveridge to survey Britain's various welfare schemes. Churchill's coalition government commissioned the report to counter Nazi propaganda and defuse popular domestic pressure for wartime reforms while Britain faced the threat of a German invasion, but Beveridge had other ideas. Taking his assignment as a directive to bring about nothing less than universal "freedom from want," he drafted a hugely ambitious government-sponsored social security program based on the assumption that scientific advances and a modest redistribution of income could eliminate poverty. Although the Conservative members of the War Cabinet strongly opposed the "Beveridge plan," it was hugely popular with the general public and serving soldiers. In 1943 the British Trade Union Congress went a step further in releasing a "four decencies" manifesto, modeled on Franklin Roosevelt's "Four Freedoms" declaration, that called on the authorities to promise returning veterans a decent job, home, social security scheme, and education.[18] Recognizing that the war-weary public needed to believe that their sacrifices of men and material would lead to a better world and improved living standards, the coalition government issued a series of policy directives (white papers) based on the Beveridge plan that became the basis of the postwar British welfare state.

Beveridge's utopian vision was expensive, however, and Britain was largely bankrupt by August 1945. Almost six years of total war had nearly destroyed the metropolitan economy, and the nation owed £2.723 billion to the members of the sterling area who had indirectly lent Britain the value of their exports and deposits in metropolitan banks. Even more serious, the net worth of its overseas holdings shifted from a positive balance of £5 billion in 1938 to a deficit of £500 million in 1945. The coalition government sold these assets, which amounted to roughly one-quarter of Britain's national wealth, to fund the war effort. The fighting also sank one-third of the merchant fleet and cut off overseas markets, thereby reducing British exports by two-thirds. Moreover, German bombing damaged British industry severely and destroyed approximately £900 million worth of machinery. Given these realities, it is easy to see how postwar commentators like Arthur Bryant could take the London victory festivities as a reminder of how much the nation had sacrificed to defeat the Nazi threat.

The many Britons who looked to the empire for assistance in reconstruction had little patience for their American ally's anti-imperial stance. The unwillingness of the United States to help fund Britain's postwar recovery contributed to the growing friction between the wartime partners that was becoming apparent at the 1946 celebrations. Aid from the United States kept the British economy going during the war, but the Americans insisted that Lend-Lease monies could not be used to rebuild export industries that might compete with their own manufacturers. The American decision to abruptly end the Lend-Lease program entirely in August 1945 was an unexpected and drastic blow that famed economist John Maynard Keynes likened to Britain's military disasters earlier in the war when he termed the move a "financial Dunkirk." The British government tried to convince the Americans to replace Lend-Lease with an interest-free grant, but Keynes could only secure a $3.75 million loan at 2 percent interest and a reduction in the Lend-Lease debt from $21 billion to $650 million.[19] In return, the Americans required the British to ratify the Bretton Woods Agreement of 1944. This concession meant Britain would have to stop propping up the value of the pound, reduce—if not eliminate—trading preferences it granted to the empire, and eventually dismantle the sterling area.

Britain therefore faced greater financial problems in the two years after the end of World War II than it had during the actual conflict. Expecting a quick return to normalcy, British voters turned Winston Churchill out of office in the 1945 elections on the assumption that the Conservative leader was ill-suited to manage postwar recovery and reconstruction. They replaced him with Clement Attlee, a Labour Party leader who ran on a platform of economic development and social reform. But Attlee was hard-pressed to make good on his electoral promises. Britain desperately needed to earn dollars to pay its debts to the United States, but it had little to export in return because its industrial base was in a shambles. The Labour government had to reduce domestic consumption drastically because it could not afford to pay for much-needed imports of food and building materials. As a result, Britain faced severe food shortages when poor weather disrupted harvests in 1946 and ration standards provided fewer calories than wartime diets. The shortage of building materials also made it difficult to accommodate the 4 million people whose homes had been destroyed in the war. This was at a time when extensive defense commitments in Asia, the Middle East, and continental Europe remained hugely expensive.

Many Britons understandably looked to the empire for help in addressing these grave and fundamental weaknesses. With the onset of the Cold War, British strategists hoped that increased imperial military and economic cooperation would allow them to stand up to the Soviet Union if the United States retreated into isolationism as it had after World War I. The Labour foreign secretary Ernest Bevin spoke of developing the empire into a "third force" that would rank with the United States and the Soviet Union as a global superpower. He envisioned defusing nationalist opposition in the colonies through economic development and vague promises of eventual self-government within the Commonwealth. Bevin also expected this new approach to rebut Britain's critics in the new United Nations, which was decidedly hostile to autocratic imperialism, who demanded that the European powers dismantle their empires.

Most important, and perhaps contradictorily, the Labour government looked to the overseas possessions to fund its ambitious plan to transform Britain into a social welfare state. Officials like Bevin, a former prominent trade unionist, and Colonial Secretary Arthur Creech Jones, a onetime socialist critic of the empire, believed that they could create a new kind of liberal imperialism that would be both moral and profitable. Creech Jones, whose appointment to oversee the Colonial Office one Conservative imperial expert likened to "making a theoretical prison reformer a prison governor," declared during the 1945 election campaign, "I do not conceive of the Empire as a vast economic asset to be developed and exploited from London for national ends."[20] Instead, the growth of a "public spirit" in the colonies through greater opportunities to participate in local government, promotion of trade unionism to foster better relations between employers and workers, stronger labor controls to prevent exploitation, and fair prices for agricultural produce would form the basis of a new humanitarian partnership of mutual benefit to Britain and subject populations.

The Labour government recognized that it would take increased investment in the empire to turn this updated version of Frederick Lugard's dual mandate into reality. To this end, it expanded the Colonial Development and Welfare Act (CDW) of 1940 to provide £120 million for the colonies in 1945 and 1946. Impressed by the apparent success of the Soviet Union's five-year plans in the 1930s, the Labour colonial experts assumed that they could reap the biggest returns on this investment through the centralized state planning that was at the core of their domestic economic policies. Largely still unaware of the scope of the famine and political purges inherent in the Stalinist model, some officials advocated incorporating the "Russian system of collectivism" and its "scientific use of land" into the individual territorial development plans that the CDW required each colony to draw up. Although these views may appear controversial in hindsight, most Britons accepted the need for some sort of central planning in the immediate postwar era. Speaking approvingly of the achievements he witnessed on a trip to Soviet Uzbekistan, Colonel C. E. Ponsonby called on each British colony to develop a state-directed development plan as part of the Conservative Party's 1945 election platform.[21] From the metropolitan perspective, this new form of seemingly rational and scientific rule offered real hope of funding the British recovery and strengthening the postwar empire.

THE END OF THE RAJ

Even as this planning took place, there was a growing acknowledgment and acceptance in both London and New Delhi that India would not play a role in the new imperial development schemes. India was already well on the way to full local autonomy when the war broke out, and the Bengal famine and the Raj's draconian suppression of the Quit India movement doomed the political reforms of the 1930s. Nor did the 1942 offer of dominion status or full independence after the war by Sir Stafford Cripps, the lord privy seal and leader of the House of Commons, do much to generate popular Indian support for the war effort. Several key members in Churchill's War Cabinet opposed the Cripps offer because they correctly recognized that it could not be withdrawn if the Indian nationalists turned it down. Once Cripps had demonstrated that Britain was prepared to surrender direct control of India when faced with the prospect of a Japanese invasion, the only significant questions remaining in the postwar era were how and when this would take place.

Although the Quit India movement and the ensuing unrest in 1942 and 1943 failed to bring about an immediate end of the Raj, it did demonstrate that Britain was losing control of India at the local level. Recruiting for the Indian Civil Service (ICS) at British universities ended entirely by 1943, and one year later a blanket invitation for British military officers in the Indian army to apply for peacetime ICS postings produced few takers. Equally problematic, by 1945 it had become politically unfeasible to charge the Indians who had defected to the Indian National Army after the fall of Singapore with treason. During the prosecution of the first batch of former INA officers, the general secretary of the Indian National Congress declared that it was the former viceroy Lord Linlithgow who should be in the dock to answer for the deaths of 3 million people during the Bengal famine. [22] As strikes and mutinies broke out among the Indian navy and paramilitary police units in the months following the Japanese surrender, it became obvious that holding India would take a massive commitment of British forces.

This was at a time when British voters had already demonstrated in the 1945 parliamentary elections that they were most concerned with recovery and reconstruction, and wartime colonial and regular army units in Asia were themselves on the verge of mutiny over the slow pace of demobilization. Moreover, the Indianization of the Indian Civil Service and the declining economic value of India meant that there were relatively few Britons with a direct stake in preserving the old order. Whereas profitable Indian loans had helped keep the British economy afloat in the interwar era, wartime spending left Britain actually owing India £1.3 billion in 1946. With no reserves left in London, the Raj also had nothing to contribute to the sterling area. Nor could India help the empire earn dollars because it too was in debt to the United States. [23] It now made political and economic sense to dismantle the Raj.

Nonetheless, Attlee could not simply withdraw from India. Unwilling to create the perception that they were forced to surrender the most important territory in the empire, British officials sought to portray their departure as the deliberate and planned withdrawal that had always been the ultimate aim of the Montagu-Chelmsford reforms. Their goal was to turn power over to a friendly regime that would respect British investments and keep India in the Commonwealth. But this would take time, and the Raj was on its last legs. In September 1946, the Viceroy Field Marshall Viscount Wavell warned that the loyalty of Indian members of the Indian Civil Service was shaky and that it would take five full British divisions to maintain order if the Indian army became unreliable. By his estimation, the Raj was destined to collapse in eighteen months.

The last British rulers of India thus had to orchestrate the transfer of power within a very narrow timeframe. This was difficult, as it was by no means clear what would replace the Raj. Constrained by liberal ideology, Lord Louis Mountbatten, whose prestige as a close relative of the British royal family led Attlee to select him as India's last viceroy, could realistically only transfer sovereignty to a popularly elected government. Unfortunately, the gradual and limited political reforms of the interwar era did not lay the groundwork for this. Instead, the Indian National Congress dominated the first postwar elections in 1945 and 1946 and won an absolute majority in eight of India's eleven provinces, with 91 percent of the non-Muslim vote. The prospect of majority rule inflamed religious and communal tensions that had been simmering throughout India since the first electoral reforms at the turn of the century.

Although Gandhi insisted emphatically that all Indians were equal regardless of faith, caste, or social class, non-Hindus and other minority groups continued to worry about their future under a Congress-dominated government. Realistic or not, these fears politicized Indian Muslims. Under the leadership of Muhammad Ali Jinnah, the Muslim League emerged as a significant political force by the start of the war. Jinnah imposed unity and discipline on the diverse and heterogeneous Muslim community through a well-organized campaign that included a network of paid speakers, nationalist songs, a Muslim national guard, and nationalistic sermons in the mosques.

The Muslim League's primary goal was to force the Raj and the INC to guarantee the rights of minorities in a national Indian constitution. Its leadership proposed redrawing administrative boundaries to create provinces with an Islamic majority and setting aside a fixed quota of legislative and executive positions for Muslims. Jinnah did not introduce the idea of a separate Muslim state until late in the war. Although Muslim students and intellectuals had been discussing uniting the northwestern provinces of Sind, Baluchistan, and the Punjab with the Northwest Frontier Province to create Pakistan since the early 1930s, Jinnah and other League leaders were initially lukewarm to the idea because they worried about what would happen to the Muslim minorities that remained within India. Initially, Jinnah's primary goal was to win autonomy for Muslims within an independent Indian federation. He only raised the possibility of partition to unite the Muslim community and gain leverage in the constitutional negotiations. He was successful in the short term, and the League won all thirty of the Muslim seats in the first postwar elections.

Mountbatten's negotiators tried to resolve these Hindu-Muslim tensions through a complex federal compromise, but Jawaharlal Nehru, who had become the main political voice of the INC, refused to go along. Recalling that the Raj had exploited Indian social divisions to remain in power, the Congress leadership insisted that India should have a unitary government and a constitution that discouraged sectarian differences. In response, Jinnah boy-cotted the 1946 constitutional negotiations and sought greater leverage through a "direct action" campaign. Intended to be peaceful protests, the various demonstrations sparked violent incidents throughout northern India, where nationalistic debates inflamed local grievances. In August 1946, a massive riot broke out in Calcutta that killed four thousand people, injured fifteen thousand more, and left another hundred thousand homeless. Muslims suffered the most in Calcutta, but in Muslim-majority areas like East Bengal, Hindus were the main victims. It took three battalions of British troops to restore order in Calcutta, and the Raj struggled to maintain order throughout the rest of the country.

Faced with the collapse of the constitutional negotiations, Mountbatten determined that the only way to extricate British forces in a timely fashion was to accept the partition of the Raj, with Pakistan and India becoming independent states as dominions within the Commonwealth. This was not what Jinnah wanted. The Muslim League had hoped to establish Pakistan as an autonomous body within a larger federation, but Mountbatten's plan made the political division of the subcontinent inevitable. Indian nationalists have charged that Mountbatten's negotiators intentionally inflamed Hindu-Muslim tensions in the hope of preserving British influence in South Asia, but the last viceroy's main goal was to wind down the Raj before Britain became embroiled in a sectarian civil war.

This rapid retreat from India had tragic consequences. The partition, which became official on August 15, 1947, was illogical, chaotic, and violent. Seeking to draw borders that would place the most Muslims in Pakistan, Mountbatten created an independent boundary commission that split the provinces of Bengal and Punjab. The Muslim half of Bengal became East Pakistan, a province over one thousand miles from the rest of Pakistan. It became the independent nation of Bangladesh after a civil war in 1971. The situation in the Punjab was equally unsatisfactory as the British ignored Sikh demands for their own state. Instead, the Sikhs, who were the majority in the province, found themselves split between the two new nations.

Over 1 million former subjects of the Raj died in the chaos and fury sparked by its drastic division. An additional 5.5 million people became refugees, which, as we shall see in chapter 6, led many to eventually emigrate to Britain. Yet partition still left 30 million Muslims within India, which amounted to about 10 percent of the total population. Recognizing the inherent dangers in breaking up the Raj, Gandhi had always aimed to create a unified state based on a secular interpretation of Indian nationalism that would defuse sectarian and caste tensions. His efforts cost him his life. After a Hindu nationalist murdered him in January 1948, the Congress Party embraced his secular nationalist ideals, but Islam became the central feature of Pakistan's national identity.

These conflicting ideologies contributed to bitter enmity between the two nations that continues to this day, particularly over the fate of Kashmir. Mountbatten, who had gone to school with many of the Indian princes, allowed the leaders of the princely states to choose whether to join India or Pakistan. This allowed Hari Singh, the maharaja of Kashmir, to take his predominately Muslim state into India. The unresolved status of Kashmir sent India and Pakistan to war in 1965 and 1971, and the development of atomic weapons by the two sister states means that a third major war in South Asia might result in a nuclear conflagration.

In the near term, the end of the Raj had significant consequences for the rest of Britain's Asian empire. Nationalist resistance to World War II in Ceylon did not match the intensity of the Indian National Congress's opposition, but it still forced Churchill's government to promise the colony full self-government after the war. The retreat from India made Ceylonese independence inevitable, and in February 1948 Ceylon became a sovereign nation within the Commonwealth. In return, the Ceylonese granted British forces continued access to the island's military bases.

To the east, Britain had little remaining use for Burma after the demise of the Raj. Freed from direct Indian control by the 1935 Government of India Act, the colony became further unmoored from the wider empire by two years of Japanese occupation. Although Churchill had expected to restore imperial authority in Burma after the war, Attlee was distracted by the events in India and was willing to reach an accommodation with the nationalist leader Aung San, despite his senior post in the Japanese puppet government. Faced with a 1946 police strike and the unavailability of Indian troops to restore order, the British authorities invited Aung San to run a transitional government and announced that the colony would become independent in 1948. This was not a particularly big sacrifice as the colony's rice, timber, and oil exports went primarily to India and thus did not contribute to the sterling area. Consequently, the British government was not particularly troubled when Aung San declared that Burma would be a republic outside the Commonwealth.

As in India, the rapid and relatively sudden end to imperial rule in Ceylon and Burma inflamed political and ethnic divisions. The new Sinhalese-dominated national government in Ceylon struck Indian migrants off the voting rolls, and even more serious problems arose when the island's Tamil community demanded 50 percent of the seats in the legislature. As in the Raj, the jarring transition to democracy and universal suffrage led a minority to fear for its rights, and Tamil efforts to create their own separate nation led to a tragic civil war that lasted for decades. In Burma, struggles among the various nationalist factions led to the assassination of Aung San and his cabinet on the eve of independence. The new government then faced a serious challenge from a communist insurgency and an alliance of minority groups known collectively as the Karen National Union.

Although British strategists were resigned to the loss of India, Ceylon, and Burma, Attlee's government was far more committed to retaining Malaya within the empire. In keeping with the postwar emphasis on greater productivity and efficiency, it hoped to weld the Malay sultanates and Straits Settlements into a more economically viable Malayan Union after the Colonial Office replaced the chaotic British Military Administration of Malaya in 1946. This was to be a first step toward the creation of a larger Southeast Asian dominion based on an inclusive nonethnic Malayan national identity. In contrast to Burma and Ceylon, Malaya still had significant value to the empire because its tin and rubber exports went primarily to the United States, thereby earning important dollar returns for Britain's postwar reconstruction between 1946 and 1952.

The ambitious plans for the Malayan Union also faced insurmountable political and social problems. First, the Malayan sultans balked at giving up their autonomy. More significantly, the attempt to create a multiracial democracy in the union by granting Chinese and Indians full citizenship touched off a popular Malay backlash. Although they outnumbered both groups, the Malays worried that the better educated and more commercially advanced immigrant communities would dominate the new government. In 1948, the United Malays National Organization forced the British administration to replace the union with the much more loosely organized Federation of Malaya. The sultans retained their authority, and only a few Indians and Chinese qualified for citizenship.

These discriminatory measures mobilized and empowered the Malayan Communist Party. This Chinese-dominated movement was a useful wartime ally, and members of its Malayan Peoples' Anti-Japanese Army marched with the Malayan contingent at the 1946 London victory celebrations. The communists were willing to work through the political process in the postwar era, but the British authorities calculated that the Malays were more useful allies. In 1947, the communists took up arms when the colonial government cracked down forcibly on their trade union activities. Within a year, five thousand guerrillas, many of whom were veterans of World War II, returned to the forests in what became known as the Malaya Emergency. They used this refuge to launch attacks on the rubber plantations and tin mines, which threatened British reconstruction. Proving remarkably difficult to defeat, the communist insurgents forced Attlee's government to commit forty thousand regular British troops and eighty thousand local militiamen to defend the federation.

MIDDLE EASTERN COMPLICATIONS

Middle Eastern oil, which represented 41 percent of the world's known reserves in 1945, was as important to postwar Britain as Malayan tin and
rubber. Calculating that reconstruction required 17 million barrels of oil per
year, imperial strategists were initially optimistic that they could maintain
influence in the region. Ernest Bevin, the Labour foreign secretary, hoped to
protect British interests through an "empire by treaty," which essentially
continued the prewar policy of forming mutually beneficial alliances with
nominally independent Arab states. These treaties allowed Britain to give up
the expense of direct rule in Egypt, Iraq, and the Transjordan while retaining
access to their military bases through reciprocal defense pacts. In theory,
these installations allowed imperial forces to block Soviet expansion in the
Middle East and defend the Suez Canal in time of war. The garrisons also
provided additional security for the British companies that were deeply involved in developing the oil fields in Arabia, Iraq, and Persia. Bevin's aim
was to win popular Arab tolerance, if not outright support, for this continued
imperial presence in the region through policies that appealed to "peasants
not pashas." This was essentially an attempt to return to the nineteenth-
century practice of informal empire.

As in Asia, however, nationalism and communal tensions complicated
and ultimately doomed Bevin's plans. Arab rulers signed the bilateral defense pacts because they were the only way to get the British to leave.
Nationalists resented having foreign bases on their soil and detested the
continued meddling in their internal affairs. Never forgetting that Britain had
intervened militarily to keep both nations from siding with the Axis powers
during the war, most Egyptians and Iraqis wanted to end all ties to their
former rulers.

The situation was particularly tense in Egypt, where the government insisted on full control of the Sudan and the end of the mutual-defense provisions of the 1936 Anglo-Egyptian Treaty. Bevin was willing to rework the
accord, but when negotiations broke down in 1946, British forces withdrew
to a zone around the Suez Canal where they had a right to maintain a ten-
thousand-man garrison. Moving well beyond the letter of the agreement,
imperial strategists developed the Canal Zone into a massive military complex consisting of ten airfields, thirty-four army bases, and almost two hundred thousand imperial troops. This blatant violation of Egyptian sovereignty
radicalized large segments of the general public and discredited the leaders of
the relatively moderate Wafd Party, who had been willing to work with
Britain during the war. Islamicist rebels assassinated two prime ministers
between 1945 and 1947, and guerrilla attacks on British military installations
undercut the security and overall value of the Canal Zone bases.

Given this implacable hostility, imperial military planners hoped that Palestine might offer a solution to their problems in Egypt. No treaties limited their freedom of action in the mandate, and it was right next to the Suez Canal. Palestine also had the industrial infrastructure to replace the repair facilities in the Canal Zone bases, and the oil pipeline and refinery at the port of Haifa provided a reliable fuel source.

The Palestine Mandate, however, proved to be anything but an asset in the new era of anti-imperial nationalism. Popular anger over continued Jewish settlement in the mandate jeopardized Britain's standing in the Middle East and undermined Bevin's peasants-over-pashas strategy. As was the case in Iraq and Egypt, many Palestinian Arabs had sympathized with the Nazis on the expectation that a German victory would end British influence in the Middle East.

Most Palestinian Jews, conversely, supported Britain on the hope that Churchill's government would reverse the prewar ban on further immigration, and they recognized that military training would be useful if the conflict with their Arab neighbors flared up again after the war. Consequently, Jews enlisted in every branch of the imperial military. In Palestine, the British trained fifteen hundred of them to operate as guerrillas if the mandate fell into German hands.

There was, however, an extremist Zionist faction, initially led by Abraham Stern, that considered Britain an illegitimate occupying power. Calling themselves "The Fighters for the Freedom of Israel," they launched a terrorist assault on the mandate government in 1939 that included bank robbery and bombing military and oil installations. British security forces killed Stern in 1942, but two years later his operatives scored a huge propaganda victory by assassinating Lord Moyne when the minister of state for the Middle East was visiting Cairo. A larger group known as the Irgun Z'vai Le'emi was initially more restrained and limited its attacks to targets associated with immigration control, but in 1944 it joined the Stern faction in a formal war on British interests. On the whole, these violent groups had relatively limited popular support, and the more realistic Jewish Agency, which represented the World Zionist Organization in Palestine, recognized that Nazism was the greater threat. Moderate Jewish leaders therefore limited themselves to criticizing British immigration policy and did their best to restrain the radicals.

The Zionists' tacit truce with Britain came to end after the war when the full extent of the Holocaust became public knowledge. The Attlee government's opportunistic decision to tilt toward the Arabs in the Arab-Zionist struggle by limiting further immigration became diplomatically embarrassing when hundreds of thousands of desperate Holocaust survivors languished in refugee camps throughout Europe. Writing sympathetically about the Zionist cause, the American journalist I. F. Stone unknowingly echoed the West Indian Rastafarians when he drew a comparison between the British colonial

administration in Palestine and the Assyrians and Romans, who had persecuted the biblical land of Israel.[24] Stone and other supportive journalists told
the world how heroic Zionist operatives struggled to smuggle as many people as they could into the mandate on decrepit ships. The Royal Navy turned
most of these floating hulks away, and several thousand refugees drowned
when their ships capsized and sank.

Even moderate Jews found this situation intolerable. In 1945, the Haga-
nah, the Jewish Agency's military arm, formed a tactical alliance with the
radicals. Together the now unified Zionists renewed the guerrilla campaign
to drive the British out of Palestine. They began by sabotaging military
installations but progressed to more terroristic operations that included
bombing British administrative offices in Jerusalem's King David Hotel and
abducting and hanging a pair of British army sergeants. They also fought
local Palestinians and the thousands of volunteers who streamed into the
mandate from neighboring Arab countries.

Mandate officials found themselves in the middle of what was rapidly
becoming an undeclared open war. Bevin had hoped that both sides would
respect Britain's avowed policy of strict neutrality, but the mounting violence made this impossible. By 1947, conditions in Palestine had become so
bad that the mandate no longer had any strategic value. Mandate officials had
to send their families back to Britain for safety while imperial troops and
policemen sheltered in fortified bases that the metropolitan press dubbed
"Bevingrads." News coverage of the Royal Navy turning away shiploads of
destitute refugees undermined Britain's international reputation. Moreover,
10 percent of the entire British military was tied down in Palestine, where the
unrest cost metropolitan taxpayers £40 million per year. In February 1947,
Attlee decided to cut his losses and refer the entire Palestinian problem to the
United Nations. The United Nations divided the mandate between the two
factions over vehement Arab objections, and full-scale war broke out between Zionist and Arab forces when Britain rapidly withdrew its military
garrison in May 1948 to escape the fighting.

As in India, imperial administrators could not to come to terms with the
nationalist aspirations of their subjects. Their failure to lay the groundwork
for a rational and orderly transfer of power led to political strife and eventually violence between communities that had previously coexisted, albeit pre-
cariously, under British rule. In the Middle East, ongoing fighting between
Arab countries and the new State of Israel forced British military planners to
fall back on their installations in Egypt to safeguard the Suez Canal and the
communication links to Asia after an expensive and highly unrealistic plan to
develop the Kenyan port of Mombasa into a substitute base fell apart.[25] As
we shall see in chapter 5, their defiance of Egyptian nationalist opposition
would have serious consequences in the 1950s.

A NEW EMPIRE?

The end of the Middle East mandates and the independence of many Asian territories increased the importance of the rest of the empire. The feasibility of the Labour government's ambitious plans for a new, mutually beneficial imperial partnership depended on its ability to reconcile metropolitan Britain's reconstruction and recovery needs with the nationalist aspirations of its remaining subjects. This was in a precarious postwar era when both the United States and the Soviet Union were openly critical of formal empire. Fully aware of these challenges after the loss of so many of their Asian and Middle Eastern territories, imperial partisans from both ends of the British ideological political spectrum believed that a revitalized and more inclusive Commonwealth offered the best chance of preserving the political, economic, and military ties that made Britain a prosperous nation and a global power. Ideally, local self-government within the Commonwealth would become a viable alternative to nationalism and full independence for the empire's remaining subjects.

The main complication was that there was no getting around the reality that subjecthood was a form of subordination. Imperial rule invariably placed the interests of metropolitan Britain and other special interest groups ahead of local populations. There was little that most Africans, Asians, or West Indians could do about this during the empire's heyday, but the dominions used their autonomy to become increasingly assertive and nationalistic. After the Axis defeat, Canada, Australia, New Zealand, and South Africa all signed the United Nations Charter individually, and their governments made it clear that they would pursue their own independent foreign policies.

In September 1945, the Canadian government went a step further in puncturing the illusion of a common imperial nationality by enacting immigration and naturalization laws that no longer conferred automatic citizenship on British subjects from other parts of the empire. The resulting Canadian Citizenship Act of 1946 further declared that all Canadian citizens were British subjects, which meant that any successful immigrant to Canada now automatically acquired citizenship in the wider empire. Seeking to preserve the integrity of the all-encompassing concept of imperial citizenship that was at the core of the Commonwealth ideal, Attlee's government gave all of the other dominions the right to pass their own citizenship laws and pushed a law through Parliament that recognized all residents of the remaining overseas territories as "British subjects."

This new and extremely broad definition of "Britishness," which was embodied in the 1948 British Nationality Act, fit the Labour Party's vision of a new, nondiscriminatory empire, and it won favor from Conservatives who believed that giving the ideal of universal imperial citizenship legal standing would preserve Britain's central leadership role within the Commonwealth.

Acknowledging the need to blunt the appeal of anti-imperial nationalism, the Conservative MP David Gammans optimistically asserted, "We have to create a sense of Empire citizenship, so that a man from Nigeria will talk about his status as a British subject permanently and with pride, just as a man would who was born in Yorkshire, or in Scotland, or in any other part of Britain."[26] In practical terms, the British Nationality Act granted all residents of the empire equal status and the right to live and work in Britain. Although this measure usefully gave legal weight to the ideal of a universal Commonwealth citizenship, chapter 6 will show how it would have profound consequences for metropolitan Britain as the empire broke up over the next three decades.

In the short term, the new nationality legislation provided a politically and diplomatically acceptable rationale for India, Pakistan, and Ceylon to remain within the Commonwealth after becoming independent republics. Although they no longer recognized the British monarch as their head of state, under the terms of the 1949 London Declaration they accepted King George VI as "the symbol of the free association of its independent member nations and as such the Head of the Commonwealth." The designation "Commonwealth country" thus replaced "dominion" in official usage, and the entire organization dropped the word British from its title to become simply the "Commonwealth of Nations." Bureaucratically, the Commonwealth Relations Office handled Britain's relations with these essentially independent states. Canada, Australia, and New Zealand were satisfied with this arrangement because they viewed Britain as their spiritual home and continued to acknowledge the king as their head of state, but in South Africa the Afrikaner-dominated Reunited National Party, which came to power in 1948, remained suspicious, if not openly hostile, to the Commonwealth ideal.

Ireland, which had already become a de facto republic before World War II, created an even bigger nationality problem when it formally declared itself a republic with no ties whatsoever to the Crown in 1948. This was its right under the 1936 Statute of Westminster, but it was impossible to achieve a total divorce from Britain when some fifty to sixty thousand Irishmen immigrated to Britain to participate in the postwar recovery. Taking important but relatively low-wage jobs, Irish laborers played an essential role in the reconstruction. This is why the British government disregarded the pronouncements coming out of Dublin and refused to treat them as foreigners. Irish citizens therefore remained entitled to all the benefits of the new welfare state and liable for national service while living in Britain. Speaking in defense of the 1948 British Nationality Act that embodied this new policy in the House of Lords, Lord Simon declared, "I do not know what would happen to many of the hospitals if all Irish nurses had to leave and return to their own country."[27] The problem with this decision to ignore Ireland's declaration of an imperial divorce was that the new nationality legislation

treated the Irish Republic as simultaneously in- and outside the Commonwealth. Nor did it resolve the status of the six counties that remained part of
Great Britain as Northern Ireland. A key factor in the British parliament's
rationale for accepting the dual national status of citizens of the Irish Republic was the grudging acknowledgment that it would have been impossible to
treat the boundary between northern and southern Ireland as an international
border.

From a practical standpoint, these broad constitutional changes meant that
Ireland, the remaining dominions, and the new Commonwealth countries
refused to play a subordinate role in Britain's postwar reconstruction. Consequently, imperial planners focused on increasing the value of their African
and West Indian territories, which still did not have the protection of self-
government, through state-directed development. Just as it was seeking to
reshape the metropolitan economy and society through an ambitious program
of nationalization, centralized planning, scientific management, and public
welfare programs, the Labour government expected to bring greater efficiency and productivity to the remaining colonies whether their subject populations wanted it or not.

In the West Indies, economic development depended on resolving the
underlying economic and political tensions that produced the strikes and riots
of the 1930s. The colonial authorities hoped to use funds from the Colonial
Development and Welfare Act to alleviate the endemic poverty that they
blamed for the unrest. Public health campaigns targeted yaws, venereal disease, tuberculosis, and malaria, while housing experts and urban development specialists drew up plans to improve conditions in the slums. Most
colonial administrations also created labor departments that promoted trade
unionism as a nonpolitical way for workers and employers to resolve their
grievances.

Measurable development in the West Indies, however, depended ultimately on the colonial authorities' ability to uncouple nationalism from radical labor activism by winning over middle-class elite moderates through
gradual political reform. In the early 1940s, British officials made plans to
expand the electorate and create greater opportunities for political participation on the condition that nationalist leaders did not threaten British economic interests. In 1944, they introduced a new constitution in Jamaica that
created a House of Representatives that was, for the first time in the West
Indies, elected by universal suffrage. There was also an upper Legislative
Council where nominated local representatives held ten of the thirteen seats.
Under this model, Jamaica and the rest of the West Indian Crown colonies
would gradually acquire more autonomy until they became self-governing
territories within a revitalized and more expansive Commonwealth.

In keeping with its preference for creating larger, more economically
manageable territories, the Colonial Office also aimed to draw the West

Indian colonies into a West Indies Federation. In 1947, Arthur Creech Jones chaired a conference of local delegates that approved the plan. In contrast to Malayan opposition to federation, West Indians backed the colonial secretary's proposal because they saw federation as the fastest route to independence. Assuming that the West Indies Federation would have a weak central government, they expected it to defer to nationalist leaders in the individual territories because Creech Jones explicitly promised that federalism would not stand in the way of self-government.[28]

These reforms only conferred the appearance of actual political power. Under the Jamaican constitution, the British governor retained control of military, foreign, and economic policy and had the authority to enact legislation without consulting the elected local representatives. This was frustrating for middle-class leaders like Norman Manley and Eric Williams, who built popular movements in Jamaica and Trinidad by embracing labor issues. Most political parties had strong union ties, and the careers of West Indian politicians depended largely on their ability to further workers' agendas. This proved difficult as the Labour government's grand development plans gradually fizzled out by the end of the 1940s. Most of its social welfare initiatives amounted to little more than pilot projects. As a result, popular discontent with British rule continued to grow, and apart from the unplanned postwar flow of migrant workers to Britain, the West Indian colonies contributed comparatively little to the empire's recovery.

The imperial planners had much higher hopes for the African colonies. No longer a forgotten corner of the empire, British Africa captured the imagination of many Britons in the postwar era. Bevin spoke wistfully of integrating the French and British colonies to create a common market that would enable both empires to end their dependence on American aid. Similarly, in 1947, Field Marshall Viscount Montgomery, chief of the Imperial General Staff, advocated creating a single unified African territory that would allow Britain to better exploit the colonies' food, mineral, and energy resources. The field marshal was no starry-eyed idealist, and his 1947 classified policy brief showed that he remained a firm believer in Frederick Lugard's dual mandate: "There will be many people in the U.K. who will oppose such a plan on the grounds that the African will suffer in the process; there is no reason whatever why he should suffer; and in any case he is a complete savage and is quite incapable of developing the country himself."[29]

Montgomery's frankness reflected the underlying realities of Britain's postwar development plans for Africa. Although Labourites with socialist leanings like Creech Jones spoke optimistically about new initiatives that would raise living standards in the colonies, they intended colonial development first and foremost to benefit Britain. This meant increasing the output of key raw materials that could be exported to the United States to earn the dollar returns essential to the postwar recovery. Throughout most of the twentieth century, a triangle trade between Britain, the empire, and North America enabled Britain to earn the dollars needed to purchase food imports by selling colonial raw materials to the United States and the rest of the dollar zone. This delicate balance was already under stress in the 1930s, and the wartime destruction of British industries led it to break down entirely. By 1947, Britain's dollar imbalance with the United States had reached $10 billion. The Labour planners had two alternatives: they could either risk damaging the recovery by reducing American imports and imposing greater austerity on the already weary and restive metropolitan population, or they could increase African exports to earn more dollars. Sir Stafford Cripps, Labour's minister for economic affairs, made this clear in a 1947 speech to a conference of colonial governors:

> It is the urgency of the present situation and the need for the Sterling Group and Western Europe . . . to maintain their economic independence that makes it so essential that we should increase out of all recognition the tempo of African economic development. We must be prepared to change our outlook and our habits of colonial development and force the pace so that within the next 2–5 years we can get a really marked increase of production in coal, minerals, timber, raw materials of all kinds and foodstuffs and anything else that will save dollars or will sell in a dollar market. [30]

The Labour colonial experts believed they could meet these unrealistic goals by transplanting their centralized development tactics to Africa, and they assumed that with some "efficient social engineering" their colonies could become "the 'granary' . . . of hungry and undersupplied Western Europe."[31]

The primary aim of colonial development was to produce these vast quantities of dollar-earning raw materials through mechanization and rational planning. The updated 1945 Colonial Development and Welfare Act aimed to meet this goal by requiring territorial governments to draw up ten-year programs for how they would use the new investment to spur agricultural expansion, build roads and power plants, and fund other essential public works projects. In 1948, the Labour government also created the Overseas Food Corporation and the Colonial Development Corporation, which aimed to use state funds (the two corporations had total reserves of £165 million) to channel capital into export-related colonial projects that had difficulty attracting private investment.[32]

At the same time, many colonial development experts finally realized that African farmers were actually well equipped to produce greater yields at lower prices. Officials in colonies without significant settler populations were better able to recognize this fact and sought to encourage and expand African agricultural production. To this end, they introduced marketing boards to tap into the wealth generated by African farmers. The metropolitan government first used these semi-official boards in the 1930s to encourage

British farmers to produce more milk, bacon, and potatoes by guaranteeing them reasonably high prices. During World War II, the government used a similar system to purchase and market West African cocoa, and by 1943 the West African Cocoa Control Board had banked reserves of roughly £3.6 million.[33] These measures ensured that the loss of markets during wartime did not hurt African producers, but the substantial surplus generated by the marketing boards provided a ready source of capital for development. In the postwar era, colonial administrations required farmers to sell their crops at prices well below international rates. This theoretically encouraged commodity production because the surplus wealth held by the marketing boards allowed them to ensure the farmers a reasonable return for their harvests in good times and bad. Instead, the marketing boards held on to the profits and helped rebuild British currency reserves and finance the postwar recovery by banking them in London. African farmers, by comparison, received only a fraction of the true value of their crops. Between 1947 and 1954, Gold Coast cocoa boards paid farmers only 37 percent of the going world rate for their produce and held on to 51 percent of the colony's cocoa earnings.[34]

These successes led the Labour development experts to conclude that African farmers and laborers were often more valuable to the postwar recovery efforts than highly centralized state-supported corporations. Yet the Colonial Office's plan to deemphasize settler agriculture and expand and "modernize" African production by sparking a grassroots agricultural revolution ran into stiff opposition from senior colonial governors who began their careers during the interwar era and continued to oppose rapid changes that threatened to disrupt "tribal culture." Creech Jones and Andrew Cohen, head of the African Division, tried to get around entrenched and unapologetic Lugardians like T. R. O. Mangin in the Gold Coast, Arthur Richards in Nigeria, and Philip Mitchell in Kenya by instituting a series of conferences at Oxford and Cambridge that would advance the careers of a new generation of more progressive administrators. Bringing together metropolitan academics and young colonial service experts, these "summer schools" issued a stream of reports that became implicit statements of official Colonial Office policy.[35]

As a whole, this new development agenda required larger and more specialized colonial bureaucracies that intervened more directly in the daily lives of African communities. In what the historian John Lonsdale famously termed the "second colonial occupation," the Colonial Office sent a new generation of specialists in agriculture, animal husbandry, soil conservation, labor relations, community education, home economics, and women's issues to the colonies.[36] Just as the metropolitan government adopted scientific statist welfare strategies to combat urban poverty in Britain, the new generation of territorial administrators now aimed to direct social improvement in African communities. Continuing a practice that began in the interwar era, many employed social anthropologists to map African administrative and cultural institutions and provide feedback on how supposedly primitive tribal peoples were adapting to the rapid changes of the postwar era.[37]

Recognizing that they would need suitably trained African partners to administer these new policies at the grassroots level, Creech Jones and his men were less committed to the rigidly doctrinaire Lugardian model of indirect rule. Even before the outbreak of World War II, colonial experts in London began to realize that uneducated tribal chiefs were ill-suited to assist in the economic development and social transformation of African societies. In 1939, Colonial Secretary Malcolm MacDonald sent Lord Hailey, a former Indian provincial governor, to Africa to investigate the possibility of introducing representative democracy into native administrations. Hailey concluded that real political advance required Western-educated Africans and proposed creating more opportunities for them to serve in the civil service and on legislative councils. These recommendations were not as progressive as they might appear. Hailey's main intent was to follow the Raj's strategy of distracting potential anticolonial nationalists with the complications of local administration, and his recommendation to retain the chiefs' autocratic powers showed that he remained firmly committed to the old model of indirect rule.

Nevertheless, Hailey's 1941 report set in motion a limited reform process that the Labourites took up in the postwar era. Colonial education experts made plans to expand secondary education and establish new university colleges throughout the empire to produce better-trained subjects who could be partners in development. Creech Jones equated tribal chiefs with right-wing British Conservatives and urged the colonial governors to promote "the development of an efficient and democratic system of local government." Africans would then move from serving on elected local bodies to seats on territorial legislative councils. The councils would eventually become national parliaments as the colonies evolved into autonomous entities within the Commonwealth. As Creech Jones put it, "It cannot be too often repeated, for the information of our critics abroad as well as of the peoples in the Colonial Empire, that we are in these territories to guide them as quickly as circumstances permit to responsible government within the Commonwealth, in conditions that ensure to the peoples fair standards of living and freedom from oppression from any quarter."[38] In answering their Lugardian critics, who claimed that Africans were not ready to take charge of their own affairs, Creech Jones's able lieutenant, Andrew Cohen, declared, "Self-government is better than good government."[39]

Very little of this actually came to pass in the near term because the colonial authorities linked the rate of political progress to the education and civic-mindedness of the African "masses." Although the promises coming out of the postwar Colonial Office sounded grand in principle, Creech

Jones's men envisioned a timetable measured in decades and generations rather than years. Nonetheless, publicizing this political blueprint allowed Britain to claim that it was fulfilling its obligations under Article 73 of the United Nations Charter, which obligated the imperial powers to "develop self-government" in their possessions, by declaring that self-rule was the ultimate goal of the Crown colony system.

IMPERIAL REALITIES

Three years after the Japanese surrender and two years after the London victory celebrations, Creech Jones provided the metropolitan parliament with a progress report on Labour's ambitious colonial development initiatives for the period from June 1947 to June 1948. Stressing the positive, he cited the transition to self-government in Ceylon and Malta, the federation of the Malay states and peninsular settlements, steps toward federation and regional integration in the West Indies and East Africa, progressive "mass-education" programs in Africa, nutritional improvement in the Gambia, and "campaigns against diseases of all kinds." The colonial secretary also paid tribute to the members of the colonial service and emphatically declared, "Britain has nothing for which to apologize in respect of her colonial policy and her activities overseas in this connection."[40]

Yet Creech Jones also had to acknowledge that there had been a "great deal of trouble in certain parts of the Empire" in the past twelve months. These troubling incidents include "outrages" against British security forces during the retreat from Palestine, rioting in the Gold Coast, and "difficulties in Malaya" (which were actually the first shots of the well-organized Chinese communist challenge to British rule). Furthermore, the colonial secretary admitted that the colonial service was having difficulty recruiting college graduates with the specialist skills needed for his ambitious development agenda, and he acknowledged that most of the territorial governments' ten-year development plans were faltering due to a shortage of capital, key inputs like steel and cement, trained staff, and, most important, cooperative African laborers.[41] Addressing the 1948 colonial summer conference on African administration a few weeks later, Creech Jones spoke even more candidly about a "troublesome period ahead." His main concern was that most subject populations "lacked the revolution of habit and mental capacity" to make sufficient use of the benefits of the "modern state" that Britain was endeavoring to introduce into its colonies. Communist instigators and anti-imperial agitators were beginning to prey upon the empire's "backward people," who were confused and "mentally discomforted" by the rapid changes that characterized the Cold War era.[42]

Creech Jones, Cohen, and their development experts hoped to thwart these conspiratorial forces by winning popular support and appeasing the more moderate nationalists by improving living standards in the truncated empire. Speaking to the British parliament in July 1948, Creech Jones warned that without the "good will of the local governments and the cooperation from the colonial peoples themselves . . . colonial development will not go far."[43] Yet, even at this point, it was clear that Labour's centralized, state-directed approach to colonial development was faltering. Most infamously, its experiment with state-directed capitalism resulted in the sprawling Tanganyika Groundnut Scheme, which covered three parcels of land equal in size to the state of Connecticut that were entirely unsuitable for peanut production. Relying largely on unqualified staff and using converted military tanks as tractors, it suffered from severe transportation bottlenecks and spent £36 million to produce just 9,162 tons of peanuts between 1946 and 1951. This worked out to almost £4 million per ton or approximately £1,785 per pound.[44] The Gambian Egg Project, which aimed to produce 20 million eggs per year for export to Europe, brought virtually no returns whatsoever because the feed crop failed and the imported chickens died off in huge numbers. The Sudanese Gezira Cotton Scheme, which the Colonial Office described as a "sort of half-way house between American Individualism and Russian Communism," was less of a debacle because it gave tenant farmers a greater role in production and a 40 percent share of the profits.[45]

Still, Creech Jones and Cohen were absolutely right to tie the long-term survival of the empire to its ability to win popular support in the colonies. They failed to realize or accept, however, that formal imperial rule was incompatible with this simple goal. Empires, by their inherently authoritarian nature, were unreformable and therefore unacceptable to all but a minority of subject populations. This was particularly true during the immediate postwar era when more and more people around the world came to consider nationalism and self-determination a basic human right.

There was little chance that very many Africans, West Indians, and Asians would accept a development agenda that privileged the interests of metropolitan Britain. Many of Creech Jones's former leftist allies at home and in the colonies understood this and became some of his harshest critics. Charging that the Labour government's policies were intended primarily to earn dollars to fund the British welfare state, the Trinidadian Marxist and Pan-Africanist George Padmore characterized its seemingly benevolent development program as "socialism at home, imperialism in the colonies."[46] On this score, those who wished to charge their self-appointed platonic guardians with hypocrisy needed only to point to the Labourite Colonial Office's opposition to collective bargaining and unfettered union organizing and its continued toleration of forced labor (under the guise of "traditional tribal obligations") in the wider empire.[47]

In most colonies it was also hard to deny that the policy of treating subject peoples as too ignorant and backward to look after their own affairs was a poorly disguised excuse for racial discrimination. During World War II military censors uncovered letters that made it clear that colonial populations who expected their contributions to the imperial war effort to bring about significant reforms would have little tolerance for explicit racism. As a group of Ugandan soldiers put it, "If one is a soldier of our Great Empire, there should be no such discrimination as that of saying 'because this is a European and this is an Indian and that [one] an African.' All are brothers and all are children of His Majesty, our King."[48] Quite a few metropolitan Britons actually shared these sentiments, and the Conservative MP David Gammans, who spoke so eloquently about the need to create a sense of "empire citizenship" during the debate over the status of Ireland, was equally committed to stamping out the colour bar in British Africa. "If we want it to be a permanent association and not something with a connotation of inferiority, we have to get rid of any implication of colour bars. The King cannot have two sorts of subjects, first class and second class." On the opposite end of the metropolitan political spectrum, the socialist colonial expert Marjorie Nicholson similarly warned that "the British Commonwealth will stand or fall on its handling of colour and race questions."[49]

Acknowledging that racism in India had hastened the demise of the Raj and that racial animosity hindered economic development, Creech Jones asked the territorial governments to report on and then strike down all overtly discriminatory laws. The Colonial Office also directed field administrators to show greater courtesy to all their subjects and looked to appoint district officers that were not "infected with racial snobbery." Although these were fine sentiments in London, there was no getting around the inherent racism that underpinned imperial rule, particularly in the African settler colonies. Seeing no reason to apologize for racial segregation in Kenya, the Lugardian governor Philip Mitchell claimed that it was actually beneficial to the majority of Africans, who generally preferred to live apart from "economically stronger races." He also reminded Creech Jones that the segregated highlands were necessary because "white settlement . . . is the framework around which the whole economy of the Colony has been constructed." Given these views, it was hardly surprising that a Kenyan civil service commission ruled that racially discriminatory pay scales were justifiable and appropriate on the grounds that educated and fully credentialed Africans were "markedly inferior to Asians [much less Europeans] in such matters as sense of responsibility, judgment, application to duty and output of work."[50]

The situation was marginally better in West Africa, where the absence of a privileged settler class allowed the Gold Coast government to appoint the first African assistant district commissioners in 1942. This was over the objections of many senior members of the colonial service who did not want to interact socially with Africans. In 1947, a Greek hotel manager in Lagos almost single-handedly derailed the Labourites' attempts to convince the world that the British Empire did not practice racial discrimination by refusing to register a senior Colonial Office welfare specialist named Ivor Cummings, who was of African descent, on the grounds that he was "black." The resulting uproar received widespread coverage in the Nigerian press and forced Arthur Richards, another of Creech Jones's problem governors, to issue an order banning racial discrimination in public venues throughout the territory. Richards made matters worse by refusing to apologize to Cummings on the grounds that he was partially to blame for the controversy by not accepting the need for "discretion" in dealing with racial matters in Nigeria.[51] Five years later, a British district officer demonstrated that little had changed when he candidly told his parents that the Nigerian civil service remained so sharply divided on racial lines that "we only have ourselves to blame if the Africans have a dislike of us."[52]

Racial discrimination endured in the wider empire largely because most senior colonial officials ultimately believed that their subjects were inherently different and unequal. Rather than promoting full equality, which would have been incompatible with the fundamentally authoritarian nature of imperial rule, they offered at best an unequal partnership, whereby Britons, as the more "advanced race," would continue to serve as trustees for the tribal masses until generations of social change under British tutelage brought them up to a more advanced level.[53] Refusing to accept that their non-Western critics had legitimate grievances, imperial partisans reassured themselves that the spreading "troubles" in the postwar empire were the result of simple misunderstandings. In the Caribbean, the Moyne Commission blamed the labor unrest of the 1930s on "confusion" among West Indians who mistakenly blamed discrimination for their poverty. It suggested that local governments defuse racial tensions by carefully explaining the reasoning behind colonial policy. The Colonial Office even considered commissioning a sociological booklet that would explain British customs and intentions to Africans. In essence, it believed that West Indian and African opposition to British imperialism was born out of ignorance rather than legitimate nationalist aspirations or objections to postwar development policy.

This explains how both the metropolitan and individual colonial governments were unprepared to deal with the widespread popular discontent resulting from frustrated nationalist ambitions, opposition to the second colonial occupation, and rejection of Labour's Anglocentric economic agenda. Confined to limited representation on local councils and still under the thumb of authoritarian chiefs, Africans lacked the political means to challenge unpopular policies or address the broader problems that influenced their daily lives. Postwar inflation cut real wages at a time when the pressure to produce cash crops for export reduced food supplies. The result was another wave of popular discontent that dwarfed prewar labor unrest and spread throughout British Africa in the late 1940s. Although workers and peasants turned to strikes and protests to express their grievances, many commercial farmers and educated elites concluded that only full independence could solve their problems.

This was particularly true in the more politically advanced West African colonies where businessmen, lawyers, wealthy farmers, and even a few forward-thinking chiefs grew impatient with the slow pace of political reform. Gold Coast officials tried to answer their concerns by introducing a new constitution in 1946 that gave Africans a majority on the legislative council. But a handpicked group of chiefs chose most of the council members, and the new system did little to satisfy popular demands for greater political representation. Widespread unrest stemming from discontent over marketing boards, government bungling of a cocoa-tree-killing blight, housing shortages, rising prices, war veterans' anger over unpaid pensions, and awareness of the British retreat from India forced the Gold Coast government back to the constitutional drawing board.

The "troubles" that Creech Jones mentioned in his 1948 parliamentary assessment were actually a riot by African ex-servicemen in the Gold Coast that resulted in the deaths of several protesters when panicked policemen opened fire on the crowd. This was not another Amritsar, but the escalating violence forced the government to call in troops from neighboring territories to restore control. Realizing that a majority of the population was turning against British rule, Labour's Africa specialist Andrew Cohen chose to accelerate Labour's timetable for self-government in the Gold Coast by making a council of elected African ministers responsible for much of the territorial government. Colonial officials had hoped that these concessions would bring moderate politicians to power, but much to their dismay, the nationalistic Convention People's Party (CPP) supplanted their more cooperative African partners by winning widespread popular support for its "self-government now" manifesto. The CPP's leader, Kwame Nkrumah, an American-educated Pan-Africanist lawyer who had helped draft the call for a complete end to British rule in Africa during the 1945 Pan-Africanist Congress, won the first elections in 1951 even though the government had imprisoned him for leading a national strike. Forced to accept reality, Governor Charles Arden-Clarke, who was one of Cohen's allies, released him from prison to become the "leader of government business" in the newly expanded legislative assembly.

The scope and rate of political change was predictably slower in East Africa, where local European communities refused to share power with Africans at any level. Secure in the knowledge that Governor Mitchell shared their view that Kenya was a "white man's colony," settler farmers in particular emerged from the war stronger and more confident that mechanization and modern agricultural techniques would free them from their reliance on low-cost African labor. It was also hardly surprising that the Kenyan government stood by as white farmers evicted over a hundred thousand of their African tenants, who were mostly from the Kikuyu community. To the south, the Tanganyikan government set aside 5 million acres of prime agricultural land for settler farms and plantations. Creech Jones's references to positive steps toward greater interterritorial cooperation in East Africa were actually a move to give the settlers greater influence by linking Kenya, Tanganyika, and Uganda through an East African High Commission that coordinated common services like customs, railways, and the postal system. As was the case before the war, the settlers hoped that these developments would lead to the creation of a self-governing "white" dominion in East Africa.

Frustrated East Africans had no opportunity to resist these policies through legal constitutional means. The displaced Tanganyikan farmers who lost their land to white settlement tried in vain to get the United Nations to intervene on their behalf. At the territorial level, colonial authorities stifled opposition by denying Africans the right to form political parties and would only recognize tribally based welfare associations. This meant that moderate leaders—like Eliud Mathu, who won widespread acclaim as the first African member of the Kenyan Legislative Council—who sought reform through the sanctioned process soon lost their popular support.

Recognizing that education and civilization had become an excuse to deny them political rights and social equality, African parents and community leaders became particularly impatient with the underfunded and inadequate colonial education system. At a time when European students in Kenya enjoyed generous state support, less than 1 percent of Africans completed secondary school. Moreover, the territorial government insisted that it was too expensive to provide a simple primary education for every African student who wanted one. This meant that very few young people could acquire the educational credentials needed to advance in colonial society. Those with insufficient schooling faced the bleak prospects of unemployment or exploitive wage labor. In 1947, the political consequences of these inequities became apparent when marginally employed Kenyan workers struck en masse to demand better pay and working conditions. They found common cause with landless Kikuyu squatters evicted from settler farms and angry unemployed young men, who had taken to calling themselves "young Hitlers."

Similarly, in 1945 and 1949, riots broke out in Uganda over low cotton prices, marketing boards, taxation, and anger over the economic influence of the South Asian immigrant community. Coffee farmers in Buganda were incensed that the price of their beans in London was roughly one hundred times what they received from the marketing boards. Gandan cotton growers also rejected the protectorate government's assertion that they lacked "the character, the competence, [and] the providence" to compete directly with the South Asians who dominated the cotton trade.[54]

More ominously, the riots showed that a younger generation of Gandan commoners was no longer content simply to complain about colonial agricultural policies or accept the authoritarian rule of an elite class that it perceived as too close to a foreign power. By 1949, a militant faction led by the African Farmers' Union and the Bataka Party directly challenged the leadership of Kabaka Mutesa II and, by extension, British imperial rule in Buganda. Edward Frederick William David Walugembe Mutebi Luwangula Mutesa ("King Freddie" in the British press) was the grandson of Mwanga, the last truly independent monarch. Apolo Kagwa and Ham Mukasa, who had attended Edward VII's 1902 coronation, were part of a group of Gandan aristocrats who ruled the kingdom as regents for his father, Daudi Chwa, the infant who had become *kabaka* after the British deposed his father, Mwanga. By the late 1940s, there was widespread dissatisfaction with the terms of the 1900 agreement that granted the Gandan aristocracy title to much of the kingdom's arable land. Many ordinary people therefore came to view the ruling regime as little more than an unrepresentative imperial proxy. The Gandan farmers in particular rejected the postwar development agenda and demanded the right to gin and market cotton on their own. In April 1949, the protectorate authorities sparked a riot against Mutesa II's government when they broke up a mass protest by the radicals in Kampala, and as in the Gold Coast one year earlier, it took troops from the neighboring British colonies to restore order.

One year later, Kenyan labor leaders called a general strike in Nairobi for similar reasons. Most workers were in dire straits as the flood of landless and unemployed young people into the city after World War II produced severe housing shortages and depressed wages. Whereas the price of corn meal, the staple food for most poor Africans, increased 600 percent between 1939 and 1948, the average pay of unskilled laborers barely returned to predepression levels.[55] African Nairobites were also upset over harsh new laws, which Mitchell had assured Creech Jones were not based on race, empowering the police to arrest anyone they even suspected of being unemployed. Celebrations marking the British government's decision to award Nairobi full city status sparked rumors that the colonial authorities were planning to seize more African land to make room for another twelve thousand European settlers.

Led by radical union bosses, the strikers hoped to do more than just win better pay and benefits. As the Kenyan novelist Ngugi wa Thiong'o, who grew up during this period, explained in *Weep Not, Child*, they aimed to begin a colony-wide protest that would undermine the very foundations of British rule. "All black people will stop working. All business in the country will come to a standstill because all the country depends on our sweat. The

Government and the settlers will call us back. But we shall say, No, no. Give us our money first. Our sweat and blood are not so cheap."[56] A few of the striking workers had served in World War II, but the colonial authorities' fear that the men who grew so impatient and militant in the Indian demobilization camps in 1945 would lead the challenge to British rule proved unfounded. Most of the men and women who joined the Nairobi protest had never been in the military. Rather, they were ordinary people whose poverty and desperation led them to defy colonial authority. Their numbers made them a much more serious threat than the largely disorganized veterans. The Kenyan authorities recognized the gravity of the situation and broke up the strike with armored cars, baton charges, tear gas, and mass arrests.

The situation was equally tense in the Union of South Africa, where the ultra-right-wing Reunited National Party won the 1948 elections. Although the dominion's economy grew markedly during the war, the boom drew huge numbers of African migrants into urban areas in defiance of pass laws that made it illegal for non-Europeans to live in cities. Fearing a rise in African militancy, both Afrikaans- and English-speaking white voters listened to the National Party's call for strict racial segregation. Hendrik Verwoerd, the nationalists' chief ideologue, claimed that apartheid, or separateness, would prevent a race war by setting primitive Africans on their own path to development. With a nod to the growing international criticism of imperial rule, he promised that the native reserves would eventually become "tribal fatherlands" that over centuries would evolve into nations under the Christian trusteeship of white South Africans.

This benevolent rhetoric provided moral cover for the continued exploitation of the African majority. Far from bringing about true segregation, apartheid accelerated the transformation of the native reserves into overcrowded rural ghettoes where Africans could only survive by becoming low-paid migrant laborers in white-owned mines and factories. Educated members of the African National Congress (ANC) initially tried to fight apartheid through constitutional means, but the new regime ignored and oppressed them. Seeking to keep South Africa in the Commonwealth, successive British governments offered little help on the grounds that the union enjoyed full self-government under the dominion system. South Africa was an important trading partner in the sterling area, and the Royal Navy viewed the Simonstown naval base, located at the southernmost tip of Africa, as a vital Cold War asset. By the end of the 1940s, the political impotency of the senior ANC leadership convinced a new generation of activists, including a young lawyer named Nelson Mandela, to adopt more confrontational tactics in challenging apartheid.

Despite these obvious signs that local resistance to the imperial system was on the verge of becoming violent, the metropolitan authorities remained reasonably confident that British rule was secure in their remaining colonies.

Creech Jones's Colonial Office believed that, in time, development, local government, and racial reconciliation would win over the "colonial masses." More pragmatic senior military and police officials hedged their bets by expanding the postwar internal security services. Acknowledging the potential consequences of the Malaya Emergency and the Gold Coast riots, in the fall of 1948 Attlee called a special meeting of the "white" dominion leaders (thereby excluding the newly independent governments of India, Pakistan, and Ceylon) to urge them to expand and coordinate their intelligence-gathering operations. The Colonial Office did its part by creating an Inspectorate General of Police to improve policing throughout the empire by providing advice on recruiting and training. Most territorial governments quietly added Special Branch units to their police forces to liaise with colonial military units and work with the metropolitan Security Service (MI5) to monitor and infiltrate nationalist organizations.[57] Ever fearful of "native uprisings," the settler colonies also raised special police paramilitary units equipped with armored vehicles and automatic weapons. Many of these new mobile forces were led by men who had begun their imperial policing careers in the Royal Irish Constabulary before moving on to India, Palestine, and then postwar Africa.

Having freed themselves from the burden of governing India and Palestine, Labour colonial experts and imperial strategists believed that it was possible to build a stronger and more viable empire through a combination of good government and judicious imperial policing. Economic development and improved social welfare would win over the non-Western "masses," while more robust security measures would rein in nationalist agitators from the "classes." Although this seemed a viable strategy in London, the next chapter will show that these were at best stopgap measures. Once it became clear that there were viable alternatives to British rule, most people were no longer willing to remain imperial subjects.

Chapter Five

The Final Retreat from Empire, 1950 to 1970

KWAME NKRUMAH AT THE UNITED NATIONS

It took only a decade for Kwame Nkrumah to go from an overcrowded and squalid Gold Coast jail cell to the lectern at the United Nations General Assembly. Speaking as the head of an African nation-state on September 23, 1960, the Ghanaian president's meteoric rise stood in stark contrast to the second British Empire's rapid disintegration during the same period. In 1957, Ghana and the Federation of Malaya both won their independence. Cyprus achieved the same status in the month preceding Nkrumah's speech to the General Assembly. The planning for an independent federation of the West Indies was well under way, and Nigeria was on schedule to become independent just eight days after President Nkrumah's New York address. More significantly, in February 1960 Prime Minister Harold Macmillan's Conservative government announced that Britain intended to withdraw from the rest of its imperial territories as rapidly as possible over the vehement objections of the settler communities in eastern and southern Africa.

This was a jarring transition. In 1950, the British Empire still seemed secure when Nkrumah marked the new year in the James Fort Prison. Even the imperial diehards who grumbled about the Gold Coast government's decision to release him after his Convention People's Party landslide electoral victory assumed that there would be a long period of tutelage and partnership before he could make good on his campaign vow of "self-government now." Few would have imagined that Britain's run as a major imperial power would end in a matter of years.

Seeking to put the best face possible on the developments that led to Nkrumah's UN address in 1960, political leaders and colonial officials claimed that the Ghanaian nation-state was the logical and expected outcome of their local self-government initiatives. Having warned the South African parliament that there was a nationalistic "wind of change" sweeping through the continent several months earlier, Macmillan told a meeting of the Joint Commonwealth Societies Council, "We recognise now the strength of the desire for the formation of new independent nations on the continent of Africa. It is a legitimate aspiration. It is one with which we are ready and willing to co-operate. We are glad to see the development of the nations in the world to which we already stand in the relationship of parents."[1] By this reasoning, the transfer of power in Africa was the culmination of a long-standing plan to transform the empire into a free commonwealth of independent nations bound together by shared history and mutual allegiance to the British Crown. Accepting that further attempts to suppress anti-imperial nationalism would be futile, Macmillan's government sought to ensure that the new rulers of the former colonies would become diplomatic partners, Cold War allies, and diligent custodians of British economic interests. For the more assertive leaders, like Nkrumah, who found the implications and conditions of full Commonwealth membership politically unacceptable, the colonial authorities offered the more informal option of "friendly association" as a way to remain within the British sphere of influence.

Nkrumah, however, had an entirely different agenda, and in the three years that elapsed between Ghanaian independence and his address to the UN General Assembly, he had already made it explicitly clear that he would not play the role of dutiful ally. Wrapped in an orange, gold, green, and brown cloth, which the *New York Times* compared to a Roman toga, the Ghanaian president earned enthusiastic applause from the Eastern Bloc countries for his verbal assault on the new imperialism.[2] Nkrumah directed his most vehement criticism at Belgium's continued meddling in the Congo, South Africa's apartheid policies and refusal to relinquish the former German colony of Southwest Africa (Namibia), Portuguese settler colonialism, and French nuclear testing in the Sahara, but he also implicitly refuted the most cherished and central ideologies of British imperial rule by declaring that "for years and years Africa has been the foot-stool of colonialism and imperialism, exploitation and degradation."[3] Although he kept Ghana in the Commonwealth after independence, Nkrumah also made it clear that he would not accept undue or overt British diplomatic guidance or economic influence. "African countries need to be on their guard against what I call clientele-sovereignty, or fake independence, namely, the practice of granting a sort of independence by the metropolitan power, with the concealed intention of making the liberated country a client-state and controlling it effectively by means other than political ones."[4] If the colonial authorities actually had a long-standing plan for the transfer of power, Nkrumah's Ghana was hardly the outcome they envisioned.

Even worse, Nkrumah's criticism of Western rule in Africa meshed neatly with the liberationist rhetoric coming out of the Soviet Union. Following the Ghanaian president to the General Assembly podium, Nikita Khrushchev enthusiastically took up his anti-imperial cudgel. Conveniently disregarding the reality that the Soviet Union was essentially the old tsarist empire under new management, the Soviet premier attacked the Western powers for using punitive expeditions, exploitive monopolies, secret tribunals, reservations (native reserves), colour bars (racial segregation), and concentration camps in their empires, and he attributed substandard life expectancies, high rates of illiteracy, and low national incomes among subject peoples to "colonial slavery."[5] Like Nkrumah, Khrushchev also took direct aim at the British Empire's central legitimizing paternalistic ideology when he declared, "The peoples of the new states have proved conclusively that they are not only able to do without the control and trusteeship of the colonial powers and government themselves, but that they are active builders of a new life and incomparably more sensible administrators and thrifty managers of their possessions, of their country's wealth, than the colonial authorities."[6]

Despite the American Secretary of State Christian Herter's declaration that Nkrumah had "marked himself as very definitely leaning toward the Soviet bloc through his rhetoric and associations in New York," Nkrumah's commitment to neutrality meant that he was definitely not a Soviet puppet. Neither was Jawaharlal Nehru, who combined a similar doctrine of Cold War impartiality with unapologetic attacks on Western imperial rule, even though India also remained a member of the Commonwealth. The Indian prime minister was one of the primary organizers of the 1955 Asian-African Conference at Bandung, Indonesia, that laid the groundwork for the Non-Aligned Movement and resolved that "colonialism in all its manifestations is an evil which should be speedily brought to an end."[7] Even the Harry Truman and Dwight Eisenhower administrations challenged the legitimacy of the new imperialism by emphasizing strenuously that the United States was not a power with imperial ambitions.

This convergence of anti-imperial nationalism and Cold War rhetoric was one of the central factors in Macmillan's decision to accelerate the timetable for winding down the empire. In 1945, Britain had been able to ensure that the original United Nations Charter made no explicit mention of decolonization apart from a vague admonition to the imperial powers to administer their colonial territories "in the interests of the inhabitants" and with an eye toward "self-government or independence" at some point in the comfortably undefined future. By the early 1960s, however, the number of independent former colonies in the General Assembly had grown large enough to force a fundamental sea change in the UN policy on formal empire. General Assembly Resolution 1514 (XV) 1960 explicitly declared that "the subjection of peoples to alien subjugation, domination and exploitation constitutes a denial of fundamental human rights."[8] The United States and Great Britain both abstained from this "Declaration on the Granting of Independence to Colonial Countries and Peoples," and there were no dissenting votes whatsoever.

At the end of World War II, the Labour Colonial Office calculated that benevolent paternalism, economic development, and expanded local governance would blunt the appeal of anti-imperial nationalism and convince subject peoples that it was possible to pursue their aspirations for self-determination under the protective umbrella of a reformed and modernized British Empire. In time, it became increasingly clear that these assumptions were unrealistic and unsustainable. The popular dissatisfaction with the empire in the 1940s led to widespread unrest in the 1950s as nationalist intellectuals found common cause with frustrated middle-class elites and restive workers, farmers, and the growing urban unemployed. Widespread opposition to the second colonial occupation and its invasive development agenda required territorial governments to adopt authoritarian countermeasures that scuttled the Labourites' experiments in gradual political reform. Imperial governance depended on the cooperation of at least a segment of the subject population to remain viable and cost-effective, but by the 1950s more and more people concluded that there were alternatives to British rule. This popular nationalism made British rule too fiscally and diplomatically expensive as the economic and strategic value of the formal empire declined steadily.

Given these realities it was understandable that metropolitan British politicians and strategists came to the conclusion that it was time to cut their losses. This was largely a rational calculation that the returns of the imperial project no longer justified their cost to the British metropole. The colonial authorities' public claims about Nkrumah's Ghana being the logical outcome of a master plan for decolonization was an attempt to make the best of a bad situation. Sally Chilver, secretary of the Colonial Social Science Research Council and the Colonial Economic Research Committee, was much more honest when she admitted that the Colonial Office sought primarily to get out "without getting one's tail caught in the door."[9] In attempting to peacefully transfer power to a sufficiently Anglicized and cooperative generation of nationalist leaders, Macmillan's government sought to preserve the economic and strategic benefits of empire without incurring the costs of direct imperial rule. In effect, this was an attempt to turn back the clock to the informal empire of the mid-nineteenth century when Britain's industrial and commercial preeminence and uncontested naval power were more than sufficient to protect its global interests. This was certainly no longer the case when Nkrumah spoke at the United Nations, but even more fundamentally, the colonial authorities actually did very little to prepare the remnants of the second British Empire for independence. Having inherited narrow representative political institutions that barely extended beyond the municipal level, stunted education systems, and neo-mercantile economies that remained geared to producing bulk raw materials for export, Nkrumah and his peers faced the daunting challenge of turning dysfunctional colonies into viable nation-states.

WANING ENTHUSIASM FOR EMPIRE

Given the pomp and ceremony celebrating the second British Empire in the first half of the twentieth century, it would be easy to imagine that its erosive decline after World War II would cause considerable anxiety and soul-searching in the British metropole. In fact, most Britons were largely unconcerned with the fate of their empire. Apart from colonial scandals in Uganda, Bechuanaland (Botswana), and British Guyana and anti-imperial insurgencies in Malaya, Kenya, and Cyprus, the metropolitan public remained largely ignorant of the fundamental changes taking place in the wider empire. As noted in chapter 1, a 1951 poll by the Government Social Survey Unit found that almost 60 percent of Britons could not name a single British colony and that 88 percent of respondents did not understand how colonies earned dollars.[10] Yet this is not to say that the events in the wider empire did not have political consequences in Britain. Although the House of Commons spent surprisingly little time debating imperial topics as the 1940s drew to a close, minority factions within the Labour and Conservative parties remained deeply concerned about such matters.

Conservative imperial partisans still believed that the empire made Britain stronger, particularly as an alternative to greater economic and political integration with continental Europe or deference to the growing power of the United States. Party activists joined with private groups like the Royal Empire Society, the Victoria League, and the British Empire Producers' Organisation to promote greater imperial integration and self-sufficiency through protective tariffs, expanded agricultural research, improved communications, and some form of common imperial citizenship. Most therefore did not oppose the Labour government's implementation of the Colonial Development and Welfare Act in the postwar years, but they distinguished themselves from their socialist rivals by arguing that private enterprise was the most effective instrument of development. Consequently, Winston Churchill and the Conservatives, who returned to office in the 1951 elections, continued many of the Labourites' colonial policies.

In shifting to the opposition, the mainstream Labour leadership paid relatively little attention to imperial matters except when colonial scandals acquired metropolitan political dimensions. This was in contrast to a broad spectrum of backbench Labourites and more ardent private organizations that became more explicitly and openly critical of the empire as an institution over the course of the 1950s. This humanitarian lobby included the Anti-

Slavery Society, the National Council for Civil Liberties, the National Peace Union, the International Conference of Free Trade Unions, Christian Action, Racial Unity, the London Missionary Society, the Moderators of the Church of Scotland, and the Africa Bureau. Each group had its own agenda, but for the most part they criticized the excesses of settler colonialism and promoted policies designed to make British rule more humane and progressive. The Movement for Colonial Freedom, however, called for self-determination and full independence for all subject peoples. Led by the parliamentarian Fenner Brockway, this loose coalition of progressive clergymen, trade unionists, and left-wing Labour activists provided political backing, legal advice, and material aid to the anticolonial nationalist movements that sprang up throughout the empire in the 1950s.[11] As would be expected, the Communist Party of Great Britain had an even more strident anti-imperial agenda. For the most part, however, the leftist critics of empire had no more influence over imperial policy in the 1950s than their right-wing counterparts.

The empire's minor role in mainstream metropolitan politics stemmed largely from its declining economic value. Initially, the remaining colonies did contribute to postwar reconstruction. Between 1945 and 1951, the Treasury spent £40 million under the Colonial Development and Welfare Act and extracted £140 million from its overseas territories in return.[12] Although this was a considerable sum in Africa, it did not come close to covering the cost of postwar reconstruction in the metropole. The most significant factors in Britain's recovery were renewed American aid under the Marshall Plan, dollar-earning exports from the entire sterling area (which included independent sovereign states), and the devaluation of the pound. Even then, the sterling area's imports and exports still remained out of balance, and the short-term economic boom resulting from the Korean War gave way to renewed inflation resulting from an unresolved dollar deficit. Acknowledging this reality, the 1952 Conference of Commonwealth Prime Ministers issued a communiqué directing that "development should be concentrated on projects which directly or indirectly contribute to the improvement of the [sterling] area's balance of payments with the rest of the world."[13]

This meant colonial economic policy was still geared toward producing dollar-earning bulk raw materials for export. The Colonial Office and individual territorial governments therefore had little choice but to continue the unpopular and invasive economic policies of the immediate postwar years. Although the spectacular failure of the Tanganyika Groundnut Scheme embarrassed Clement Attlee's government, the era of "big development" was definitely not over. The state-directed projects that were still in operation in the early 1950s included the Gezira Cotton Irrigation Scheme in the Sudan, the Sukumaland Development Scheme in Tanganyika, the Mwea and Perkerra irrigation schemes in Kenya, the Kigezi Resettlement Scheme in Uganda, and the African Farmer's Improvement Scheme and Peasant Farming

Scheme in Northern Rhodesia. The Conservatives also kept the Colonial Development Corporation (CDC) running despite the fact that many of its projects proved to be extremely inefficient and wasteful. In the West Indies, the CDC hired a hotel manager in British Honduras (Belize) before actually building a hotel, and one of its banana plantations in Dominica employed seven times the workforce of similarly sized local estates while producing only one-sixth of their output. [14]

These policies retarded economic growth in the colonies. Seeking to preserve the value of the pound, the metropolitan Treasury blocked territorial governments from using their dollar earnings to buy machinery and construction materials that could be used for actual local development. Furthermore, the unpopular marketing boards that had sparked political unrest in Uganda and the Gold Coast in the late 1940s were still in operation and continued to bank their growing cash reserves in London. Making no apology for privileging metropolitan British interests, Sir Charles Lockhart of the Overseas Food Corporation reminded the African colonial governors in 1953 that "development" meant the "development of agriculture," and he ruled out any sort of colonial industrialization on the grounds that it drew investment and manpower away from "primary" agricultural production. [15] By the time Churchill turned over the prime ministership to Anthony Eden in 1955, these unpopular and inefficient development strategies were not generating sufficient returns to justify their expense and diplomatic and political costs. The development of synthetic alternatives to colonial raw materials, the expansion of metropolitan agriculture, and compelling American pressure for Britain to allow open trade with full sterling convertibility raised significant questions about the overall economic value of the empire.

The Conservative governments of the early to mid-1950s were not yet ready to accept these economic realities. This was particularly true in Malaya, where, as noted in chapter 4, the ongoing Emergency, essentially a Chinese communist revolt, cost the Treasury roughly £6 million per year in 1951. [16] Although it had limited popular support, the Malayan Races Liberation Army waged a tenaciously effective insurgency against the colonial infrastructure. Beginning in 1948, it disrupted rubber and tin production by attacking mines and plantations and terrorizing the local workforce. Three years later, the guerrillas assassinated Malaya's British high commissioner, Sir Henry Gurney. Although these were considerable blows, retreat was out of the question, for Malayan tin and rubber were strategic commodities and important dollar-earning exports. General Sir Gerald Templer, who became high commissioner in 1952, therefore undertook a comprehensive counterinsurgency campaign that won over the Malays with political reforms and isolated the guerrillas by confining their civilian supporters to fortified villages. With large numbers of regular British army units tied up in the Korean War, Templer fought the insurgents with local security forces and imperial troops from Fiji and East and Central Africa. These tactics, which had their origins in the South African War, brought the Emergency to a close in 1955, thereby allowing British administrators to resume planning for a larger self-governing Malayan federation.

Colonial officials were also moving gradually but steadily toward federation in the West Indies. Acknowledging the minimal returns of their ambitious postwar development plans, they saw an even greater need to create a more economically viable administrative unit by uniting the small island colonies. By the early 1950s, most individual territories had acquired a large measure of autonomy as democratically elected politicians assumed responsibility for local administration. The Colonial Office hoped these reforms would reduce the labor unrest that plagued the West Indian territories and was generally willing to allow the new leaders a free hand so long as they did not challenge Britain's economic or strategic interests in the region.

The 1953 elections in Guiana, the only British colony on mainland South America, demonstrated the limits of this policy by bringing to power a regime whose radical policies threatened British sugar and bauxite production in the territory. Led by Cheddi Jagan, an American-trained dentist with strong socialist leanings, the new government intervened firmly on the side of Guyanese workers in their struggles with foreign employers. Claiming that Jagan had a pro-communist agenda to nationalize the economy and drive all Europeans out of the territory, Churchill's government suspended the constitution and sent in troops to remove him from office. The Guyanese case sent a powerful message to the other West Indian colonies that there were sharp limits to self-rule within the empire.

Moreover, unrest in the British West Indies persisted because political gradualism and local self-rule were not much use to the landless and urban unemployed. By the 1950s, pervasive slums were a central part of life in most major West Indian cities. Lacking basic services like running water and sewers, these could be difficult places to live where too many people survived through petty trading and criminal activity. Overlooked by both the colonial administration and middle-class politicians, slum residents created a new urban culture that celebrated the defiance of authority and nurtured new styles of music that, as we shall see in chapter 6, had a strong influence on youth culture in metropolitan Britain. On Trinidad, groups of tough young men like the saga boys were popular heroes in the 1940s. In Jamaica, the gangster Ivanhoe "Rhygin" Martin became famous for his gunfights with the police. By the 1950s, many of these outcast groups had formed alliances with Rastafarians and other independent Christian groups that stood outside mainstream society. Their increasing militancy and defiance tested the limits of Britain's constitutional reforms. Local politicians won a measure of political power in the 1950s, but the Guyanese case demonstrated that they risked British intervention if they attempted to address what they saw as the root causes of urban poverty by ending the economic privileges enjoyed by foreign employers and other colonial special interests.

This was also the case in British Africa, where the pace of constitutional advance was considerably slower. In 1951, the Gold Coast was the only African territory to win a measure of self-rule on the West Indian model. Responding to the strikes and riots of the late 1940s, the 1949 Coussey Constitution established an elected legislative council that chose eight of the seats on the eleven-person executive council. According to the Colonial Office blueprint for local self-government, Andrew Cohen and the Gold Coast authorities expected that the relatively moderate and cooperative class of cocoa-growing elites would seize this opportunity. Instead, Kwame Nkrumah won over the electorate with his call for immediate independence. He drove this point home through a program of nonviolent "positive action," which resulted in the general strikes that landed him in prison. Although Nkrumah had an unsigned British Community Party membership card in his pocket when the Gold Coast police arrested him, chapter 4 has shown that Governor Charles Arden-Clarke felt he had no choice but to release him from prison after his Convention People's Party (CPP) won a decisive victory in the 1951 elections. The Gold Coast prison director resigned in protest rather than report to one of his former prisoners.

Once Nkrumah realized that the British government was serious in its intention to withdraw from West Africa, he became a cooperative partner. Declaring that "we shall give the constitution a chance," he accepted an arrangement where he served as prime minister under the supervision of a British governor until the Gold Coast became fully independent in 1957. This arrangement reassured potential foreign investors and donors, and senior colonial officials answered South African criticism that their "weakness and capitulation" was a "betrayal of the white race in Africa" by insisting that the compromise would "promote goodwill and retain [British] influence" in the region.[17]

At first glance, the Gold Coast reforms appeared to fulfill the basic demands of the African nationalists, but as in India, the prospect of independence inflamed ethnic and social divisions as rival factions competed to inherit power from the colonial regime. Nkrumah was a popular leader who had established himself as a respected anticolonial voice in the wider Pan-Africanist movement, but he faced significant challenges to his authority in the Gold Coast itself. Leaders of the Asante community, recalling that they once had a powerful precolonial empire, sought to reassert their autonomy after independence by insisting that the new state adopt a federal system of government. They demanded thirty reserved seats in the legislature and greater control of their cocoa earnings. This was a significant claim, for in 1955 the Gold Coast's cocoa exports totaled £66 million, which was approximately 69 percent of the colony's entire export revenue.[18] Led by a group of young men calling themselves the National Liberation Movement (NLM), Asante militants drove Nkrumah's supporters from their territory. The situation grew so tense by 1954 that worried colonial officials drew up plans to evacuate the colony in the event of civil war. Nkrumah cleverly resolved the problem by using age and class appeals to divide the Asante and isolate the NLM. In 1956, he convinced Asante chiefs and wealthy farmers to support his government in return for a promise that he would guarantee their influence and status after independence.

These sorts of compromises papered over the deep cleavages that existed in most African colonies. Frederick Lugard and the other architects of British colonial Africa drew arbitrary territorial boundaries that rarely reflected pre-existing political, ethnic, and religious affinities and identities. As a result, most colonies had diverse populations with little in common beyond the shared experience of living under British rule. This was not much of a problem before World War II when it appeared that the empire would last for centuries. But the prospect of autonomy, if not independence, led diverse African communities to worry about their status in a postcolonial nation-state where an elected majority would be able to impose its will on the rest of the population.

British officials hoped a federal system, in which specific regions or communities were assured a measure of autonomy, might defuse some of these tensions. In Nigeria, where Lugard had joined northern Muslim savanna lands with the wealthier and largely Christian southern forest belt to reduce administrative costs, the colonial authorities proposed a postcolonial federation consisting of three separate eastern, western, and northern regions. Each would have its own legislative assembly, executive government, and civil service. Federation was supposed to keep Nigeria intact, but unfortunately it reinforced the divisions between northern Muslims and members of the predominately Christian Ibo and Yoruba communities. Some nationalists suspected that the federation plans were part of a plot to weaken the postcolonial Nigerian state, but Britain's primary concern was to withdraw as smoothly as possible from West Africa.

Mindful of French plans to grant self-rule to their colonies, British officials were most concerned with engineering an orderly transfer of power because they did not want to be left as the sole imperial power in the region. Their primary goal was to protect British economic interests by transferring power to cooperative African governments. Thus, at the stroke of midnight on March 6, 1957, the Gold Coast became the sovereign nation of Ghana. In ceremonies that included joyous street celebrations and a formal flag-lowering ceremony that became a model for the various transfers of power to follow, Nkrumah was careful to balance his declaration that the populace had regained its "lost freedom" with reassurances that Ghana would remain within the Commonwealth. When the United Nations voted unanimously to admit the new African nation-state several days later, the British UN representative triumphantly declared it a "proud day" that demonstrated the flexible and democratic bonds that united the British family of nations. [19]

Although the Gold Coast's rapid but bumpy progress to self-rule and nationhood could be seen as the logical end point of the postwar Labour government's local self-government initiatives, this strategy was only feasible in West Africa, where there were no entrenched settler communities. Self-government and planned decolonization looked very different in Britain's eastern, central, and southern African territories during the 1950s. In Kenya and Northern and Southern Rhodesia, privileged settler minorities, which had no intention of withdrawing from Africa, tenaciously defended the racist institutions that underpinned their political preeminence and allowed them to exploit African land and labor. In 1955, there were 200,000 Rhodesians and 6 million African subjects in British Central Africa; in the East African colonies, the ratio was 60,000 Europeans to 18 million Africans. [20] The decentralized nature of British imperial rule meant that the authorities in London actually had limited control over individual territorial governments, which allowed conservative colonial officials and politically influential settlers to block the West African model of decolonization. Their intransigence also prevented the Colonial Office from granting Ghanaian-style self-rule to colonies like Uganda, Tanganyika, and Nyasaland, which did not have significant European populations, because Africans in Kenya and the Rhodesias would have demanded the same concessions.

At first, these limitations did not particularly trouble imperial policy makers because they had no intention of imposing a West African solution on their settlement colonies. Even the Labour colonial experts who aspired to reform the British Empire accepted that the European populations in Africa were there to stay. So instead of planned decolonization, they offered their subjects "partnership" in "multiracial" societies that would progress toward nationhood through a series of gradual constitutional reforms. Implicit in this arrangement was an assumption that Africans had to accept a period of continued political subordination in return for the economic prosperity that would come when the new colonial development policies bore fruit. Once the African majority reached an equal level of "civilization" with the European settlers, they would share power in fully democratic societies. In the short term, however, they would have to be the junior members of the partnership because they were constitutionally unequipped to mix with Westerners on equal terms. In opposing a motion in the House of Commons to ban racial discrimination in the empire, several prominent Conservative imperial partisans claimed that this social colour bar was necessary because Africans could not handle alcohol or firearms, believed that sexual intercourse with a "white woman of any age" was a cure for venereal disease, and put infant boys to sleep by the "the excitation of their uro-genital organs." [21]

These stereotypes and prejudices dictated that Africans could never come to power in the settler colonies. Therefore the multiracial constitutions granting Africans a greater measure of representation still allocated legislative seats based on ethnic quotas that did not reflect their numerical superiority. Although the precise ratios varied from territory to territory, European settler representatives (known as "unofficials") and appointed members of the administration invariably retained control over legislative and executive councils. In effect, multiracialism preserved settler privilege and colonial control while creating the illusion of democracy and self-government.

In the years following World War II, the Labour Colonial Office justified this institutional inequality by asserting that a long period of European minority rule was necessary because of the "present inability of the majority to stand alone in the strenuous conditions of the modern world."[22] The proponents of multiracialism claimed that it would draw capital to British Africa by assuring foreign investors that the territories would remain politically stable under British influence. Although this view seemed reasonable and valid to the well-meaning colonial authorities in London, in Africa multiracialism was little more than an excuse for preserving institutionalized racial discrimination. In public, the Kenyan government insisted that it had no laws that explicitly discriminated on the basis of race, but in 1949 Governor Philip Mitchell admitted to the Colonial Office that a wide array of Kenyan regulations and statutes prevented Africans from living permanently in European areas in the "white highlands," used public health as an excuse to mandate urban segregation, barred "natives" from consuming "spirituous liquors," criminalized "illicit sexual connections" with white women, and made "civilization" the basis for civil service pay grades.[23]

In the Rhodesias, formal discriminatory laws barred non-Europeans from skilled and semiskilled trades in urban areas, and the settler population insisted on a wide-ranging program of social segregation that humiliated Africans on a daily basis. Banned from European restaurants, hotels, and public transportation, they had to enter post offices through separate doors and purchase food through small hatches cut into the outer walls of grocery stores. The situation was particularly bad in Southern Rhodesia, where unchecked postwar immigration taxed the resources of the colony. Nevertheless, the Rhodesian authorities insisted that high living standards for Europeans had to be maintained to ensure that new arrivals did not "degenerate quickly, and become 'poor whites' or intermarry with the natives."[24] African interests, by comparison, were secondary, and most Southern Rhodesians agreed with their prime minister, Godfrey Huggins, when he declared, "Yes, it will be a partnership—such as exists between a horse and rider."[25]

Given these realities it was understandable that most educated Africans were unmoved by the idealistic rhetoric of multiracialism. Tom Mbotela, an African nominated member of the Nairobi City Council, asserted forcefully that the settlers were in Kenya to make a comfortable home for themselves and not as "trustees for the African people." Dismissing the fundamental premise of multiracialism, he maintained that arguing that "the African had not reached a comparable stage of civilisation does not make the African a less rightful owner of the African continent."[26] If Mbotela, whose nomination to the city council marked him as an African "moderate," rejected the central premise of Labour's new imperial policy, then there was little hope of winning over the greater subject population.

The authorities in London ignored these realities and reassured themselves that polite manners, patience, and expressions of goodwill could mitigate the inherent discrimination of settler colonialism. This paternalistic optimism informed their grand designs for African federations, which were the logical extension of the long-standing British policy of joining smaller territories together to create larger, more governable and economically viable political units. Theoretically, these federations were a framework for multiracial partnership that would provide a viable alternative to the West African model of decolonization. But while this strategy produced Australia and Canada in the nineteenth century, Britain's federation-building efforts in the West Indies, Malaya, the Persian Gulf, and Africa during the post–World War II era floundered because they sought to unite disparate and unwilling populations who insisted on self-government, if not national independence, on their own terms.

This was particularly true in East and Central Africa, where educated Africans recognized that expatriate Europeans would dominate any federation, which was precisely why the settler communities supported federation building so enthusiastically. Vehement African opposition in Uganda and Tanganyika to any formal relationship with settler-dominated Kenya forced the Labour Colonial Office to create the East African High Commission, which was an economic rather than a political unit, as a substitute for a formal federation in the years after World War II. Most East Africans were not convinced. Government assurances that the commission's sole function was to promote development and coordinate common services like the railways and the postal service failed to allay suspicions that it was a thinly disguised stepping-stone to a formal political federation that would have enshrined settler privilege.

The Central African Federation (CAF) was even more controversial. Combining Northern and Southern Rhodesia into a single self-governing dominion had been a cherished goal of the local settler community since the 1920s, but the deeply racist Southern Rhodesian colour bar made this a political impossibility in metropolitan Britain. In the aftermath of World War II, the Rhodesians initially had to settle for the Central African Council, which served most of the same economic functions as the East African High Commission. However, the growing influence of the Union of South Africa in the region, particularly after the right-wing National Party came to power in 1948, forced the Colonial Office to reconsider its opposition to creating some form of formal political federation in Central Africa. It did not matter that most Africans believed the CAF would lead to increased European immigration, thereby blocking their progress toward self-government and eventual independence on the West African model. Arthur Creech Jones's Africa expert, Andrew Cohen, pressed on by drawing up a plan in cooperation with the Commonwealth Relations Office (CRO), which had jurisdiction over Southern Rhodesia and the High Commission Territories of Swaziland, Basutoland, and Bechuanaland, to link the Nyasaland and Northern Rhodesia protectorates with the colony of Southern Rhodesia.

Fearing that the steady postwar migration of Afrikaners northward would pull the Rhodesias into South Africa's orbit, or worse actually absorb them as a fifth province of the union, the Labour Africanists concluded that a federation was the only way to keep Central Africa British, given that there was actually very little the metropolitan government could do to impose its will on the Rhodesian settlers. Southern Rhodesia's prime minister, Godfrey Huggins, and the Northern Rhodesian settler leader Roy Welensky were well aware of this weakness. Seeking to bring the federation into being as swiftly as possible, they exploited the Labour government's South African phobias by calling for the abolition of the Central African Council and threatening to sabotage the Colonial Office's multiracial constitutional experiments in Northern Rhodesia.

The Rhodesians' goals for the Central African Federation made the Labourites' naive aspirations for multiracial cooperation entirely unworkable. In February 1949, Huggins, Welensky, and their allies convened a conference at Victoria Falls, where they drew up a blueprint for the CAF that guaranteed their dominance of the proposed federation by equating one hundred Africans with a single European for the purposes of determining representation in the new federal legislature. Although Cohen grumbled that the formula was hardly "consistent with the currently accepted doctrine about the rights of man," he still insisted that the CAF was necessary on the grounds that federation would mobilize resources for development and keep South Africa's new apartheid policies out of the Rhodesias.[27] This did not mean that Cohen was pro-settler. Rather, he considered it politically impractical and economically unwise to try to pave the way for planned West African–style decolonization by dislodging expatriate Europeans.

It mattered little that both educated and ordinary Africans vehemently rejected any political arrangement that placed them at the mercy of the Rhodesian settlers. Although conventional imperial rule could be frustrating and occasionally humiliating, Colonial Office supervision was far preferable to the Rhodesian colour bar. As one Scottish journalist put it, "Colour prejudice in Northern Rhodesia is not the worst in the world, but it is probably the worst in any British colony."[28] This is why the African population of the Nyasaland Protectorate was virtually unanimous in its opposition to Labour's federation plans. Having a settler population that numbered only in the thousands, they recognized that inclusion in the proposed federation would seriously damage their chances for self-government. Cohen dismissed these fears in insisting that Nyasaland had to be included in the CAF because a federation required more than two territories. He also wanted it to offset the Rhodesian settler influence in the federal government. Brushing aside Governor G. F. T. Colby's private but increasingly insistent appeals for his territory to be left out of the CAF, Cohen was adamant that in the long run federation would benefit Nyasaland's African population by facilitating the flow of migrant labor to the Rhodesias and attracting foreign investment to the admittedly impoverished protectorate.

In taking this position Creech Jones, Cohen, and their counterparts in the Commonwealth Relations Office, which was much more inclined to sympathize with the Rhodesian settlers, refused to accept the reality that the proponents of the CAF-supported federation intended to stifle African nationalism. Along with the nationalist government in South Africa and imperial partisans in metropolitan Britain, the Rhodesians were particularly revolted by the developments in the Gold Coast. Under the doctrine of multiracialism, full participatory democracy and national self-determination became the equivalent of "racialism" (i.e., racism) because it meant that an African majority would disenfranchise the privileged settler minority. According to the Conservative colonial secretary Oliver Lyttelton, who enthusiastically took up the cause of federation after the Labour government fell in 1951, universal suffrage would have "handed over to primitive and largely illiterate people the task of not only running but building a modern state." Lyttelton went on to add, "It is difficult to see how anyone, however starry-eyed, imagines that the complete swamping of the European vote by 20 to 1 could do other than lead to political disaster, administrative chaos, and the strangling of all the skills and capital which are required to bring these countries to prosperity and sound government."[29] By this rather twisted reasoning, multiracialism became the moderate middle ground between the extremism of South African apartheid and the African nationalism of Nkrumah's Gold Coast. South Africa and the Gold Coast thus became the dual bogeys that justified the Central African Federation, and in public the CAF's supporters rebutted left-wing humanitarian criticism of the federation by promising that it was the most effective means of containing the union's extremist apartheid policies.

Behind the scenes, the Labour government proved surprisingly willing to conciliate the South Africans. This was particularly true in the case of Seretse Khama. Seretse was the recognized heir to the Ngwato paramount chieftaincy, which was the largest and most important "native unit" in the Bechuanaland Protectorate. A grandson of the ruling dynasty's founder, Khama III, he succeeded to the chieftaincy at age four and grew up under the regency of his father's half-brother Tshekedi, a strict authoritarian who became one of Britain's most reliable allies in southern Africa during the interwar years. In 1948, Seretse alienated both his uncle and the British authorities by marrying a young Englishwoman named Ruth Williams while studying law in London. Tshekedi, whose long-standing opposition to interracial intimacy was in keeping with the sexual mores of neighboring South Africa, opposed the marriage adamantly. Claiming that Seretse's rash decision to wed a European without consulting his elders marked him as unfit for the chieftaincy, he tried to use the wedding as an opportunity to supplant his nephew permanently. This strategy backfired, however, when a mass gathering of Ngwato male elders voted overwhelmingly to support Seretse, a landslide that most British observers attributed to an expression of "no confidence" in Tshekedi.

By all rights this relatively minor dynastic squabble should have remained confined to Bechuanaland, but Seretse's marriage to a European coincided with the National Party's rise to power in neighboring South Africa. The Labour Commonwealth Relations Office therefore became deeply concerned that South African and Rhodesian settler opposition to Seretse's marriage would provide the union with the excuse to intervene in Bechuanaland, Basutoland, and Swaziland and provide an opportunity for the nationalist regime to forge closer ties to the Rhodesias. In 1949, the South Africans drove this point home by declaring Ruth Khama a "prohibited immigrant" in the union. This created a significant problem because the Bechuanaland Protectorate's capital was at Mafeking, which was inside the borders of the Orange Free State.

Although most all metropolitan British politicians expressed revulsion at the National Party's racist apartheid policies, which included a law outlawing "mixed marriages," British strategists still believed that it was essential to keep South Africa from leaving the Commonwealth. But the Labourites could and would not admit that their desire to appease the union had an impact on their policies in the High Commission Territories. Instead, British High Commissioner Evelyn Baring recommended that the CRO use a relatively obscure rule giving the Bechuanaland government the authority to "confirm" all new paramount chiefs in the protectorate to block Seretse from power. Tshekedi helpfully provided additional cover by asking for a formal judicial inquiry to determine whether his nephew's marriage had rendered him unfit to serve as paramount chief. Yet the commission of inquiry headed by the chief justice for the High Commission Territories created more problems than it solved when it reported in November 1949 that Seretse's "prospects of success as a Chief are as bright as those of any Native in Africa with whom we have come in contact," while still ruling that his marriage disqualified him for the chieftainship because it had offended the Union of South

Africa. Concluding that "a friendly and co-operative Union of South Africa and Southern Rhodesia is essential to the well-being of the [Ngwato] and indeed the whole of the Bechuanaland Protectorate," Chief Justice Sir Walter Harrigan recommended that Seretse be exiled from the protectorate on the grounds that his continued presence would make effective administration impossible by "unsettling the tribe."[30]

The Harrigan report was so politically embarrassing that the British government never released it to the public, but this did not prevent the Labour Commonwealth Relations Office from using its conclusion that Seretse constituted a threat to the "peace and good order in the [Ngwato] reserve" as an excuse to banish him. In February 1950, the CRO invited him to London to discuss the situation and offered him an allowance of £1,100 per year to follow the example of Britain's King Edward VIII by abdicating and going into exile. When Seretse declined, the Commonwealth secretary, Patrick Gordon Walker, refused to allow him to return to Bechuanaland, which prompted the rightful Ngwato chief to hold a press conference to demand the release of the Harrigan report and to cable his supporters in Bechuanaland, "Tribe and I tricked."[31]

The resulting furor forced Gordon Walker to stretch the truth mightily by telling the House of Commons that South African racial sensibilities had no impact on his decision to exile Seretse for five years. Instead, he insisted that he had acted to prevent the clash between Seretse's and Tshekedi's followers from disrupting the protectorate. Unconvinced by these feeble excuses, Seretse's many supporters charged the Labour government with betraying the color-blind ideals of the Commonwealth by caving into South African racism. Left-wing imperial critics joined with noteworthy Britons of non-European descent, like the famed West Indian cricketer Learie Constantine, to form the Seretse Khama Fighting Committee, and even the Conservative party leader Winston Churchill, who had no doubts about the merits of the empire, called the CRO's tactic of luring Seretse to London under false pretenses a "very disreputable transaction." In answering these charges and defending his decision to ignore the overwhelming preference of the Ngwato people for Seretse, Gordon Walker clung tenaciously to the doctrine of colonial trusteeship. Reminding his critics that the Ngwato "were not a sovereign people," the Commonwealth secretary insisted that the CRO had acted appropriately because "we must stay [in Bechuanaland] to preserve order and good government, and to preserve the integrity of the territory, we have responsibility, and we must have rights to go with that responsibility."[32]

The paternalistic assumption that the vast majority of Africans were still too backward to make informed political judgments also provided the Colonial and Commonwealth Relations offices with the excuse to continuing planning for a Central African Federation. In February 1951, Gordon Walker embarked on a tour of southern Africa that convinced him that friendly containment of South Africa and good relations with the Rhodesians was the only way to prevent the National Party's racism from spreading northward. "Should we, intentionally or by default, throw British communities in East and Central Africa into the arms of the Union our whole work in Africa would be undone. The policies that we detest in the Union would be established far to the North and in the heart of this part of our Colonial Empire. Millions of Africans would be subjected to oppression. Terrible wars might even be fought between a white-ruled Eastern Africa and a black-ruled Western Africa."[33] For Gordon Walker, appeasing the Rhodesians was the key to avoiding this racial Armageddon. Turning a deaf ear to the concerns of the vast majority of southern Africans, he concluded that the native policies of settler-dominated Southern Rhodesia and the Colonial Office's Nyasaland and Northern Rhodesia protectorates were essentially compatible in that their ultimate objective was "the economic, social and political advancement of the Africans in partnership with the Europeans." He attributed the colour bar and the seemingly obvious differences in how the three territories treated Africans to minor local disparities in "method and timing." By this rather remarkable reasoning, Gordon Walker concluded that Britain was obliged to ignore African opinion. "By listening to the protests of Africans and others against any truck with Southern Rhodesia we would in the end betray our trust to the Africans by being unable effectively to protect them against South African Native policy."[34]

Andrew Cohen and James Griffiths, who had replaced Creech Jones as colonial secretary in 1950, shared most of these views, including the need for haste in creating the Central African Federation. In March 1951, the Colonial and Commonwealth Relations offices jointly hosted a conference of Rhodesian and Nyasaland administrators in London that drew up the formal federal blueprint. At a time when the Gold Coast was well on the way to full self-government and independence, the officials planned for a settler-dominated federal legislature with authority over external affairs, defense, immigration, higher education, and economic policy. The Labourites convinced themselves that Africans would be protected by keeping Northern Rhodesia and Nyasaland under Colonial Office jurisdiction, giving each territory control over its own native policies, creating a federal African Affairs Board, and appointing a minister for African interests with a seat in the federal cabinet. The board and the minister would then check discriminatory legislation by referring it to the British parliament for review. Cognizant of the near universal African opposition to the scheme, Griffiths publicly assured African leaders and the members of the metropolitan humanitarian lobby that the British government would not allow federation to go forward without African support. Behind the scenes, Cohen minuted, "We must not . . . simply take the line which is likely to be most popular with Africans. It is also our business to do what we believe is in [their] genuine interest."[35]

The CAF's Labour sponsors thus plunged ahead with their plan on the assumption that the economic benefits of federation would eventually produce a prosperous African middle class that would work in partnership on relatively equal terms with the Rhodesian settlers. The Conservatives generally agreed with all of these assumptions and quickly issued a statement that they would continue the push for federation in Central Africa when they came to power in October 1951. Highly effective lobbying by bureaucrats like Andrew Cohen in the Colonial Office and his counterpart, G. H. Baxter, in the CRO ensured that the new and relatively inexperienced Tory ministers accepted the central premises of the federal project.[36] Like their predecessors, they believed that most Africans were not equipped mentally to make informed political choices, and they trusted that greater foreign investment and economic development through territorial integration would eventually generate popular support for the CAF.

The most significant difference in the Conservatives' approach to federation was that they tended to openly favor the settlers. Lord Milverton (Arthur Richards), who had opposed Creech Jones's imperial reform program as the governor of Nigeria, told the House of Lords, "The Europeans [in Central Africa] are just as much entitled to have their interests safeguarded as are the Africans. Some of us to-day are so busy in being fair to other people that we have no time . . . to be fair to our own people."[37] To this end, the Conservative Colonial and Commonwealth Relations offices allowed the Southern Rhodesians to strip out many of the measures intended to protect Africans at the federal level. The final CAF blueprint dropped the minister for African interests and diluted the authority of the African Affairs Board considerably.

Colonial Secretary Oliver Lyttelton and his counterpart in the CRO, Lord Salisbury, strove futilely to find a few cooperative Africans who would consent to the new plan, but the most influential chiefs and community leaders in Nyasaland and Northern Rhodesia boycotted the conferences that finalized the arrangements for federation. In April 1952, an African nominated member of the Northern Rhodesian legislature told a London press conference, "Southern Rhodesia has put Africans down in the ditch and we cannot see how federation with it will lift us up in any way." In Nyasaland, one hundred chiefs signed a petition to the Crown that declared, "We are not willing to purchase economic advancement by the sacrifice of political rights and civil liberties which we believe would result from surrendering us into the power of European settlers." Kamuzu Hastings Banda, a Nyasaland medical doctor practicing in London who would eventually become the first president of independent Malawi, infuriated the colonial experts by rebutting the case for federation point by point. Declaring that it was absurd to conclude that there was no difference between the Southern Rhodesian colour bar and the native policies of the two northern protectorates, he pointed out that the CRO had never intervened in Southern Rhodesia to block discriminatory legislation.

Banda also rightly pointed out that federation would actually accelerate the northern migration of right-wing Afrikaners, and in his opinion the best way to keep Central Africa British was to give Africans full political rights.[38]

Once out of power, Creech Jones and Griffiths joined the metropolitan humanitarian lobby in adding their voices to these protests. Insisting vehemently that federation should not be imposed from above, they attacked the final version of the CAF in Parliament and the metropolitan press. The Conservatives justifiably pointed out that they were following through on their predecessors' plan, but intense criticism from Central Africa posed a huge problem. British missionaries and journalists reported that opposition to the CAF in Nyasaland and Northern Rhodesia was virtually universal, and multiple African delegations visited London to express their opposition. Faced with this wholesale rejection of federation, the CAF's supporters fell back on the old imperial gambit of depicting the African critics as a small, unrepresentative, and self-interested clique of detribalized elites (the "classes") who either intimidated or agitated illiterate tribesmen (the "masses") into opposing what was ultimately in their best interests. In parliamentary debates, many of the Tory proponents resorted to gross stereotypes to make their case. Julian Amery claimed that most Africans were no more politically aware than ancient Britons at the time of the Roman invasion, while Archer Baldwin declared, "One has only to go a few yards off the highway to find oneself in an African reserve, where the people are living as they have done for 1,000 years."[39] Still, there were cautionary voices from the Conservative camp. Recalling that dismissing popular anti-imperialism as the work of a few disgruntled agitators had left the Raj unprepared for the explosive growth of Indian nationalism, the venerable empire expert Lord Hailey warned,

> I am told . . . that we must not make . . . too much of African opinion because there is no such thing as African opinion . . . but only a certain number of vocal Africans who lead others along the path they have chosen for them. Well, I used to hear a great deal of that kind of argument when I first went to India. . . . But gradually we came to learn for ourselves the truth that . . . a number of advanced and . . . aggressive people [had] assumed leadership of the country for the mass of the people. . . . Sooner or later we have to reckon with that class of opinion [in Central Africa], and it would be exceedingly unsafe to neglect it now.[40]

Although Hailey was to prove prescient, the federation plans were too far along to be abandoned or even modified. On August 1, 1953, the British government legislated the Central African Federation into existence. The mood in London was optimistic and self-congratulatory. In South Africa, Prime Minister D. F. Malan withheld comment, but he also made the metropolitan backers of federation squirm by declaring that Godfrey Huggins had assured him that Southern Rhodesia supported the union's apartheid policies.

Africans in the Rhodesias were sullen but hopeful that the CAF might actually force a relaxation of the colour bar. Nyasaland, by comparison, erupted in violence. In suppressing widespread riots and protests, particularly in the southern province, the security forces killed eleven and injured seventy-two. The government had to depose and exile several prominent chiefs who had ordered their communities to ignore unpopular agricultural and forestry regulations. The protests even marred the grand plans to celebrate Queen Elizabeth II's coronation. The Nyasaland Boy Scouts refused to play their assigned roles in the typically elaborate ceremonies, and students at the Lubwa mission school in Northern Rhodesia threw down their cakes and sweets, defaced their special coronation medals, and sang nationalist protest songs. They uprooted a special coronation tree so many times that the school authorities had to replant it in a secret location.[41]

It is tempting to conclude that Labour's African specialists would have been more inclined to respect African opinion and abandon their federation plans if they had remained in power, but only the Labour Party's most extreme left wing actually questioned the authoritarian paternalism that was integral to imperial rule. Imperial matters in the early 1950s only generated significant political controversy when the Conservative Colonial and Commonwealth Relations offices took mutually agreed-upon policies further than the Labourites were willing to go. This was the case with many of the festering African problems they inherited on coming to power in 1951. Concluding that an ongoing noncooperation campaign organized by Seretse Khama's supporters was risking South African intervention and blocking the Bechuanaland administration's plans to appoint a new paramount chief, in March 1952 the Commonwealth secretary provoked an outcry in the protectorate and the House of Commons by deciding to banish Khama and his family permanently rather than reviewing his case after five years, as Gordon Walker had planned.

Churchill's government adopted permanent exile as the solution to a problem in the Kingdom of Buganda that was also arguably the result of Labour's colonial policies. In this case, Andrew Cohen, who had left the Colonial Office to assume the governorship of Uganda after the Conservative electoral victory, touched off another enormous imperial controversy by deposing and banishing Kabaka Mutesa II in November 1953. "King Freddie" was the kind of tradition-bound aristocrat that the Labour Africanists viewed as an impediment to development and local representative government. More fluent in English than Luganda, the thirty-fifth *kabaka* was a Cambridge classmate of Colonial Secretary Oliver Lyttelton's son and had shared a cigarette with George VI as an honorary colonel in the elite Grenadier Guards. But he also scandalized the Anglican clergy in Uganda by having extramarital affairs with several women, including his own wife's sister.

The actual crisis that led Cohen to exile Mutesa began in July 1953 when Oliver Lyttelton told an overwhelmingly pro-settler audience at the East African Dinner Club that the next step in the federation-building process was to bring political unity to Kenya, Uganda, and Tanganyika. Mutesa and the Gandan *lukiko* (parliament) reacted with alarm and demanded that the British government shift responsibility for the Kingdom of Buganda from the Colonial Office to the Foreign Office as the first step toward independence on the Gold Coast model. Dismissing the Colonial Office's assurances that they would not be forced into an East African federation against their will, they disrupted Cohen's local self-government plans by refusing to nominate three Gandan representatives to the expanded territorial legislative council on the grounds that doing so would have suggested that the Kingdom of Buganda was a mere province of Uganda.

In Cohen's eyes, this was Mutesa's greatest sin. The Ugandan governor cared little about the *kabaka*'s private life, apart from worrying that Mutesa might not be able to attend state functions if the Anglicans excommunicated him for adultery, but standing in the way of Cohen's grand development plans was unacceptable. Brushing aside Mutesa's insistence that as *kabaka*, he had to respect the wishes of the *lukiko*, Cohen expected him to follow his own example in pushing through the CAF by ruling benevolently but despotically. Mutesa, for his part, disparaged Cohen's brand of authoritarian development colonialism: "Sir Andrew Cohen arrived with a host of ideas which were to benefit Uganda whether Uganda liked them or not. Where the ideas of the country did not fit, it was the country that was going to be altered."[42] As the deadlock dragged on over several months in the fall of 1953, the *kabaka* and his advisors steadfastly refused to appoint the legislative council representatives or acknowledge that Buganda was an inherent part of the Uganda Protectorate because doing so would have violated the democratic principles of Gandan parliamentary procedure. Moreover, continuing pressure for democratic reform from the Ugandan National Congress and the Gandan populists who were behind the 1949 unrest covered in chapter 4 meant that Mutesa could not afford to side with the colonial regime against the *lukiko*.

Having tried angry lectures, sincere appeals of friendship, and finally an ultimatum, Cohen and Lyttelton agreed that their only recourse was to depose King Freddie and replace him with his elder brother, who they assumed would be more cooperative. On November 30, 1953, the governor handed Mutesa a document that withdrew British recognition of his kabakaship because he had violated the terms of the 1900 Uganda Agreement by failing to accept British "advice." The protectorate government prepared for potential unrest by mobilizing the army, and the commissioner of police was on hand with a police detachment to place Mutesa under arrest and escort him to the airport, where a plane was set to take him to London.

Cohen had apparently calculated that his strong record of promoting development and local self-government would protect him from criticism in metropolitan Britain, but he soon found, much to his dismay, that his heavy-handed tactics had turned the *kabaka* into a sympathetic figure. Mutesa's elite friends from his Cambridge days stuck with him, his fellow exile Seretse Khama expressed solidarity, and the left wing of the Labour Party rallied to his cause despite the fact that they also professed to respect Cohen as a liberal-minded colonial administrator. A delegation from Buganda soon arrived in London to affirm that Mutesa remained the legitimate ruler of Buganda and to lobby for his return, thereby demonstrating that Cohen had inadvertently succeeded in uniting the disparate Gandan factions against British rule.

This set the stage for one of the oddest parliamentary confrontations of the 1950s, in which James Griffiths, the former colonial secretary who had appointed Cohen, attacked the Conservative government for exiling a "feudal monarch" whom the Labourites claimed to hold in low regard. Lyttelton found himself in the equally unusual position of defending Cohen's actions by citing the Ugandan governor's excellent record on development. The colonial secretary also made a pious speech professing how much he did not want to have to approve Mutesa's exile: "It was extremely painful to me because of the dignified and correct bearing of the Kabaka in all these matters. It was more painful to me because he was member of my university and of my regiment, and a friend of my son's at Cambridge." In this Lyttelton was being more than a bit disingenuous. The notes of British cabinet discussions reveal that in private he told his fellow government ministers that the *kabaka* could never return to Buganda because he "has lived with own sister, had child by her, as well as sister-in-law. Long record of homo-sexuality also: with English men: which persists. Treats his wife v. badly: allows her only £300 [per annum] while he spends thousands."[43] These scandalous rumors accusing the *kabaka* of incest and homosexuality circulated widely in London during the early months of his exile, and they did little to help the government's cause because they were unsubstantiated. This led many of Mutesa's supporters, including many senior British clergymen, to suspect that he was the victim of a Colonial Office smear campaign.[44]

Collectively, the British government's heavy-handed tactics in exiling Seretse Khama and Mutesa and implementing the CAF over near-universal African opposition reflected a willful disregard for the changing realities in Africa in the early 1950s. The result was a series of embarrassing but largely manageable imperial controversies. The situation in Kenya during this period was much more serious. The first signs that landlessness and unemployment, resulting from the wholesale eviction of African laborers (squatters) from the settler-controlled white highlands and rising population pressure in the native reserves, had driven substantial numbers of Kikuyu, who constituted the largest African community in the colony, to desperation came in the late 1940s. Angry young people challenged the authority of elders and colonial chiefs compromised by their role in colonial administration, maimed settler cattle, and began to stockpile homemade guns and firearms stolen from settler homesteads and state armories.

The Kenyan security services were entirely unaware of these developments until the early 1950s when small, loosely organized bands of Kikuyu guerrillas began to raid police stations, attack mission converts, and assassinate high-ranking chiefs and moderate African political figures. Tom Mbotela, the Nairobi City Council man who had spoken so eloquently against partnership and multiracialism, was one of their victims. These killings undermined the very foundations of British imperial rule in Kenya by attacking the colonial regime's most important African intermediaries. Most alarming to the settlers, however, was the relatively small number of cases in which the insurgents slaughtered isolated European farm families. All told, only thirty-two European civilians died during what became known as the Mau Mau Emergency, but the killing of Western women and children by armed bands of African men played upon the deepest and most fundamental fears of the settlers, who now realized the full implications of living as a privileged minority among a sea of poor and desperate people.

Even more alarming, it soon became apparent that the Kenyan police were entirely unequipped to deal with the bands of fighters who hid in the forests or Nairobi's African slums. In October 1952, Evelyn Baring, who became governor of Kenya after serving as the British high commissioner in South Africa, had little choice but to declare a state of emergency in the colony. This gave him the authority to detain nearly two hundred suspected subversives, including Jomo Kenyatta, without trial. Baring also had to call in a brigade of troops from the regular British army in an effort to restore order. This admission of weakness and unpreparedness was a particularly embarrassing development for the Kenyan government because it had to draw on British imperial forces that were already stretched thin in Korea, Malaya, and West Germany.

Unwilling to accept that the sudden explosion of pent-up violence was due to their misrule and failed trusteeship, the colonial authorities groped for explanations. Since the rebellious Kikuyu committed spectacular acts of violence and bound themselves together with a variety of secret and seemingly alien oaths, the Kenyan authorities concluded that the revolt stemmed from an inability to cope with Western "modernity." As the government's official report put it, "[Mau Mau] arose from the development of an anxious conflictual situation in people who, from contact with an alien culture, had lost their 'magic' modes of thinking." The missions viewed the uprising as a "demonic upsurge of the old heathen faith—and the communalism which required every member of the tribe to submit to the sanctions of the tribal spirits."[45]

The very term "Mau Mau," which had no actual meaning in any Kenyan language, lent credence to these lurid and tribalistic interpretations. It mattered little that insurgents did not use the term and actually called themselves the Kenya Land Freedom Army (KLFA). Alternatively and quite illogically, some imperial partisans, who recalled that Kenyatta had visited the Soviet Union in the 1930s, tried to tie the Emergency to the Cold War by attributing it to Soviet "subversion."

On the surface, the Mau Mau Emergency shared several commonalities with the Emergency in Malaya. Both were guerrilla wars in which small bands of lightly armed men operating from the protection of dense forests initially managed to stand up to the military might of the British Empire. But the Malayan rebels were avowed Chinese communists who struggled to win support from the greater Malay population, while most Kikuyu were tacit Mau Mau supporters. The colonial regime was fortunate that the revolt did not spread to the other Kenyan communities. The Mau Mau Emergency was, at its core, a Kikuyu civil war rather than an atavistic backlash against the modern world or a nationalist anticolonial uprising. Lacking the means and opportunity to attack the institutions of British rule directly, the guerrillas lashed out at the colonial regime's Kikuyu allies in their own community. The Mau Mau hard men targeted the chiefs, wealthy farmers, mission converts, and other "loyalists" whose ties to the Kenyan state allowed them to prosper at the expense of the majority. Alarmed at the realization that perhaps 90 percent of the Kikuyu population had taken some form of Mau Mau oath, the Kenyan government raised a twenty-five-thousand-man loyalist "home guard" to respond to these attacks and limit further spread of the contagion.

The distinction between home guardsman and KLFA soldier was never clear-cut. Unwilling and intimidated conscripts filled out the ranks of both forces, and many people adopted the pragmatic solution of supporting the loyalists by day and the KLFA by night. It was also not unusual for the Emergency to split families, and the noted Kenyan novelist Ngugi wa Thiong'o had a brother on each side of the conflict. This intimacy often had fratricidal consequences as both factions resorted to arson, intimidation, terror, and even mass murder. This was the case with the infamous Lari massacre in which members of the same small community used the Emergency as an excuse to refight old battles over land and cooperation with the colonial regime. The resulting violence left more than four hundred men, women, and children dead.[46] The nuances of these sorts of tragic incidents were lost on the colonial authorities, and they used the Lari slaughter and other equally internecine explosions of violence to bolster their claims that Mau Mau was a savage tribal uprising and not a consequence of their own misrule.

FROM THE SUEZ CRISIS TO THE WIND OF CHANGE

In Britain the general public largely accepted the Kenyan explanation for
Mau Mau, and only the small humanitarian lobby and the left wing of the
Labour Party raised doubts about the colonial government's handling of the
Emergency. The metropolitan government's stubborn and largely bipartisan
commitment to multiracialism in Africa demonstrates that planned decolonization was only for West Africa. By the end of 1953, the controversies in
Central Africa, Bechuanaland, Uganda, and even Kenya had produced minimal political consequences at home, and the Labour Party's attempt to introduce a motion censuring the Conservative government for its mishandling of
African affairs went nowhere in the Commons. Far from paying a price for
their imperial partisanship, the Tories emphasized imperial themes in their
successful election campaigns during the 1950s.

Neither Winston Churchill nor Anthony Eden, who succeeded him as
prime minister, ever had any intention of dismantling what was left of the
empire. In the mid-1950s, many Britons would have agreed that this was the
correct course. Reassuring themselves that the fundamental challenges to
British rule in East and Central Africa were the work of a few opportunistic
agitators, the leaders of the main political parties naively continued to place
their faith in multiracialism and partnership. The Commonwealth was important, as were good relations with its newest members, but the rising anti-
imperial challenge from the new nations in South Asia that came out of the
April 1955 Asian-African Conference in Bandung was of little consequence
for most imperial strategists at this point. From Malaya to the West Indies,
colonial officials sought to use gradual constitutional reform to co-opt moderate political leaders and blunt the appeal of nationalism, and it is quite
possible that they would have tried to prolong the empire's life span more
tenaciously had not events in the Middle East forced a hard reconsideration
of its diplomatic, political, economic, and moral costs.

Although Britain had given up the Palestine, Iraq, and Transjordan mandates by this time, it still had significant strategic Middle Eastern interests in
the 1950s. The oil fields in Iraq, Arabia, and Iran (Persia) remained vitally
important to the metropolitan economy, and the Suez Canal remained an
essential link to Australia, New Zealand, and the remaining Asian half of the
empire. British strategists tried to share the cost of defending their interests in
the region by creating a Middle Eastern Defence Organization that would
have included the United States, France, Turkey, and the emerging Arab
nations, but the plan fell apart when the Egyptians and Syrians refused to
join. With the old Labour strategy of courting "peasants not pashas" producing few results, Churchill's government relied on the sprawling Suez Canal
Zone bases, along with a string of lesser fortified military installations in

Malta, Cyprus, Iraq, and Aden, to exert regional influence and deter Soviet expansion.

The great weakness of this strategy was that it underestimated the intensity of local hostility toward even informal imperial influence. In 1951, a new nationalist regime in Iran under Prime Minister Muhammad Mosaddeq lost patience with foreign control of its natural resources and cancelled Britain's oil concessions. The outgoing Labour government considered military intervention to protect British investors but had to back down because Britain's armed forces, already stretched to the limit with the loss of the Indian army, were not up to the task. Although they could still buy Iranian oil, Churchill and the Conservatives were determined to keep a stronger hold on their remaining Middle Eastern assets.

The Crown colony of Cyprus, which had been a key British base since the late nineteenth century, was central to this strategy. Its ports and airfields had become even more strategically important after the loss of Palestine, and it hosted an important radio listening post and the British army's general headquarters for military intelligence for the Middle East. Rather than seeking independence, Greek Cypriots, who constituted roughly 80 percent of the population, demanded to be united with Greece. Led by a Cypriot veteran of the Greek army named Georgios Grivas and Archbishop Makarios III, the leader of the Orthodox Church on the island, the National Organization of Cypriot Struggle (known by the Greek acronym EOKA) launched a guerrilla war against British rule in 1955. Although the conflict was relatively small at its outset, the government of Cyprus had to declare a state of emergency because its security forces were entirely unprepared to deal with an anticolonial insurrection.

The center of Britain's Middle Eastern problems, however, lay in Egypt. With Palestine gone, the Suez Canal Zone bases became even more central to British defense planning, and in the early 1950s the size of the imperial garrison was over forty thousand troops. The continued presence of these foreign soldiers, coupled with ongoing controversies over the status of the Sudan and anger over Britain's role in the creation of the new Israeli state, made Egyptian public opinion profoundly anti-British. This left King Farouk's government little room to maneuver. Over the course of the 1940s, radical nationalists and Islamicists assassinated two prime ministers they judged too willing to compromise on Arabist and Islamic ideals. It was therefore not surprising or unexpected that Prime Minister Mustafa El-Nahas voided the Anglo-Egyptian Treaty and the Sudanese Condominium Agreement, whereby Britain and Egypt shared in the government of the Sudan, when negotiations over the Suez Canal Zone broke down in 1951. The Egyptians stepped up the pressure by withdrawing the civilian labor force from the Suez bases, which forced the Middle East Land Forces Headquarters to recruit over ten thousand East African pioneers (military laborers) to keep the installations running. Much more seriously, Egyptian irregulars placed the Suez Canal Zone under siege by launching guerrilla attacks on British military personnel and property. In January 1952, these confrontations erupted into a series of pitched battles that led to serious anti-Western rioting throughout the country.[47]

This aggressively nationalist stance did not, however, generate much support for the Egyptian king and his unpopular government. In July 1952, a military faction known as the Free Officers used the widespread rioting sparked by British attempts to disarm Egyptian policemen in the Suez to overthrow King Farouk. General Mohammed Neguib formally led the soldiers, but a young colonel named Gamal Abdel Nasser soon emerged as the true ruler of Egypt. At first the British government hoped that the new regime would be more open to negotiation, but Nasser kept up the pressure on the Suez Canal Zone bases and established the "Voice of Cairo" to broadcast anti-imperial propaganda to East Africa. The situation grew so bad by 1954 that John Strachey, a former secretary of state for war in the Labour government, described the Suez as "little more than a concentration camp in which an enormous proportion of the overseas part of our Army has to spend at least some of its overseas service."[48]

These developments eventually forced Churchill to accept that Britain's position in Egypt was no longer tenable. The Suez bases drained dwindling military resources, hindered recruitment, and cost £50 million per year. Using the excuse that the Soviet's new hydrogen bomb had rendered the bases indefensible, the Conservative government withdrew from both the Suez and the Sudan. This was over the strenuous objections of a hard-core pro-empire faction of their own parliamentary block known as the "Suez Group." In return, the Egyptians acknowledged Sudanese independence and granted Britain the right to reoccupy the Suez if a foreign power threatened the canal.

To compensate for this strategic retreat, the British government revived plans for a Middle Eastern mutual-defense alliance. In 1955, Pakistan, Iraq, and Turkey joined Britain in the Middle East Treaty Organization, popularly called the Baghdad Pact. Iran, whose nationalist government fell from power in 1953 in an American-sponsored coup, also became a member. Although this was primarily an anti-Soviet alliance, Nasser found it threatening because he recognized that the Baghdad Pact would isolate Egypt if the British convinced more Arab states to join. He therefore forged a mutual-defense arrangement with Syria and turned to the Soviet Union to end his reliance on Western military aid. When Britain and the United States responded by withdrawing funding from the Aswan Dam project, Nasser took the drastic step of nationalizing the Suez Canal in July 1956.

Nasser's tactics threatened both British interests in the Middle East and the security of the eastern half of the empire. In the late nineteenth century, Britain had dealt with nationalist threats to the canal by invading Egypt. This, however, was no longer feasible in the post–World War II era when international opinion had turned against imperial adventures. Instead, Anthony Eden, who succeeded an ailing and aging Winston Churchill as the Conservative prime minister, hatched a scheme with France and Israel to overthrow Nasser. The French were angered by Egypt's interference in the Algerian War, while the Israelis worried that Soviet weapons would tip the balance of power in the region. Israel put the plan in motion with a preemptive strike on Egypt in October 1956, thereby allowing Britain and France to pose as peacekeepers and reoccupy the Suez Canal Zone.

The failure of Eden and his allies to recognize that Cold War politics now trumped imperial security doomed the plan from the start. The United Nations General Assembly voted overwhelmingly to call for an immediate cease-fire, but the greatest casualty of the ill-considered plan was, at least in the short term, Anglo-American relations. Fearing that the Soviets would exploit the non-Western world's near universal hostility to the Suez invasion, the Eisenhower administration openly condemned the exercise as a colonial occupation. Alan Foster Dulles, the American secretary of state, threatened to end U.S. support for Britain's application for a loan from the International Monetary Fund if it did not withdraw its forces from Egypt. The value of the pound sterling dropped alarmingly, and critics around the globe pointed out that Eden's invasion of a sovereign nation, which unfortunately coincided with the Soviet military intervention in Hungary, had helped to legitimize the communist bloc's suppression of a legitimate nationalist revolution. A Canadian plan for a UN peacekeeping force gave Britain cover to withdraw in December 1956, but the humiliating reverse forced Eden to resign under the pretext of poor health.

In the wake of the Suez Crisis, Harold Macmillan, the new Conservative prime minister, adopted a more realistic view of the empire. The Conservative right wing and imperial partisans in general blamed the United States for opportunistically seeking to supplant Britain in Asia, Africa, and the West Indies, but it was hard to deny that the Suez debacle exposed Britain's fundamental military weakness and growing diplomatic isolation on questions of empire. Moreover, by this point it had become clear that the great postwar experiment in development colonialism would not produce its promised dividends. Britain's balance-of-payment problems led the Treasury to stiffen its opposition to making more development grants from metropolitan resources, particularly as the private sector was unwilling to invest in the remaining imperial territories. Just as the Indian Civil Service had struggled to recruit British university graduates after World War I, the colonial service, which became Her Majesty's Overseas Civil Service in 1956, now found it difficult to convince young Britons that the British Empire would survive long enough to provide them with stable and sufficiently lucrative careers. Quite understandable fears that postcolonial governments would not honor employment contracts or pension promises meant that half of the administrative posts in East Africa were vacant in 1955. [49]

Mindful of these realities, Macmillan asked the Colonial Office to estimate the value of the remaining African colonies to Britain. The report, issued in June 1957, concluded that decolonization in West Africa was not detrimental to British interests, but it warned that a retreat from East and Central Africa would lead to a loss of markets, capital flight, contraction of the sterling area, and greater Soviet intrusion in the region. However, the Colonial Office also concluded that no single territory was valuable enough to influence wider British policy decisions. These findings did not mean that Macmillan had immediate plans to retreat from British Africa, but they did signal that the metropolitan government's support for formal empire was weakening.

British military strategists similarly decided that nuclear arms had made colonial armies and massive base complexes unnecessary. This reconsideration began before the Suez invasion with a comprehensive review of imperial defense by the former Malayan high commissioner Sir Gerald Templer. In his April 1955 report, Templer pointed out that the empire's remaining small and undertrained colonial military units had little strategic value in the new nuclear age. Drawing on his experience with the Malayan Emergency, Templer also concluded that the postwar emphasis on colonial development had created many of Britain's overseas security problems by drawing resources away from the internal security forces. [50] In the aftermath of the Suez debacle, the British government undertook a further review of its defense needs in 1957 under the supervision of Minister for Defence Duncan Sandys. Mindful of the rising costs of imperial security, Sandys concluded that the Warsaw Pact nations were the most significant threat to metropolitan Britain and took Templer's recommendations a step further in arguing that British defense spending should be devoted primarily to developing a more robust and sophisticated nuclear deterrent. These conclusions dovetailed with Macmillan's cost-benefit analysis of decolonization. The result was an overall revision of defense strategy that emphasized nuclear weapons and relied on a pared-down network of military bases in relatively stable territories like Gibraltar, Malta, Aden, and Singapore to protect Britain's foreign interests.

This new imperial realism also applied to the economic sphere. Just as strategic policy reviewers adopted a more realistic approach to imperial defense, many industrialists, investors, and speculators concluded there was more profit to be made outside the empire and the sterling area. By the mid-1950s, the colonies and dominions provided only about one-tenth of British imports and exports. [51] The system of reciprocal tariff preferences between Britain and the empire dating from the Great Depression era had much less value when nonimperial customers were ready to purchase colonial minerals and cash crops. As currency pressures on the pound eased after 1952, there was also not as much need to use these exports to earn dollars. Moreover, the colonial sterling reserves became less important when wealthy oil-producing nations began to bank their earnings in London, and the sterling area, which included many nonimperial territories and countries, played a lesser role in the metropolitan economy as members drew down their reserves from these same institutions. By the end of the decade, the British government was managing budget deficits with loans from the International Monetary Fund, whose leaders required Britain to apply for membership in the European Common Market as a condition for further funding. Although France eventually vetoed the application, it was becoming clear that Europe was now economically more important than the waning empire and perhaps even the Commonwealth.

This shift from formal empire to informal influence that began with the demise of the Raj became more urgent in the late 1950s. As would be expected, the Suez Crisis accelerated the British disengagement from the Middle East. One complication was that the EOKA's guerrilla campaign and open fighting between the island's Greek and Turkish communities made it difficult to leave Cyprus. It took UN pressure and assistance from the Greek and Turkish governments to negotiate the accord that made the former Crown colony a republic in 1960. Under the terms of the agreement, the Cypriot Greeks and Turks shared power while Britain retained control of the island's military bases.

Things did not go as smoothly in the Arab heartland, where a cabal of military officers in Iraq overthrew and executed King Faysal II and his relatively pro-British prime minister Nuri al-Sa'id in 1958. The Iraqi revolution left Aden as the primary British military base in the area. The Baghdad Pact survived, but it became the Central Treaty Organization under largely U.S. sponsorship. Aiming to safeguard the strategic port of Aden, protect British oil interests in Arabia, and compensate for the loss of key airbases in Cyprus and Iraq, the British government convinced cooperative local shaykhs to accept the Federation of Arab Emirates of the South in 1959. At that moment, at least, the shaykhs' fear of the Egyptian radical Arab nationalism that had helped bring down the Hashemite regime in Iraq was greater than their aversion to British federation building.

Similarly, British strategists remained equally committed to federation building in Asia and the West Indies. In Malaya, where there were few troublesome settlers, it was a relatively easy matter to continue the ongoing transfer of power to moderate local nationalists. Unlike in Central Africa, British officials had some success in persuading the Malay, Indian, and Chinese communities to come to terms by allowing only multiracial political parties to participate in elections. In 1955, the Alliance Party, which consisted of the United Malays National Organization (UMNO), the Malayan Chinese Association, and the Malayan Indian Congress, won all but one of the fifty-two seats on the federal council. Tunku Abdul Rahman, the UMNO president, became chief minister and led the constitutional negotiations that resulted in Malaya's independence in 1957. Singapore remained a Crown colony until 1961, when it joined with Malaya and the former British possessions of Sarawak and North Borneo to form the Malaysian federation. With most communist Chinese leaders dead or in detention, Abdul Rahman and his allies agreed that the new nation would remain in the Commonwealth and the sterling area, respect foreign investment in rubber and tin production, and grant Britain continued access to its military bases.

The prospects for federation in the West Indies appeared similarly promising as the 1950s drew to a close. In 1956, the British government took the initial step of creating an administrative union of the ten British territories in the region with an appointed governor-general retaining control of defense, finances, and foreign affairs. Two years later, the West Indies Federation achieved full self-government with Sir Grantley Adams, the premier of Barbados, becoming the federal prime minister. The new entity covered eight thousand square miles and had a population of 3 million people. Rather ominously, however, it was also much weaker than the other British-sponsored federations. It failed to provide for a customs union, free movement of people, a common currency or postage, and even the power to tax.

The weak federal model in the West Indies thus contrasted sharply with the Macmillan government's determination to make the CAF work and to retain the eastern and southern African colonies. Still pinning their hopes on federation building and multiracial partnership, Conservative colonial policy makers still believed they could hold back the tide of African nationalism through economic development, gradual constitutional reform, and interracial friendship. In a book promoting careers in the Overseas Civil Service, a senior colonial official warned new recruits, "Do not, whatever you do, go ashore in your first Colony with the idea that you are one of a master race, come with a mission to administer an inferior people. . . . One tactless, ignorant or stupid remark by one junior officer may undo the work of years."[52] In practice, neither the Colonial Office nor individual territorial governments took tangible steps to open the senior ranks of the civil service, police, and military to Africans. Social and racial segregation remained a fact of life in most of British Africa, and many of the die-hard traditionalists in the colonial service who never lost their faith in tribal chiefs and Lugardian indirect rule continued to distrust the younger generation of educated Africans. Although the end of British rule in much of Asia and the West Indies was clearly in sight by the late 1950s, the Colonial Office continued to assure potential recruits that there would be no drop off in the demand for administrative officers in the remaining empire.[53]

This institutional naiveté was out of step with the swiftly changing political realities in Africa. Although metropolitan imperial partisans and senior colonial officials were certain that the end of imperial rule was still comfortably far off, mounting African opposition forced concessions as the decade progressed. The colonial authorities repeatedly told the populations of Bechuanaland and Buganda that the banishment of Seretse Khama and Kabaka Mutesa II was irrevocable and permanent, but both returned home from exile relatively quickly. Mutesa's restoration in October 1954 was particularly painful for Governor Andrew Cohen and the Ugandan administrative officers, for they had spent the better part of a year unsuccessfully trying to convince the Gandans to select a new *kabaka*.

Instead, the Gandans gave them a lesson in how indirect rule really worked. In a sophisticated campaign of resistance, combining legal action, deft propaganda, high political lobbying, and grassroots activism, Gandans worked together to remind Cohen and Oliver Lyttelton's Colonial Office how much local cooperation it took to run an African colony. They declared a day of mourning to lament the government's actions, boycotted colonial institutions ranging from Anglican church services to soccer matches, wore barkcloth coats and dresses in place of Western-style cotton clothing, and jeered Cohen when he appeared in public. In court, three members of the *lukiko*, advised by sympathetic British legal experts, challenged Cohen's right to depose Mutesa under the terms of the 1900 Uganda Agreement. The Uganda National Congress, which was one of the *kabaka*'s harshest critics, organized a general strike and boycott of foreign-owned shops, and Mutesa's wife, who most likely had little affection for her adulterous husband, wrote to Queen Elizabeth II, Indian prime minister Jawaharlal Nehru, and Kwame Nkrumah to express her "misery" at the loss of her spouse. Similarly, an association of elite Gandan women led by the wives of two of the regents that Cohen had appointed to rule in Mutesa's place collected money to support the *kabaka* in London and lobbied the colonial government for his return. When Cohen asked the *katikiro* (prime minister), Paulo Kavuma, to draw up a list of enemies for arrest and detention, he responded, "At the head of the list . . . must be my wife, for even she, though she loved me, was my enemy because of what had happened to the Kabaka while I was the Katikiro. After her the whole people of the Baganda were my enemies."[54]

In deciding to exile the *kabaka*, Cohen had rightly concluded that Mutesa's personal conduct had made him unpopular with a significant portion of the general public. However, the governor's authoritarian tactics rallied people from across the ideological spectrum, and indeed throughout the entire protectorate, to his cause. Gandan partisans viewed the *kabaka*'s deposition as an attack on their jealously guarded sovereignty, while the Uganda National Congress took it as a violation of the principles of self-rule. Faced with this uncharacteristically united front, there was little Lyttelton could do but search for a face-saving way to send Mutesa home. This came in the form of a special committee chaired by Sir Keith Hancock, director of the Institute of

Commonwealth Studies, which brokered an agreement whereby the Gandans agreed to choose representatives for the territorial legislative council in return for the right to select their own *kabaka*, who would rule as a constitutional monarch. This compromise paved the way for Mutesa's jubilant return in October 1954. Cohen claimed to be happy to have him back, but the debacle had clearly damaged his prestige. The *lukiko* shouted him down when he tried to announce the Hancock Committee's findings, and he lost his plumed gubernatorial hat when a crowd led by small children throwing stones and dust chased him from the parliament building.

In Bechuanaland, the end of Seretse's exile initially appeared far less triumphal and significant. Although the bulk of the Ngwato populace never stopped supporting their rightful paramount chief, the Commonwealth Relations Office, with its jurisdiction over the High Commission Territories, was far less concerned with African opinion. The Anglo-American Corporation's interest in developing Bechuanaland's significant mineral reserves forced the CRO to become more flexible because the Ngwato and the other main "tribes" owned the protectorate's mineral rights collectively. Anglo-American therefore needed the signature of the paramount chiefs to begin prospecting for diamonds in the tribal reserves, but the Ngwato threatened to disrupt their development plans by steadfastly refusing to choose a replacement for Seretse. The Commonwealth secretary allowed him to return home in 1956 on the condition that he open the way for a new paramount chief by renouncing all claims to hereditary rule. Seretse accepted these conditions, but he remained an enormously popular and influential private citizen.

This was in contrast to Mutesa's improving political fortunes in the second half of the 1950s. Although the *kabaka* was supposed to become a constitutional monarch with limited powers under the compromise that brought him back from London, in the short term his enhanced status allowed him to reward his allies with land grants and government appointments and to remove the chiefs and senior officials who had allied themselves with the colonial administration. Cohen damaged his plan to manage the transition to self-government in Uganda through his mishandling of Mutesa's exile, and the overall security situation deteriorated steadily in the late 1950s as the Uganda Police struggled to retain control and prevent the tensions between the reenergized Gandan nationalists and the Uganda National Congress, which had returned to its long-standing policy of opposing Gandan separatism, from fracturing the protectorate.

To the east, by comparison, the Conservative government could take some reassurance in the military defeat of the Kenya Land Freedom Army. Although in the early days of the Mau Mau Emergency the Kenyan authorities were certain that they were facing a well-organized and entrenched conspiracy, they were fortunate that the KLFA's leadership was divided among itself and had little popular support beyond its Kikuyu base. The colonial regime would have been in a much more precarious position if the revolt had spread to the colony's other communities. Initially, loosely organized bands of Kikuyu fighters moved relatively easily throughout the central Kenyan highlands because they had the element of surprise, but in targeting the Kikuyu chiefs and other loyalists, they failed to exploit this advantage by attacking vulnerable strategic targets like the railway, water supply, and electrical grid. By 1955, the British counterattack had largely ended their military effectiveness by driving them deep into the forests for protection. [55]

The Kenyan government's brutal counterinsurgency tactics, however, did far more to damage the long-term viability of imperial rule in East Africa than the lightly armed bands of Kikuyu fighters. The colonial authorities' inability to distinguish a loyalist from a Mau Mau guerrilla forced them to resort to the draconian tactic of incarcerating almost the entire Kikuyu population. This included rounding up and detaining virtually every Kikuyu person in Nairobi. Coming to the panicked conclusion that only 1 percent of the community was "reliable," the police and administration assumed that all Kikuyu were guilty until proven innocent. They detained without trial anyone even suspected of supporting the Mau Mau and used forced relocations to incarcerate everyone else in fortified villages built on the Malayan model. Only documented loyalists vetted by special screening teams and hooded informants escaped the net, and by the end of the military phase of the Emergency, there were roughly seventy thousand people undergoing state-sponsored "rehabilitation" in detention camps scattered in the remote corners of the colony, with about 1 million more in the new villages.

As in Malaya, it was a relatively simple matter to defeat the rebels once they were cut off from their civilian base of support, and Britain's military triumph was absolute and conclusive. According to official estimates, the army and security forces killed at least eleven thousand Kikuyu fighters by 1956. By comparison, the insurgents killed less than two hundred policemen and soldiers and approximately eighteen hundred "loyal" African civilians. [56] In the short term, the counterinsurgency operations and mass detentions succeeded in rescuing the settlers and preserving their political and social preeminence in the colony.

Yet this victory came at a considerable cost. By mid-1959, the British and Kenyan governments had spent over £55 million on the Emergency. This was a politically unacceptable expense during the era of postwar austerity and economic retrenchment, but the brutal conduct of the Kenyan settlers and security forces in suppressing the revolt was equally damaging. At first, the metropolitan press told the public that the Kenyan authorities were bravely fighting to contain a savage tribal uprising, but soon reports that this entailed summary executions, torture, fabrication of evidence, detention without trial, forced labor, and other gross violations of human rights began to filter out of the colony. The realization that the Kenyan government was tolerating, if not actively engineering, a program of state-sponsored terrorism damaged Britain's international reputation and its relations with the new non-European members of the Commonwealth. At home, the dirty war in Kenya further undermined public faith in the empire and the humanitarian ideals of development colonialism.

To make matters worse, the Mau Mau scandals coincided with renewed controversy over the character and conduct of the Central African Federation. Although Andrew Cohen and the other architects of the CAF had promised that development and prosperity would overcome African opposition to the scheme, it took only a few years for most people to realize that the Rhodesian promises to respect African interests were merely a ruse to win British support for federation. Many Southern Rhodesians had been born in the colony, but a large portion of them were recently arrived lower-middle-class Britons drawn by good weather, inflated wages resulting from the colour bar, low taxes, cheap African servants, and the promise of upward social mobility. Many colonial officials in the northern protectorates looked down on them as "low-grade," and the British humor magazine *Punch* referred to Southern Rhodesia as "a first-class country for third-class whites." Constituting less than 3 percent of the CAF's 7 million people, the European immigrants were determined to protect their privileges. To this end, Godfrey Huggins, Roy Welensky, and the other Rhodesian leaders would threaten periodically to declare themselves independent of British rule by undertaking their own "Boston Tea Party" in Central Africa.

Forced to acknowledge that they had little political or military leverage in Central Africa, the authorities in London allowed the Rhodesians to modify the central features of the federation. In 1957 and 1958, the federal assembly enacted a pair of constitutional measures that gave Africans greater representation while diluting their political influence through higher property and education voting qualifications and by giving Europeans a greater say in selecting the new African legislators. When the African Affairs Board, which was supposed to have the power to block this kind of discrimination, referred the issue to the British government, the Conservative majority in Parliament ignored the board's concerns and approved the measures on the grounds that they encouraged interracial partnership. This was over the vehement objections of the Northern Rhodesian and Nyasaland governments. Upon leaving his post in 1956, Nyasaland governor Sir Geoffrey Colby reported that his administration was now uniformly opposed to federation. His Northern Rhodesian counterpart, Sir Arthur Benson, was even more direct. Officially, he complained that the Southern Rhodesians never intended the CAF to be anything more than a "springboard" to the creation of a settler-dominated self-governing dominion in Central Africa, and in a private letter to a friend in the Colonial Office he went even further: "You know that [the federal election law] is wrong and I know that it is wrong and what is more our [political] masters know that it is wrong. But they don't give a damn. .... I have taken and kept as much as possible to myself the utter cynicism and complete lack of interest in the welfare either of the Federation or of Africa as a whole or of Britain's position in Africa."[57] Far from being moved by these heartfelt appeals, the Conservative government insisted that it was still possible to make the CAF work. Commonwealth Secretary Lord Home pushed the Colonial Office to make it clear to colonial administrators in Nyasaland and Northern Rhodesia that "federation has come to stay," and he called for the transfer of civil servants "whose heart is not in the task."[58]

Although many imperial partisans and bureaucrats in the Commonwealth Relations Office openly favored the Rhodesian settlers, they continued to claim that federation was in the best interests of the CAF's African majority. Economic development remained the central premise of this increasingly obvious fabrication. The Conservative government insisted that the CAF had made "spectacular progress" since 1953, but most of its seeming prosperity and increased foreign investment was due to the global boom in copper prices. In this sense, the CAF's primary function was to divert the earnings of the Northern Rhodesian Copperbelt to the Southern Rhodesian settlers. Governor Colby also complained that the federal treasury skimmed off customs duties and tax receipts, which were Nyasaland's main source of revenue, and actually spent very little on development projects in the protectorate. Moreover, the CAF's protectionist economic policies actually hurt poor Africans by eliminating subsidies on corn meal and increasing the cost of living through tariffs on inexpensive clothing and other basic consumer goods. Despite these realities, the federation's defenders continued, in what one noted economic historian has called "a curious violation of the laws of arithmetic," to insist that the CAF drove economic growth in Nyasaland and would eventually win over Africans throughout the federation through agricultural development and improved social services.[59]

These promises may have still sounded plausible in London, but they fooled very few people in Central Africa. Marginal economic growth, if it existed at all, did nothing to mitigate racial discrimination in the CAF. Far from eliminating or even relaxing the colour bar, the federation, as predicted, further institutionalized and spread racial discrimination in employment and most every aspect of urban life. In the Rhodesias, Africans had to enter post offices through separate doors and needed a specially stamped form from their employers to claim a package. Similar systems were in place for buses and hospitals, and Africans could buy meat, which was invariably substandard, only at select butcher shops. Even the Rhodesian Boy Scouts and Olympic Organizing Committee refused to consider relaxing their segregationist policies. On country roads, Europeans entertained themselves with "munt scaring" ("munt" was a corruption of the word for "person" that became a racial slur in the Rhodesias), which entailed aiming their cars at African bicyclists. [60]

It was therefore entirely understandable that Africans in Nyasaland continued to worry that the Conservative government would eventually turn them over to the Southern Rhodesians, particularly after it caved into Rhodesian demands for an early review of the federal constitution in 1960. Most observers rightly took this as a first step to granting the federation total self-government, de facto dominion status, and Commonwealth membership on par with the newly independent Gold Coast. The preamble to the CAF's constitution explicitly stated that Northern Rhodesia and Nyasaland would remain under Colonial Office supervision for as "long as their respective people so desire," but in 1958 the Commonwealth secretary argued that Britain should be prepared to transfer the two protectorates directly to the federation. "We shall probably . . . have to stretch the interpretation of the 1953 pledges, so as to be able to hand over the Northern Territories within a reasonable time. . . . We should not allow factious opposition from Africans in Northern Rhodesia and Nyasaland to deflect us from a policy of building up a strong Federation." [61]

Although they were not a party to British cabinet deliberations, it was not difficult for the young and relatively inexperienced leaders of the Nyasaland African Congress (NAC) to intuit the CRO's agenda. Recognizing that it was essential to have a say in the pending 1960 federal review, the NAC demanded an elected African majority on the Nyasaland legislative council. When the protectorate government balked, they invited Kamuzu Hastings Banda, the U.S.-trained medical doctor who had represented their interests in London during the 1953 anti-CAF campaign, back to Nyasaland in July 1958 to assume the Congress leadership. Two decades later, the Colonial Secretary Alan Lennox-Boyd recalled Banda telling him, "I go back to break up your bloody federation." [62]

Although many of the younger NAC leaders favored a Mau Mau–style campaign of violence against European settlers and businessmen, Banda's strategy was to follow the example of the Indian nationalists by rendering the protectorate ungovernable through mass noncooperation. This campaign entailed refusing to vote in local elections, boycotting European- and Asian-owned businesses, withholding taxes, and staging increasingly large and provocative mass demonstrations. As was the case in the Bechuanaland and Buganda protests earlier in the decade, African women played a central role in these efforts. The Congress Women's League was particularly effective in challenging the notions of gender propriety that underpinned Western rule in Africa by making rude and insulting gestures toward scandalized settlers and colonial officials.

By early 1959, the protests had grown too large for the police to control, but apart from the vandalism of government property and some stones thrown at settler cars, there were no significant attacks on Europeans. Never-theless, the government panicked when the Nyasaland Special Branch warned that the NAC was planning a mass slaughter of Europeans in the protectorate. This "murder plot" (as it became known in the British press) supposedly entailed the sabotage of airfields, roads, telephone lines, bridges, and power plants and the execution of all colonial administrators, their African allies, and their wives and children. Although these warnings came entirely from informers of questionable reliability, Governor Sir Robert Ar-mitage, who had survived an assassination attempt by EOKA guerrillas as governor of Cyprus, felt he had no choice but to declare a state of emergency.

Taking inspiration from the Southern Rhodesian government's mass ar-rest of five hundred African nationalists a month earlier, he authorized a similar roundup of the Nyasaland African Congress leadership. In the pre-dawn hours of March 3, 1959, the Nyasaland security forces launched Opera-tion Sunrise. Before the day was out, they had arrested 208 "hard-core" Congress members and flown them to federal prisons in the Rhodesias for detention without trial. As was the case during Kenya's Mau Mau Emergen-cy, the security forces swept up anyone with even the faintest connection to the NAC, which was an entirely legal political organization before the state of emergency. By November 1959, there were over two thousand Nyasaland-ers in federal prisons. Banda and the senior Congress leadership received relatively good treatment, but federal security officers subjected many rank-and-file NAC members to beatings, sleep deprivation, and other forms of illegal coercion in an effort to get them to confirm that there was indeed a murder plot.[63] The Nyasaland authorities claimed these drastic extralegal measures had preemptively suppressed the kind of mass anti-imperial upris-ings that had led to so much loss of life in the Punjab after World War I and Kenya in the early 1950s.

They were unprepared for the resulting popular backlash. The protecto-rate government lost control of large sections of the Northern Province for more than a week and had to rely extensively on the federal police and military to deal with mass protests and widespread acts of sabotage. After some deliberation, the Colonial Office gave the Royal Rhodesian Air Force permission to fire on crowds of rioters if they first conducted "preliminary dummy runs" to show their intentions.[64] Fortunately, unlike in the Amritsar case some four decades earlier, there were no air attacks on civilians, but in a little more than a month, the largely Rhodesian security forces killed fifty-one African men and women and wounded a great many others through gunfire and baton charges. The worst incident took place in northern Nyasa-land, where a detachment of outnumbered Rhodesian reservists in the all-European Royal Rhodesian Regiment killed twenty-two people by firing into a dense crowd of protestors at Nkata Bay. In contrast, there were no European casualties during the Emergency, despite the fact that many civilians found themselves in the hands of angry African crowds.[65]

The slaughter at Nkata Bay, which appeared to confirm the worst fears of the CAF's critics, produced a political backlash in London. Calling on the metropolitan and federal authorities to either charge or release Banda and the rest of the detainees, left-wing members of Parliament (MPs) and the rest of the humanitarian lobby rejected the Nyasaland governor's claim that the Nyasaland African Congress was planning a Mau Mau–style uprising and charged the Conservative Colonial Office with unfairly depicting a legitimate nationalist movement as a terrorist enterprise. Kanyama Chiume, a senior NAC leader who escaped detention because he was in London, worked with the Committee of African Organizations to call a mass protest in Hyde Park and challenged Colonial Secretary Lennox-Boyd to repeat the government's murder plot charges outside the Commons, where he could be sued for libel.

In answering these criticisms, the CAF's supporters in Parliament fell back on the standard excuse that Africans were too primitive to be trusted with political rights, but this stereotype finally rang hollow in an era when the West African colonies were on the verge of independence.[66] Macmillan had little choice but to appoint a commission to report on the circumstances in Nyasaland that led to the state of emergency and the violence resulting from Operation Sunrise. As with the Hunter Committee that investigated the post–World War I Punjab uprising and Amritsar killings, the Conservative government intended the commission to defuse a metropolitan political controversy by finding that the incidents of violent conduct by imperial security forces were either justified or due to the unauthorized actions of individuals.

It therefore came as a rude shock that the commission, which was made up entirely of reliable Conservative Party members and chaired by the respected high court judge Sir Patrick Devlin, found that "Nyasaland is—no doubt only temporarily—a police state, where it is not safe for anyone to express approval of the policies of the Congress party [and it is] unwise to express any but the most restrained criticism of government policy."[67] The Devlin Commission's conclusion that the state of emergency was justified because the government was losing control and some Congress members were planning violence without Banda's approval came as little comfort, particularly when the commissioners also found that the Nyasaland government's official report on the Emergency tried to make Banda appear more radical by omitting key words from his speeches. Equally damning was their finding that the security forces had used "unnecessary and illegal force" during Operation Sunrise and in the suppression of the ensuing mass protests. Further investigations revealed that the Rhodesian Special Branch had coerced detainees into making false confessions and coached them in how to give false testimony to the commission.[68]

Even more problematically for Macmillan's government, the Devlin Commission's report on July 17, 1959, came on the heels of the Colonial Office's admission that the Kenyan government's scheme to rehabilitate the most hard-core Mau Mau guerrillas still in custody had gone horribly wrong. Anxious to close down the sprawling network of detention camps, Kenyan prison officials concluded that the detainees' fear of their primitive oaths was preventing them from accepting the colonial regime's version of redemption. More specifically, the prisoners, who had spent years incarcerated without trial, had to confess that they had taken an oath to gain release and reabsorption into civil society. Tens of thousands of people took part in this charade to secure their freedom, but in 1959 a defiant group of slightly less than one hundred men held up the rehabilitation process by refusing to cooperate. In response, the prison authorities concocted a fantastic scheme to demonstrate that the oaths had no power by forcing the most defiant and committed prisoners to violate their vows by undertaking simple manual agricultural labor. Much like the Gandans and Ngwato, who stubbornly insisted on choosing their own leaders, and the Nyasalanders, who objected to the CAF, the detainees would be compelled by African prison wardens to pull weeds and thus recognize that the "tribal superstitions" preventing them from cooperating with the government had no power over them. Instead, in March 1959 the plan resulted in a mass beating whereby the African prison guards ended up clubbing eleven men to death.

Although the Kenyan authorities at first tried to claim that the victims had died from drinking contaminated water, the truth soon came out and triggered one of the most serious of the postwar colonial scandals in metropolitan Britain. The resulting investigations found that the use of violent force to compel prisoners to work was illegal.[69] Deeming the deaths to have been murders, a government critic in the House of Lords called the Hola scandal the "most shameful single event that has occurred in our Colonial history." Left-wing Labourites in the Commons were equally scathing, but the most damning criticism of the Kenyan colonial regime came from the Conservative MP Enoch Powell. Rejecting suggestions that the detainees were not entitled to the full protection of British justice because they were in some way "subhuman," as one of his Conservative colleagues had suggested, he declared, "We cannot say, 'We will have African standards in Africa, Asian standards in Asia and perhaps British standards here at home.'"[70]

Powell's genuine anger over the damage that the colonial scandals were doing to Britain's honor and prestige reflected a disenchantment with the empire lobby in the Conservative Party and metropolitan Britain in general. As Europe became more economically important than the Commonwealth or the remaining imperial territories, there was a growing bipartisan consensus that resources devoted to colonial development and police actions could be better spent on expanding social services at home. Macmillan himself was not a strong supporter of settler colonialism, and in 1943 he had proposed buying out and repatriating the Kenyan settlers while serving as a junior minister in the wartime coalition government. Having won a conclusive victory in the 1959 elections, which both removed some of the most ardent imperial partisans from Parliament and demonstrated that the metropolitan electorate was largely unconcerned with colonial issues, Macmillan was free to reconcile Britain's West and Central African policies by replacing multiracialism with nonracialism. In a sweeping policy review that coincided with the unfolding Hola and Nyasaland scandals, he reaffirmed that "self-government" was the main goal of colonial policy throughout the empire, but this no longer meant that Britain would mandate a particular constitutional model or continue to insist that the remaining colonies serve a "lengthy apprenticeship" before becoming nations.[71] The growing international rejection of formal empires that was apparent in the United Nations General Assembly's enthusiastic support for Nkrumah's vehement denunciation of "colonial slavery" also had an impact on the Conservative prime minister's pragmatic calculations.

Macmillan announced this shift in British colonial policy during a tour of Africa. Speaking to the South African parliament in February 1960, he declared that it was futile to resist the popular demand for complete self-rule: "The wind of change is blowing through this continent, and, whether we like it or not, this growth of national consciousness is a political fact."[72] After more than a decade of bipartisan wishful thinking by Labour and Conservative governments, a British prime minister finally acknowledged that the African rejection of foreign colonial rule was total and uncompromising. Right-wing Afrikaners were entirely unmoved by Macmillan's warning and believed they could contain African nationalism through violent repression. One month after the prime minister's call for accommodation and reconciliation, the South African security forces murdered over sixty unarmed African protesters in the black township of Sharpeville. In 1961, the nationalist regime severed all formal political ties with Britain by declaring South Africa a republic. The ruling Afrikaners were motivated in part by lingering anger over their treatment in the South African War and resistance to cultural Anglicization, but they also rejected the new Commonwealth, where Africans now had equal status as the rulers of sovereign states.

For the rest of British Africa, the now famous "wind of change" speech meant that the decolonization timetable was measured in years rather than decades. As had been the case in India, Palestine, and Cyprus, Britain's remaining African possessions would progress rapidly to independence regardless of their internal stability or economic viability. The increasingly overt hostility toward formal empires in the United Nations dictated the need for haste as Britain's rivals and former subjects used the British Empire to score political and diplomatic points. By 1960, the Israelis and Irish republicans had joined the Soviets, Chinese, Indians, and Egyptians in offering aid and support to aspiring African nationalists. Seizing the opportunity to remind the world of his country's painful history of British rule, the Irish Republic's *taoiseach* (prime minster), Sean Lemass, served notice that Ireland intended to play a role in African affairs by declaring, "We have . . . ourselves experienced all the teething troubles of nation building. Irish people have a natural sympathy with countries coming to independent status."[73] With French and Belgian decolonization well under way by 1960, expediency replaced tutelage as Macmillan's government scrambled to ensure that Britain would not suffer the ignominy of being the last imperial power in Africa.

These developments came as a shock in East and Central Africa. As late as 1959, the Colonial secretary, Alan Lennox-Boyd, had told the East African governors that independence was at least ten to fifteen years away. Moreover, British military strategists, who were curiously unaware of the implications of Macmillan's policy review, still considered Kenya a "fortress colony." Assuming that it would remain under British control for decades after the defeat of the Kenya Land Freedom Army and the end of the Mau Mau Emergency, they spent roughly £8 million to turn Kenya into a base for a new air mobile strategic reserve that would protect British interests in Arabia and the Indian Ocean.[74] Mau Mau detainees built the Eastleigh airfield and Kahawa army barracks in eastern Nairobi, and between 1958 and 1961 the regular army brigade stationed there deployed to Jordan, Aden, and Kuwait. This strategically important garrison made the settlers feel secure and made African independence seem reassuringly remote.

The Kenyan administration shared these assumptions and was caught entirely off guard when, as one former civil servant put it, "everything changed in 1960."[75] It was a relatively straightforward matter to transfer power in Uganda and Tanganyika because they lacked significant settler populations. In both territories elected African leaders served as prime ministers under colonial governors for a short transition period until they achieved full independence. This went smoothly in Tanganyika, where Julius Nyerere, a highly popular figure in the nationalist struggle, inherited power at the end of 1961. The situation was more complex in Uganda, where, like the Asante in the Gold Coast, Mutesa and the Gandan elites tried in vain to recreate the old Kingdom of Buganda. Instead, British officials left Uganda with a constitution that created a strong unitary central government while granting limited federal status to Buganda and the other southern preconquest states of Toro, Ankole, Bunyoro, and Busoga when it became a sovereign nation in 1962. A northerner named Milton Obote, whose Uganda People's Congress descended from the old Uganda National Congress, became the first prime minister, with a frustrated and disgruntled Mutesa assuming the largely symbolic and powerless national presidency.

   Although Kenya was arguably the most politically sophisticated of the three East African territories, the thorny question of the fate of the expatriate Europeans delayed the colony's independence. The settlers complained bitterly that Macmillan had betrayed them, and their supporters in Britain fought hard to block the transfer of power to an elected African majority. But Macmillan's conclusive victory in the 1959 elections gave him the political security to reach an accord with the nationalists, and a group of newly elected Conservative MPs who were far less invested in the empire made his task easier. Putting the matter bluntly, one of them shocked the settler leader Michael Blundell by declaring, "What do I care about the f--king settlers, let them bloody well look after themselves."[76] In practice, however, the settlers definitely did not have to look after themselves. Mindful of both the political and economic costs if displaced Britons returned home as refugees, Macmillan's government forced the new African regime to borrow extensively to buy, at grossly inflated prices, the land of any farmer wishing to leave. It tried to protect those who stayed by imposing a federal system on Kenya that had an extremely weak central government with minimal influence over tribally based "regions." This would mean that the settlers would simply become another minority "tribe" with the constitutional guarantee of autonomy in the postcolonial era.

   Prime Minister Jomo Kenyatta, whom many of the settlers and metropolitan Conservatives still considered the sinister force behind the Mau Mau, was a willing partner in this process. Calculating that expelling the settlers and nationalizing British assets would isolate Kenya and dry up foreign investment, he retained much of the colonial administration intact, glossed over human rights violations in the Mau Mau detention camps, and backtracked from his earlier suggestions that independence would lead to land redistribution. Striking a conciliatory note, he invited the settlers to stay if they were willing to help build the new Kenya: "The foundation of our future must lie in the theme: forgive and forget."[77] Nonetheless, Kenyatta moved quickly to replace Britain's highly unworkable experiment in federal regionalism with a strong central government once Kenya became independent in late 1963. Many of the supporters of the Kenya Land Freedom Army felt betrayed by his moderate land policies, but his former settler critics, who once branded him a devil worshipper, now hailed him as a great statesman.

   The Central African Federation presented a more complex problem. Although Macmillan's "wind of change" dislodged the East African settlers, their Rhodesian counterparts would not be swept aside so easily. The copper boom of the 1950s created an artificial air of prosperity, and their greater numbers gave them an equally unrealistic sense of security. Even as it became obvious that the rest of British Africa was on its way to independence and majority rule, their powerful Conservative allies in Britain insisted that the CAF could still be saved. The fact-finding Monckton Commission, which toured the federation in early 1960 as a precursor to the long-anticipated federal constitutional review, refused to acknowledge that the "pathological" African opposition to federation it encountered rendered multiracial partnership unworkable. Overlooking a precipitous drop in global copper prices and the fact that insecurity was scaring off foreign investment, the commissioners, who were all Conservatives or local Central African appointees, continued to believe that the CAF's economic benefits outweighed its political costs. The Monckton Commission did not ignore the shifting political realities in Africa entirely. Much to the dismay of the Rhodesians, it also recommended that Northern Rhodesia and Nyasaland should be allowed to withdraw from the CAF in seven years if their populations remained adamantly opposed to federation. This was the CAF's death knell because the African hostility toward settler rule was nearly universal and uncompromising.

Winding down the federation would not be easy, for the Rhodesians' control over the federal police and armed forces gave them the means to defy London. The federal authorities did their best to prevent the British government from negotiating with Banda and Northern Rhodesia's Kenneth Kaunda, and rumors circulated that they might be intending some sort of coup to prevent African nationalists from coming to power in the northern protectorates. The Colonial Office dismissed these concerns as fantastic, but in August 1960 the federal military commander in Nyasaland asked his superiors for two army battalions to prevent Banda's newly constituted Malawi Congress Party from using "intimidation" to win the upcoming elections: "I feel if something of the sort is not done here very soon one can write their territory off as being a black state . . . agitating for independence continually. . . . Time is running out rapidly unless something to ease the political situation is put into effect by the Army now."[78] This never came to pass, and after Banda won a decisive electoral victory in July 1961, Macmillan's government gave him the right to withdraw Nyasaland (which was soon to become Malawi) from the CAF one year later. After another round of constitutional negotiations, Kaunda eventually won the same concession for Northern Rhodesia (Zambia). In June 1963, representatives from all three territories met once again at Victoria Falls, where the Rhodesians had plotted to create the federation almost two decades earlier, to work out the terms of its demise by the end of the year.

Macmillan's "wind of change" shift also meant the Rhodesians and South Africans would never realize their dream of annexing the High Commission Territories. Instead, they became independent nations as Swaziland, Lesotho (Basutoland), and Botswana (Bechuanaland) between 1966 and 1968. Not surprisingly, Seretse Khama, who had reentered politics as a private citizen, was Botswana's first president. In 1966, Queen Elizabeth II appointed the man whom the colonial authorities had deemed "unfit" to rule because of his "irresponsibility" in choosing an English wife a knight commander of the

Most Excellent Order of the British Empire. In 2008, Sir Seretse and Ruth Khama's son Ian became Botswana's fourth president.

Decolonization in the rest of southern Africa did not bring about an immediate end to European minority rule in Southern Rhodesia or the demise of the colour bar. Determined to resist until the bitter end, Prime Minister Ian Smith banned African political parties and renewed the Rhodesians' long-standing threat to declare their independence. Their allies in Britain defended them tenaciously. In debating the Devlin Report, Edward Turnour, a Conservative peer who had opposed Irish home rule nearly sixty years earlier as a twenty-one-year-old unionist MP, reminded Macmillan's government that the Curragh Mutiny broke out when pro-union British army officers refused to disarm the Irish Volunteers. Warning against trying to similarly impose some form of African home rule in Southern Rhodesia, he recalled, "Ulster was prepared to fight and Ulster managed to get its own way."[79] These sentiments were very much in play as the CAF broke up, and senior metropolitan commanders warned of Curragh-type insubordination if British soldiers received orders to move against their kith and kin. Rhodesia's later-day Ulster Volunteers were actually in little danger because, regardless of the domestic political consequences, the British military simply did not have the resources to depose them.

Secure in this knowledge, Ian Smith announced a Unilateral Declaration of Independence (UDI) on November 11, 1965, that made Southern Rhodesia a republic. Claiming that Harold Wilson's newly elected Labour government intended to transfer power to Soviet-supported African nationalists, he ordered a state of emergency and the mass arrests of African political leaders. Although UDI could easily be construed as treason, Smith appealed for metropolitan support by recalling the pioneering spirit of Rhodesia's British founders and stressing his people's continued affection for the Crown. Recognizing that it was both politically and militarily impossible to use force against the Rhodesians, Wilson tried to compel them to give way through economic sanctions. This strategy was not universally popular in Britain, and many Conservatives equated Wilson's support for African nationalism with Neville Chamberlain's appeasement of Nazi Germany. On the opposite end of the ideological spectrum, Kwame Nkrumah and the other African Commonwealth leaders demanded that Britain take military action against a criminally racist regime.

Although the sanctions took an economic toll, South Africa and Portugal, which controlled neighboring Angola and Mozambique until 1975, helped the Rhodesians survive by providing access to the outside world. Their support gave Smith the means to fight a fruitless but bloody holding action against African guerrilla forces led by Robert Mugabe and Joshua Nkomo. Eventually, the end of Portuguese colonial rule and sheer exhaustion forced the Rhodesians to allow Britain to finally broker the transfer of power to the nationalists in 1979. Most Rhodesians had little choice but to stay in the new Zimbabwe because, unlike in Kenya, the British government now felt no obligation to buy them out after they had declared their independence.

Conceived as a result of the postwar Labour government's well-meaning but ultimately arrogant experiment in development colonialism, the Central African Federation was an unquestionable disaster. For the noted historian Ronald Hyam, it was "the most controversial large-scale imperial exercise in constructive state-building ever undertaken by the British government. It appears now as a quite extraordinary mistake, an aberration of history . . . like the Crusader Kingdom of Jerusalem."[80] In this sense, the most fundamental flaw of the British imperial federation-building project was that it sought to yoke together diverse groups of people with decidedly different and incompatible nationalist agendas.

This did not mean that all federations were doomed to fail. In 1963, Malaya joined Singapore and several former British possessions on the island of Borneo in a Federation of Malaysia. Singapore withdrew from the federation two years later, but Malaysia survived as one of Britain's more successful federal creations. Economically robust, it was large enough to fend off aggressive Indonesian claims on its territory in the mid-1960s.

In the Caribbean, the West Indies Federation's biggest flaw was that it came ten years too late. West Indian political elites had embraced federalism in the 1940s because they saw it as the fastest route to political autonomy. But in the post-Suez era, the prospect of full national independence loomed for each West Indian colony. Unwilling to weaken their political power or subsidize less viable territories like the Leeward and Windward Islands, Eric Williams of Trinidad and Tobago and Jamaica's Norman Manley embraced local nationalism and insisted that the federation have a weak central government. Together, Trinidad and Jamaica had over three-quarters of the federal population, and by 1960 they had diversified their economies to rely less on cash crop exports and more on manufacturing, mining, and tourism. Worried that migrants from less prosperous territories would threaten their improving living standards, the Trinidad and Jamaican governments blocked free movement within the federation and denied the federal government the power to impose taxes or customs duties.

This made the West Indies Federation far too anemic to survive the heady nationalism of the early 1960s. Lacking the ability to raise revenue through taxes or tariffs, it depended on direct contributions from member governments for its income. Jamaica and Trinidad and Tobago had expected Britain to shoulder the costs of federation, but in 1960 they found themselves providing over 80 percent of the federal government's operating revenues. British federation builders had promoted federalism to reduce the cost of colonial administration and refused West Indian calls for direct grants to the Caribbean colonies. As a result, nationalist politicians came to view the federation as an expensive and unnecessary check on their autonomy.

Metropolitan planners hoped that the West Indies Federation would achieve full sovereignty in 1962, but in 1961 Jamaicans voted to secede in a referendum on the federation. The Jamaican withdrawal left Trinidad and Tobago with the primary burden of supporting the federal government, and Eric Williams had little choice but to opt for full independence as well. The eight remaining colonies were still willing to make a go of the West Indies Federation if Britain would provide financial support. But Macmillan's government had no intention of devoting its limited resources to failing imperial projects. In December 1961, the Colonial Office declared that Britain could not increase its support beyond the already promised £2 million per year due to the necessity of fiscal austerity at home. Even worse, Britain's entry into the European Common Market threatened the imperial preferences that made West Indian sugar and bananas competitive on global markets. These developments set the remaining West Indian colonies on the path to full independence when the rest of the federation broke up in 1962.

The Federation of Arab Emirates of the South, which became the Federation of South Arabia with the addition of Aden in 1963, was even more problematic. Although they generally supported Macmillan's "wind of change" policy, imperial strategists sought to retain the Aden base to protect British oil interests in Arabia and the Persian Gulf. In 1961, Aden proved its worth as a staging area when Macmillan's government had to rush seven thousand troops (some of them from the base in Nairobi) to defend the newly independent Kingdom of Kuwait, which supplied 40 percent of Britain's oil needs, from an invasion by a hostile Iraqi regime that claimed sovereignty over the new state. But the Federation of South Arabia was highly unstable because the local shaykhs that Britain counted on to keep popular Arab nationalism in check were ineffective allies. Seeking to build support for federation in its last strategic asset in the Middle East, Macmillan's government was far more generous with development aid than it was in the West Indies.

This strategy was largely ineffective, and British forces became embroiled in a civil war between rival Yemeni groups, which both opposed the federation. The result was yet another failed federation and an ultimately futile campaign against a tenacious group of popular insurgents. Unable to resolve the conflict through diplomatic or military means, Wilson's Labour government gave up control of Aden in 1967. Federations were not destined to fail, but most of Britain's creations were untenable because they were intended to preserve British influence. Moreover, even postcolonial attempts to create federations in East Africa and between Egypt and Syria floundered because the new nationalist rulers were unwilling to share power or compromise their sovereignty.

With Aden gone, all that remained of the British Empire was a small collection of Pacific and Atlantic islands and Hong Kong. Even then, some controversies remained. Spain continued to demand the return of Gibraltar, and in 1982 Argentina launched a full-scale military invasion in an ill-fated attempt to assert sovereignty over the Falkland Islands. Closer to home, marginalized Northern Irish Catholics, who rejected the unionist assertion that Northern Ireland was an organic part of Great Britain, insisted that the six northern counties had to be reunited with the Republic of Ireland. In 1969, these tensions erupted in another burst of vicious civil conflict between republican and unionist militias that eventually forced the British government to reinstitute direct rule in Northern Ireland. Although the status of the six Irish counties remains unsettled to this day, the Good Friday Agreement of 1998, one year after Hong Kong's return to China, opened the way for a cease-fire, disarmament, and eventually power sharing between the two Irish factions.

THE AFTERMATH OF EMPIRE

In April 1960, Harold Macmillan spoke to the Joint Commonwealth Societies Council about his recent African tour and the motives behind the wind of change speech in South Africa. Acknowledging that decolonization was now inevitable, he mapped out his hopes for the democratic political evolution of Britain's former possessions. "We are glad to see the development of the nations in the world to which we already stand in the relationship of parents. Like all parents we would like to see our children take after us. We would like to see them follow in our footsteps not only in their independence but in their free institutions. We think a country is only truly free when all the inhabitants of it are secure in their rights and understand their duties."[81]

Macmillan's criteria constituted a reasonable metric for evaluating Britain's imperial legacy, but it is fair to assume that he would have been profoundly disappointed by the state of most former British territories after independence. The partition of the Raj produced two hostile nuclear powers on the South Asian subcontinent, and Sri Lanka (formerly Ceylon) endured a protracted ethnic civil war. Many of the former African colonies abandoned or radically revised their constitutions to create single-party regimes, and far too many of the nationalist heroes of the independence struggle became authoritarian, if not openly corrupt, rulers. Several of them, including Kwame Nkrumah, fell victim to military coups. By the end of the 1960s, the British-imposed federal systems in Nigeria and Uganda had ended in civil war. Moreover, most of the new nations in Africa and the West Indies remained largely poor and underdeveloped for decades after independence.

Imperial partisans took little responsibility for these circumstances and continued to insist that the end of the British Empire was the culmination of a grand strategy of gradual constitutional reform leading ultimately to full Commonwealth membership. By this reasoning, the political and economic problems that plagued so many former British territories could have been avoided if their subjects and allies had had the patience to allow this planned decolonization to run its proper course. Ex-colonial officials often suggested, some times quite openly, that the nationalist leaders had demanded power before they were ready to exercise it properly. In explaining why the Westminster-style constitutions that Britain had left behind in Africa proved problematical, a former deputy governor of Tanganyika once again claimed that Africans were psychologically unable to grasp the fundamentals of parliamentary democracy because their tribal mentality was incompatible with modernity and the "Western way of life."[82] Although economic necessity and diplomatic considerations led the metropolitan governments of the 1960s to distance Britain from its empire by closing down the Colonial Office, pensioning off or reassigning colonial administrators, and celebrating Commonwealth solidarity, a great many imperial partisans held themselves blameless for problems in the "developing world."

These biases rest on the assumption that the flag-raising rituals that were the centerpiece of fifty years of independence ceremonies marked a conclusive transfer of power from a colonial to a nationalist regime. The cheering crowds that attended these grand pageants assumed that their newly won sovereignty would entail the freedom to break with the past and make their own choices about how to govern themselves. This was often not the case. The failure of development colonialism meant that most new nations inherited understaffed and untrained bureaucracies, inadequate education systems, and one-dimensional neo-mercantile economies that still depended on the export of one or two raw commodities. Moreover, there were few people with the political expertise, education, or training to run a modern state. In other words, the new nations differed very little from their colonial predecessors. Many African states retained colonial bureaucratic institutions like the autocratic system of district commissioners and appointed chiefs. These imperial methods of administration were so ingrained that it was difficult for committed nationalists to abandon the decentralized and largely unaccountable systems of local governance.

The British Empire's political heirs also found that they had far less economic autonomy than they expected. In most territories the transfer of power came with a requirement that the new rulers guarantee to remain within the sterling zone and promise not to threaten foreign investment or commercial interests by nationalizing privately owned assets like mines, plantations, or settler farms. This meant that it was extremely difficult to depart from the imperial neo-mercantilist policies that emphasized the production of raw materials for export and discouraged the development of enterprises that might compete with metropolitan commercial interests. Even in India, which was the most industrialized of Britain's non-Western possessions, the Raj did not actively support local manufacturers until the 1930s.

It was also extremely risky to seek alternatives to the Western development model. The example of British Guiana demonstrates that nationalist leaders like Cheddi Jagan, who tried to improve social welfare by taking greater control of their economies or turning to communist countries for development aid, faced isolation, intervention, and possibly even deposition. Although the Labour government itself nationalized key British industries after World War II, during the Cold War the United States and the other capitalist powers equated socialist development strategies with Soviet Marxist-Leninism. Developing countries had to respect foreign ownership of their key economic assets if they wished to receive Western economic and military aid. Only large and relatively self-sufficient nations like India could afford the risk of nationalizing key industries after independence. Given these realities, frustrated East Africans came to describe the transfer of power as mere *uhuru wa bendera* (flag independence) once they discovered how little real control they had over their own economic affairs.

Moreover, few former colonies had the expertise or administrative capacity to attempt such a radical break with their imperial past. Even the most passionate anti-imperial nationalists, like Kwame Nkrumah, had little choice but to continue to rely on expatriate British administrators, policemen, military officers, educators, technicians, and development experts well after their flags replaced the Union Jack. A great many of these "seconded" civil servants were the very same people who ran the later British Empire. A recent study of former British colonial officials found that nearly one-third of them continued to work in the same country after the transfer of power.[83] The Colonial Office may have disappeared in 1966, but the Ministry of Overseas Development allowed many former colonial officials, like Andrew Cohen, who became its permanent secretary after serving as Britain's representative to the United Nation's Trusteeship Council, to extend their careers. In the late 1960s, Cohen oversaw an Overseas Aid Scheme that loaned out nine thousand British administrators to friendly African governments. It often took more than a decade before the public sectors in the new nations were entirely indigenous, and even then British-sponsored training schemes and institutes of administration produced most of the new African bureaucrats.

Cohen and many of the other former colonial experts still continued to see agriculturally focused centrally planned development as the best means of achieving industrialization and economic growth. In sending one thousand agronomists to Africa in 1967, Cohen declared, "To improve her agricultural productivity and to exploit her natural resources, Africa needs science."[84] These assumptions also shaped the World Bank's policies in the West Indies,

Africa, and Asia as many former British colonial agricultural officers rose to prominent positions in its aid and development branches.

Predictably, these repurposed colonial experts still favored large-scale high-prestige projects, but so did many of the African rulers who learned to place their faith in state-sponsored development during their formative years in the lower rungs of the colonial administration. Even Julius Nyerere's bold socialist plan to nationalize foreign capital assets in Tanzania (the result of the union of Tanganyika and Zanzibar) and fund indigenous industrialization through state-sponsored communal agricultural was not as much a radical departure from the colonial past as it appeared. Inspired as much by Labour's post–World War II development colonialism as by Soviet and Chinese collectivization, the program of *ujamaa* (family solidarity) employed a high level of state coercion. Just as Andrew Cohen and the Labour development experts believed that it was acceptable to use authoritarian methods to achieve noble goals, Nyerere's government tried to achieve greater production and economies of scale by compelling peasant farmers to move into new centralized villages. Although the *ujamaa* project was more successful than the spectacularly disastrous Tanganyika Groundnut Scheme, the two development initiatives were both born of a faith in top-down centralized planning.

In Ghana, Nkrumah's construction binge, military expansion, and generous grants to Pan-Africanist allies left the nation so hard-pressed by 1961 that he had to meet government expenses by raiding the Cocoa Marketing Board, raising taxes, and forcing Ghanaian workers to join a mandatory national savings plan.[85] His plan to generate cheap hydroelectric power for aluminum smelting and other industrial projects by damming the Volta River was even more problematic. First proposed by British development experts during the colonial era and completed in 1965 at a cost of approximately £130 million, the Akosombo Dam put the Ghanaian government deeply in debt, displaced eighty thousand people, and spread the waterborne disease schistosomiasis while failing to produce the promised industrial growth.

Recognizing the public anger over the failure of political independence to bring immediate economic benefits, the new national rulers knew that it would be difficult to remain in power by winning elections. Many therefore fell back on the same kind of authoritarian tactics that the colonial authorities had used against them. Preventative detention acts in Ghana, Kenya, and Malawi allowed the new regimes to detain their political rivals without trial in camps where they suffered human rights abuses on par with the worst excesses of the colonial prisons. By the end of the 1960s, many African prime ministers rewrote the constitutions Britain had left them to solidify their hold on power by creating single-party states. In 1966, Jomo Kenyatta made the Kenya African National Union the sole national party by using the Preservation of Public Security Act, a holdover from the colonial era, to detain members of the rival Kenya People's Union without trial. In Malawi, Kamuzu Hastings Banda used the Malawi Congress Party to make himself president for life.

This return to authoritarianism left force as the only viable option for removing an unpopular ruler. Consequently, incidents of military intervention in African politics became depressingly more common by the mid-1960s. Even Kwame Nkrumah, who was one of the most respected Pan-Africanist leaders of the colonial era, fell victim to the temptations of political office, and in 1966 his own army officers were sufficiently fed up with his economically disastrous experiment in state socialism to overthrow him. In Uganda, Milton Obote put an end to Buganda's nationalist aspirations by using the army to back his suspension of the federal constitution in what the local British defense attaché termed a "coup d'état against his own government."[86] In 1966, military units under the command of Idi Amin drove Kabaka Mutesa into his last and final exile by launching a full-scale assault on his palace. Five years later Amin deposed Obote, thereby subjecting Uganda to eight years of tyranny and terror. Britain's federal experiment in Nigeria had similarly tragic consequences when the Eastern Region declared its independence in 1967. In the resulting Biafran war of succession, more than half a million people died of violence, disease, and starvation before the federal government defeated the secessionists in 1970.

The troubling history of Britain's former African colonies shows that the nationhood and formal political sovereignty resulting from the transfer of power did not bring about a clean break with the imperial past. There were considerable continuities in the development era, which stretched roughly from 1939 to the crash in commodity prices resulting from the Arab oil embargo and global recession in 1973. It was also asking a great deal of the first generation of nationalist rulers to respect constitutions and the electoral process given that they had come of age under an authoritarian system that provided little exposure to democracy and frequently bent the law to suit its own purposes. Given these realities, it is an open question as to how much the despotism, corruption, and economic mismanagement that plagued far too many former British territories were the result of the failings of the new national regimes or the continuation of an imperial legacy.

Chapter Six

Global Legacies of the British Empire

In October 1979, a self-titled album by a band called the Specials reached the seventh spot on the album charts at a time when the national temper was fraying in metropolitan Britain. Coming at the end of a decade of racial unrest, generational friction, right-wing extremism, aggressive policing, rising unemployment, and a wave of strikes that threatened to paralyze the country, Margaret Thatcher and the Conservative Party won a decisive but divisive electoral victory in May 1979 by promising to rein in the excesses of the postwar welfare state, uphold law and order, and defend British values. The Specials offered both a political and social rebuttal to this agenda. With a sound that blended punk rock with ska, a Jamaican style of music, the band offered a powerful critique of postimperial British society.

Although African American and West Indian musical styles had long been popular in Britain, the arrival of hundreds of thousands of South Asians, West Indians, Africans, and other subject peoples from the various corners of the empire in the 1950s and 1960s provoked a popular backlash against non-European migrant communities. Ironically, it became easier to move from the colonies to the metropole as the British Empire wound down. For many Britons, it was one thing to have an abstract sense of belonging to a larger multiethnic empire but quite another to have former colonial subjects as neighbors and fellow citizens. Both new arrivals and "black Britons," who often had deep family roots in Britain, endured discrimination in housing and employment and suffered frequent harassment, which often turned violent, as they went about their daily lives. Lynval Golding, the Specials' Jamaican-born rhythm guitarist, recalled the racism he faced in school upon arriving in Britain in 1965: "It shocked me really bad. . . . They spat at me and called me names. I just wasn't used to that kind of thing . . . in Jamaica."[1] More often than not, the perpetrators of these violent attacks were bands of young, disaffected "white Britons" known as skinheads. By the mid-1970s, racial tensions simmered as Britons of West Indian and South Asian descent began to fight back against the police and the skinheads.

It was significant that the Specials, an integrated band that included white Britons and West Indian migrants from Coventry, would attract such a large following. Ska had been popular in Britain since the late 1960s, when the song "The Israelites" by Desmond Dekker became the first Jamaican recording to top the British popular music charts. The children of the first generation of immigrants created a British version of these West Indian musical traditions in bands like Steel Pulse, which was formed by three friends from the Handsworth area of Birmingham to play reggae music. Initially, the skinheads and other groups of working-class young people embraced this music because they found it rebellious and entertaining, but by the mid-1970s popular music came to reflect the fractious state of British society by becoming much more segregated in terms of race. Punk rock was predominately white, whereas many young black Britons turned to a slower, more politically charged Rastafarian version of reggae that depicted racist Britain as an oppressive modern-day Babylon.

The Specials reversed this trend by combining punk rock with older West Indian musical styles to create a new, distinctly British version of ska that had appeal across the racial spectrum. This included innovative covers of classic West Indian hits like "A Message to You Rudy" and "Gangsters" and their own songs that urged racial tolerance and understanding. The most telling lyrics of "Doesn't Make It Alright" urged young Britons not to divide themselves on the basis of being "black" or "white."[2] Although the group also wrote high-minded songs attacking neo-fascist groups like the British National Party and the National Front, the Specials made their most powerful political statement with vibrant, punched-up, highly danceable music that drew punk rockers, Rastafarians, and a new generation of skinheads. A reviewer for the *New Music Express* was entirely won over: "Although the predominant musical influence is black (ska, bluebeat, reggae and soul), [their first mainstream album is] wrapped in ferocious rock 'n' roll: the kind of hybrid that so many other British bands have tried to contrive . . . but, in comparison, failed to make convincing. . . . From Coventry, featuring two blacks and five whites, The Specials instinctively 'feel' the true realities of Britain's multi-racial youth."[3] Taking these ideals a step further, the band's label, 2 Tone Records, featured a black-and-white checkerboard and a silhouette of a man, who could be either white or black, dressed in a style first popularized by an earlier generation of Jamaican gangsters, consisting of a black suit, white shirt, black tie, sunglasses, and porkpie hat.

Jerry Dammers, the Specials' founder, made it clear that 2 Tone was not a political party. "It was never that. The Specials were just pointing out things that the politicians conveniently chose to forget about. . . . I see 2 Tone as a little club, and if you liked the music, then you were part of the club."[4] The fact that lots of people liked the music gave the band a broad cross-cultural following. Golding recalled that the Specials appealed to the "strictest Rastas," who cared most about reggae music and "not about whether it's black or white people playing it," and Rico Rodriguez, the band's renowned Jamaican trombonist who had played with Prince Buster, the Skatalites, and other seminal Jamaican groups, dismissed accusations that the Specials were "stealing reggae or ska music from the black man" as "just poor foolishness, just pure f--kery."[5] On the other end of the spectrum, the Specials had such a huge following among young skinheads that the National Front viewed them as a corrupting threat and attacked their shows as part of a futile effort to recruit working-class youth to their right-wing anti-immigrant cause.

By 1979, there was no denying that the Specials' version of ska had become a distinctly British art form. Describing their appeal in cruder, simpler terms, comedian and DJ Mark LaMaar recalled, "First, they looked f--king great. . . . Second, they sounded f--king great. Thirdly, they thought f--king great."[6] The Specials' fame proved short-lived as the band soon split up over the usual sorts of personal tensions and artistic differences that frequently bedevil successful music groups, but its broad popularity in post-colonial Britain demonstrated that imperial rule often had unintended consequences. Whereas earlier generations of Britons would have scoffed at West Indian music as primitive and discordant, the Specials showed that their children and grandchildren had now made it their own.

Ignoring these imperial complexities, the celebrated economic historian Niall Ferguson has approvingly noted that the British Empire was a powerful medium of cultural exchange. "No organization in history has done more to promote the free movement of goods, capital and labour than the British Empire in the nineteenth and early twentieth centuries. And no organization has done more to impose Western norms of law, order and governance around the world."[7] These Western norms, which Ferguson defined as representative democracy, banking and fiscal systems, responsible bureaucracy, Protestantism, the ideal of personal liberty, and even team sports, were just what Harold Macmillan had in mind in 1960 when he expressed hope that the newly independent African colonies would follow in Britain's footsteps.

Many imperial partisans expected the Commonwealth to encourage this trend, and the 1971 Commonwealth Declaration of Principles announced that member nations would work together against racism, colonialism, and global economic inequality. Unfortunately many Commonwealth countries, particularly the single-party regimes in Africa and Asia, did not live up to these high ideals. Although the Commonwealth acquired significant global weight through its sponsorship of the Commonwealth Games and promotion of a wide range of development and social welfare initiatives, it had very little influence on the internal affairs of the former British colonies. Apart from drawing the national boundaries of most of the English-speaking world, the British Empire's positive conventional political and economic legacy has been relatively limited.

Ferguson's mistake, which is common to many historians of conventional empire, was to confuse imperial rule with the organic and ongoing processes of global change that shape human history. The twentieth-century Western empires were actually part of a larger set of processes that we now call globalization. In social science terms, globalization can be defined as "the process whereby individual lives and local communities are affected by economic and cultural forces that operate world-wide. In effect it is the process of the world becoming a single place."[8] Although the term only came into widespread use in the last three decades, these forces were well underway by the time of the ancient Chinese, South Asian, Near Eastern, and Roman empires, and they accelerated markedly after the advent of industrialization and global capitalism in the nineteenth century. Global change was never even or uniform, and successful empire builders exploited imbalances in globalization to conquer and rule populations who had lost the ability to defend themselves. More significantly, the broad changes that Ferguson attributes to the British Empire would have eventually reached the various corners of the world on their own. In this sense, imperial rule was an attempt to control the nature and trajectory of globalization to serve Britain's national ends.

Although this was a feasible proposition in earlier eras, the second British Empire of the late nineteenth century was born of a temporary technological imbalance that allowed the new imperialists to conquer much of the non-Western world quickly and cheaply. Imperial partisans assumed that this arrangement would last for centuries, but, as we saw in the last chapter, the second British Empire's demise was predictable and inevitable.

Nonetheless, the empire still left a significant and long-lasting informal cultural mark on the contemporary world. Ferguson's claims for the transformative power of imperial rule are true to a point, but one could also amend his contention to say that no organization in history has done more to spread South Asian, West Indian, and, to a lesser degree, African and East Asian norms and cultural institutions around the globe. The British Empire was a web of multidirectional exchanges that allowed peoples, ideas, and commodities to move more easily across national and geographic boundaries. So while the empire brought British settlers to North America, Australia and New Zealand, and Africa, it also shifted South Asian laborers, merchants, investors, students, and diplomats to the Caribbean, southern and eastern Africa, and eastern Asia. This South Asian diaspora included both the Sikh soldiers and policemen who upheld the empire and the militant Sikhs in the Ghadr movement who sought to bring it down. Similarly, Irish administrators, policemen, and missionaries served the empire faithfully, while Irish republicans used imperial networks to offer support and advice to their fellow nationalists in Africa and Asia. Careful inspection reveals that the British Empire was not as "British" as it appeared.

Although the political legacy of the British Empire is fairly obvious, its informal networks of exchange helped inspire new cultures and identities that endured long after the last British army detachment hauled down the Union Jack. British administrators, missionaries, and settlers set out to remake local non-Western communities in their own image through Christian evangelism, Western education, and capitalist enterprise. Secure in their notions of cultural and moral supremacy, they were confident that their rule uplifted and developed backward peoples. In reality, the empire produced new identities and cultures that were the unplanned result of multiple and overlapping informal interactions between Britons and their subjects. These exchanges were never unidirectional, and Britain itself was changed by the imperial experience of ruling such a diverse range of peoples. Those who felt threatened by the large numbers of migrants from the former colonies in the post–World War II era were haunted by a fear that the empire had changed what it meant to be British. In recent decades migration from Africa and Asia has become a fact of life in most western European nations, even those that did not have colonies. Imperial rule, however, determined the scope and impact of the seismic social changes that have transformed contemporary Britain. The globalizing British Empire produced new and unexpected cultural norms in the colonies, but it also transformed the metropolitan heartland into a more diverse and multiethnic society that was ready to embrace the music of the Specials.

LOCAL LEGACIES

The borders of postcolonial nation-states are the British Empire's most obvious political bequest to the non-Western world, but the new or reimagined ethnicities that emerged during the new imperial era are arguably its more significant legacy. The codification, if not outright invention, of larger and more rigid national and collective identities was an evolving global process in the nineteenth and twentieth centuries. Driven largely by population growth, improved communications, more powerful state bureaucracies, and the spread of literacy and printing, this was a phenomenon that would have continued whether the new imperialism had occurred or not. Nevertheless, the western European empires exerted a powerful influence on the character and composition of these new identities through the simple mechanics of imperial rule. This did not mean, however, that their attempts to regulate and control the processes of identity formation always achieved the desired results.

As we saw in chapter 1, British administrators sought to make sense of non-Western societies by sorting subject peoples into the more familiar categories of religion, caste, and tribe. These classifications made it easier to understand, divide, and administer colonized majorities. As was often the case with imperial policy, India served as the model for the rest of the empire. Officials in the Raj considered some foraging and pastoral communities to be tribes, but they primarily used religion and Hindu castes to classify and divide most South Asian societies. Yet "tribe" and "caste" were not, at least originally, Indian terms. Tribe had its origins in the Latin *tribus*, and caste came from *castus*, the word for "species or breed" that the Spanish used to denote gradations of racial mixing in their American colonies. Introduced into India by the Portuguese, the term caste helped British rulers make sense of the complex societies of the South Asian subcontinent.

Assuming that Indian caste and religious identities were fixed and unchanging, administrators, military recruiters, and judges used them as the basic building blocks of imperial rule. The numerous subdivisions of the main castes, known as *jatis*, became the basis for regulating social institutions like adoption, marriage, divorce, and inheritance. Indian army officers believed that some castes and *jatis* were naturally inclined to produce good soldiers, and recruiting handbooks provided detailed guidance on how to recognize which groups were truly "martial races" and which were not. British authorities also believed that certain communities were biologically and culturally inclined to break the law, and the Criminal Tribes Act allowed the government to restrict the movement and civil rights of any "tribe, gang or class of persons" by designating them a "criminal tribe." Beginning in the late nineteenth century, regular censuses institutionalized these stereotypes and biases by attempting to sort and categorize the entire South Asian subject population on the basis of caste, tribe, and religious community.

Governmental attempts to codify identity for the purposes of imperial rule inspired Indians to rework these categories to seek greater social and economic standing. Census takers in Bengal were surprised to find that local communities believed that the true purpose of the census was to fix the rank and social precedence of each caste, and the enumerators received hundreds of petitions from self-appointed spokesmen for these groups demanding new names, greater status, or inclusion in a more prestigious caste. These realities demonstrate that imperial categories of identity were also useful to subject peoples. As the eminent South Asia expert Christopher Bayly has observed, "The British . . . did not invent caste or construct religious identities *ex nihilo*. What they did was to provide conditions, practical and ideological, which allowed people to reproduce these forms of social power and division."[9] To this end, the caste obligations on "unclean" groups that Gandhi fought so hard to eliminate provided cheap labor for elites and helped validate elite claims to land and status in the colonial courts. Nor was it difficult for an individual to change her or his identity simply by playing on the relative ignorance of British officials. This explains how many of the supposedly martial race soldiers in the Indian army were actually members of other castes masquerading as members of the Raj's favored communities.

In British Africa, many territories tried to address these uncertainties and develop more precise systems of governance and indirect rule by employing noted anthropologists like E. E. Evans Pritchard (Sudan) and Meyer Fortes (the Gold Coast) to identify and codify tribal institutions and cultural values. In making the case that anthropologists should be part of the administration of every colonial territory, Isaac Schapera, who engaged in similar work for the Bechuanaland Protectorate, argued, "The administrator needs to know something about the people among whom he is working. He cannot keep them in order and settle their disputes unless he is familiar with their system of government and law."[10] By assuming that these collective identities were more important than individual rights in non-Western societies, colonial regimes could also appear liberal and benevolent by posing as the guardians of religious tradition or tribal custom. As the Kenyan administrator H. E. Lambert put it, "The conservation of the soul of an African tribe is as essential as the conservation of its soil."[11]

Yet, as in India, British officials and their academic allies were never powerful enough to control the processes of identity formation. The survival of colonial-era tribal designations after independence further demonstrates that subject peoples co-opted and reshaped official identities to suit their own needs. The colonial governments' insistence on assigning rights to groups rather than individuals created powerful incentives for local communities to work within these categories. At the most fundamental level, indirect rule made customary authority the key to political power and economic enrichment, and most African territories continued the Indian practice of using categories of identity to determine where people could legally reside, with whom they could interact, and if they could join the police or army.

Religious leaders, chiefs, elders, and mission school graduates therefore vied to have the colonial authorities acknowledge and authenticate their interpretation of local tradition. Echoing Christopher Bayly on caste, the noted Africanist historian John Iliffe succinctly put it as follows: "Europeans believed Africans belonged to tribes; Africans built tribes to belong to."[12] True enough, but no state, least of all the anemic colonial governments of British Africa, could simply impose new identities. If Africans used the colonial categories of tribe, they did so on their terms. Cultural brokers often exploited official biases to transform relatively fluid preexisting identities into usefully defined tribes during the colonial era. Migrant workers from

Portuguese East Africa (Mozambique) began calling themselves Lomwe to convince the Nyasaland government to accord them rights as a tribe. In Kenya, members of seven culturally related subcommunities that British officials termed "Nandi-speaking peoples" reclassified themselves in the late 1940s. Perceiving the need for a counterweight to their more populous Kikuyu and Luo neighbors, they adopted the collective name Kalenjin, meaning "I tell you," from the opening salutation the military authorities used in radio broadcasts to Nandi-speaking soldiers during World War II. [13] In the national era, Daniel arap Moi, the second president of contemporary Kenya, demonstrated that the Kalenjin identity was not an artificial colonial creation by using it to generate support for his highly authoritarian regime.

Although they did not fully grasp the flexibility of tribe and caste, British officials defended these categories of identity tenaciously because they were the foundation of colonial administration. They were particularly distrustful of ideas, institutions, and practices that blurred or eroded ethnic or religious boundaries. H. E. Lambert, the Kenyan administrative officer who fretted about the "soul" of the tribe, warned that Western culture and Christianity, which left "scars on the body politic of the tribe," were inherently "detribalizing." [14] In this Lambert was entirely correct, for the central features of British rule were incompatible with his idealized notions of egalitarian tribal collectivism. Christian evangelism helped legitimize the imperial project, but mission converts rejected the authority of tribal chiefs on the grounds that they were pagans. Settlers, mine owners, and other foreign investors depended on low-cost African labor, but wage labor had no place in Lambert's romanticized tribal world because it led to personal enrichment, social stratification, and individualism.

Tribe and caste appeared to be viable categories of identity and colonial administration in the countryside, but they could not stand the strains of urban life. Recognizing that urbanization was an inherent aspect of twentieth-century globalization, most territorial governments went to great lengths to restrict the mobility of rural peoples for fear that it would lead to subversive political activity and detribalizing social change. After all, if a person married someone from another tribe, into what category would their children fall? Not only were urban areas the birthplace of African nationalist movements, but tribal peoples could also mix and intermarry in cities, and much to the chagrin of the missionaries, Muslim evangelists won many converts among them. However, keeping people penned up in the countryside was difficult, if not impossible, for cities were the central nodes of commerce and governance in the British Empire, and urbanization was an inherent byproduct of imperial rule.

Some imperial cities were significant urban centers in precolonial times, but others grew up entirely under the British Empire. Cities were the primary nodes of the entire imperial network. As noted in chapter 1, the Raj built

New Delhi to make a political statement. Intended as an answer to the Indian nationalists, its wide boulevards, gothic palaces for Indian princes, and stately government buildings theoretically demonstrated the power and longevity of British rule at a time when British rule in India was failing. Although African cities were not as grandiose, British urban planners primarily intended them, particularly those in the settler colonies, to be extensions of Europe. The territorial governments in West Africa accepted a segregated African urban presence, but most other colonies would only allow Africans to enter cities legally as temporary laborers. These migrants were supposed to work for a fixed period before returning to their families in the countryside. As a result, most eastern, central, and southern African cities did not provide basic municipal services for Africans.

West African cities did have sanctioned African neighborhoods, but city planners used the Indian model of public health as an excuse to keep them separate from European residential areas. This reinforced an informal colour bar, and it was a tacit admission that the colonial regime lacked the resources to create healthy living conditions for the entire urban population. Using the excuse that non-Westerners harbored malaria and other contagious diseases, they created parks and greenbelts, which often doubled as golf courses, to separate the two communities. The Ugandan government even used part of its public health budget to maintain the greens and fairways in Kampala and other urban centers.

In terms of policy, the imperial authorities endeavored to maintain a sharp distinction between the "native" countryside and the "civilized" city. This was unworkable in practice. Colonial cities were unquestionably difficult places to live for most non-Westerners, particularly if they were illegal migrants or squatters, but they still were tremendously appealing spaces for a great many people. They were outside the reach of chiefs and other "traditional" rural authorities, which meant that a migrant often did not have to pay taxes or accept tribal discipline. There were also relatively lucrative urban wage-earning jobs that simply did not exist in rural peasant economies. This was particularly true for female migrants whose work as domestic servants, nannies, hotel owners, petty traders, brewers of illicit alcohol products, and sex workers gave them a measure of autonomy that was unheard of in the patriarchal countryside. City life was also fun and entertaining, and the music of the Specials, at least in part, had its origins in the seemingly oppressive West Indian slums. Finally, there was almost always more food in the colonial cities than in the hinterlands and native regions during the famines that periodically gripped the empire in the first half of the twentieth century.

Given these realities, most territorial governments were virtually powerless to check or control urban migration. In the first four decades of the twentieth century, India's urban population increased from 28.2 to 49.7 million people. City dwellers thus amounted to roughly 12 percent of the total population of the Raj. In Africa and the West Indies, the most rapid spurt in urban growth followed World War II. Between 1940 and 1960, the population of the Nigerian city of Lagos nearly tripled to 312,000 people, while Nairobi's jumped from 65,000 to 210,000 residents. The Union of South Africa experienced the highest rates of urban migration in British Africa as wartime industrialization and the collapse of agriculture in the native reserves inspired more people to seek their fortunes in the cities. Similarly, impoverished rural migrants doubled the population of Kingston, Jamaica, to approximately 123,000 in the two decades after World War II.[15]

Few colonial cities were prepared to deal with this unplanned and technically illegal influx of people. The explosive growth of informal urban settlements, if not outright slums, was an inherent part of urbanization in the British Empire. Although the urban authorities and European settlers complained bitterly that these unplanned neighborhoods fostered crime and disease, they lacked the coercive means to prevent people from leaving the countryside. Even if they could wall off the rural areas, shutting down the flow of migrants entirely was never a viable option because the colonial urban economy depended on cheap labor. The colonial cities would have also been far less congenial for Westerners if this flow of marginal people dried up. Without poorly paid labor migrants, there would have been no one to build affordable but comfortable housing, pave the roads, cart away the trash and raw sewage, tend the gardens, or mind their children.

These realities did not, however, provide a sufficient incentive for the colonial city fathers to give the informal settlements even the most basic amenities. For decades the Nairobi City Council tried to drive a settlement of Sudanese veterans off a choice parcel of land that was uncomfortably near the city center and an upscale settler neighborhood by denying them running water and simple sewage facilities. District administrators rejected their repeated appeals for clean water and other basic services on the grounds that it would be used for illegal distilling and make the slum too "attractive residentially." Instead they would only agree to provide these most fundamental requirements for daily life if the Sudanese agreed to surrender their claims to the neighborhood they called Kibera (from their word for "forest"). This policy of malignant neglect, which lasted into the postcolonial era, turned Kibera, which had a population density of forty-nine thousand people per square mile in 1993, into one of the most notorious (but widely celebrated by aid agencies and documentary filmmakers) slums in all of contemporary Africa.[16]

From the standpoint of the colonial regime, informal settlements like Kibera were more than simple public health hazards. In the decades after World War II, the population of most West Indian and African cities was under the age of eighteen. Inadequate and underfunded schools provided few opportunities for employment beyond the informal sector, and the inherent economic hardship of urban life weakened families. Predictably, crime and delinquency ran rampant. The Johannesburg townships and the other main South African urban centers fostered a distinct gangster culture that rejected both governmental and parental authority. Wearing stylish Western clothing and speaking their own distinct urban argot, these *tsotsis* valued daring criminality and disdained manual labor as effeminate. In interwar Dar es Salaam, the rootless *wanaharamu* (sons of sin) survived through violence and petty thieving. These urban social problems invariably had political implications. Although the *tsotsis* were largely apolitical, the South African townships were centers of support for the African National Congress, and a Tanganyikan social welfare expert worried that young townsmen, whom he described as the "African equivalent of the English teddy-boy[s]," would ally with radical nationalists. "[They are] waiting for a *Fuehrer* [i.e., a Nazi-style leader] to give respectability to their longing to be admired, to be feared, to have a place in the sun."[17]

These anxious colonial officials failed to recognize that the colonial slums were also creative spaces that nurtured new cultures and art forms. In East African coastal cities, young Swahili-speaking workers created a new form of entertainment, known as Beni, during the early decades of the twentieth century. Beni celebrations consisted of elaborate, stylized competitions between rival societies dressed in European clothing and military uniforms dancing to the music of brass bands. In addition to providing hugely popular entertainment, they were in effect satirizing European culture. In Mombasa, the two main groups were the Kingi (king) and the Scotchi (Scots). Similarly, West Indians on Barbados organized themselves into associations known as landships. Modeled on the hierarchy of the Royal Navy, each group was a "ship" with a "crew" that wore uniforms, adopted naval ranks, and provided each other with mutual assistance during hard times. By the 1930s, sixty different "ships" came together to form a "fleet" known as the Barbados Landship Association.

This urban creativity also extended to clothing. Influenced by American western films, aggressive and defiant young men in Dar es Salaam, very much like the young Asante members of the National Liberation Movement discussed in chapter 5, dressed in wide hats, multicolored shirts, blue jeans, and neckerchiefs. Characters in gangster movies similarly inspired mobsters like Boysie Singh of Trinidad and Jamaica's Ivanhoe Martin, both popular cult figures, by dressing well and standing up to the police. In doing so they contributed to the slum culture that produced the ska music styles that so influenced the Specials some forty years later.

Lacking the means to prevent people from coming to the cities, the colonial authorities tried to limit the destabilizing and potentially subversive aspects of urban culture. Just as they believed that it was possible to remake and uplift rural tribal societies, they sought to channel young townsmen into more constructive endeavors. Missionaries and government social welfare experts tried to capture and discipline urban youth with a variety of activities ranging from evening schools, to vocational training, to Boy Scout troops.

Organized sports in particular offered the promise of teaching non-Westerners from all walks of life to accept British notions of discipline, cooperation, and fair play. Most colonial schools included team sports in their curricula, and Lord Harris, the Trinidadian-born governor of Bombay in the 1890s, promoted cricket to encourage educated Indians to embrace imperial values. By the early twentieth century, a hugely popular Bombay cricket tournament known as the Quadrangular pitted Parsi, Hindu, Muslim, and European teams against each other. The colonial military authorities tended to prefer boxing over cricket, but in the 1950s the Kenyan governor balked at allowing Ugandan soldiers like Idi Amin to fight their counterparts in the British army on the grounds that interracial matches would undermine support for the war against the Mau Mau guerillas.[18] The Kenyan authorities were much more comfortable with a plan by a pair of district officers for the "Kalenjin Games," an athletic festival intended to popularize the new tribal identity. Although it is doubtful that this exercise in tribal engineering had much success along those lines, it did help lay the groundwork for Kenya's future dominance in track-and-field events. Imperial sponsorship of team sports also helped make games like soccer (football), rugby, and cricket national pastimes in most former British territories.

Alternatively, athletics could also reinforce anti-imperial defiance. As noted in chapter 2, Michael Cusask founded the Gaelic Athletic Association, which revived and reinterpreted "ancient" Irish sports as an alternative to "foreign" British-sponsored games. In time, the association became one of the cornerstones of the Irish nationalist movement. As was the case with other forms of Western popular culture, subject peoples invariably turned the empire's approved sports to their own ends. In South Africa, working-class Muslim members of the Western Province Coloured Rugby Union developed a more aggressive physical style of play as a challenge to Christian elites and the more established City and Suburban Rugby Union, which refused to admit Muslim players.

Cricket was by far the most complex of the imperially sanctioned games. Although its supporters, like Lord Harris, himself a top-class cricketer, depicted cricket as an egalitarian game and popularized it to promote an inclusive multiethnic view of the empire, white South Africans and West Indian planters tried to use the sport to strengthen racial privilege and exclusivity. The famed bowler Palwankar Balloo was a cornerstone of the Hindu team in the Bombay tournament, but neither his Brahmin teammates nor his European opponents would socialize with him off the field because he was a *Dalit* (untouchable). In South Africa, European teams insisted on strict racial segregation and objected to playing mixed opponents at the international level.

For many people in the cricket establishment, non-Westerners lacked the culture and discipline to play the game properly. Subject peoples throughout the empire proved them wrong. Recognizing that they could gain respectability, social status, and perhaps even political autonomy by winning at cricket, West Indian, Asian, and African teams regularly beat white sides at their own game. This is why the Indian nationalist press compared the Hindu team's victory in the 1906 Bombay tournament to Japan's naval triumph over Russia one year earlier.

In the Caribbean, West Indian players developed their own aggressive style of powerful batting and fast bowling that angered the colonial cricket establishment by creating a less genteel version of the game. Learie Constantine, the premier Trinidadian cricketer, approached an international cricket competition, or Test match, as a "battle," and black cricket clubs often defeated white clubs. Eventually it finally dawned on the West Indian colonial cricket associations that they needed these players to remain competitive in imperial Test matches, which were the game's most prestigious and important global tournaments. Skilled cricketers like Constantine and George Headley of Jamaica helped break down the segregation in colonial society by gradually remaking West Indian cricket into a game that stood for merit, democracy, and social justice.

In 1926, the federation of West Indian cricket associations gained full membership in the Imperial Cricket Conference. This Test status qualified them to join the ranks of the top national and territorial teams, which included England, India, and all of the dominions with the exception of Canada. The West Indian side that competed in its first Test match against England in 1928 included both black and white cricketers, who played together on the pitch but did not mix socially afterward. These divisions were unworkable, and the West Indian establishment had no choice but to accept the desegregation of its most popular game.

C. L. R. James, a Trinidadian cultural historian and political activist, wrote about cricket's anticolonial potential in *Beyond a Boundary*, a book widely recognized as one of the most thoughtful studies of the game. Recalling his anger over the cricketing authorities' preference for race over merit in choosing the West Indian Test teams, James wrote, "My Puritan soul burnt with indignation at injustice in the sphere of sport. . . . Cricket had plunged me into politics long before I was aware of it. When I did turn to politics I did not have much to learn."[19] In the early 1930s, James moved to Britain with Learie Constantine, who became a paid player for Nelson Cricket Club in the professional Lancashire league, and made a name for himself as the cricket writer for the *Manchester Guardian*. In addition to winning fame for his athletic skills, Constantine earned a law degree and an MBE (Member of the British Empire) for his service as a welfare officer during World War II. In 1954, he returned to the West Indies to enter politics and eventually became a government minister and diplomat for Trinidad and Tobago. His fame in both Britain and the West Indies is an exemplary illustration of the ability of subject peoples to turn the popular culture of the empire to their own ends and to claim parts of it as their own.

IMPERIAL NETWORKS

The travels of Learie Constantine and C. L. R. James between Britain and the West Indies were a small part of the substantial population shifts facilitated by the second British Empire. The empire was a vast, but often unseen, transportation network that spread a wide variety of peoples around the globe. Imperial propaganda created an impression that non-Western subjects were fixed in traditional societies and that only elite delegations and small groups of students ever visited the imperial center. Most Britons believed that Britain remained separate and distinct from the rest of its empire, but in reality it was quite feasible to move from one colony to another or to the metropole itself. The British Nationality and Status of Aliens Act of 1914 established that a British citizen was "any person born within His Majesty's dominions and allegiances." This legitimizing ideology that all colonized peoples were equal subjects of a benevolent British monarch meant that they were entitled to travel freely within the empire. Although imperial theorists like Frederick Lugard worried that mass movements of non-Europeans might swamp "white lands," there were no legal barriers to migration to metropolitan Britain before 1960. As a result, these imperial population shifts contributed to the rise of multicultural societies around the globe.

Mass migration has been an inherent part of the globalization process over the past two centuries, but empires shaped its trajectories, character, and consequences. Although the most substantial flow of migration to the dominions took place in the 1800s, large numbers of metropolitan Britons continued to move to the overseas imperial territories after the turn of the century. Approximately 3.4 million people left Britain in the first four decades of the twentieth century, with the vast majority continuing to settle in Canada, Australia, New Zealand, and South Africa. Seeking an escape from the hardship and austerity of post–World War II reconstruction, an additional 1 million Britons migrated to the overseas empire between 1945 and 1957.

Many settlers left of their own accord, but colonial governments and private organizations recruited others. Prior to World War I, most dominions sponsored migration to increase their European populations, while the British government encouraged English speakers to settle in South Africa in a futile effort to dilute the political influence of the Afrikaners. Charitable organizations like the Salvation Army and the East End Emigration Fund tried to entice the urban poor to go overseas to reduce overcrowding in British cities.

As noted in chapter 3, after World War I the British government passed the Empire Settlement Act and established the Oversea Settlement Committee in a largely unsuccessful attempt to strengthen ties to the dominions while reducing postwar unemployment and exporting potentially disruptive ex-servicemen. In providing financial assistance to suitable migrants, imperial partisans also hoped to dilute the influence of French Catholics in Canada and Irish republicans and Bolsheviks in Australia. There was also talk of preventing a "yellow flood" of Asians from filling up lands that were suitable for European settlement. In keeping with the spirit of the times, voluntary organizations like the British Boy Scout Association did their part by publicizing the benefits of migration within the empire. The dominions, however, were not willing to accept metropolitan Britain's castoffs and imposed strict property and occupational immigration requirements, and the interwar migration campaign fell far short of its target quotas. Disregarding this poor track record, the post–World War II Labour government sponsored another attempt to direct mass migration to the empire. Ignoring a growing metropolitan labor shortage, it once again subsidized overseas settlement for veterans to bolster British influence in the Commonwealth.

Only a minuscule percentage of these private and state-sponsored British migrants went to the Crown colonies and other non-Western territories. The few who did, however, created influential "islands of white" in eastern and central Africa.[20] There were also small permanent British populations in India and the West Indies dating back to the seventeenth and eighteenth centuries. Although it was often lonely and intimidating to live among non-Western majorities, the colonies offered migrants a comfortable upper-middle-class standard of living, complete with servants and grand homes, that would have been out of reach in metropolitan Britain. This explains why thousands of Britons disregarded the growing strength of anticolonial nationalism in the 1950s in deciding to emigrate to the Central African Federation and Kenya.

As the previous chapters have shown, the settlers guarded their white islands fiercely. They marked their distance from non-Western majorities through racial segregation and by creating an idealized mirror image of British society in the colonies. This involved importing British food and building Anglican churches, private clubs, taverns, golf courses, and Masonic lodges. Britons living under the Raj shunned Anglo-Indians, who traced their origins to eighteenth-century unions between British soldiers and Indian women, because their very existence blurred cultural boundaries. Class was also an issue, and most governments in settler colonies used unapologetically eugenicist laws to project an illusion of European racial supremacy by banning poor European migrants. In the eyes of the colonial elites, the lower classes lacked the resources to sustain the required levels of middle-class gentility and were far too willing to mix with subject populations.

Imperial partisans celebrated the men and women who sought to make a permanent home in the non-Western parts of the empire as pioneering heroes, and most people in the metropole were largely unaware that, in global terms, Indian migration within the British Empire was as significant as the mass movement of Britons. Some Indians followed long-standing precolonial trade routes to East Africa and greater South Asia. By the nineteenth century, most were indentured servants who worked on plantations throughout the empire on contracts that were supposed to send them home to the Raj after a set number of years. In the West Indies, South Asian migrant laborers filled part of the labor gap resulting from the emancipation of African slaves. Others worked on sugar plantations in South Africa, Mauritius, and Fiji or helped produce Ceylonese tea, Burmese rice, and Malayan rubber. Precise figures are not available, but by the outbreak of World War I, there were roughly 430,000 Indians in the West Indies, 1.5 million in Ceylon, 2.6 million in Burma, and 250,000 in Malaya.[21]

Some of these migrants eventually returned to India, but others settled permanently in their host territories. Labor shortages in Guiana and Trinidad led the colonial authorities to encourage the South Asians to stay, thereby making them the majority community in Guiana and 30 percent of the Trinidadian population. Territories like Mauritius and the South African province of Natal were unwilling to tolerate new non-European communities. These governments had only marginal success in expelling Indian workers with expired contracts because they lacked the legal tools to discriminate against British imperial subjects.

Indian nationalists had put an end to foreign labor recruitment in the Raj by the interwar period, but the indentured labor system left significant Indian migrant communities scattered throughout the empire. Sometimes the former indentured laborers blended with their hosts through intermarriage, but South Asians in Trinidad were numerous enough to retain a distinctive identity. During World War I, Muhammad Orfy's East Indian Destitute League lobbied the Trinidadian government to repatriate poor ex-migrants to India, and the East Indian National Association became a political force in the 1920s. The Hindu missionaries and cultural leaders who visited the colony regularly in the 1930s inspired Trinidadian Indians to become even more politically active with news of the achievements of the Indian National Congress. Concerned primarily with protecting their rights as a minority, their East Indian Democratic Labour Party emerged as a key part of the opposition bloc in the Trinidad and Tobago parliament during the 1950s. This diasporic community continued to nurture its distinct identity in the postwar era. When West Indian cricketers competed against India in a 1971 test match, Trinidadian Indians sparked a national controversy by cheering loudly for the visitors.

South Asians presented an even thornier political problem in East Africa. As part of an ancient network of trade and commerce in the Indian Ocean predating the birth of Christ, the region had well-established economic and cultural ties to the South Asian subcontinent. The British rulers of India took over these networks, and Kenya was virtually an extension of the Raj at the turn of the twentieth century. Kenyan administrators, many of whom began their careers in India, based the colony's laws on the Indian penal code. Moreover, Aden, British Somaliland, Mauritius, the Seychelles, and Kenya (until the 1920s) all used the rupee as their primary currency. South Asian workers built the Kenya-to-Uganda railway and, contrary to the boasts of the settlers, provided most of the skilled and clerical labor that made Kenya into a viable colonial state.

Economic opportunity drew steady numbers of Indian immigrants to East Africa in the early decades of the twentieth century, and the postal authorities noted that they sent thousands of rupees back to India each month. In Uganda, a handful of South Asian entrepreneurs pioneered the protectorate's cotton and sugar-refining industries, and by the 1930s more than 80 percent of Uganda's exports of these commodities went to the Raj. Some officials, like British Central Africa commissioner Sir Harry Johnston, encouraged South Asian migration to further spur economic development and argued that the region could become "the America of the Hindu."[22] Alibhoy Mulla Jeevanjee and other local Indian notables agreed emphatically. Backed by the government of the Raj, in 1919 the East African Indian leaders urged the Allied powers to make German East Africa (Tanganyika) an Indian colony as a reward for the wartime sacrifices of Indian soldiers.

The Kenyan settlers opposed these proposals vehemently and lobbied the Colonial Office to ban further South Asian immigration. Their demands were unrealistic. The colonial authorities could not openly discriminate against East African Indians because they would have played into the hands of the Indian National Congress if they even suggested that South Asians were not equal members of the empire. The Colonial Office's 1923 declaration that African interests were paramount in Kenya was in part a stratagem to protect the settlers because it prevented South Asians from buying African tribal land. These rules effectively confined Indians to urban areas and ensured that they would not compete with European farmers. Even with these restrictions, Indian immigration to Kenya continued throughout the interwar era. By 1931, Indians outnumbered the settlers in the colony 39,644 to 16,812. Some of these Kenyan Indians were descended from earlier generations of traders, but over twenty-five thousand of them were recent arrivals who had been born in India.[23]

South Asian relations with Kenya's African majority were equally complex. Africans resented Indian domination of the commercial sector and often clashed with the Goan clerks and civil servants who ran remote government offices for the colonial administration. On the other hand, during the interwar years Indian lawyers and politicians like Isher Dass kept Jomo Kenyatta's

Kikuyu Central Association (KCA) up-to-date with the Indian National Congress's campaign against the Raj, and in the late 1930s they advised Samuel Muindi on how to use passive resistance to thwart the colonial regime's attempt to force the Kamba to sell their cattle to a South African meatpacking company at below-market prices. During the Mau Mau Emergency, radicals like the trade union leader Makhan Singh joined Kenyatta and the other KCA leaders in detention.

This radicalism helped some South Asians become citizens in good standing in Kenya, Uganda, and Tanzania after independence. Interestingly, very few members of this diasporic community returned to India or Pakistan, which had been independent nations for more than decade by the time of the transfer of power in East Africa. Nevertheless, lingering popular bitterness over the comparatively privileged position that the South Asians enjoyed under British imperial rule left them in a precarious position, and many people hedged their bets by retaining their British passports. As their situation became even more uncertain over the course of the 1960s, large numbers of East African Indians used these passports to emigrate not to India but to Britain itself. The Ugandan military dictator Idi Amin made matters worse by expelling the entire Ugandan South Asian community in 1972 on the grounds that they "milked the cow, but did not feed it to yield more milk."[24] As we shall see later in this chapter, the result was an enormous popular backlash against non-Western immigrants in metropolitan Britain that led directly to an overhaul and gradual elimination of Britain's policies on open Commonwealth immigration.

At the turn of the twentieth century, few imperial partisans would have envisioned the need for such draconian measures. They were proud that Britain was the center of the empire's economic and social networks and accepted that their subjects had been traveling to the imperial metropole as diplomats, tourists, students, freed slaves, and merchant seamen for centuries. Some of these visitors stayed for a few months; others passed out of official sight by settling permanently and blending into the larger population. Their relatively small numbers did not threaten the illusion of national homogeneity, but their presence demonstrates that British society was never as "white" as the critics of postcolonial migration to Britain wanted to believe.

This gradually became more evident as the second British Empire expanded and enhanced the networks of trade and culture that brought non-Westerners to Britain. The migration began as a trickle of students, political leaders, and merchant seamen but grew into a flood of migrant workers after World War II. Keeping subject peoples fixed in place was one of the unspoken central functions of formal imperial rule, and it is telling that the empire's demise actually increased the flow of permanent settlers from the former colonies. Ever since the ancient Romans worried about the contaminating influence of Greek culture, empire builders have fretted that colonial rule, which required high levels of intimacy and cross-cultural exchange, would cause them to be changed or swallowed up by the people they conquered. It is rather unlikely that the empire would have generated so much popular support if Britons had realized that it would accelerate Britain's transformation into a multiethnic society.

From the subject's point of view, particularly before World War II, one of the most compelling reasons to visit the imperial metropole was that the authoritarian and discriminatory laws and social institutions that made life so difficult in the colonies did not apply in Britain. Although non-Westerners sometimes faced racial abuse and harassment in their daily lives, the average Briton saw no need to uphold the strict social segregation that was the cornerstone of imperial rule in the overseas empire. Subject peoples were free to attend school, petition Parliament, run for local office, and interact openly with ordinary Britons. The colonial regimes therefore tried to ensure that only the most politically reliable people visited Britain. Lacking the legal authority to issue blanket travel bans, they relied on a highly bureaucratic passport application process and the expense of ship and plane tickets to limit access to the metropole. This meant that it usually took some form of official sponsorship and financial support to visit the imperial "homeland."

Although Indian princes made frequent trips to Britain, most South Asian visitors at the turn of the century were students. Young men seeking a career in government had to take the Indian Civil Service exam in Britain, which was virtually impossible to pass without a degree from a metropolitan university. Some who went to study stayed on for decades, and several Indians actually won seats in the British parliament. Politics proved a powerful lure for many educated expatriates, and some became quite respectable by British standards. Sir Mancherjee Bhownagree, the Conservative member of Parliament for the London neighborhood of Bethnal Green, had little use for the Indian National Congress and spoke strongly against Indian home rule.

In other cases, however, a visit to the United Kingdom could lead to difficult political complications for colonial governments. From the Raj's standpoint, princely tours of Britain were not much of a problem because the worst thing that could happen was that, like Seretse Khama, a prince might come home with a European wife. As noted in earlier chapters, however, South Asian students presented a greater problem. Many followed in the footsteps of Mohandas Gandhi and the founders of the Indian National Congress, who had all studied in Britain, by moving into nationalist politics. A small handful of radical students went much further in seeking to overthrow the Raj and assaulting senior imperial officials. The severity of these attacks ranged from Vasudeo Bhattacharyya punching Sir William Lee-Warner, a former secretary of the India Office's political department, in the face for calling him a "dirty n--ger" to Madan Lal Dhingra's assassination of Sir William Curzon Wyllie. Shapurji Saklatvala, who first arrived in London as a medical student, returned in 1921 as the representative of the All-India Trade Union Congress. In the 1920s, he won the parliamentary seat for Battersea North while running as a self-declared communist. Much to the frustration of the Raj's security services, metropolitan civil liberty safeguards made London an incubator for revolutionary nationalism. This was as true for Ireland as it was for India.

Although the most influential South Asian visitors to pre–World War II Britain tended to be aristocrats or students, the early British Caribbean community represented a much broader cross section of West Indian society. Some were professionals like C. L. R. James and Henry Sylvester Williams, a Trinidadian lawyer who organized the First Pan-Africanist Congress in London in 1901 to draw attention to abuses in the African colonies. Many, however, were merchant seamen. Some of these sailors were highly politicized and spread the anti-imperial teachings of Marcus Garvey as they moved back and forth between the Caribbean, Africa, Britain, and the United States. After World War I, migrant munitions workers and veterans of the Royal West Indies Regiment, which the British government disbanded in Britain, swelled their ranks.

Although celebrated artists and athletes like Learie Constantine faced comparatively less discrimination, ordinary West Indians found it more difficult to fit into British society because they were more numerous and tended to come from lower-class backgrounds. This led to trouble when they competed with working-class Britons for jobs and women. In 1919, a string of race riots erupted in the port cities of Cardiff, Liverpool, and Tyneside as mobs attacked "colored" sailors, demobilized veterans, and laborers. Sir Ralph Williams, a colonial administrator who served in Bechuanaland and Barbados, invoked imperial racial and gender biases to justify the violence. "To almost every white man and woman who has lived a life among coloured races, intimate association between black or coloured men and white women is a thing of horror. . . . It is an instinctive certainty that sexual relations between white women and coloured men revolt our very nature."[25] In the interwar years, the metropolitan and colonial governments in Africa and the Caribbean therefore sought to repatriate as many of these poor and lower-middle-class non-European migrants as possible. Embittered by this ill treatment, many of the West Indians returned home ready to embrace anti-imperial nationalism.

Educated West Indians were less likely to face mob violence, but they too experienced racial discrimination when they sought full access to British society. The highly trained Jamaican physician Harold Moody had trouble getting work in hospitals and municipal medical services because, as the Chamberwell Board of Guardians put it, "the poor people would not have a 'n--ger' attend them."[26] Whereas poorer West Indians defended themselves with their fists, Moody and his peers turned to political activism. In 1931, he founded the League of Coloured Peoples to improve race relations and protect the interests of non-Europeans in Britain. As a devout Christian, Moody shied away from aggressive tactics and preferred to work through petitions and newspaper editorials. Similarly, James and Constantine used their fame and the popularity of cricket in northeastern England as an opportunity to tell ordinary Britons that there was a valid case for West Indian independence.

By the 1930s, many of the West Indians and Africans in Britain were ready to take a more confrontational approach. George Padmore, an American-educated Trinidadian, continued the Pan-Africanist work of Henry Sylvester Williams and the African American intellectual W. E. B. DuBois in seeking to unite all peoples of African descent in a common front against racism and imperialism. In contrast to Moody, Padmore was an avowed Marxist who founded the International African Service Bureau to aid subject peoples throughout the empire. Much to the alarm of the Special Branch, he took Jomo Kenyatta, who was in Britain to deliver a petition to Parliament asking for the return of Kikuyu lands, to visit the Soviet Union. Contrary to the Kenyan government's charges, Kenyatta was no Bolshevik, but his time in Britain gave him the opportunity to build alliances with Fenner Brockway and the rest of the metropolitan humanitarian lobby and to earn a degree in social anthropology while studying with Bronislaw Malinowski at the London School of Economics. Having spent World War II in Britain, Kenyatta helped Padmore, Kwame Nkrumah, C. L. R. James, and several other prominent British-based activists organize the 1945 Fifth Pan-Africanist Congress in Manchester to coordinate the anti-imperial struggle in Africa and the West Indies. As noted in chapter 4, whereas earlier congresses had pushed Britain to govern its colonies more fairly, the Manchester delegates called for the "complete social, economic and political emancipation" of the imperial territories.[27]

There was little that the Colonial Office or metropolitan security services could do about Padmore's activities because he and his allies enjoyed the full protection of British law. The Special Branch kept the Pan-Africanists under close surveillance but did not interfere with their right to free speech. Radicals like I. T. A. Wallace-Johnson, who was one of Padmore's close allies, spent a great deal of time in West African jails for sedition, but he was relatively free to speak and write what he pleased when he was in Britain. As Kwame Nkrumah put it, "I quickly felt at home in England. . . . Nobody bothered about what you were doing and there was nothing to stop you getting on your feet and denouncing the whole of the British Empire."[28] The future Mau Mau detainee Bildad Kaggia warmly recalled how well he was treated by working-class British families, whom he found refreshingly different from Kenya's "bossy DCs and settlers," when he visited Britain as a soldier in 1945.

In this sense London played a central role in the eventual demise of the British Empire by serving as a meeting ground for young activists and nationalists from across the political spectrum. Radicals like Padmore, Nkrumah, Wallace-Johnson, Peter Abrahams, Eric Williams, and the African American actor and singer Paul Robeson interacted with Kenyatta (who was actually quite conservative), Seretse Khama, and, by the 1950s, even the exiled Bugandan Kabaka Mutesa II. Although few members of Labour's left wing shared their aspirations for national independence at this point, many of them, like Fenner Brockway, also moved easily within these circles.

Much of this activity took place during the 1940s as social segregation was becoming more of a liability. During World War II, it was hard to portray the empire as an egalitarian multiracial institution when its subjects faced racial abuse and discrimination. The British government was embarrassed profoundly by press accounts of how Learie Constantine, the deputy president of the Indian Legislative Assembly, and a pair of Sikh Victoria Cross winners were refused service in London hotels and restaurants. The postwar Labour government's attempt to reform the empire through development colonialism and multiracial cooperation provided an additional incentive to make metropolitan Britain appear more welcoming to non-Europeans.

The British Nationality Act of 1948, which granted all residents of the empire common citizenship, gave these ideals formal legal status by stipulating that the residents of the colonies had the same rights as metropolitan Britons. In passing this legislation Clement Attlee's government sought primarily to promote Commonwealth unity by regularizing the citizenship laws in the self-governing dominions and, to a lesser degree, blunting the appeal of anti-imperial nationalism in the African, Asian, and West Indian colonies. In answering Conservative charges that the law was unworkable because non-Westerners had a different standard of civilization, Attlee's lord chancellor William Jowitt painted a grand picture of a unified empire: "We can say that people who come from one part of the British Empire shall not be allowed in and people from another part shall be allowed in, but in this great metropolitan centre of the Empire I hope we never shall say such a thing; I hope we shall always extend to all British subjects the same rights and the same privileges as members of a family."[29] In the Commons, David Maxwell Fyfe offered a similar defense of the law: "If we create a distinctive citizenship for Britain and the Colonies, inevitably . . . differentiation will creep in. We must maintain our great metropolitan tradition of hospitality to everyone from every part of our Empire."[30]

In pushing through this legislation, Attlee's government did not expect any changes in the volume or character of imperial migration. Assuming that it would take generations before the empire's backward peoples reached the civilizational level of the self-governing dominions, the Labourites expected that the British Nationality Act would only apply to the relatively small numbers of politicians, professionals, and students who visited Britain on a short-term basis. They never imagined that it would open the door for over four hundred thousand West Indians, Indians, Pakistanis, Africans, and Hong Kong Chinese to settle in Britain between 1946 and 1962.

This sudden inward migration of subject and formerly subject peoples began when individual West Indians, driven by high unemployment and oppressive poverty in the Caribbean, responded to the metropolitan postwar labor shortage. By 1948, Britain faced a shortfall of 250,000 workers due to a declining birthrate, wartime casualties, and delays in demobilization. Most of the unfilled positions were low-paying semiskilled jobs in hospitals, foundries, and textile mills that metropolitan Britons shunned. The Labour government initially recruited workers from European refugee camps and enacted registration laws discouraging less productive occupations like shoe shining, bookmaking, and nightclub bouncing, but these measures failed to produce enough cheap labor to drive the postwar recovery.

Many West Indians, however, were willing to take Britain's unappealing jobs. Having read about the labor shortage in imported British newspapers, roughly one hundred Jamaican workers, many of whom had served in the United Kingdom during the war, booked passage to Britain in 1947. They largely went unnoticed, but one year later the British press covered the arrival of another contingent of five hundred West Indians on the SS *Empire Windrush*, a former troop ship. Caught off guard by the appearance of so many non-European workers, the Ministry of Labour tried to settle the immigrants in small groups around the country to ensure they did not form "ghettos."

Although Britain faced a serious labor shortage, the West Indian workers created a political problem for Attlee. Ten members of his own party openly called for stricter immigration controls on non-Europeans. "The British people fortunately enjoy a profound unity without uniformity in their way of life, and are blest by the absence of a colour racial problem. An influx of coloured people domiciled here is likely to impair the harmony, strength and cohesion of our public and social life and to cause discord and unhappiness among all concerned."[31] Some politicians even suggested that the *Windrush* migration had been organized by the Soviets to increase racial tensions in Britain. Others argued that West Indians were too lazy and vulnerable to the cold to work in the United Kingdom.

Attlee, however, had few options. His government hoped to send the West Indians to Tanganyika to work on the ill-fated groundnut scheme but lacked the legal authority to force British subjects to take specific jobs. Under the terms of the 1948 Nationality Act, the West Indians were free to enter Britain and work where they pleased. The Labour government would have created serious political problems throughout the empire and Commonwealth if it tried to deny West Indians their legal right to enter the United Kingdom at a time when it was still recruiting foreign laborers in Europe.

The British authorities therefore turned to subtler tactics to discourage further immigration. Colonial Office representatives toured the West Indies telling would-be migrants that the jobs listed in British newspapers were only temporary positions and directed shipping companies to look out for stowaways. The complication was that British employers actually needed the West Indians. Facing a shortage of fifty thousand nurses for the newly inaugurated National Health Service, the Ministry of Health began recruiting West Indian nurses in 1949. Private employers seeking factory workers, bus drivers and conductors, porters, secretaries, and guards were also more than willing to hire migrants who arrived on their own initiative. The one limitation was that most would not employ West Indian men in positions where they might interact with "white" women.

In the 1950s, the rate of West Indian arrivals increased markedly after the American 1952 McCarren-Walter Immigration Act made it harder to reach the United States. Over the course of the decade, there was also an extremely sharp spike in South Asian migration as Indians and Pakistanis used their status as Commonwealth citizens under the 1948 Nationality Act to enter Britain. Although it seemed illogical that tens of thousands of people would choose to live under their former imperial rulers instead of their own democratically elected national governments, the turmoil caused by the partition of the Raj made the relative stability and economic opportunity in metropolitan Britain appealing. A British university degree was also still an important credential for young Indians seeking a career in the civil service or the professions. Although South Asians sent home a steady stream of remittances, the governments of India and Pakistan actively sought to limit lower-class migration through property and literacy requirements for passports on the grounds that uneducated people would damage their national prestige by creating a poor impression in Britain. These measures were largely ineffective, and the influx of people from the South Asian subcontinent continued unabated into the late 1950s. Africans, by comparison, lacked the information, economic resources, and travel opportunities to join this inward imperial migration.

Although some migrants eventually returned home, many started their families and became permanent British residents. Some London neighborhoods took on a distinctly West Indian air with Jamaicans settling in Brixton, Trinidadians and Barbadians in Notting Hill, Guyanese in Tottenham and Wood Green, and Montserratians in Finsbury Park. Many Britons were profoundly unsettled by these developments, particularly when the new arrivals stood out by introducing new cultural styles and cheering enthusiastically for visiting West Indian cricket teams.

In 1951, the ultra-right-wing Union Movement took up the issue in its party paper by attacking the "coloured invasion" and publishing stories depicting immigrants as savages, drug dealers, criminals, and rapists. Although there is no point in dignifying these slurs with a refutation, it is interesting to note that many immigrants found British life equally barbaric. Like the Specials' rhythm guitarist Lynval Golding, the Oxford-trained sociologist Stuart Hall was shocked by the racism he encountered in a place that West Indians had been taught was the welcoming center of the Commonwealth. "The word 'black' had never been uttered in my household or anywhere else in Jamaica in my hearing, in my entire youth and adolescence."[32] West Indians also complained that Britons did not bathe enough, sold their bread unwrapped, and used newspapers to wrap fish and chips. Muslim South Asians similarly protested that the six inches of warm water provided in public bathhouses, which reflected the shortages that bedeviled Britain after World War II, forced people to "wash in their own dirt."[33] Kwame Nkrumah and Seretse Khama also found postwar London an austere, frigid, and uninviting place as they scrambled for the scraps of coal that fell from passing trucks to heat their small flats. More significantly, the immigrants rightly pointed out that their critics confused poverty with culture, and Nkrumah observed that living conditions in London's East End were worse than the "meanest kind of African mud hut."[34]

At first, overt hostility and aggression toward immigrants was limited to the far-right fringe, but the backlash became more serious when packs of disaffected adolescents, particularly those known as teddy boys, began to assault randomly selected individuals. There were also reports of motorists trying to run down "coloured" men in crosswalks. Frustrated by the failure of the postwar welfare state to provide suitable jobs and a decent standard of living, they blamed the new arrivals for their lack of prospects. In this sense the teddy boys were the ideological forerunners of the skinheads who disrupted the Specials' shows in the late 1970s.

These social tensions exploded in the summer of 1958 when West Indians in Nottingham and London's Notting Hill neighborhood fought back against their tormentors with their fists and improvised gasoline bombs. The rioting spread to neighboring communities as running battles erupted between immigrants and gangs of teddy boys, neo-fascists, and unaffiliated local youths. Most of the 140 people arrested during the unrest were not West Indians, but the willingness of young immigrants to meet violence with violence unnerved people and turned popular opinion against the open-door policy within the Commonwealth. With the newspapers running regular stories like "102 More Jamaicans Arrive," mobs in London carried banners that read "Deport All N--gers."[35]

As would be expected, the racial violence of 1958 reverberated throughout the Commonwealth. The Nigerian minister of health Ayo Rosiji blamed the unrest on West Indian migrants and assured the British public that West Africans were only in Britain to study and not to settle. In the Central African Federation, Rhodesian newspaper editorials hoped that metropolitan Britons would now have a more realistic appreciation of the "colour problem's complexities." Norman Manley, the chief minister and future president of Jamaica, urged his people to do a better job of integrating themselves into metropolitan British life, but he also insisted on the right of free movement within the Commonwealth. Making an argument that British settlers in Africa would have been forced to agree with, he declared, "More people leave England every year than come into it. And they leave for precisely the same reason as we come here. They are looking for better opportunities in life."[36] Quite insightfully, the poet and playwright Adil Jussawalla linked the Notting Hill riots to the end of empire. Invoking many of the same sentiments that Ham Mukasa felt on his visit to London a half century earlier, he also questioned the meaning of imperial hospitality: "If the British were ever tolerant of foreigners on their own shores (being notoriously intolerant of them abroad) it was because they had nothing to lose. They were in a ruthlessly powerful position where they could be sanctimonious, make concessions, entertain their subjects lavishly . . . and be liked for it. Now, with an Empire lost, with the coloured population of Britain rising . . . discrimination is open, violent and bloody."[37]

On the other hand, social advancement was possible for high-profile immigrants. Learie Constantine served as Trinidad's high commissioner (the equivalent of an ambassador in the Commonwealth) from 1961 to 1964, and five years later he became the first West Indian to sit in the House of Lords as Baron Constantine of Maraval and Nelson. Looking back on how the celebrated cricketer became so popular, C. L. R. James recalled that the process of assimilation cut both ways: "When [Constantine] finally decided to leave, all Nelson asked him to stay. He had conquered the hearts of the Nelson people. That story is sufficiently known. What is not known is that the Nelson people conquered him."[38]

Although the antimigrant backlash of the late 1950s definitely made life worse for more ordinary non-Europeans in Britain, it did not slow the overall rate of immigration. In fact, the transfer of power in Africa and the West Indies actually increased the numbers of former colonial subjects moving to Britain. In 1961, the annual rate of migration reached 136,000.[39] Britain's jobs remained appealing because the empire's neo-mercantile economic legacy meant that independence did not decrease unemployment in the ex-colonies significantly. Commonwealth membership meant that the door to Britain was still open for most West Indians, Africans, and South Asians, and the new national governments lacked the means and incentive to continue the colonial policy of discouraging emigration.

Faced with the prospect that this steady stream might turn into a flood, in 1962 Parliament passed the Commonwealth Immigrants Act requiring all immigrants to apply for an official employment voucher before coming to Britain. By mandating the issue of only eighty-five hundred vouchers per year, the law effectively put a hard cap on immigration. It also empowered the police to deport migrants who committed a crime within five years of their arrival. The new restrictions did not end the controversy over British identity. Immigration remained a significant political issue, with a Conservative candidate using the slogan "If you want a n--ger neighbor vote Labour" to win the parliamentary seat for Smethwick. The Labour Party, however, adopted an equally tough stance on the migrant question and cut the annual quota of labor vouchers after coming to power in 1964. Both parties embraced a bipartisan immigration policy that tempered entrance restrictions with legal efforts to combat racial discrimination in metropolitan society.

During the colonial era, British officials had tried to use the Commonwealth ideal of universal imperial citizenship to maintain close ties to the dominions and convince South Asians, Africans, and West Indians that they did not need separate nations. By the late 1960s, however, the Commonwealth had lost much of its strategic and economic importance, and the British government was not particularly troubled by Australian objections to the 1962 Commonwealth Immigrants Act's passport controls. For some Britons, the Commonwealth had become a threat to their very national identity.

These fears became more pronounced in 1967 when the government of Kenya instituted an "Africanization" program that removed Indians from the civil service and required all non-Kenyan passport holders to take out work permits. Most East African Indians still held British passports as "British overseas citizens," and a loophole in the 1962 immigration law allowed the dependents of Commonwealth citizens already in Britain to join their relatives. Fearing that they would no longer be able to make a living in Kenya, over thirteen thousand of them sought passage to Britain.

Televised images of masses of South Asians lining up for plane tickets in Nairobi returned the immigration question to the forefront of British politics. The National Front, an ultra-right-wing coalition of neo-fascist and racial nationalist groups, emerged as a political force by calling for the repatriation of all immigrants. Enoch Powell, a high-ranking member of the Conservative Party who had won widespread respect a decade earlier for his eloquent criticism of his own party's handling of the Hola camp killings, warned that non-European immigration was about to plunge Britain into the same kind of ethnic turmoil that produced the 1968 race riots in American cities. In what has become known as his "rivers of blood" speech, he declared, "As I look ahead, I am filled with foreboding. Like the Roman, I seem to see 'the River Tiber foaming with much blood.' That tragic and intractable phenomenon which we watch with horror on the other side of the Atlantic . . . is coming upon us here by our own volition and our own neglect. Indeed, it has all but come."[40] Powell's inflammatory language cost him his party leadership position, but, much to the chagrin of the Labour Party, the wave of sympathy strikes that broke out across the nation to protest Powell's removal showed that many British workers shared his views. This popular support for even tighter restrictions on immigration contributed to the passage of the 1968 Commonwealth Immigrants Act, which required would-be immigrants to have been born, naturalized, or adopted in the United Kingdom. This permitted most residents of the dominions to enter Britain, but by creating two categories of British passport holders, it stripped the East African Indians of their right to travel freely in the Commonwealth.

Three years later, Edward Heath's Conservative government went a step further by pushing through the 1971 Immigration Act, which rescinded the promise of universal Commonwealth citizenship entirely. It required "British overseas citizens" wishing to enter Britain to have a special work permit that had to be renewed each year. Although international pressure forced Britain to admit the thirty thousand Indians that Idi Amin summarily expelled from Uganda one year later, the 1971 Immigration Act finally and conclusively severed the central threads of the British Empire's global migration network. Henceforth, there would be no further mass population transfers between Britain and its former imperial possessions. There were, however, hundreds of thousands of former colonial subjects who were now legal citizens of the new multiethnic postimperial Britain.

COLONIZING BRITAIN?

The British people themselves were thus transformed by the experience of having a global empire. Just as imperial rule introduced Africans and Asians to the West's ideas, values, and material culture, Britons also borrowed, both intentionally and unintentionally, from their colonial subjects. Indirect rule required British officials to govern as local rulers, while settlers and other employers had to learn the languages and customs of their workers. Missionaries studied local cultures to refine their evangelical message, and they created written versions of African and Asian languages as part of their efforts to produce a more accessible bible. These people introduced non-Western culture and customs to Britain when they retired. After World War II, West Indian and South Asian migrants further contributed to the hybridization of British culture. Ironically, although many Britons may have lamented the loss of their ethnic homogeneity, over time they came to appreciate the food and music of the very people they sought to keep at arms' length through the increasingly restrictive immigration bills.

One the most significant and revealing legacies that the British Empire bestowed on metropolitan culture was a broader and richer diet. During the heyday of the new imperialism, special interest groups used food to demonstrate the benefits of empire to the British public. In the 1920s, the Empire Marketing Board sent sixty thousand copies of a recipe for "An Empire Christmas Pudding," supposedly concocted by King George V's personal chef, to grocery stores throughout the United Kingdom.

> 1 lb Sultans & 1 lb Currants from Australia
> 1 lb Stoned Raisins from South Africa
> 6 oz Minced Apples from Canada
> 1 lb Bread Crumbs from the United Kingdom
> 1 lb Beef Suet from New Zealand
> 6 oz Candied Peel from South Africa
> 8 oz Flour from the United Kingdom
> 4 Eggs from the Irish Free State
> 1/2 oz Ground Cinnamon from Ceylon
> 1/3 oz Ground Cloves from Zanzibar
> 1 pinch Pudding Spice from India
> 1 tablespoon Brandy from Cyprus
> 2 tablespoons Rum from Jamaica
> 1 pint Old Beer from England[41]

The empire also made it easier for Britain to remain a nation of tea drinkers. The British had consumed Chinese-grown tea for centuries, but India and Ceylon became their main source of the beverage in the twentieth century. In the 1950s, Britons were drinking an average of nearly six cups of tea per day, much of which came from the Commonwealth and former imperial territories.[42]

The empire also helped make once exotic foodstuffs like cocoa and tropical fruit into common fare for the average family. In 1900, the British government required the shipping company of Elders, Dempster and Company to import twenty thousand bananas into Britain per week as a condition of the subsidy to carry mail to and from the West Indies. Although the company initially had to give the fruit away because it was so exotic, by 1924 the British public was consuming over 11 million bunches of bananas per year.

In terms of the overall volume of imports, the colonies were never able to supply all of Britain's tropical produce needs, but the empire still played a key role in shaping metropolitan tastes. When World War II severed Britain's commercial links with the tropics, consumers missed their bananas and made do with mashed turnips flavored with banana "essence." When the fruit reappeared in the postwar era, parents had to teach their children to eat them like ice cream cones instead of corn on the cob. The commodity boom of the 1950s restored bananas and other tropical products to an increasingly central place in British diets, which in turned helped sustain the fragile economies of the British West Indies.

More significantly, the imperial experience produced new hybrid metropolitan cuisines. By the 1990s, there were more than seven thousand Indian restaurants in Britain.[43] Most offered a distinctive menu featuring curries of varying degrees of spiciness. Yet "curry" had no specific meaning in actual Indian cooking. It emerged in the nineteenth century as a generic term for a sauce flavored with a mixture of spices including turmeric, coriander, cumin, ginger, fenugreek, and various kinds of pepper. The dish became an integral part of the Raj's culture. Indian army officers prided themselves on their ability to eat the hottest versions of the dish, while the wives of Indian Civil Service bureaucrats made it part of their regular family fare. These expatriate Britons took their taste for curry with them when they returned home, and it became a regular feature in metropolitan cookbooks by the twentieth century.

It did not take South Asians in Britain long to recognize curry's potential. In 1926, an Anglo-Indian medical student founded the first Indian restaurant in Britain on London's Regent Street. Serving a variety of dishes ranging from game to beef curry, Veeraswamy acquired a prestigious clientele, including Edward Prince of Wales, Charlie Chaplain, and Indira Gandhi. It was not until the 1960s, however, that South Asian cooks, who were mostly male migrants, developed the staple curries with standardized ingredients and Anglicized names that are featured in most of Britain's Indian restaurants. Starting with a basic sauce, they varied its temperature to create mild (korma), medium (madras), and very hot (vindaloo) versions of the dish. This cuisine could hardly be called traditional by South Asian standards.

Curry, along with an Anglo-Chinese cuisine that was similarly invented by immigrants from Hong Kong and greater China, became a staple fixture of contemporary British culture. Initially, a taste for Chinese or Indian food was a mark of sophistication, but these dishes soon became common fare for all social classes. In the 1990s, a national poll found that chicken tikka masala, an entree of diced chicken in curry sauce that was once unknown in India, was Britain's favorite dish. In another survey, three-quarters of all Britons reported that they cooked an Indian meal at least once per month.[44] Extremely hot vindaloo curry ironically became the staple food of the hyper-aggressive, hard-drinking hooligans who preyed on immigrants and "coloured Britons." The dish was so distinctively British that English football (soccer) fans adopted "Vindaloo Vindaloo" as their national chant in the 1998 World Cup competition.

As with curry, the imperial experience helps explain the popularity of the Specials and the rise of new musical forms in late-twentieth-century Britain. Although it took longer for South Asian "Bollywood" films and musical genres like bhangra to develop a large popular following in the metropole, West Indian migrants had a much more immediate influence on the listening tastes of young Britons. The ska favored by the Specials was a Jamaican import that grew out of a complex blend of African music, European folk melodies, and American rhythm and blues. Initially known as mento, Jamaican popular music featured social commentary set to a highly danceable beat. Jamaican entrepreneurs in the 1950s created a market for recorded mento and other kinds of local music by staging impromptu dances backed by enormous mobile amplifiers drawing over thirty thousands watts. These "sound systems," as they were popularly known, helped mento evolve into ska by featuring music with deep and heavy danceable baselines. In the 1960s, ska became the favored music of rebellious young Jamaicans and Kingston gangsters, known collectively as rude boys, by blending local styles with interpretations of international hits like the theme music of the James Bond movies. The song track from the 1961 film *The Guns of Navarone* was covered by a wide variety of bands, including the Specials. By the end of the decade, ska gave way to reggae, which combined the mento tradition with the drumming and Pan-Africanist ideology of the Ethiopian, or Rastafarian, movement.

Jamaican migrants took their music with them on their travels. Mento musicians had been playing in Britain since the interwar period, and Seretse Khama first found common ground with his future wife, Ruth Williams, in their shared interest in jazz and calypso music. But the sound system tradition of the 1950s had the greatest impact on popular metropolitan culture. Preferring their "own sort of music," Jamaican migrants played imported ska recordings in nightclubs throughout London, Manchester, and Birmingham. Rico Rodriguez, the trombonist who backed the Specials in the late 1970s, played in many of these clubs in the early 1950s. Young Britons discovered ska records in the 1960s when independent "pirate" radio stations broadcasting from ships in international waters to get around the British Broadcasting Company's state-mandated monopoly of the airwaves began playing the music of the West Indian immigrants.

Like curry, ska and reggae became popular with outcast youths who perceived "black" culture as masculine, defiant, and cool. Ironically, the first generation of skinheads in the late 1960s played a significant role in the commercial success of West Indian music because they liked its heavy base lines and gangster connotations. Similar to the earlier teddy boys and overlapping with the football (soccer) hooligan culture, these working-class youths despised the privileges and pretensions of 1960s middle-class "hippy" bohemian culture. Wearing the proletarian garb of steel-toed work boots, rolled-up jeans, suspenders, and a close-cropped haircut, they embraced violence and confrontation. By the 1960s some London gangs even had a few West Indian members, but the skinheads continued in the teddy boy tradition of harassing immigrants by shifting to attacks on Indians and Pakistanis. Considering them too feminine and different, they singled out South Asians, particularly after Powell's race-baiting "rivers of blood" speech, for what became known as "paki-bashing."

Regardless of the fact that many of the skinheads' targets had been born in Britain, "black" became linked with "immigrant." Even though most were now citizens in good standing, by the 1970s these "black Britons" faced increased abuse from both the skinheads and the police, who placed their neighborhoods under close surveillance ("under heavy manners") and used antivagrancy laws as an excuse to stop and search them. Deploying tactics pioneered in Ireland and the colonies, the London Metropolitan Police Service's Special Patrol Group, which acquired a reputation for brutality and civil rights abuses, was ready to step in if these marginalized groups protested collectively. This is what happened in 1976 in Notting Hill after members of the West Indian community tried to prevent the police from arresting an accused pickpocket. As was the case in 1958, gangs of "white" youths joined in the fighting as the clash with police erupted into another full-scale riot.

Although the original skinheads did not support any particular political party, the 1970s also saw a skinhead revival that was far more militant and extreme in dress—which now entailed shaved heads, tattoos, and military clothing—and espoused an anti-establishment ideology. On the left, the young punk rockers shared their alienation and hostility toward all forms of authority. In 1977, the Sex Pistols provided an entirely different perspective on the celebration of Queen Elizabeth II's twenty-fifth anniversary on the throne by singing, "God save the Queen, a fascist regime."[45] These developments coincided with a spike in popular support for the National Front, which garnered almost 250,000 votes in the 1977 elections. Seeking to broaden their support among working-class youths, the rightists created the Young National Front (YNF) to co-opt the skinheads and punks. The YNF made little headway in this regard, and the Sex Pistol's Johnny Lydon (aka Johnny Rotten) dismissed them as "loathsome slugs."

The Specials were born of this era. In blending ska with punk rock, they created a new musical style and promoted an ideology that reclaimed West Indian music for the Left. They rejected both white supremacy and the aggressive backlash it inspired in the immigrant communities. Their 2 Tone icon, which acquired the nickname "Walt Jabsco," combined the clothing of the Jamaican rude boy and the British skinhead and could be seen as either a white or black man. More significantly, the Specials used the anti-establishment ethos of the 1970s to promote an aggressive tolerance in their music. The song "Do the Dog" disgustedly warned of the consequences of pointless racialized violence and cautioned that the result would be punks, "Teds," National Front members, Rastafarians, mods, rockers, hippies, and skinheads pointlessly fighting until they were all dead.[46] The Specials were not the only group expressing these sentiments, and they drew some of their largest audiences in the Rock against Racism (RAR) concerts that the new generation of musicians organized in response to anti-immigrant statements by popular mainstream artists like Eric Clapton. In this sense, the RAR was the Left's answer to the National Front.

The Specials stayed together for only a few years, and the overall social impact of their 2 Tone label should not be overstated. Indeed, some of the worst race riots in the postcolonial era occurred in 1981 after Margaret Thatcher's Conservative Party returned to power on an explicitly anti-immigrant platform. Nevertheless, by playing Anglicized versions of West Indian gangster music in a racially mixed group, the band became a potent force in the ongoing struggle to define the nature and character of contemporary British society. In effect, the Specials and their 2 Tone colleagues embraced the British Empire's multiethnic legacy.

Although the formal empire withered away over the last decades of the twentieth century, its complicated legacy still exerted a powerful influence on political and cultural debates in both Britain and its formal imperial possessions. In 1997, the same year that Britain returned Hong Kong to China, Queen Elizabeth and her consort, Prince Philip, marked the fiftieth anniversary of Indian independence by visiting Amritsar and the memorial to the victims of the massacre at the Jallianwala Bagh nearly eight decades earlier. However, she stopped short of apologizing for General Dyer's actions and instead expressed only her "sadness" that the deaths had occurred. Yet neither the Queen's failure to take responsibility for the killings, nor Philip's unfortunate assertion that the memorial's claim that two thousand people died at the Jallianwala Bagh was exaggerated because he had gotten the correct number from Dyer's son, caused much outcry in India. The Foreign Secretary Robin Cook's support for third-party mediation in the Kashmir dispute, which the Indian government interpreted as being pro-Pakistan, produced considerably more anger and controversy. Noting that Tony Blair's Labour government was looking to win the support of Sikh voters in Britain, the Indian magazine *Frontline* observed that the queen's visit "was not, in any meaningful sense, about India at all."[47]

Seven years after the royal visit to Amritsar, four children of immigrants blew themselves up on the London subway in July 2005, killing over fifty people. Three of the assailants were Muslims of South Asian descent, and the fourth was a West Indian convert to Islam. Although terrorism experts had warned that Islamic radicals might target the Underground, the British public was shocked to discover that the bombers were locally born and not foreign operatives of al Qaeda. British Muslim leaders condemned the attack, and Prime Minister Tony Blair declared his government's intention to revoke the citizenship of naturalized residents who did not respect "the British way of life."[48]

The young bombers committed suicide to oppose Britain's involvement in the American invasion of Iraq, but many political commentators also concluded that their alienation was the result of Britain's failure to develop into a truly multiethnic society. So it is tempting to say that as native-born Britons, theirs was a much different vision of the "British way of life." However, in commenting on Blair's underlying motives for arranging Queen Elizabeth's 1997 visit to the Amritsar memorial, Praveen Swami insightfully noted that the British Empire's legacy actually offered a way for its former subjects to become fully British: "For Asian migrants in the United Kingdom, the Empire provides a vital, if misguided, defence against racism, emphasizing the historic linkages between their state of origin and white Britain, thus legitimising their presence in that country. Labour's multiculturalism is in fact founded on the 'imperial heritage': a politics that subsumes minority cultures within a broader narrative of England and the Empire."[49] At a time when the devolution of substantial legislative authority from the metropolitan parliament in London to the National Assembly for Wales, the Northern Ireland Assembly, and the Scottish parliament raises fundamental questions of what it means to be British, the empire and its legacy remain a significant source of cohesion for the United Kingdom.

This is one reason why the Conservative Prime Minister David Cameron, whose great-grandfather voted to censure Secretary of State Edwin Montagu over his decision to force General Dyer to retire in 1920, went a step further than Queen Elizabeth and actually expressed remorse for Dyer's actions when he visited the Amritsar memorial in February 2013. Mindful that there were some eight hundred thousand British Sikhs in politically important constituencies in the London and East Midlands regions, Cameron wrote that the killings were "deeply shameful" in the Amritsar memorial book and declared, "So many British people can trace their roots to this part of northern India. Punjabis make an extraordinary contribution to British life. Sikhism is one of the key faiths not just of India, but of Britain now too."[50]

Chapter Seven

Epilogue

In late December 1963, more than a year after Uganda's independence, Ali Kisekka, the representative for Mengo South, launched a fiery attack on a group of expatriate Britons from the floor of the National Assembly. Enraged by the disrespect they had allegedly shown his nation, he shouted, "Seize their passports, publicly flog them at Kampala's independence arch." Other members of Parliament charged that the Britons, who were mostly civil servants working on loan for the Ugandan government, were members of a subversive group with ties to the American Ku Klux Klan, and Prime Minister Milton Obote joined the chorus of denunciations by calling them "snakes in our pot."[1] As would be expected, these vehement accusations touched off a relatively serious diplomatic incident at a time when the British government was working strenuously to forge good relations with its former African colonies.

Given the level of the Ugandans' outrage and the problems that it caused for Anglo-Ugandan relations, it seems remarkable that the whole scandal was the result of a raucous Christmas party that coincided with the celebrations marking the transfer of power in neighboring Kenya on the night of December 11, 1963. It was hosted by a group of four Britons in their mid- to late twenties at a large neocolonial-style house in the elite Kampala neighborhood of Tank Hill. Calling themselves the "Sludge Drinkers' Syndicate," the organizers sent out invitations to approximately two hundred Westerners from the United States and a range of European countries that read, "Greets to our right trusted and well-beloved . . . we the League of Ex-Empire Loyalists do request and require your presence at a bottle Colonial sundowner . . . to celebrate the end of the white man's burden." The invitation instructed the guests to RSVP by "native bearer in cleft stick or tom-tom . . .

or shrunken head." The dress was to be on the theme of *Sanders of the River*.[2]

In other words, they were planning the kind of frivolous cocktail party that British administrators, military officers, and settlers had been holding in every corner of the second British Empire for more than a century. One year earlier, the group's party commemorated Hannibal crossing the Alps, and the organizers most likely were inspired by the looming transfer of power in Kenya in choosing the theme for their 1963 holiday celebration. Taking the *Sanders of the River* directive to heart, many of the guests arrived wearing pith helmets, mosquito boots, and other items of clothing that might have been worn by the fictitious Nigerian district commissioner R. G. Sanders. A female employee of the Save the Children charity wore a *busuuti* dress, which had become a symbol of Ugandan nationalism, and a much more daring young woman fashioned a bikini out of the Union Jack. In addition to marking the end of imperial rule in Kenya, the party seems to have also had an informal sewage theme, perhaps because one of the organizers was an engineer for the Mengo Municipal Council. The punch bowl was a newly purchased, but unused, toilet and the guests sang a rowdy rugby song, which Obote later would recite from the floor of the Ugandan National Assembly:

> The sewage works will soon break down,
> The place will stink like mad.
> But it isn't bad for the African? It's what we've always had.
> We are bound to make a few mistakes,
> We haven't got the brains,
> And also it's undignified
> For men to clean out drains.[3]

At the stroke of midnight, they also sang "God Save the Queen" as a radio broadcast described the lowering of the Union Jack in Nairobi.

The party broke up at 5:00 a.m. on the morning of December 12, and none of the organizers thought much more about it until the Ugandan police raided the house five days later. They were responding to stories that a group of Britons had trivialized, if not openly mocked, African nationalism. In the Ugandan National Assembly, Kisekka claimed that the woman wearing the *busuuti* dress was pulled around by a rope around her neck to show "that when an African becomes independent, that is how he treats the women." Another parliamentarian gave voice to the entire assembly when he declared that the "motive behind this is racialism."[4] The youth wing of the ruling Uganda People's Congress were among the primary instigators of the resulting scandal. Their Buganda branch secretary declared that "an insult to Kenya is indeed an insult to Uganda," and a mob of youth wingers forcibly marched the editor of the *Uganda Argus*, who had not been at the party, around Kampala's main market with a bunch of bananas on his head. More seriously, arsonists burned the house on Tank Hill to the ground.

Fearing for their safety, the party organizers met with Obote to assure him personally that they had meant no disrespect, but it probably did not help matters that they had called themselves the "League of Ex-Empire Loyalists." This could easily be confused with the actual League of Empire Loyalists, which was a far-right group that eventually became part of the National Front. The British high commissioner tried to defuse the situation by formally apologizing for what the Commonwealth Relations Office (CRO) termed a "piece of horse-play [that] certainly appears to have been in poor taste." Nevertheless, the Ugandan government served deportation orders on the group along with the woman wearing the *busuuti* dress and eight British employees of the police and prisons department who had also been at the party. This most likely ended any chance of reemployment in another Commonwealth country. In explaining the reasons for taking such a drastic step, Minister of Internal Affairs Felix Onama declared that the behavior of the former civil servants "reflects very badly on their loyalty as servants of the Uganda Government."[5]

The group soon found themselves back in London, where the British government's decision to apologize for the party created a minor political furor. Using a debate over a bill that recognized Uganda's status as a republic within the Commonwealth, a Conservative MP accused the CRO of practicing "appeasement" and demanded compensation for the sacked civil servants. None was forthcoming. The American news magazine *Time* cheekily referred to the incident as "a white man's hangover," but one of the party organizers, who continued to vehemently protest his innocence, had no choice but to observe, "These chaps have no sense of humor at all."[6]

In dismissing the Ugandan objections to the Tank Hill party, the organizers and their defenders failed to realize that their former subjects never found the experience of imperial rule to be particularly funny. In a scathing attack on the young Britons' conduct, a Ugandan MP recalled, "Most of us . . . who have been born and bred in this country under the colonial regime have suffered different kinds of humiliations at different stages of our life, right from childhood to the present day." And Prime Minister Obote, in noting that there were no Africans at the party, asked, "If the [organizers] have African friends how is it possible that they can organise a party of some 200 people before they come the first of their African friends?"[7]

These poignant critiques of imperial society underscore that the legitimizing narrative of empire required Ugandans to play the role of simple primitives who surrendered their sovereignty, and often their personal dignity, in exchange for the benefits of Western civilization. As Colonial Office bureaucrat turned academic Kenneth Robinson put it, "Africa ceased to be the Dark Continent only by becoming the colonial continent."[8] In making this frequently voiced generalization, Robinson and the rest of the imperial partisans made the mistake, often self-servingly, of conflating poverty with cultural inferiority. To this, Jomo Kenyatta offered a withering rebuttal that exposed the underlying self-interest of the new imperialism: "Africans are not hostile to Western civilization as such; they would gladly learn its techniques and share in the intellectual and material benefits which it has the power to give. But they are in an intolerable position when the European invasion destroys the very basis of their old tribal ways of life, and yet offers them no place in the new society except as serfs doomed to labour for bare subsistence."[9]

On a more personal level, the Kenyan novelist Ngugi wa Thiong'o never forgot the shame and embarrassment of being arrested and detained for weeks without trial in a crowded and filthy cell simply because he was a young, educated Kikuyu with a promising future. "What can top this absurdity of my being held in a garrison for nothing more criminal than stating that I have been to Alliance [high school]? Wrestling with these memories has neither helped numb the pain I feel nor blunted the humiliation."[10]

Imperial partisans and colonial administrators reassured themselves that they, and not disgruntled elites like Kenyatta and Ngugi (the "classes"), represented the interests of the largely illiterate subject "masses." This was how the Raj failed to recognize the threat posed by the Indian National Congress, and it explains why the postwar British government ignored the near universal African opposition to the Central African Federation and multiracial constitutions. As the majority of people who lived under the second British Empire were illiterate, and thus relatively voiceless at the metropolitan level, it was easy for the imperial experts to tell themselves that they, and not the scheming Indian baboo or the upstart detribalized trousered African, were the legitimate trustees of simple tribesmen, peasants, nomads, and other sorts of "traditional" peoples.

Yet ordinary people throughout the empire actually did "speak back" to their British rulers in countless, but less orthodox, ways. Had the imperial authorities known how to listen, they would have been alarmed and upset to learn that their subjects often considered them the uncouth barbarians. Although the imperial apologists liked to list stamping out slavery and cannibalism as one of their achievements, there were widespread rumors in Central Africa that colonial officials and settlers kidnapped people to eat or to drain their blood to make quinine. Similarly, many people worried that the Central African Federation put drugs in beer to make them sterile so as to open more land for European settlement.[11] These stories were of course untrue, but so were most of the accounts of cannibalism and barbarism in preconquest Africa. And it goes without saying that for centuries Britain and many other civilized Western nations played a central role in the Atlantic slave trade.

The vast majority of Britons were unaware of these anti-imperial sentiments and accepted the second British Empire's official legitimizing narrative without question. But the transformation of the former British territories into independent sovereign nations forced them to confront the profound and deep-seated resentment of their former subjects. Kwame Nkrumah's fierce speeches at the United Nations, the biting criticism in Ngugi's novelistic treatment of life under British rule, and even the scandal over the Tank Hill party were all part of a global shift in sentiment that made formal empire immoral and illegitimate. This trend has continued in recent years, particularly as the release of previously embargoed or secret archival records from the colonial era have exposed the brutal tactics of the colonial security services. This was a key factor in the British government's 2013 decision to pay £20 million in compensation to Kenyan survivors of the Mau Mau counterinsurgency operations and detention camps.

As we have seen, a substantial majority of the metropolitan British population did not pay much attention to imperial issues or scandals. But the stigmatization of formal empire in the post–World War II era was profoundly unsettling to colonial officials, politicians, intellectuals, and a fair number of ordinary Britons. In the 1920s, Frederick Lugard offered the reassurance that "British rule has promoted the happiness and welfare of the primitive races," which was a conviction that Conservative MP George Beresford Craddock still shared three decades later: "I believe that we in this country through the British Empire and Commonwealth have made a great contribution to the scheme of things in the world, and that is something we should be proud of. I believe the best chance for the welfare of the African peoples, materially, morally and spiritually, will come from their continued protection by the strong arm of Britain."[12] These were sincere sentiments. Although there is no defending the colour bar or the racist excesses of settler colonialism, most young Britons who went into colonial administration genuinely believed that they ruled in the best interests of their subjects. The director of the Imperial Institute in the 1950s emphasized this to potential recruits for the Overseas Civil Service when he told them that they should be more open in expressing this compassion. "Most of us who work with the Colonial peoples become very attached to them; we do give them our hearts, but the trouble is that we are often too reserved to admit our affection and much too shy to show it."[13] In the present day, many of the well-meaning men and the few women who were dedicated colonial administrators or missionaries under the British Empire would surely have become "development" specialists with the World Bank and other nongovernmental aid organizations.

On the conservative side of the British ideological spectrum, many politicians and academics never lost faith in Lugard's dual mandate. Certain that the empire was a noble enterprise that made Britain a great power while simultaneously civilizing its non-Western subjects, they resented its stigmatization in the Cold War era. Sir Arthur Hilton Poynton, the last permanent undersecretary of state in the Colonial Office, did not like the term "decolonization" because it was "flavoured with the garlic of guilt," and in 1979 he lamented that there was "a generation growing up who have been brain-washed into thinking that colonialism is synonymous with exploitation."[14]

It also rankled that the Soviet Union, which ruled the former Russian imperial lands brutally, could position itself as the champion of colonized peoples simply by denying that it was an empire. In 1962, after noting in a debate in the United Nations General Assembly that both Azerbaijan and Ceylon had come under imperial rule in 1815, the British representative Sir Patrick Dean reminded the delegates that Ceylon became an independent nation in 1947, and he asked the Soviet ambassador when Azerbaijan would achieve the same status. Dean had a valid point, but he made little headway in convincing the new African and Asian members of the United Nations that Britain's empire was progressive and benevolent.

Although British imperial partisans had always viewed the Russian tsar-ist, then Soviet empire as a hostile rival, many never forgave the United States for its failure to support their empire. Echoing Arthur Bryant's senti-ments at the 1946 London victory parade, Niall Ferguson sees America's anticolonial meddling during World War II as a betrayal that forced Britain to sacrifice its empire to save the world from the evils of Japanese and German imperialism. The Conservative historian and peer Max Beloff took this argument a step further in charging the postwar U.S. government with leaving the world vulnerable to "deprivation, famine, civil and tribal war, and even genocide" by actively instigating the "catastrophe of decolonization."[15]

On both ends of the political spectrum, British imperial partisans and British imperial critics agreed that the Americans were hypocritical for fail-ing to admit that they, too, were an imperial power. D. N. Pritt, the unapolo-getically Stalinist lawyer who defended a wide range of African and Asian nationalists, titled his book attacking American imperialism *Star-Spangled Shadow*. Some fifty years later the historian David Cannadine expressed frustration at America's imperial myopia: "In both public and academic life, the presumption is that empire happens elsewhere—neither here in America, nor where America has outposts overseas."[16] To be sure, the United States conquered and colonized the Philippines at the dawn of the new imperial era. The Monroe Doctrine and military intervention in Caribbean nations made America the dominant, albeit informal, imperial power in the Western Hemi-sphere. The rise of the U.S. dollar as a global currency, the Cold War era's worldwide network of military bases, and the ubiquity of American popular culture convinced Bernard Porter that "America's early-twenty-first century 'hegemony' was already greater than that of any empire in history."[17]

The British Empire's partisans frequently invoked a tu quoque (you did it too) defense in answering U.S. attacks on their policies. Alan Burns, who served as both the governor of the Gold Coast and the British representative to the United Nations Trusteeship Council, which oversaw the old League of Nations mandates, batted away criticism of the Mau Mau detention camps by reminding Americans of their misconduct in the Philippines. Although this was self-serving, Burns was correct in pointing out that American policies toward non-Westerners could be contradictory and equally brutal. President Dwight Eisenhower rebuked the State Department's South African bureau chief for expressing "regret" over the Sharpeville massacre, and State Department officials under his Democratic successor, John F. Kennedy, initially supported South Africa as a strategically important "white redoubt" against radical "black" nationalism. The Central Intelligence Agency's Phoenix Program in South Vietnam, which killed or "neutralized" approximately eighty thousand Viet Cong supporters and sympathizers in the 1960s, dwarfed the Kenyan colonial regime's Mau Mau counterinsurgency campaign.[18]

The assumption of racial inferiority that was an inherent part of British imperial rule was hardly unique in the twentieth century. As we have seen, the most extreme British imperialists often used the racial slur "n--ger," but this hateful form of verbal abuse was far more common in the segregated American South. It was also no accident that the struggles for decolonization in the British Empire and desegregation in the United States took place at the same time. In 1958, the Notting Hill riots coincided with the Eisenhower administration's decision to use the American military to force the Little Rock, Arkansas, school board to comply with the Supreme Court's landmark *Brown v. Board of Education* ruling that racial segregation in American public schools was unconstitutional. On August 27, 1958, Britain's *Daily Express* printed a widely reproduced cartoon titled "Holier Than Thou" showing the segregationist Arkansas governor Orval Faubus and the South African prime minister Daniel Malan smiling knowingly at Harold Macmillan's embarrassment over the racial violence in Britain.

As was the case with the Soviet anti-imperial propaganda, pointing out the hypocrisy of the British Empire's critics did not negate the validity of their charges. From the standpoint of subject peoples, it mattered little whether the United States or the Soviet Union behaved better or worse than their British rulers. On this score, many imperial apologists found themselves in the difficult position of actually trying to prove that the empire brought substantial and measurable benefits. L. H. Gann and Peter Duignan attempted to do this by citing figures for school enrollments, railway and road construction, wage labor, and other quantifiable metrics of westernization that took place under British rule. To this list of achievements, Ferguson added "credible monetary regimes," transparent fiscal systems, and expanded commodity production.[19]

As we have seen in earlier chapters, the benefits of British imperialism were hardly shared equally between ruler and subject, and in Central Africa most of the infrastructural advances that so impressed Gann and Duignan were for the exclusive use of the settler class. For George Orwell the British Empire was always a "money-making concern," and he made a direct link between the wealth of the empire and living standards in metropolitan Britain. "We all live by robbing Asiatic coolies, and those of us who are 'enlightened' all maintain that these coolies ought to be set free; but our standard of living, and hence our 'enlightenment', demands that the robbery shall continue."[20]

Imperial partisans like Frederick Lugard would have rebutted this charge by arguing that under the dual mandate, British rule benefited both the metropolitan and subject populations. We have, however, seen that the empire's development record was often quite poor. In 1950, more than three-quarters of the Indian population was still employed in the agricultural sector where low yields, population pressure, and persistent social inequality kept living standards low. In British Africa, even Andrew Cohen admitted that the colonial governments did not make a sufficient investment in peasant agriculture or in the public sector.[21] Moreover, many of the empire's dubious development strategies lingered on well after the transfer of power as colonial administrators and technicians assumed leadership positions in the World Bank and other nongovernmental aid organizations. It was therefore scarcely surprising that a 1981 audit of a twenty-year $58 million World Bank rural development program in Malawi that was planned and run by a former Kenyan agricultural expert had failed to improve soil fertility or crop production significantly.[22]

Ultimately, however, imperial balance sheets and cost-benefit analyses are ineffective tools for deciding whether the second British Empire was "good" or "bad." It was neither. The Western empires born of the new imperialism in the late nineteenth century were instruments of global change, and historical change on this scale invariably benefits some and harms others.[23] These sorts of changes were never even or uniform, and the new imperialists exploited a short-term technological and commercial imbalance in the scope of globalization to conquer and rule non-Western populations that had temporarily lost the ability to defend themselves. Yet they also helped accelerate and smooth out these global changes by introducing new political, cultural, and commercial institutions into subject societies. In doing so British imperialists inadvertently taught their subjects the meaning of nationalism, capitalism, human rights, and racism, thereby setting in motion the second British Empire's surprisingly quick demise.

The Western empires that emerged from the new imperial era were thus short-lived anachronisms. As a liberal democracy underwrote their project, imperialists like Frederick Lugard had to cloak the empire's underlying authoritarianism behind a humanitarian facade. In this sense, the British, French, and, to a lesser extent, German, Portuguese, Dutch, and American empires were part of the totalitarianism that influenced so much of twentieth-century history. As George Padmore put it, "Imperialism, whatever its high pretensions to philanthropy, cannot be anything else but Fascist in its actual operation. It is founded on the lust for power and the greed for gain, and finds its excuse in theories about the superiority of one race over another."[24] Yet the British commitment to civilization and moral uplift was not entirely window dressing, and the various imperial scandals that occasionally generated controversy in the metropolitan parliament demonstrated that the new imperialism was not compatible with democratic liberalism. Although the Kenyan and Rhodesian settlers were ready to fight until the bitter end, most Britons lacked the will to hold the empire together by force. The second British Empire was thus actually surprisingly weak when it mattered. Faced with the choice of "shoot or get out," time and time again the metropolitan government chose to get out.

In declining the opportunity to become an Officer of the Most Excellent Order of the British Empire (an OBE) in 2003, the novelist Doris Lessing famously remarked that she could not do so because the British Empire no longer existed. And while Britain still has sovereignty over the Falkland Islands, Gibraltar, and several other small former imperial outposts, this is unquestionably true. Nevertheless, as we have seen in the preceding chapters, the British Empire remains at the center of intense political, academic, and popular debates.

Quite remarkably, scholars and public intellectuals still cannot agree on the empire's origins, purpose, life span, and inherent nature. This is because they are viewing the various corners of the empire from vastly different perspectives. The second British Empire seemed relatively orderly and rational from the wood-paneled office of the colonial secretary in London and in the Colonial Office records that now reside in the British National Archives. Debates in the Houses of Lords and Commons, which served as something of an imperial Greek chorus, showcased the noblest and the basest motives behind the imperial project. From this perspective, the self-governing dominions often got lumped in with the decidedly non-self-governing, non-Western protectorates. This gave metropolitan imperial partisans and scholars a great deal of freedom to portray the British Empire as strong, rational, and progressive.

It was only at the territorial level that a more nuanced view of the empire emerged. In New Delhi and the other capital cities of the empire, stately governors' mansions and large stone monuments projected a sense of permanency and power, but the correspondence, directives, and reports produced by the secretariat, which were the paper residue of the colonial bureaucracy, expose the improvised, inefficient, and often contradictory nature of British imperial rule. More often than not, poor communications allowed field administrators to ignore official directives and policy debates taking place in London. Even in the 1950s, it took a week for the Ugandan colonial government to discuss confidential matters with the Colonial Office as it relied on letters hand-delivered by British airline pilots because it took too much effort to code and decode telegrams.[25] These territorial administration records largely have survived in the national archives of the former colonies, but the most sensitive and controversial material tended to disappear into bond fires on the eve of the transfer of power or, in the case of Uganda, were dumped into Lake Victoria under the guise of being sent for "cleaning" before being turned over to Obote's government.[26]

These missing records made it possible to portray the second British Empire as humane and progressive. The vast collection of memoirs and popular histories produced by British settlers, which predictably cast a heroic and rosy light on colonial society, further feed popular Western stereotypes of African and Asian exoticism and backwardness. The mission schools and government offices that produced and employed the small class of educated elites provided a decidedly different perspective on the nature of British imperial rule. This was also true for the peasant farms, mining camps, military and police barracks, and urban slums where the vast majority of Britain's non-Western subjects experienced the realities of the new imperialism. As most were largely illiterate, they tended to drop out of the historical record, and so we know far less about the day-to-day realities of life under the empire. The scholars who have labored to bring these people back into the light of history by collecting their oral histories and traditions, reading between the lines of official records, and studying material conditions under which they lived and worked have produced interpretations of the empire that differ markedly from the histories written from the vantage point of London, the imperial capitals, or comfortable settler homes. Given that the British Empire continues to be a common reference point for foreign policy, economic planning, and popular culture in both the Western and non-Western worlds, it is worthwhile to keep these varying perspectives in mind.

British Empire Timeline

1171	Henry II begins the era of English imperial influence in Ireland
1627	English settlement of Barbados
1655	England captures Jamaica from Spain
1707	Act of Union joins England and Scotland to create Great Britain
1757	Battle of Plassey; British East India Company wins the right to administer the Mughal province of Bengal
1763	Treaty of Paris cedes New France (Quebec) to Britain
1775–1783	Britain loses control of thirteen North American colonies
1801	Act of Union creates the United Kingdom of Great Britain and Ireland
1806	Britain acquires permanent control of the Cape Colony
1819	Stamford Raffles acquires the island of Singapore for Britain
1834	Abolition of slavery in the British Empire
1842	Hong Kong acquired under Treaty of Nanking
1852	New Zealand Constitution Act grants responsible government to New Zealand
1857	Indian Mutiny
1858	Government of India Act creates the Raj by transferring the assets of the British East India Company to the Crown

1862	John Hanning Speke "discovers" that Lake Nyanza/Victoria is the source of the White Nile
1865	The House of Common's Select Committee on Africa recommends no further expansion in West Africa
1867	British North America Act creates Canada
	Colonial Office assumes responsibility for the Straits Settlements (Penang, Malacca, and Singapore)
1875	Benjamin Disraeli purchases a controlling interest in the Suez Canal for Britain
1878	Cyprus Convention gives Britain the right to administer the island
1882	British occupation of Egypt
1884–1885	Conference of Berlin partitions Africa
1899–1902	South African War
1900	Uganda Agreement
1901	Commonwealth of Australia
	First Pan-Africanist Congress in London
1902	Apolo Kagwa, Ham Mukasa, and the Gandan delegation visit Britain
1905	Partition of Bengal
1907	Tata steel plant at Jamshedpur opened
1909	Indian Councils Act (Morley-Minto reforms)
1910	Union of South Africa
1911	King George V's Coronation Durbar in Delhi
1912	Third Irish Home Rule Bill
1914–1918	World War I
1915	Ghadr revolt
1916	Easter Rising in Dublin
	Sykes-Picot Agreement partitions the Ottoman Empire between Britain and France
1917	Balfour Declaration expresses British sympathy for a Jewish national home in Palestine
1918	Strike by the Royal West Indies Regiment
1919	Amritsar massacre

	Government of India Act (Montagu-Chelmsford reforms)
	Dáil Éireann (Irish Assembly)
1919–1922	Mohandas Gandhi's satyagraha campaign against the Raj
1920	Government of Ireland Act
1921	Anglo-Irish Treaty establishes the Irish Free State and Northern Ireland
1922	Publication of Frederick Lugard's *The Dual Mandate in British Tropical Africa*
1924	Global tour by the Royal Navy's Special Service Squadron
1929	End of the Iraq Mandate
1931	Inauguration of New Delhi
	Statute of Westminster affirms that the dominions are equal, self-governing institutions within the Commonwealth
1932	Ottawa Agreement on imperial preferences
1935	Government of India Act introduces dyarchy (joint rule) to the central government of the Raj
1936	Anglo-Egyptian Treaty establishes a mutual-defense pact and restricts the imperial garrison to the Suez Canal Zone
1936–1939	Arab Revolt in Palestine
1937	Constitution of Ireland
1938	West Indies Royal (Moyne) Commission reports on the causes of labor unrest in the West Indies
1939–1945	World War II
1940	Colonial Development and Welfare Act
1941	Atlantic Charter
1942	Fall of Singapore to Japan
	Quit India movement
1942–1943	Famine in Bengal and East Africa
1945	Fifth Pan-Africanist Congress in Manchester, United Kingdom
1946	Canadian Citizenship Act
	London Victory Parade
1946–1951	Tanganyika Groundnut Scheme
1947	Independence and partition of the Raj into India and Pakistan

1948	British Nationality Act
	Ceylon independence
	Federation of Malaya
	Gold Coast riots
	Malaya Emergency
	Reunited National Party comes to power in South Africa, beginning of the apartheid era
	The SS *Empire Windrush* arrives in Britain carrying five hundred West Indian migrants
1951	Elections put the Gold Coast on the path to independence
1952	Mau Mau Emergency in Kenya
1958	Race riots in Nottingham and the Notting Hill neighborhood in London
1962	Commonwealth Immigrants Act limits on immigration from the Commonwealth
1968	Enoch Powell's "Rivers of Blood" speech
1971	Immigration Act rescinds the promise of universal Commonwealth citizenship
1997	Hong Kong returns to Chinese sovereignty as a self-governing territory
2013	The British government agrees to compensate Kenyan survivors of Mau Mau detention camps

Notes

1. INTRODUCTION

1. Edward A. Gargan, "Hong Kong Still Carries Britannia's Indelible Mark," *New York Times*, June 29, 1997.

2. Simon Jenkins, "Tears Mingle with Monsoon Rain as Retreat Is Beaten," *Times*, July 1, 1997.

3. Edward A. Gargan, "China Resumes Control of Hong Kong, Concluding 156 Years of British Rule," *New York Times*, July 1, 1997.

4. John Fortescue, *Narrative of the Visit to India of Their Majesties King George V. and Queen Mary and of the Coronation Durbar Held at Delhi 12th December 1911* (London: Macmillan and Co., 1912), 154.

5. Times Special Correspondents, "The Coronation Durbar," *Times of London*, December 13, 1911.

6. "The Maharaja Who Chose to Insult the King Emperor," *India Today*, December 11, 2011.

7. Ronald Hyam, "The British Empire in the Edwardian Era," in *Oxford History of the British Empire*, Vol. 5: *The Twentieth Century*, ed. Judith Brown and William Roger Louis (New York: Oxford University Press, 1999), 48.

8. Richard Koebner and Helmut Dan Schmidt, *Imperialism: The Story and Significance of a Political Word, 1840–1960* (Cambridge: Cambridge University Press, 1964), 10.

9. Great Britain, House of Commons, *Report from the Select Committee on Africa (Western Coast)* (London: n.p., 1865), iii.

10. C. Braithwaite Wallis, *The Advance of Our West African Empire* (London: T. Fisher Unwin, 1903), 280.

11. Quoted in Dane Kennedy, *Islands of White: Settler Society and Culture in Kenya and Southern Rhodesia, 1890–1939* (Durham, NC: Duke University Press, 1987), 130.

12. Quoted in Robin Moore, "Curzon and Indian Reform," *Modern Asian Studies* 27 (1993): 724.

13. F. D. Lugard, "The Colour Problem," *Edinburgh Review* 233 (April 1921): 280–81; Great Britain, Colonial Office, *Colonial Office Summer Conference on African Administration: African Local Government*, Fourth Session, August 20–September 1, 1951 (London: Colonial Office, 1951), 19–20.

14. Ewart Grogan and Arthur Sharp, *From Cape to Cairo: The First Traverse of Africa from South to North* (Freeport, NY: Books for Libraries Press, 1972), 356.

15. Evelyn Baring, Earl of Cromer, *Ancient and Modern Imperialism* (London: John Murray, 1910), 74.

16. Home Secretary James Ede, Great Britain, House of Lords Debates, "British Nationality Bill," HL Deb June 21, 1948, Vol. 156, cc992–1083.

17. Home Secretary James Ede, Great Britain, House of Lords Debates, "British Nationality Bill," HL Deb June 21, 1948, Vol. 156, cc992–1083.

18. David Goldsworthy, *Colonial Issues in British Politics, 1945–1961* (Oxford: Clarendon Press, 1971), 399.

19. Lance Davis and Robert Huttenback, *Mammon and the Pursuit of Empire: The Political Economy of British Imperialism, 1860–1912* (Cambridge: Cambridge University Press, 1986), 270.

20. Kenneth Bradley, *A Career in the Oversea Civil Service* (London: H. M. Stationery Office, 1955), 38; Terence Gavaghan in A. H. M. Kirk-Greene, ed., *The Transfer of Power: The Colonial Administrator in the Age of Decolonisation* (Oxford: University of Oxford Interfaculty Committee for African Studies, 1979), 126.

21. W. McGregor Ross, *Kenya from Within: A Short Political History* (London: George Allen and Unwin, 1927), 444.

22. Anthony Kirk-Greene, *On Crown Service: A History of H. M. and Overseas Civil Services* (London: I. B. Tauris, 1999), 114.

23. P. E. Mitchell, "Indirect Rule," *Uganda Journal* 4 (1936): 102.

24. Gavaghan in Kirk-Greene, *The Transfer of Power*, 125.

25. Thomas Metcalf, "'A Well Selected Body of Men': Sikh Recruitment for Colonial Police and Military," in *Beyond Sovereignty: Britain, Empire and Transnationalism, c. 1880–1950*, ed. Kevin Grant, Philippa Levine, and Frank Trentmann (London: Palgrave Macmillan, 2007), 146.

2. THE EMPIRE AT HIGH TIDE

1. Ham Mukasa, *Uganda's Katikiro in England: Being the Official Account of His Visit to the Coronation of His Majesty King Edward VII*, ed. and trans. Ernest Millar (London: Hutchinson and Co., 1904), 193–94.

2. Mukasa, *Uganda's Katikiro in England*, 201–2.

3. Mukasa, *Uganda's Katikiro in England*, xi.

4. Mukasa, *Uganda's Katikiro in England*, 186.

5. Mukasa, *Uganda's Katikiro in England*, vi.

6. Mukasa, *Uganda's Katikiro in England*, 44.

7. Mukasa, *Uganda's Katikiro in England*, 159.

8. J. M. Gray, "Mutesa of Buganda," *Uganda Journal* 1 (1934): 22.

9. Ham Mukasa, "Some Notes on the Reign of Mutesa," *Uganda Journal* 1 (1934): 131; Ham Mukasa, "Some Notes on the Reign of Mutesa," *Uganda Journal* 2 (1934): 69–70.

10. The book was the published version of Kenyatta's master's thesis at the London School of Economics. Jomo Kenyatta, *Facing Mount Kenya: The Tribal Life of the Gikuyu* (New York: Vintage Books, 1965), 41–42.

11. P. J. Cain and A. G. Hopkins, *British Imperialism: Innovation and Expansion, 1688–1914* (London: Longman, 1993), 113, 173–77.

12. Cain and Hopkins, *British Imperialism*, 452; Ronald Hyam, "The British Empire in the Edwardian Era," in *Oxford History of the British Empire*, Vol. 5: *The Twentieth Century*, ed. Judith Brown and William Roger Louis (New York: Oxford University Press, 1999), 50.

13. R. F. Foster, *Modern Ireland, 1600–1972* (London: Penguin Books, 1988), 437; Donal McCarthy, "From Parnell to Pearse," in *The Course of Irish History*, ed. T. W. Moody and F. X. Martin (Lanham, MD: Roberts Rinehart Publishers, 1995), 301.

14. Neil Charlesworth, *British Rule and the Indian Economy, 1800–1914* (London: Macmillan Press, 1982), 44, 51; B. R. Tomlinson, *The Economy of Modern India, 1860–1970* (Cambridge: Cambridge University Press, 1993), 13–14.

15. Charlesworth, *British Rule and the Indian Economy*, 129–32.

16. David Potter, *India's Political Administrators, 1919–1983* (Oxford: Clarendon Press, 1986), 83.

17. Leonard Thompson, *A History of South Africa* (New Haven, CT: Yale University Press, 1985), 173; W. M. Hailey, *Native Administration in the British African Territories, Part I East Africa: Uganda, Kenya, Tanganyika* (London: n.p., 1950), 117, 120.

18. Jane Burbank and Frederick Cooper, *Empires in World History: Power and the Politics of Difference* (Princeton, NJ: Princeton University Press, 2010), 8.

19. Charlesworth, *British Rule and the Indian Economy*, 27; Tomlinson, *The Economy of Modern India*, 32.

20. John Stuart, "Beyond Sovereignty? Protestant Missions, Empire and Transnationalism, 1890–1950," in *Beyond Sovereignty: Britain, Empire and Transnationalism, c. 1880–1950*, ed. Kevin Grant, Philippa Levine, and Frank Trentmann (London: Palgrave Macmillan, 2007), 103–4.

21. Philippa Levine, "Orientalist Sociology and the Creation of Colonial Sexualities," *Feminist Review* 65 (2000): 13–14.

22. Ronald Hyam, *Empire and Sexuality: The British Experience* (Manchester: Manchester University Press, 1990), 171–72.

23. Terence Gavaghan, *Of Lions and Dung Beetles* (Devon: Arthur Stockwell, 1999), 66.

24. Memorandum by the East African Women's League, January 14, 1924, Rhodes House Library, Oxford, Mss. Afr. s. 633 Box 10.

25. Tommy Gee in Douglas Brown and Marcelle Brown, eds., *Looking Back at the Uganda Protectorate: Recollections of District Officers* (Perth, Australia: Frank Daniels, 1996), 89.

26. Diana Heath, "Bureaucracy, Power and Violence in Colonial India: The Role of Indian Subalterns," in *Bureaucracy and Empire*, ed. Peter Crooks and Timothy Parsons (Cambridge: Cambridge University Press, 2013), xxx, 21–22.

27. Quoted in Nicholas Mansergh, *The Commonwealth Experience* (New York: Frederick Praeger, 1969), 171.

28. Geoffrey Hodges, "African Manpower Statistics for the British Forces in East Africa, 1914–1918," *Journal of African History* 19 (1978): 115.

29. Krishan Saini, "The Economic Aspects of India's Participation in the First World War," in *India and World War I*, ed. DeWitt Ellinwood and S. D. Pradhan (Columbia, MO: South Asia Books, 1978), 143–45, 173.

30. T. R. Sareen, *Select Documents on the Ghadr Party* (New Delhi: Mounto Publishing House, 1994), 156–60.

3. THE EMPIRE BETWEEN THE WARS, 1918 TO 1939

1. Anthony Clayton, *The British Empire as a Superpower, 1919–39* (Athens: University of Georgia Press, 1986), 1.

2. Frederick Lugard, *The Dual Mandate in British Tropical Africa* (London: Archon Books, 1965), 205.

3. Frederick Lugard, "The White Man's Task in Tropical Africa," *Foreign Affairs* 5 (1926): 59.

4. Lugard, *Dual Mandate*, 108, 198.

5. Lugard, *Dual Mandate*, 195–96; Lugard, "The White Man's Task in Tropical Africa," 65.

6. Lugard, *Dual Mandate*, 117.

7. Taraknath Das, "The Progress of the Non-violent Revolution in India," *Journal of International Relations* 12 (1921): 207, 211–12.

8. Matlubul Hasan Saiyid, *Mohammad Ali Jinnah: A Political Study* (Lahore: Sheikh Muhammad Ashraf, 1945), 238–39.

9. India Committee on Disturbances in Bombay, Delhi, and the Punjab, *Evidence Taken before the Disorders Inquiry Committee*, Vol. 3: *Amritsar* (Calcutta: Superintendent Government Printing, 1920), 175–76, 180–82.

10. Government of India, Home Department, Political Section, *Correspondence between the Government of India and the Secretary of State for India on the Report of Lord Hunter's Committee, Command Paper 705* (London: H. M. Stationery Office, 1920), 23; R. E. H. Dyer, *Army. Disturbances in the Punjab, Command Paper 771* (London: H. M. Stationery Office, 1920), 25; India Committee on Disturbances, *Evidence*, Vol. 3: *Amritsar*, 112.

11. India Committee on Disturbances, *Evidence*, Vol. 3: *Amritsar*, 202–3 (emphasis in original).

12. India Committee on Disturbances, *Evidence*, Vol. 3: *Amritsar*, 112, 118, 126.

13. India Committee on Disturbances, *Evidence*, Vol. 3: *Amritsar*, 204.

14. India Committee on Disturbances, *Evidence*, Vol. 3: *Amritsar*, 126.

15. India, Committee on Disturbances in Bombay, Delhi, and the Punjab, *Report of the Committee Appointed in the Government of India to Investigate the Disturbances in the Punjab* (London: H. M. Stationery Office, 1920), 121, 125–30, 132–34.

16. India, Committee on Disturbances in Bombay, Delhi, and the Punjab, *Report of the Committee Appointed in the Government of India to Investigate the Disturbances in the Punjab*, 122.

17. India, Committee on Disturbances in Bombay, Delhi, and the Punjab, *Report of the Committee Appointed in the Government of India to Investigate the Disturbances in the Punjab*, 115.

18. Secretary of State for India, "Indian Disorders Committee: Conclusions," May 6, 1920, Great Britain, the National Archives (TNA) CAB 24/105.

19. Dyer, *Army. Disturbances in the Punjab*, 4–5.

20. Great Britain, House of Lords Debates, "Punjab Disturbances: The Case of General Dyer," HL Deb July 19, 1920, Vol. 41, cc222–307; Great Britain, House of Commons Debates, "Army Council and General Dyer," HC Deb July 8, 1920, Vol. 131, cc1705–819.

21. F. D. Lugard, "The Colour Problem," *Edinburgh Review* 233 (April 1921): 267.

22. Secretary of State for India, "The Mesopotamian Mandate," October 9, 1920; Major N. N. E. Bray, "Mesopotamia: Causes of Unrest—Report No. II," October 18, 1920, TNA CAB 24/112.

23. Viscount Milner, Secretary of State for the Colonies, "Report of the Special Mission to Egypt: General Conclusions," May 17, 1920, TNA, CAB 24/112.

24. Clayton, *The British Empire as a Superpower,* 85–90.

25. Alvin Jackson, *Ireland, 1798–1998: War, Peace and Beyond*, 2nd ed. (Oxford: Wiley-Blackwell, 2010), 267–70.

26. House of Commons Debates, "Army Council and General Dyer," July 8, 1920.

27. "Har Dayal, Rebel, Recants His Views," *New York Times*, June 8, 1919.

28. George Antonius, *The Arab Awakening* (New York: Capricorn Books, 1965), 276.

29. Tanganyika Education Conference, *Conference between Government and Missions: Report of Proceedings 5–12 October 1925* (Dar es Salaam: Government Printer, 1925), 79.

30. Tanganyika Education Conference, *Conference between Government and Missions*, 76.

31. Lugard, *The Dual Mandate*, 217.

32. House of Commons Debates, "Army Council and General Dyer," July 8, 1920.

33. Imperial Conference, Inter-imperial Relations Committee, "Report Proceedings and Memoranda," November 18, 1926, TNA, E (I.R./26) Series.

34. D. K. Fieldhouse, "The Metropolitan Economics of Empire," in *Oxford History of the British Empire*, Vol. 5: *The Twentieth Century*, ed. Judith Brown and William Roger Louis (New York: Oxford University Press, 1999), 101.

35. Quoted in Madhavi Kale, "Screening Empire from Itself: Imperial Preferences, Represented Communities, and the Decent Burial of the Indian Cinematograph Committee Report, 1927–28," in *Beyond Sovereignty: Britain, Empire and Transnationalism, c. 1880–1950*, ed. Kevin Grant, Philippa Levine, and Frank Trentmann (London: Palgrave Macmillan, 2007), 209.

36. Elizabeth Wallace, *The British Caribbean: From the Decline of Colonialism to the End of Federation* (Toronto: University of Buffalo Press, 1977), 31.

37. Claude Markovitz, ed., *A History of Modern India, 1480–1950*, trans. Nisha George and Maggy Hendry (London: Anthem Press, 2002), 440–42.

38. P. J. Cain and A. G. Hopkins, *British Imperialism: Crisis and Deconstruction, 1914–1990* (London: Longman, 1993), 81, 93.

39. Neeti Nair, "Bhagat Singh as 'Satyagrahi': The Limits to Non-violence in Late Colonial India," *Modern Asian Studies* 43 (2009): 659–62, 668–69.

40. Quoted in Richard Toye, *Churchill's Empire: The World That Made Him and the World He Made* (New York: St. Martin's Griffin), 176.

41. Charles Smith, "Communal Conflict and Insurrection in Palestine, 1936–48," in *Policing and Decolonisation: Politics, Nationalism and the Police, 1917–65*, ed. David Anderson and David Killingray (Manchester: Manchester University Press, 1992), 69–71.

42. Bridget Brereton, *A History of Modern Trinidad, 1783–1962* (London: Heinemann, 1981), 173.

43. George Orwell, *The Collected Essays, Journalism and Letters of George Orwell*, Vol. 2: *1940–43*, ed. Sonia Orwell and Ian Angus (London: Secker and Warburg, 1968), 73.

44. Quoted in S. N. Bogonko, "African Political Associations and the Quest for Secular Education in Kenya, 1920–1934" (Kenyatta University College Department of History Staff Seminar Paper, February 8, 1984), 12.

45. Lord Altrincham (Edward Grigg), *Kenya's Opportunity: Memories, Hopes, and Ideas* (London: Faber and Faber, 1955), 116.

46. Bertram Francis Gordon Cranworth, *A Colony in the Making: Or Sport and Profit in British East Africa* (London: Macmillan and Co., 1912), 85.

47. Quoted in Carina Ray, "'The White Wife Problem': Sex, Race and the Contested Politics of Repatriation to Interwar British West Africa," *Gender and History* 21 (2009): 639.

48. House of Commons Debates, "Army Council and General Dyer," July 8, 1920.

49. House of Commons Debates, "Army Council and General Dyer," July 8, 1920.

50. India Committee on Disturbances in Bombay, Delhi, and the Punjab, *Evidence Taken before the Disorders Inquiry Committee*, Vol. 1: *Delhi* (Calcutta: Superintendent Government Printing, 1920), 172.

51. Eamon de Valera, *India and Ireland* (New York: Friends of Freedom for India, 1920), 12, 15.

52. House of Commons Debates, "Army Council and General Dyer," July 8, 1920.

53. "Amritsar," *Times*, June 6, 1924; "Lord Olivier and the O'Dwyer Case," *Times*, August 28, 1924; "General Dyer: The Amritsar Shooting," *Times*, July 25, 1925.

54. "Shooting of Sir M. O'Dwyer," *Times*, April 2, 1940; "Murder of Sir Michael O'Dwyer: Indian Sentenced to Death," *Times*, June 6, 1940; Derek Sayer, "British Reaction to the Amritsar Massacre 1919–1920," *Past and Present* 131 (1991): 163–64.

4. THE 1940S

1. Great Britain, *Official Programme of the Victory Celebrations, 8th June 1946* (London: H. M. Stationery Office, 1946).

2. "Britain's Tribute to War Victors," *Times*, June 10, 1946.

3. "Britain's Tribute to War Victors."

4. Cyril Falls, "Aftermath of War, Victory—Consequences and Disappointments," *Illustrated London News*, June 15, 1946, 642.

5. Arthur Bryant, "Our Note Book," *Illustrated London News*, June 15, 1946, 640.

6. Great Britain, *Malayan Victory Contingent* (London: n.p., 1946), 1–2; Christopher Bayly and Tim Harper, *Forgotten Wars: Freedom and Revolution in Southeast Asia* (Cambridge, MA: Harvard University Press, 2007), 101–6, 109.

7. Report of Morale of British, Indian and Colonial Troops of Allied Land Forces, Southeast Asia, November–December 1945, January 1946, Great Britain National Archives, Great Britain, the National Archives (TNA) WO 203/2268.

8. Report of Morale of British, Indian and Colonial Troops of Allied Land Forces, Southeast Asia, February–April 1945, TNA, WO 203/9544; Commander-in-Chief India to Secretary of State for War, November 5, 1945, Liddell Hart Centre (LHC), King's College London, Dimoline Papers, IX/3; General Sir Richard O'Connor to General Officer Commanding the East Africa Command, LHC, Dimoline Papers, X/5.

9. 11 Division Circular, December 4, 1945, LHC, Dimoline Papers, IX/2; A. J. Knott, "East Africa and the Returning Askari: The Effect of Their War Service," *Quarterly Review* 285 (January 1947): 101.

10. *Illustrated London News*, June 15, 1946, 648.

11. Great Britain, *Malayan Victory Contingent,* 4–6.

12. Arthur Bryant, "Our Note Book"; "London's Great Day," *New York Times*, June 9, 1946.

13. "An Open Letter from the Editors of *Life* to the People of England," *Life* 1 (October 1942) (emphasis in original).

14. Indivar Kamtekar, "The Shiver of 1942," *Studies in History* 18 (2002): 87–88.

15. Jomo Kenyatta, *Kenya: The Land of Conflict* (London: Panaf Service Ltd., 1944), 21.

16. Quoted in William Roger Louis, *Imperialism at Bay: The United States and the Decolonization of the British Empire, 1941–1945* (New York: Oxford University Press, 1978), 14.

17. George Padmore, ed., *History of the Pan-African Congress* (London: Hammersmith Bookshop, 1945).

18. William Beveridge, *Social Insurance and Allied Services* (London: H. M. Stationery Office, 1942); "T.U.C. and Post-war Plans: Charter Based on the 'Four Decencies,'" *Glasgow Herald*, August 13, 1943.

19. D. K. Fieldhouse, "The Metropolitan Economics of Empire," in *Oxford History of the British Empire*, Vol. 5: *The Twentieth Century*, ed. Judith Brown and William Roger Louis (New York: Oxford University Press, 1999), 95; L. J. Butler, *Britain and Empire: Adjusting to a Post-imperial World* (London: I. B. Tauris, 2002), 31, 60, 64.

20. Lord Rennell, A. Creech Jones, and C. E. Ponsonby, "Africa and the British Political Parties," *African Affairs* 44 (1945): 111–14; David Goldsworthy, *Colonial Issues in British Politics, 1945–1961* (Oxford: Clarendon Press, 1971), 50.

21. Kenya, Post-war Employment Committee, *Report of the Sub-committee on Post-war Employment of Africans* (Nairobi: Government Printer, 1943), 17–19; Rennell, Creech Jones, Ponsonby, "Africa and the British Political Parties," 115–19.

22. Bayly and Harper, *Forgotten Wars*, 88–90.

23. P. J. Cain and A. G. Hopkins, *British Imperialism: Crisis and Deconstruction, 1914–1990* (London: Longman, 1993), 196–97.

24. I. F. Stone, *Underground to Palestine* (New York: Pantheon Books, 1978), 5.

25. Construction of a Stores Holding Area in East Africa, October 5, 1947, Great Britain, the National Archives (TNA), WO 216/247.

26. Great Britain, House of Commons Debates, "Orders of the Day—Colonial Affairs," HC Deb July 8, 1948, Vol. 453, cc589–705.

27. Great Britain, House of Lords Debates, "Eire and the Commonwealth," HL Deb December 15, 1948, Vol. 159, cc1051–140; Kathleen Paul, "Communities of Britishness: Migration and the Last Gasp of Empire," in *British Culture and the End of Empire*, ed. Stuart Ward (Manchester: Manchester University Press, 2001), 187.

28. H. V. Wiseman, *The West Indies: Towards a New Dominion?* Research Series No. 130 (London: Fabian Colonial Bureau, 1948), 3–4.

29. Report of the Chief of the Imperial General Staff's African Tour, December 1947, TNA WO 216/675.

30. Speech by Sir S. Cripps to the African Governors' Conference, Economic Development in Africa, November 12, 1947, in *British Documents on the End of Empire*, Series A, Vol. 2: *The Labour Government and the End of Empire, 1945–51*, ed. Ronald Hyam (London: H. M. Stationery Office, 1992), 298–302.

31. Rita Hinden, *Common Sense and Colonial Development,* Research Series No. 131 (London: Fabian Colonial Bureau, 1949), 15.

32. Hinden, *Common Sense and Colonial Development,* 9.

33. Great Britain, Colonial Office, *Report on Cocoa Control in West Africa, 1939–1943, and Statement on Future Policy* (London: H. M. Stationery Office, 1944), 6.

34. Basil Davidson, *The Black Man's Burden* (London: James Curry, 1992), 210.

35. Great Britain, Colonial Office, *Colonial Office Summer Conference on African Administration, First Session, 18th–28th August 1947* (London: Colonial Office, 1948); Anthony Kirk-Greene, *On Crown Service: A History of H. M. and Overseas Civil Services* (London: I. B. Tauris, 1999), 60.

36. John Lonsdale and D. A. Low, "Introduction: Towards the New Order, 1945–1963," in *History of East Africa,* ed. D. A. Low and A. Smith (Oxford: Clarendon Press, 1976), 3:43.

37. I. Schapera, "Anthropology and the Administrator," *Journal of African Administration* 3 (1951): 133.

38. Great Britain, House of Commons Debates, "Orders of the Day—Colonial Affairs," HC Deb July 8, 1948, Vol. 453, cc589–705.

39. Ronald Robinson, "Sir Andrew Cohen: Proconsul of African Nationalism, 1909–1968," in *African Proconsuls: European Governors in Africa,* ed. L. H. Gann and Peter Duignan (New York: Free Press, 1978), 360.

40. Great Britain, House of Commons Debates, "Orders of the Day—Colonial Affairs," HC Deb July 8, 1948, Vol. 453, cc589–705.

41. Great Britain, House of Commons Debates, "Orders of the Day—Colonial Affairs," HC Deb July 8, 1948, Vol. 453, cc589–705.

42. Great Britain, Colonial Office, *Colonial Office Summer Conference on African Administration: The Encouragement of Initiative in African Society, Second Session, 19th August–2nd September 1948* (London: H. M. Stationery Office, 1948), 10, 15.

43. Great Britain, House of Commons Debates, "Orders of the Day—Colonial Affairs," HC Deb July 8, 1948, Vol. 453, cc589–705.

44. J. S. Hogendorn and K. M. Scott, "The East African Groundnut Scheme: Lessons of a Large Scale Agricultural Failure," *African Economic History* 10 (1981): 108.

45. Great Britain, Colonial Office, *Colonial Office Summer Conference on African Administration: Agricultural Development in Africa, Third Session, 15th–27th August 1949* (London: Colonial Office, 1949), 13; Mike Cowen, "Early Years of the Colonial Development Corporation: British State Enterprise Overseas during Late Colonialism," *African Affairs* 83 (1984): 68–99.

46. George Padmore, "Imperialism: London and Paris Styles," *Pan-Africa: Journal of African Life and Thought* 1 (July 1947): 16.

47. Great Britain, Colonial Office, *Colonial Office Summer Conference on African Administration: African Local Government, Fourth Session 1951,* 106; Paul Keleman, "Planning for Africa: The British Labour Party's Colonial Development Policy, 1920–1964," *Journal of Agrarian Change* 7 (2007): 85.

48. Petition of 442 Motor Transport Company, February 14, 1943, Kenya National Archives (KNA), MD 4/5/137/150a.

49. Great Britain, House of Commons Debates, "Orders of the Day—Colonial Affairs," HC Deb July 8, 1948, Vol. 453, cc589–705; Marjorie Nicholson, *Self-Government and the Communal Problem: A Study of Colonial Constitutional Problems Arising in Plural Societies,* Research Series No. 126 (London Fabian Colonial Bureau, 1948), 9.

50. Memorandum on Legislation Involving Racial Discrimination, TNA, CO 859/129/1; Mitchell to Creech Jones, February 28, 1949, Confidential Report by Governor and Memoranda on What Legislation Is Discriminatory, TNA, CO 859/129/1; Great Britain, Colonial Office, *Report of the Commission on the Civil Services of Kenya, Tanganyika, Uganda, and Zanzibar* (London: H. M. Stationery Office, 1948), 39–40; Kirk-Greene, *On Crown Service,* 99.

51. John Flint, "Scandal at the Bristol Hotel: Some Thoughts on Racial Discrimination in Britain and West Africa and Its Relationship to the Planning of Decolonization," *Journal of Imperial and Commonwealth History* 12 (1983): 88–89.

52. A. H. M. Kirk-Greene, ed., *The Transfer of Power: The Colonial Administrator in the Age of Decolonisation* (Oxford: University of Oxford Inter-faculty Committee for African Studies, 1979), 85.

53. Arthur Creech Jones, "British Colonial Policy: With Particular Reference to Africa," *International Affairs* 27 (1951): 179, 182.

54. Uganda Protectorate, *Report of the Commission of Inquiry into the Disturbances in Uganda during April, 1949* (Entebbe: Government Printer, 1950), 66–70.

55. Notes on Cost of Living Increase in Kenya, November 12, 1945, National Library of Scotland, Church of Scotland Mission Archives, ACC 7548-B269.

56. Ngugi wa Thiong'o, *Weep Not, Child* (Oxford: Heinemann, 1989), 50–51.

57. Philip Murphy, "Intelligence and Decolonization: The Life and Death of the Federal Intelligence and Security Bureau, 1954–63," *Journal of Imperial and Commonwealth History* 29 (2001): 106–7; Christopher Andrew, *Defend the Realm: The Authorized History of MI5* 9 (New York: Vintage Books, 2010), 451–52.

5. THE FINAL RETREAT FROM EMPIRE, 1950 TO 1970

1. Harold Macmillan, "Africa," *African Affairs* 59 (1960): 193.

2. Dana Adams Schmidt, "Nkrumah Speaks," *New York Times*, September 23, 1960.

3. Kwame Nkrumah, *Osagyefo at the United Nations* (Accra: Ghana Government Printer, 1960), 1.

4. Nkrumah, *Osagyefo at the United Nations*, 4.

5. N. S. Khrushchov, *Freedom and Independence for All Colonial Peoples* (Moscow: Foreign Languages Publishing House, 1962), 21–22, 61.

6. Khrushchov, *Freedom and Independence for All Colonial Peoples*, 21.

7. George McTurnan Kahin, *The Asian-African Conference: Bandung, Indonesia, April 1955* (Ithaca: Cornell University Press, 1956), 81.

8. United Nations General Assembly, *Resolutions Adopted by the General Assembly* (New York: United Nations, 1950–1976).

9. Quoted in David Mills, "Anthropology at the End of Empire: The Rise and Fall of the Colonial Social Science Research Council, 1944–1962," in *Empires, Nations, and Natives: Anthropology and State-Making*, ed. Benoit de L'Estoile, Federico Neiburg, and Lygia Sigaud (Durham, NC: Duke University Press, 2005), 160.

10. David Goldsworthy, *Colonial Issues in British Politics, 1945–1961* (Oxford: Clarendon Press, 1971), 399.

11. Goldsworthy, *Colonial Issues in British Politics,* 276–78.

12. Basil Davidson, *The Black Man's Burden* (London: James Curry, 1992), 219.

13. Great Britain, Colonial Office, *Colonial Office Summer Conference on African Administration: Rural Economic Development, Fifth Session, 17–29 August 1953* (London: Colonial Office, 1953), 18–19.

14. Mike Cowen, "Early Years of the Colonial Development Corporation: British State Enterprise Overseas during Late Colonialism," *African Affairs* 83 (1984): 68–71.

15. Great Britain, Colonial Office, *Summer Conference on African Administration: Rural Economic Development, 1953*, 22–23.

16. Goldsworthy, *Colonial Issues in British Politics*, 23; Nicholas White, "Capitalism and Counter-insurgency? Business and Government in the Malayan Emergency, 1948–57," *Modern Asian Studies* 32 (1998): 173–76.

17. "Gold Coast Self-Rule Sped—London Hopes It Will Retain Ties," *New York Times*, January 18, 1954.

18. Thomas Brady, "Gold Coast: Laughter, Wealth, Freedom," *New York Times*, October 7, 1956.

19. Lindesay Parrott, "U.N. Unanimous on Ghana Entry," *New York Times*, March 8, 1957.

20. Kenneth Robinson, "Colonial Issues and Policies with Special Reference to Tropical Africa," *Annals of the American Academy of Political and Social Science* 298 (March 1955): 93.

21. Great Britain, House of Commons, "Colour Bar (Abolition)," HC Deb May 1, 1953, Vol. 514, cc2505–95.

22. Great Britain, Colonial Office, *Colonial Office Summer Conference on African Administration: African Local Government, First Session* (London: H. M. Stationery Office, 1947), 123.

23. Confidential—Memorandum on Legislation Involving Racial Discrimination: Report by Governor and Memoranda on What Legislation Is Discriminatory, 1949, Kenya Governor to Colonial Secretary, February 28, 1949, Great Britain, the National Archives (TNA), CO 859/129/1.

24. J. Kennedy to P. Liesching, Opinion in Southern Rhodesia, January 11, 1950, and J. Kennedy to Gordon Walker, Southern Rhodesia—Economic Problems, November 10, 1950, DO 35/3681, in *British Documents on the End of Empire: Central Africa*, Series B, Vol. 9: *Part I Closer Association, 1945–1958*, ed. Philip Murphy (London: H. M. Stationery Office, 1992), 130, 143.

25. Quoted in Jan-Bart Gewald, "Rumours of Mau Mau in Northern Rhodesia, 1950–1960," *Afrika Focus* 22 (2009): 44.

26. Fabian Colonial Bureau, *The Kenya Controversy*, Controversy Series No. 4 (London: Fabian Publications, 1947), 10.

27. Minutes by Andrew Cohen, March 7–23, 1949, in Murphy, *British Documents on the End of Empire: Central Africa*, Series B, Vol. 9, *Part I*, 102–3.

28. From *The Scotsman* and cited by G. M. Thomson in Great Britain, House of Commons Debates, "Central African Federation," HC Deb May 4, 1953, Vol. 5157, cc37–167.

29. Oliver Lyttelton, *The Memoirs of Lord Chandros: An Unexpected View from the Summit* (New York: New American Library, 1963), 373.

30. Walter Harrigan et al., "Report of the Judicial Enquiry Re Seretse Khama of the Bamangwato Tribe," *Botswana Notes and Records* 17 (1985): 57, 59–63.

31. "Seretse's Challenge to Government: Findings of Inquiry," *Times*, March 9, 1950.

32. Great Britain, House of Commons, "Tribal Chief, Bechuanaland (Recognition)," HC Deb March 8, 1950, Vol. 472, cc285–97; Great Britain, Commonwealth Relations Office, *Bechuanaland Protectorate: Succession to the Chieftainship of the Bamangwato Tribe* (London: H. M. Stationery Office, 1950): 5–7.

33. Visit by the Secretary of State for Commonwealth Relations to the Union of South Africa, Southern Rhodesia and the Three High Commission Territories of Basutoland, the Bechuanaland Protectorate, and Swaziland, April 16, 1951, TNA, CAB 129/45/C.P. (51) 109.

34. Visit by the Secretary of State for Commonwealth Relations to the Union of South Africa, Southern Rhodesia and the Three High Commission Territories of Basutoland, the Bechuanaland Protectorate, and Swaziland, April 16, 1951, TNA, CAB 129/45/C.P. (51) 109; Memorandum by the Secretary of State for the Colonies and the Secretary of State for Commonwealth Relations, Closer Association in Central Africa, May 3, 1951, TNA, CAB, 129/45/C.P. (51) 122.

35. Minute by A. B. Cohen, Northern Rhodesia, December 21, 1950, CO 537/5895, in Murphy, *British Documents on the End of Empire: Central Africa*, Series B, Vol. 9: *Part I*, 149.

36. Philip Murphy, "'Government by Blackmail': The Origins of the Central African Federation Reconsidered," in *The British Empires in the 1950s: Retreat or Revival?* ed. Martin Lynn (New York: Palgrave Macmillan, 2006), 65.

37. Great Britain, House of Lords, "Central African Federation," HL Deb July 7, 1952, Vol. 177, cc726–832.

38. Minutes of a Meeting with the Anti-slavery and Aborigines Protection Society, Colonial Office Record, July 13, 1951, CO 1015/55, in Murphy, *British Documents on the End of Empire: Central Africa*, Series B, Vol. 9: *Part I*, 163–65; "Africans and Federation: Reasons for Refusal to Attend Talks," *Times*, April 24, 1952; A. Creech Jones, ed., *A Petition to Her Majesty Queen Elizabeth II against Federation Made Chiefs and Citizens of Nyasaland* (London: Africa Bureau, 1953), 10.

39. Great Britain, House of Commons, "Central African Federation," HC Deb March 4, 1952, Vol. 497, cc208–339; House of Commons Debates, "Central African Federation," HC Deb May 4, 1953, Vol. 5157, cc37–167.

40. Great Britain, House of Lords, "Central African Federation," HL Deb July 7, 1952, Vol. 177, cc726–832.

41. Nyasaland Boy Scout Association Annual General Meeting, June 11, 1954, Kenya Scout Association Archives, KBSA/C/67; At Ipenburg, *"All Good Men": The Development of Lubwa Mission, Chinsali, Zambia, 1905–1967* (Frankfurt: Peter Lang, 1992), 212.

42. Mutesa II, King of Buganda, *Desecration of My Kingdom* (London: Constable, 1967), 113–14.

43. Great Britain, House of Commons, "Kabaka of Buganda (Deposition)," HC Deb December 2, 1953, Vol. 521, cc1229–86; Great Britain, Cabinet Minutes, December 15, 1953, C.C. 79 (53), 349, TNA, CAB 195/11.

44. Kevin Ward, "The Church of Uganda and the Exile of Kabaka Muteesa II, 1953–55," *Journal of Religion in Africa* 28 (1998): 430.

45. J. C. Carothers, *The Psychology of Mau Mau* (Nairobi: Government Printer, 1955), 15; "Mau Mau Movement in Kenya," by R. G. M. Calderwood, December 21, 1952, National Library of Scotland, Church of Scotland Mission Archives (CSM) ACC 7548-B271.

46. David Anderson, *Histories of the Hanged: The Dirty War in Kenya and the End of Empire* (New York: Norton, 2005), 127–30.

47. Michael Thornhill, *Road to Suez: The Battle for the Canal Zone* (London: Stroud, 2006).

48. Great Britain, House of Commons, "Army Estimates, 1954–55," HC Deb March 11, 1954, Vol. 524, cc2450–503.

49. Anthony Kirk-Greene, *On Crown Service: A History of H. M. and Overseas Civil Services* (London: I. B. Tauris, 1999), 65–69.

50. General Sir Gerald Templer, "Report on Colonial Security," April 23, 1955, TNA, CAB 129/76.

51. L. J. Butler, *Britain and Empire: Adjusting to a Post-imperial World* (London: I. B. Tauris, 2002), 106–8.

52. Kenneth Bradley, *A Career in the Oversea Civil Service* (London: H. M. Stationery Office, 1955), 21, 37.

53. Great Britain, Colonial Office, *Summer Conference on African Administration: A General Review of Progress in Local Government in British African Territories, Ninth Session, 25 August–6 September 1958* (London: Colonial Office, 1958), 33, 91; Bradley, *A Career in the Oversea Civil Service*, 6.

54. Paulo Kavuma, *Crisis in Buganda, 1953–1955: The Story of the Exile and Return of the Kabaka, Mutesa II* (London: Rex Collins, 1979), 40, 47–56.

55. Appreciation by the Commander-in-Chief of the Operational Situation in Kenya in July 1955, by Secretary of the War Council, August 4, 1955, Kenya National Archives (KNA) WC/CM/1/5/704.

56. Great Britain, Colonial Office, *Historical Survey of the Origins and Growth of Mau Mau, Command 1030* (London: H. M. Stationery Office, 1960), 316.

57. Sir A. Benson to W. L. Gorell Barnes, December 30, 1957, in Murphy, *British Documents on the End of Empire: Central Africa*, Series B, Vol. 9: *Part I*, 386.

58. Lord Home to Lennox Boyd, July 31, 1956, CO 967/295, in Murphy, *British Documents on the End of Empire: Central Africa*, Series B, Vol. 9: *Part I*, 386.

59. Arthur Hazlewood, "The Economics of Federation and Dissolution in Central Africa," in *African Integration and Disintegration*, ed. Arthur Hazlewood (London: Oxford University Press, 1967), 223.

60. Lynette Schumaker, "A Tent with a View: Colonial Officers, Anthropologists, and the Making of the Field in Northern Rhodesia, 1937–1960," *Osiris* 11 (1996): 252.

61. Secretary of State for Commonwealth Relations, "Problems That Lie Ahead in the Area of the Federation of Rhodesia and Nyasaland," November 12, 1958, TNA CAB/129/95/c. (58) 232.

62. A. H. M. Kirk-Greene, ed., *The Transfer of Power: The Colonial Administrator in the Age of Decolonisation* (Oxford: University of Oxford Inter-faculty Committee for African Studies, 1979), 3.

63. John McCracken, "In the Shadow of Mau Mau: Detainees and Detention Camps during Nyasaland's State of Emergency," *Journal of Southern African Studies* 37 (2011): 538, 541–44.

64. Macmillan Minute for Lennox-Boyd, Nyasaland Emergency Use of Aircraft, March 7, 1959, PREM 11/2787, M 80/59 in Philip Murphy, ed., *British Documents on the End of Empire: Central Africa*, Series B, Vol. 9: *Part II, Crisis and Dissolution, 1959–1965* (London: H. M. Stationery Office, 1992), 28.

65. Great Britain, Colonial Office, *Report of the Nyasaland Commission of Inquiry, Command 814* (London: H. M. Stationery Office, 1959), 3–4, 107–8, 125.

66. Great Britain, House of Lords, "Unrest in Nyasaland," HL Deb March 24, 1959, Vol. 215, cc198–362.

67. Great Britain, Colonial Office, *Report of the Nyasaland Commission of Inquiry*, 1.

68. Great Britain, House of Commons, "Nyasaland (Report of Commission of Inquiry)," HC Deb July 28, 1959, Vol. 610, cc317–454.

69. Great Britain, Colonial Office, *Documents Relating to the Deaths of Eleven Mau Mau Detainees at Hola Camp in Kenya, Command 778* (London: H. M. Stationery Office, 1959), 15.

70. Great Britain, House of Commons, "Hola Camp, Kenya (Report)," HC Deb July 27, 1959, Vol. 610, cc181–262; Great Britain, House of Lords, "The Hola Camp Disaster," HL Deb July 29, 1959, Vol. 218, cc895–924.

71. Draft Statement on British Colonial Policy in Africa, June 22, 1959, TNA, PREM 11/2583.

72. "Mr. Macmillan's Appeal to South Africans," *Times*, February 4, 1960.

73. Taoiseach's Statement to the International Social Study Congress at Dublin, June 26, 1960, Irish National Archives (INA) H34/733.

74. Conclusions of the East African Land Forces Conference, July 25, 1958, KNA, LF 1/154/12.

75. John Johnson in John Johnson, ed., *Colony to Nation: British Administration in Kenya, 1940–1963* (Banham, Norfolk: Erskine Press, 2002), 218.

76. Michael Blundell, *So Rough a Wind: The Kenya Memoirs of Sir Michael Blundell* (London: Weidenfeld and Nicolson, 1964), 266.

77. Jomo Kenyatta, *Suffering without Bitterness* (Nairobi: East African Publishing House, 1968), xv.

78. Commander Nyasaland Area to Federal Army Chief of Staff, August 19, 1960, Malawi National Archives, F/248/2072/CAC/155/3/G (Ops)/25.

79. Great Britain, House of Lords, "Unrest in Nyasaland," HL Deb March 24, 1959, Vol. 215, cc198–362.

80. Ronald Hyam, "The Geopolitical Origins of the Central African Federation: Britain, Rhodesia and South Africa, 1948–1953," *Historical Journal* 3 (1987): 145.

81. Macmillan, "Africa," 193.

82. John Fletcher-Cooke, "The Failure of the 'Westminster Model' in Africa," *African Affairs* 63 (1964): 206.

83. Joseph Hodge, "Modernizing Mission: Approaches 'Developing' the Non-Western World after 1954," *Journal of Modern European History* 8 (2010): 25.

84. Andrew Cohen, "Development in Africa: The Problems of Today," *African Affairs* 67 (1968): 50.

85. Central Intelligence Organization, Freedom of Information Act Electronic Reading Rooming, http://www.foia.cia.gov, Central Intelligence Agency #1, SNIE 64.1-61: Prospects for Ghana, Declassified by: 050315, January 21, 1976 [1].

86. Quarterly Report, Colonel V. J. Senior, April 26, 1966, THA, DO 213/213/3.

6. GLOBAL LEGACIES OF THE BRITISH EMPIRE

1. Paul Williams, *You're Wondering Now: A History of the Specials* (Dunoon, Scotland: S. T. Publishing, 1995), 8.

2. The Specials official website: http://www.thespecials.com/music.

3. Tony Stewart, "Review of the Specials," *New Music Express*, October 20, 1979.

4. Williams, *You're Wondering Now*, 4.

5. Chris Salewicz, "The Specials: Stop the Tour, I Want to Get Off," *New Music Express*, September 27, 1980.

6. "The Band," The Specials, http://www.thespecials.com/the_band.html.

7. Niall Ferguson, *Empire: How Britain Made the Modern World* (London: Penguin Books, 2003), xxi.

8. Bill Ashcroft, Gareth Griffiths, and Helen Tiffin, *Key Concepts in Post-colonial Studies* (London: Routledge, 1998), 110.

9. C. A. Bayly, *Empire and Information: Intelligence Gathering and Social Communication in India, 1780–1870* (Cambridge: Cambridge University Press, 1996), 168.

10. Isaac Schapera, "Anthropology and the Administrator," *Journal of African Administration* 3 (1951): 129.

11. H. E. Lambert, "Disintegration and Reintegration in the Meru Tribe," January 9, 1940, Kenya National Archives (KNA), DC MRU 4/5.

12. John Iliffe, *A Modern History of Tanganyika* (New York: Cambridge University Press, 1979), 318.

13. R. B. Boeder, *Silent Majority: A History of the Lomwe in Malawi* (Pretoria: Africa Institute of South Africa, 1984), 75; A. T. Matson, "Reflections on the Growth of Political Consciousness in Nandi," in *Hadith 4: Politics and Nationalism in Kenya*, ed. B. A. Ogot (Nairobi: East African Publishing House, 1972), 20.

14. Lambert, "Disintegration and Reintegration in the Meru Tribe."

15. Bill Freund, *The Making of Contemporary Africa: The Development of African Society since 1800* (Bloomington: Indiana University Press, 1984), 192–94; Judith Brown, *Modern India: The Origins of an Asian Democracy* (Oxford: Oxford University Press, 1994), 110.

16. District Commissioner Nairobi to Provincial Commissioner Central Province, May 16, 1938, KNA, MAA 2/1/3/I/76a; James Karuga, *Action towards a Better Nairobi: Report and Recommendations of the Nairobi City Convention* (Nairobi: Nairobi City Convention, 1993), 33–34.

17. J. A. K. Leslie, *A Survey of Dar es Salaam* (London: Oxford University Press, 1963), 112–13.

18. Annual Historical Report, 4 KAR, 1952–3, Great Britain, the National Archives (TNA), WO 305/257; Governor's Private Secretary to Deputy Chief of Staff, East Africa Command, January 13, 1954, KNA, GH 4/457/20.

19. C. L. R. James, *Beyond a Boundary* (Durham, NC: Duke University Press, 1993), 65.

20. This telling phrase comes from Dane Kennedy, *Islands of White: Settler Society and Culture in Kenya and Southern Rhodesia, 1890–1939* (Durham, NC: Duke University Press, 1987).

21. David Northrup, *Indentured Labor in the Age of Imperialism* (Cambridge: Cambridge University Press, 1995), 60–65.

22. Robert Blyth, *The Empire of the Raj: India, Eastern Africa, and the Middle East, 1858–1947* (London: Palgrave Macmillan, 2003), 94.

23. William Malcolm Hailey, *An African Survey: A Study of Problems Arising in Africa South of the Sahara* (London: Oxford University Press, 1938), 335.

24. Quoted in William Kuepper, G. Lynne Lackey, and E. Nelson Swinerton, *Ugandan Asians in Great Britain: Forced Migration and Social Absorption* (New York: New Viewpoints, 1975), 5.

25. Quoted in Peter Fryer, *Staying Power: Black People in Britain since 1504* (Atlantic Highlands NJ: Humanities Press, 1984), 311.

26. Fryer, *Staying Power*, 326.

27. George Padmore, ed., *History of the Pan-African Congress* (London: Hammersmith Bookshop, 1945), 5.
28. Kwame Nkrumah, *The Autobiography of Kwame Nkrumah* (London: Thomas Nelson and Sons, 1957), 48.
29. Great Britain, House of Lords Debates, "British Nationality Bill," HL Deb June 21, 1948, Vol. 156, cc992–1083.
30. Great Britain, House of Commons Debates, "British Nationality Bill," HC Deb July 7, 1948, Vol. 453, 385–510.
31. Quoted in Clive Harris, "Post-war Migration and the Industrial Reserve Army," in *Inside Babylon: The Caribbean Diaspora in Britain*, ed. Clive Harris and Winston James (London: Verso, 1993), 23–25.
32. Stuart Hall, "Negotiating Caribbean Identities," *New Left Review* 209 (1995): 8.
33. Christina Hardyment, *Slice of Life: The British Way of Eating since 1945* (London: BBC Books, 1995), 133.
34. Nkrumah, *The Autobiography of Kwame Nkrumah*, 58.
35. "Further Racial Incidents," *Times*, September 3, 1958; "102 More Jamaicans Arrive," *Times*, September 4, 1958.
36. "West Indians Give Mr. Manley Enthusiastic Reception," *Times*, September 8, 1958.
37. Adil Jussawalla, "Indifference," in *Disappointed Guests: Essays by African, Asian and West Indian Students*, ed. Henri Tajfel and John L. Dawson (London: Oxford University Press, 1965), 130.
38. James, *Beyond a Boundary*, 124.
39. Richard Thurlow, *Fascism in Britain: A History, 1918–1985* (Oxford: Basil Blackwood, 1987), 243.
40. The full text of the speech is reprinted in "Enoch Powell's 'Rivers of Blood' Speech," *Daily Telegraph*, November 6, 2007.
41. Derek Oddy, *From Plain Fare to Fusion Food: British Diet from the 1890s to the 1990s* (Woodbridge Suffolk, UK: Boydell Press, 2003), 118.
42. Geoffrey Warren, ed., *The Foods We Eat* (London: Cassell, 1958), 8–9.
43. Hardyment, *Slice of Life*, 136.
44. Richard Jones, "The New Look—and Taste—of British Cuisine," *Virginia Quarterly Review* 79 (2003).
45. "God Save The Queen 7"," Sex Pistols, http://www.sexpistolsofficial.com/records/god-save-the-queen-7.
46. The Specials official website: http://www.thespecials.com/music.
47. Praveen Swami, "The Queen in Amritsar," *Frontline: India's National Magazine* 14 (1997).
48. Alan Cowell, "After Coordinated Bombs, London Is Stunned, Bloodied and Stoic," *New York Times*, July 7, 2005.
49. Swami, "The Queen in Amritsar."
50. "We Must Never Forget What Happened Here," *Daily Mail*, February 19, 2013.

7. EPILOGUE

1. "White Party House Burnt Down," *Times*, December 23, 1963; "Uganda: That Was the Party That Was," *News Check on South Africa and Africa*, January 3, 1964, 12; "The White Man's Hangover," *Time* 83, January 3, 1964, 46.
2. "Uganda: That Was the Party That Was."
3. "The White Man's Hangover"; Gordon Dyus, *Twilight of the Bwanas: An Account of Life in East Africa during the Colonial Period* (Bloomfield, IN: Xlbris Corp, 2011), 174–78.
4. Uganda, *Uganda Parliamentary Debates (Hansard), Second Series, Volume 22, National Assembly Official Report, Second Session 1963–4, Part Four of Second Meeting, 16th, 17th, 18th, 19th and 20th December 1963* (Entebbe: Government Printer, 1963), 790–91.

5. "Uganda Expels Organizers of House Party," *Times*, December 24, 1963; Dyus, *Twilight of the Bwanas*, 178.

6. Great Britain, House of Commons, "Uganda Bill," HC Deb February 13, 1964, Vol. 689, cc565–84; "Uganda: That Was the Party That Was"; "The White Man's Hangover."

7. Uganda, *Uganda Parliamentary Debates*, 799, 805.

8. Kenneth Robinson, "Colonial Issues and Policies with Special Reference to Tropical Africa," *Annals of the American Academy of Political and Social Science* 298 (March 1955): 84.

9. Jomo Kenyatta, *Kenya: The Land of Conflict* (London: Panaf Service Ltd., 1944), 22.

10. Ngugi wa Thiong'o, *In the House of the Interpreter: A Memoir* (New York: Pantheon Books, 2012), 199.

11. Political Intelligence Bulletin, No. 4, 1943, Malawi National Archives, S34/1/4/1; Luise White, "Cars Out of Place: Vampires, Technology, and Labor in East and Central Africa," in *Tensions of Empire: Colonial Cultures in a Bourgeois World*, ed. Frederick Cooper and Laura Ann Stoler (Berkeley: University of California Press, 1997), 450; Jan-Bart Gewald, "Rumours of Mau Mau in Northern Rhodesia, 1950–1960," *Afrika Focus* 22 (2009): 45.

12. Frederick Lugard, *The Dual Mandate in British Tropical Africa* (London: Archon Books, 1965), 619; Great Britain, House of Commons, "Colour Bar (Abolition)," HC Deb May 1, 1953, Vol. 514, cc2505–95.

13. Kenneth Bradley, *A Career in the Oversea Civil Service* (London: H. M. Stationery Office, 1955), 22.

14. A. H. M. Kirk-Greene, ed., *The Transfer of Power: The Colonial Administrator in the Age of Decolonisation* (Oxford: University of Oxford Inter-faculty Committee for African Studies, 1979), 34, 65.

15. Max Beloff, "The End of the British Empire and the Assumption of Worldwide Commitments by the United States," in *The "Special Relationship": Anglo-American Relations since 1945*, ed. William Roger Louis and Hedley Bull (Oxford: Oxford University Press, 1986), 249; Niall Ferguson, *Empire: How Britain Made the Modern World* (London: Penguin Books, 2003), 351–55.

16. D. N. Pritt, *Star-Spangled Shadow* (London: Frederick Muller, 1947), 102; David Cannadine, "'Big Tent' Historiography: Transatlantic Obstacles and Opportunities in Writing the History of Empire," *Common Knowledge* 11 (2005): 384.

17. Bernard Porter, *Empire and Superempire: Britain, America and the World* (New Haven, CT: Yale University Press, 2006), 130.

18. Ryan Irwin, "A Wind of Change? White Redoubt and the Postcolonial Movement in South Africa, 1960–1963," in *Race, Ethnicity, and the Cold War: A Global Perspective*, ed. Philip Muehlenbeck (Nashville, TN: Vanderbilt University Press, 2012), 42, 45; William Rosenau and Austin Long, *The Phoenix Program and Contemporary Counterinsurgency* (Santa Monica, CA: Rand Corporation, 2009), 13.

19. L. H. Gann and Peter Duignan, *Burden of Empire: An Appraisal of Western Colonialism in Africa* (Stanford, CA: Stanford University Press, 1971), x, 367; Ferguson, *Empire*, xx, 360.

20. Sonia Orwell and Ian Angus, eds., *The Collected Essays, Journalism and Letters of George Orwell*, Vol. 2: *1940–43* (London: Secker and Warburg, 1968), 186–87.

21. Claude Markovitz, ed., *A History of Modern India, 1480–1950*, trans. Nisha George and Maggy Hendry (London: Anthem Press, 2002), 430–31; Andrew Cohen, "Development in Africa: The Problems of Today," *African Affairs* 67 (1968): 44–45.

22. Joseph Hodge, "Modernizing Mission: Approaches 'Developing' the Non-Western World after 1954," *Journal of Modern European History* 8 (2010): 40–41.

23. Bill Ashcroft, Gareth Griffiths, and Helen Tiffin, *Key Concepts in Post-colonial Studies* (London: Routledge, 1998), 110.

24. George Padmore, "Imperialism: London and Paris Styles," *Pan-Africa: Journal of African Life and Thought* 1 (July 1947): 3.

25. Douglas Brown and Marcelle Brown, eds., *Looking Back at the Uganda Protectorate: Recollections of District Officers* (Perth, Australia: Frank Daniels, 1996), 113.

26. Michael Tuck and John Rowe, "Phoenix from the Ashes: Rediscovery of the Lost Lukiiko Archives," *History in Africa* 32 (2005): 404.

Selected Bibliography

DOCUMENTS AND MEMOIRS

Advisory Committee on Native Education in the British Tropical African Dependencies. *Education Policy in British Tropical Africa*. London: H. M. Stationery Office, 1925.

Dyer, R. E. H. *Army. Disturbances in the Punjab, Command Paper 771*. London: H. M. Stationery Office, 1920.

Government of India. *Coronation Durbar Delhi 1911*. Calcutta: Superintendent Government Printing, 1911.

———. *The Ghadr Directory: Containing the Names of Persons Who Have Taken Part in the Ghadr Movement in America, Europe, Africa and Afghanistan as Well as in India*. New Delhi: Government of India, 1934.

Government of India, Home Department, Political Section. *Correspondence between the Government of India and the Secretary of State for India on the Report of Lord Hunter's Committee, Command Paper 705*. London: H. M. Stationery Office, 1920.

Great Britain, Colonial Office. *Closer Association in Central Africa: Statement by His Majesty's Government in the United Kingdom, 21st November 1951*. London: H. M. Stationery Office, 1951.

———. *Education for Citizenship in Africa*. London: H. M. Stationery Office, 1948.

———. *Report of the Commission of Enquiry into Disturbances in the Gold Coast, 1948*. London: H. M. Stationery Office, 1948.

———. *Report of the Nyasaland Commission of Inquiry, Command 814*. London: H. M. Stationery Office, 1959.

———. *Summer Conference on African Administration: African Local Government*. London: H. M. Stationery Office, 1947.

Great Britain, Commonwealth Relations Office. *Bechuanaland Protectorate: Succession to the Chieftainship of the Bamangwato Tribe*. London: H. M. Stationery Office, 1950.

India, Committee on Disturbances in Bombay, Delhi, and the Punjab. *Report of the Committee Appointed in the Government of India to Investigate the Disturbances in the Punjab*. London: H. M. Stationery Office, 1920.

James, C. L. R. *Beyond a Boundary*. Durham, NC: Duke University Press, 1993.

Kaggia, Bildad. *Roots of Freedom, 1921–1963*. Nairobi: East Africa Publishing House, 1975.

Lugard, Frederick. *The Dual Mandate in British Tropical Africa*. London: Archon Books, 1965.

Lyttelton, Oliver. *The Memoirs of Lord Chandros: An Unexpected View from the Summit*. New York: New American Library, 1963.

Macmillan, Harold. "Africa." *African Affairs* 59 (1960).
Mukasa, Ham. *Uganda's Katikiro in England: Being the Official Account of His Visit to the Coronation of His Majesty King Edward VII.* Translated and edited by Ernest Millar. London: Hutchinson and Co., 1904.
Mutesa II, King of Buganda. *Desecration of My Kingdom.* London: Constable, 1967.
Ngugi wa Thiong'o. *In the House of the Interpreter: A Memoir.* New York: Pantheon Books, 2012.
Nkrumah, Kwame. *The Autobiography of Kwame Nkrumah.* London: Thomas Nelson and Sons, 1957.
Padmore, George, ed. *History of the Pan-African Congress.* London: Hammersmith Bookshop, 1945.
Stone, I. F. *Underground to Palestine.* New York: Pantheon Books, 1978.
Uganda Protectorate. *Withdrawal of Recognition from Kabaka Mutesa II of Buganda.* London: H. M. Stationery Office, 1953.
Wiseman, H. V. *The West Indies: Towards a New Dominion?* Research Series No. 130. London: Fabian Colonial Bureau, 1948.

SECONDARY SOURCES

Anderson, David, and David Killingray, eds. *Policing and Decolonisation: Politics, Nationalism and the Police, 1917–65.* Manchester: Manchester University Press, 1992.
Bayly, Christopher, and Tim Harper. *Forgotten Wars: Freedom and Revolution in Southeast Asia.* Cambridge, MA: Harvard University Press, 2007.
Beaumont, Joan. "Great Britain and the Rights of Neutral Countries: The Case of Iran, 1941." *Journal of Contemporary History* 16 (1981).
Beckles, Hilary. *A History of Barbados: From Amerindian Settlement to Nation-State.* Cambridge: Cambridge University Press, 1990.
Bennett, Judith. "War, Emergency and the Environment: Fiji, 1939–1946." *Environment and History* 7 (2001).
Boahen, A. A. *African Perspectives on Colonialism.* Baltimore: Johns Hopkins Press, 1987.
Brereton, Bridget. *A History of Modern Trinidad, 1783–1962.* London: Heinemann, 1981.
Brereton, Bridget, and Kevin Yelvington, eds. *The Colonial Caribbean in Transition.* Gainesville: University Press of Florida, 1999.
Brown, Judith. *Modern India: The Origins of an Asian Democracy.* Oxford: Oxford University Press, 1994.
Cain, P. J., and A. G. Hopkins. *British Imperialism: Crisis and Deconstruction, 1914–1990.* London: Longman, 1993.
Chander, Sunil. "Congress-Raj Conflict and the Rise of the Muslim League in the Ministry Period, 1937–39." *Modern Asian Studies* 21 (1987).
Clayton, Anthony. *The British Empire as a Superpower, 1919–39.* Athens: University of Georgia Press, 1986.
Daly, W. M. *Empire on the Nile: The Anglo-Egyptian Sudan.* Cambridge: Cambridge University Press, 1986.
DeWitt, Ellinwood, and S. D. Pradhan, eds. *India and World War I,* Columbia, MO: South Asia Books, 1978.
Dimeo, Paul. "'With Political Pakistan in the Offing . . .': Football and Communal Politics in South Asia, 1887–1947." *Journal of Contemporary History* 38 (2003).
Flint, John. "Planned Decolonization and Its Failure in British Africa." *African Affairs* 82 (1983).
Foster, R. F. *Modern Ireland, 1600–1972.* London: Penguin Books, 1988.
Fraser, Cary. *Ambivalent Anti-colonialism: The United States and the Genesis of West Indian Independence, 1940–1964.* Westport, CT: Greenwood, 1994.
Fryer, Peter. *Staying Power: Black People in Britain since 1504.* Atlantic Highlands, NJ: Humanities Press, 1984.

Gallagher, John. "Nationalism and the Crisis of Empire, 1919–1922." *Modern Asian Studies* 15 (1981).

Ghosh, Durba. "Terrorism in Bengal: Political Violence in the Interwar Years." In *Decentering Empire: Britain, India and the Transcolonial World*, edited by Durba Ghosh and Dane Kennedy. New Delhi: Orient Longman, 2006.

Goldsworthy, David. *Colonial Issues in British Politics, 1945–1961*. Oxford: Clarendon Press, 1971.

Greenough, Paul. "Indian Famines and Peasant Victims: The Case of Bengal in 1943–44." *Modern Asian Studies* 14 (1980).

Guha, Ramachandra. "Cricket and Politics in Colonial India." *Past and Present* 161 (1998).

Hardyment, Christina. *Slice of Life: The British Way of Eating since 1945*. London: BBC Books, 1995.

Hastings, Adrian. "Were Women a Special Case?" In *Women and Missions: Past and Present*, edited by Fiona Bowie, Deborah Kirkwood, and Shirley Ardener. Oxford: Berg Publishers, 1993.

Hazlewood, Arthur. "The Economics of Federation and Dissolution in Central Africa." In *African Integration and Disintegration*, edited by Arthur Hazlewood. London: Oxford University Press, 1967.

Holland, Robert. "The Imperial Factor in British Strategies from Attlee to Macmillan, 1945–63." *Journal of Imperial and Commonwealth Studies* 12 (1984).

Hsu, Immanuel C. Y. *The Rise of Modern China*. 5th ed. New York: Oxford University Press, 1995.

Hyam, Ronald. "The Geopolitical Origins of the Central African Federation: Britain, Rhodesia and South Africa, 1948–1953." *Historical Journal* 3 (1987).

Hyam, Ronald. "The Political Consequences of Seretse Khama: Britain, the Bangwato and South Africa, 1948–1952." *Historical Journal* 29 (1986).

Jackson, Alvin. *Ireland, 1798–1998: War, Peace and Beyond*. 2nd ed. Oxford: Wiley-Blackwell, 2010.

James, Winston, and Clive Harris, eds. *Inside Babylon: The Caribbean Diaspora in Britain*. London: Verso, 1993.

Jeffrey, Keith. *The British Army and the Crisis of Empire, 1918–22*. Manchester: Manchester University Press, 1984.

Kamtekar, Indivar. "The Shiver of 1942." *Studies in History* 18 (2002).

Kennedy, Dane. *Islands of White: Settler Society and Culture in Kenya and Southern Rhodesia, 1890–1939*. Durham, NC: Duke University Press, 1987.

Kirk-Greene, Anthony. *On Crown Service: A History of H. M. and Overseas Civil Services*. London: I. B. Tauris, 1999.

Krozewski, Gerold. "Finance and Empire: The Dilemma Facing Great Britain in the 1950s." *International History Review* 18 (1996).

Louis, William Roger. "Introduction." In *Oxford History of the British Empire*. Vol. 5: *The Twentieth Century*, edited by William Roger Louis. New York: Oxford University Press, 1999.

Mansergh, Nicholas. *The Commonwealth Experience*. New York: Frederick Praeger, 1969.

Markovitz, Claude, ed. *A History of Modern India, 1480–1950*. Translated by Nisha George and Maggy Hendry. London: Anthem Press, 2002.

McD Beckles, Hilary. *The Development of West Indies Cricket: The Age of Nationalism*. London: Pluto Press, 1998.

Metcalf, Thomas. "'A Well Selected Body of Men': Sikh Recruitment for Colonial Police and Military." In *Beyond Sovereignty: Britain, Empire and Transnationalism, c. 1880–1950*, edited by Kevin Grant, Philippa Levine, and Frank Trentmann. London: Palgrave Macmillan, 2007.

Murphy, Philip. "'Government by Blackmail': The Origins of the Central African Federation Reconsidered." In *The British Empires in the 1950s: Retreat or Revival?* edited by Martin Lynn. New York: Palgrave Macmillan, 2006.

Nair, Neeti. "Bhagat Singh as 'Satyagrahi': The Limits to Non-violence in Late Colonial India." *Modern Asian Studies* 43 (2009).

Nauright, John. "Masculinity, Muscular Islam and Popular Culture: 'Coloured' Rugby's Cultural Symbolism in Working-Class Cape Town c. 1930–1970." *Journal of the History of Sport* 14 (1997).

Nevo, Joseph. "Al-Hajj Amin and the British in World War II." *Middle Eastern Studies* 20 (1984).

Oddy, Derek. *From Plain Fare to Fusion Food: British Diet from the 1890s to the 1990s.* Woodbridge Suffolk, UK: Boydell Press, 2003.

Pearce. R. D. "The Colonial Office and Planned Decolonisation in Africa." *African Affairs* 83 (1984).

Potter, David. *India's Political Administrators, 1919–1983.* Oxford: Clarendon Press, 1986.

Ray, Carina. "'The White Wife Problem': Sex, Race and the Contested Politics of Repatriation to Interwar British West Africa." *Gender and History* 21 (2009).

Ritscherle, Alice. "Disturbing the People's Peace: Patriotism and 'Respectable' Racism in British Responses to Rhodesian Independence." In *Gender, Labour, War and Empire: Essays on Modern Britain*, edited by Philippa Levine and Susan Grayzel. London: Palgrave Macmillan, 2009.

Sachar, Howard. *A History of Israel.* New York: Alfred Knopf, 1988.

Saunders, Kay. "The Dark Shadow of White Australia: Racial Anxieties in Australia in World War II." *Ethnic and Racial Studies* 17 (1994).

Scobie, Edward. *Black Britannia: A History of Blacks in Britain.* Chicago: Johnson Publishing, 1972.

Silverfarb, Daniel. *The Twilight of British Ascendancy in the Middle East: A Case Study of Iraq, 1941–1950.* New York: St. Martin's Press, 1994.

Smith, Mark. "Windrushers and Orbiters: Towards an Understanding of the 'Official Mind' and Colonial Immigration to Britain, 1945–51." *Immigrants and Minorities* 10 (1991).

Smith, Simon, ed. *Reassessing Suez 1956: New Perspectives on the Crisis and Its Aftermath.* London: Ashgate, 2008.

Southard, Barbara. "Colonial Politics and Women's Rights: Woman Suffrage Campaigns in Bengal, British India in the 1920s." *Modern Asian Studies* 27 (1993).

Spencer, Ian. "Settler Dominance, Agricultural Production and the Second World War in Kenya." *Journal of African History* 21 (1984).

Stockwell, A. J. "'The Crucible of the Malayan Nation': The University and the Making of a New Malaya, 1938–62." *Modern Asian Studies* 43 (2009).

Tomlinson, B. R. *The Economy of Modern India, 1860–1970.* Cambridge: Cambridge University Press, 1993.

Vatikiotis, P. J. *The History of Egypt.* 3rd ed. Baltimore: Johns Hopkins University Press, 1980.

Wallace, Elizabeth. *The British Caribbean: From the Decline of Colonialism to the End of Federation.* Toronto: University of Buffalo Press, 1977.

White, Nicholas. "The Business and Politics of Decolonization: The British Experience in the Twentieth Century," *Economic History Review* 53 (2000).

Index

About the Author

Timothy Parsons holds a joint appointment as a professor of African history in the History Department and the African and African American Studies Program at Washington University in St. Louis, where he also directs the International and Area Studies Program. His primary publications include *The Rule of Empires: Those Who Built Them, Those Who Endured Them, and Why They Always Fall* (2010); *Race, Resistance and the Boy Scout Movement in British Colonial Africa* (2004); *The 1964 Army Mutinies and the Making of Modern East Africa* (2003); *The African Rank-and-File: Social Implications of Colonial Service in the King's African Rifles, 1902–1964* (1999); and *The British Imperial Century, 1815–1914: A World History Perspective* (1999).